shôjo

shô•jo (sho'jo) n. **1.** Manga appealing to both female and male readers. **2.** Exciting stories with true-to-life characters and the thrill of exotic locales. **3.** Connecting the heart and mind through real human relationships.

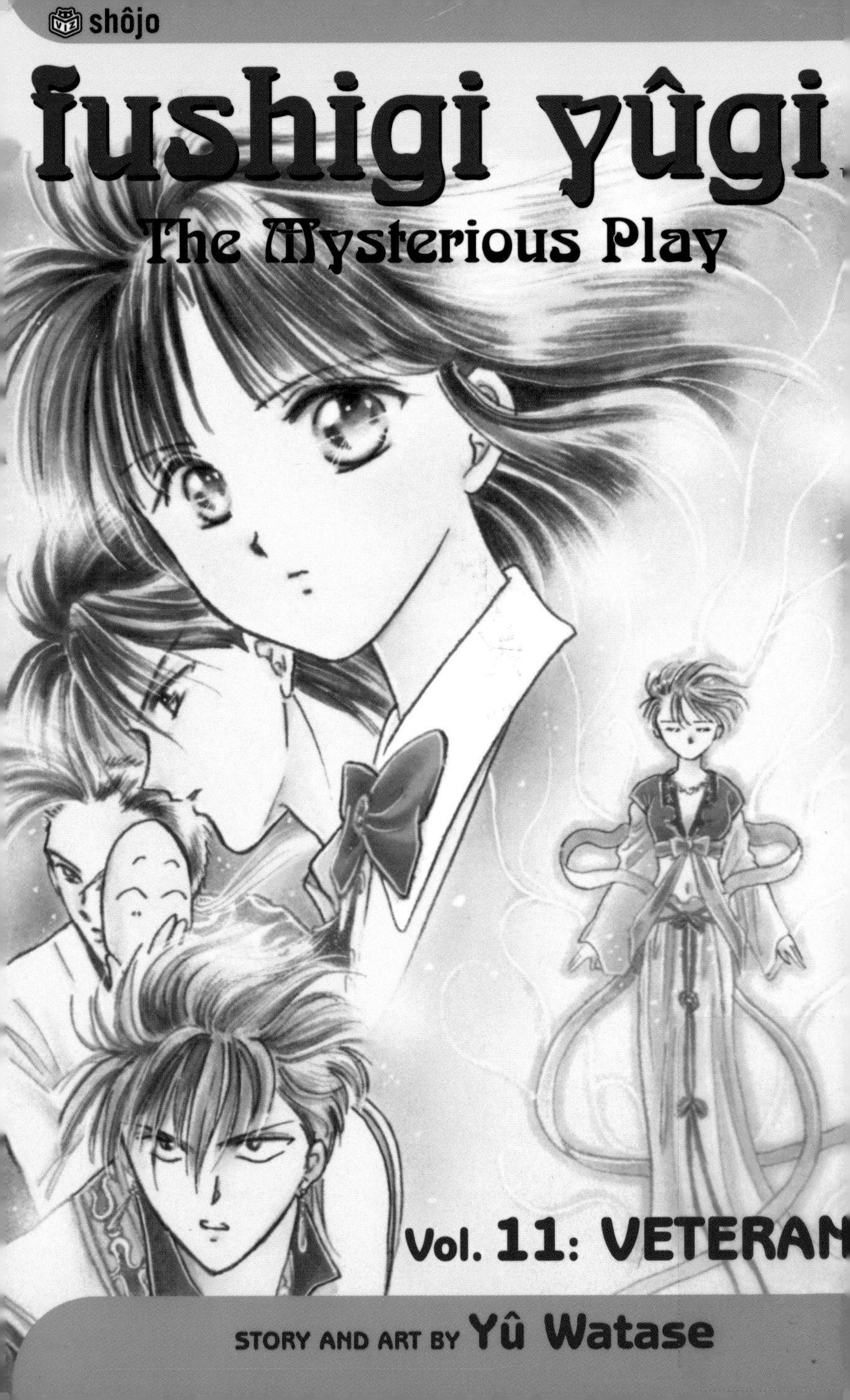
shôjo
fushigi yûgi
The Mysterious Play
Vol. 11: VETERAN
STORY AND ART BY Yû Watase

fushigi yûgi™

The Mysterious Play
VOL. 11: VETERAN

Story & Art By
YÛ WATASE

FUSHIGI YÛGI
THE MYSTERIOUS PLAY
VOL. 11: Veteran
SHÔJO EDITION

This volume contains the FUSHIGI YÛGI installments from Animerica Extra
Vol. 7, No. 2, through No. 4, in their entirety.

STORY AND ART BY YÛ WATASE

English Adaptation/Yuji Oniki
Translation Assist/Kaori Kawakubo Inoue
Touch-up & Lettering/Bill Spicer
Touch-up Assist/Walden Wong
Design/Hidemi Sahara
Shôjo Edition Editor/Elizabeth Kawasaki

Managing Editor/Annette Roman
Editor-in-Chief/Alvin Lu
Production Manager/Noboru Watanabe
Sr. Director of Licensing & Acquisitions/Rika Inouye
V.P. of Marketing/Liza Coppola
Executive Vice President/Hyoe Narita
Publisher/Seiji Horibuchi

Printed in Canada

Published by VIZ, LLC
P.O. Box 77010
San Francisco, CA 94107

Shôjo Edition
10 9 8 7 6 5 4 3 2 1
First printing, June 2004

www.viz.com   store.viz.com

CONTENTS

STORY THUS FAR

Chipper junior high school girl Miaka is physically drawn into the world of a strange book—*THE UNIVERSE OF THE FOUR GODS*. Miaka is offered the role of the lead character, the priestess of the god Suzaku, and is charged with a mission to save the nation of Hong-Nan, and in the process have three wishes granted. While Miaka makes a short trip back to the real world, her best friend Yui is sucked into the book only to suffer rape and manipulation, which drives her to attempt suicide. Now, Yui has become the priestess of the god Seiryu, the bitter enemy of Suzaku and Miaka.

The only way for Miaka to gain back the trust of her former friend is to summon the god Suzaku and wish to be reconciled with Yui, so Miaka reenters the world of *THE UNIVERSE OF THE FOUR GODS*. The Seiryu warriors ruined Miaka's first attempt to summon Suzaku, but the oracle, Tai Yi-Jun, has a new mission for Miaka and her Celestial Warriors of Suzaku—to obtain treasures from the countries of the other two gods, Genbu and Byakko, that will allow them to summon Suzaku.

Only seconds after obtaining the first treasure, it is stolen from Miaka's hand by the Seiryu Warriors, leaving her wracked with guilt. Miaka, falling for a Seiryu trick, tries to get the treasure back, but instead is trapped by Nakago, who is intent on forcing sex on her. Ashamed and confused, Miaka flees from her companions only to be rescued by an old foe, the Seiryu warrior Amiboshi, who claims to have no memory of ever meeting her before. Aided by Tamahome, and surprisingly, the Seiryu warrior Suboshi, Miaka escapes the clutches of Tomo. Miaka's quest to rekindle Tamahome's love takes a bizarre turn when she runs into not only Nakago, but her former friend Yui as well. Their reunion turns bittersweet; Miaka falls under Seiryu warrior Miboshi's spell and is unable to speak!

THE UNIVERSE OF THE FOUR GODS is based on ancient Chinese legend, but Japanese pronunciation of Chinese names differs slightly from their Chinese equivalents. Here is a short glossary of the Japanese pronunciation of the Chinese names in this graphic novel:

CHINESE	JAPANESE	PERSON OR PLACE	MEANING
Hong-Nan	Konan	Southern Kingdom	Crimson South
Qu-Dong	Kutô	Eastern Kingdom	Gathered East
Bei-Jia	Hokkan	Northern Kingdom	Armored North
Tai Yi-Jun	Tai Itsukun	An Oracle	Preeminent Person
Shentso-Pao	Shinzahô	A Treasure	God's Seat Jewel

CHAPTER SIXTY
RAY OF RESURRECTION

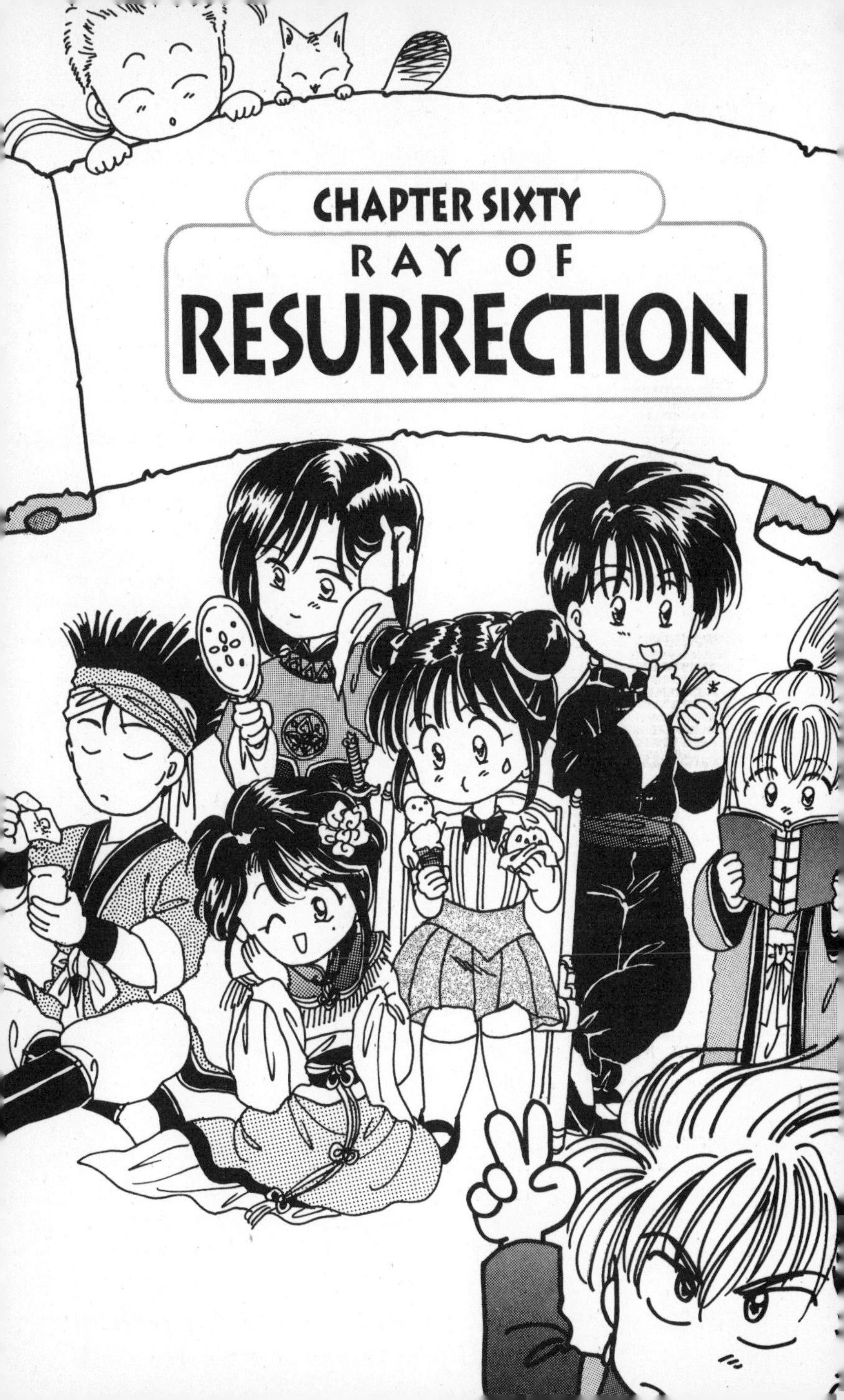

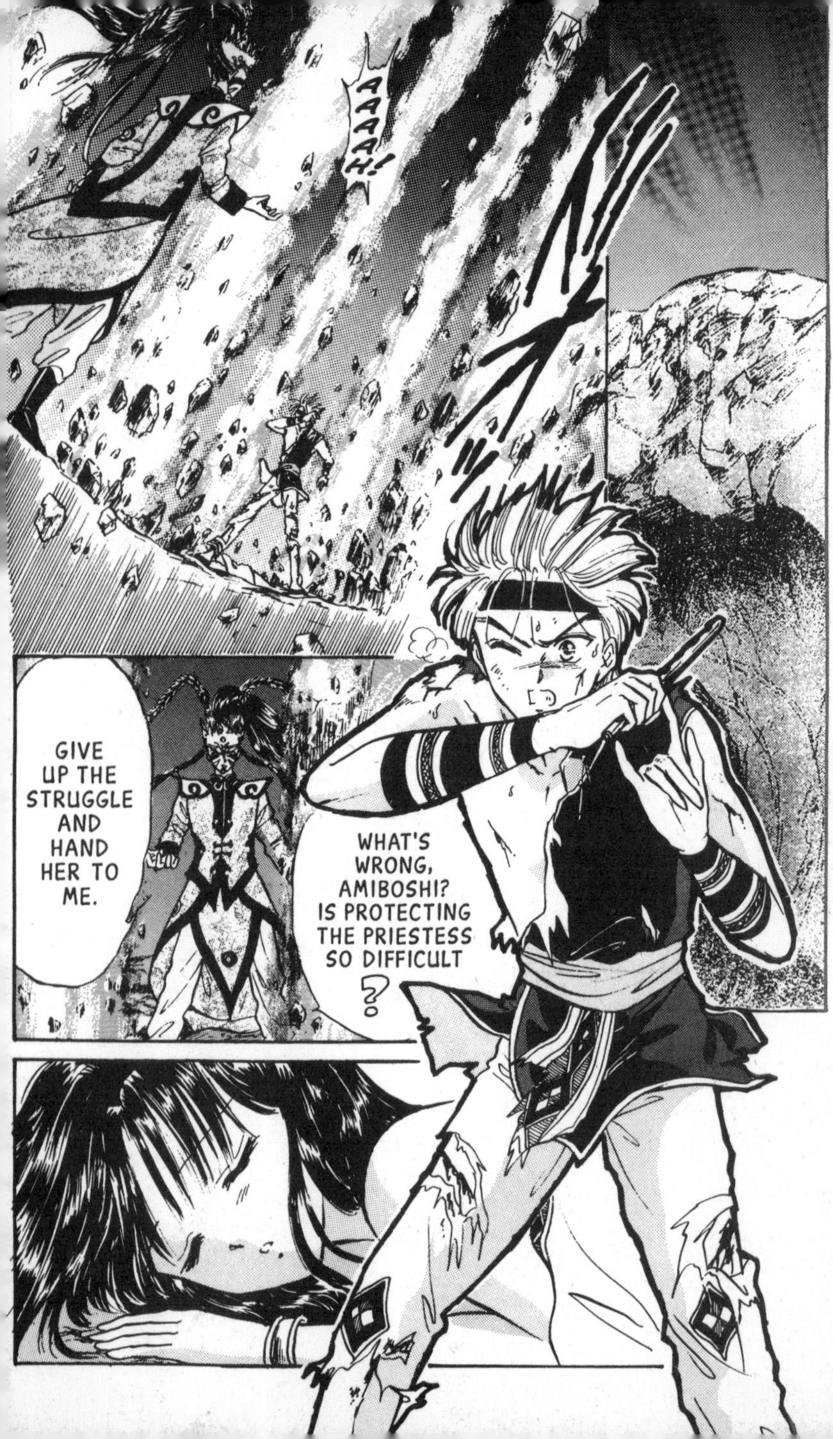
AAAAAH!
WHAT'S WRONG, AMIBOSHI? IS PROTECTING THE PRIESTESS SO DIFFICULT?
GIVE UP THE STRUGGLE AND HAND HER TO ME.

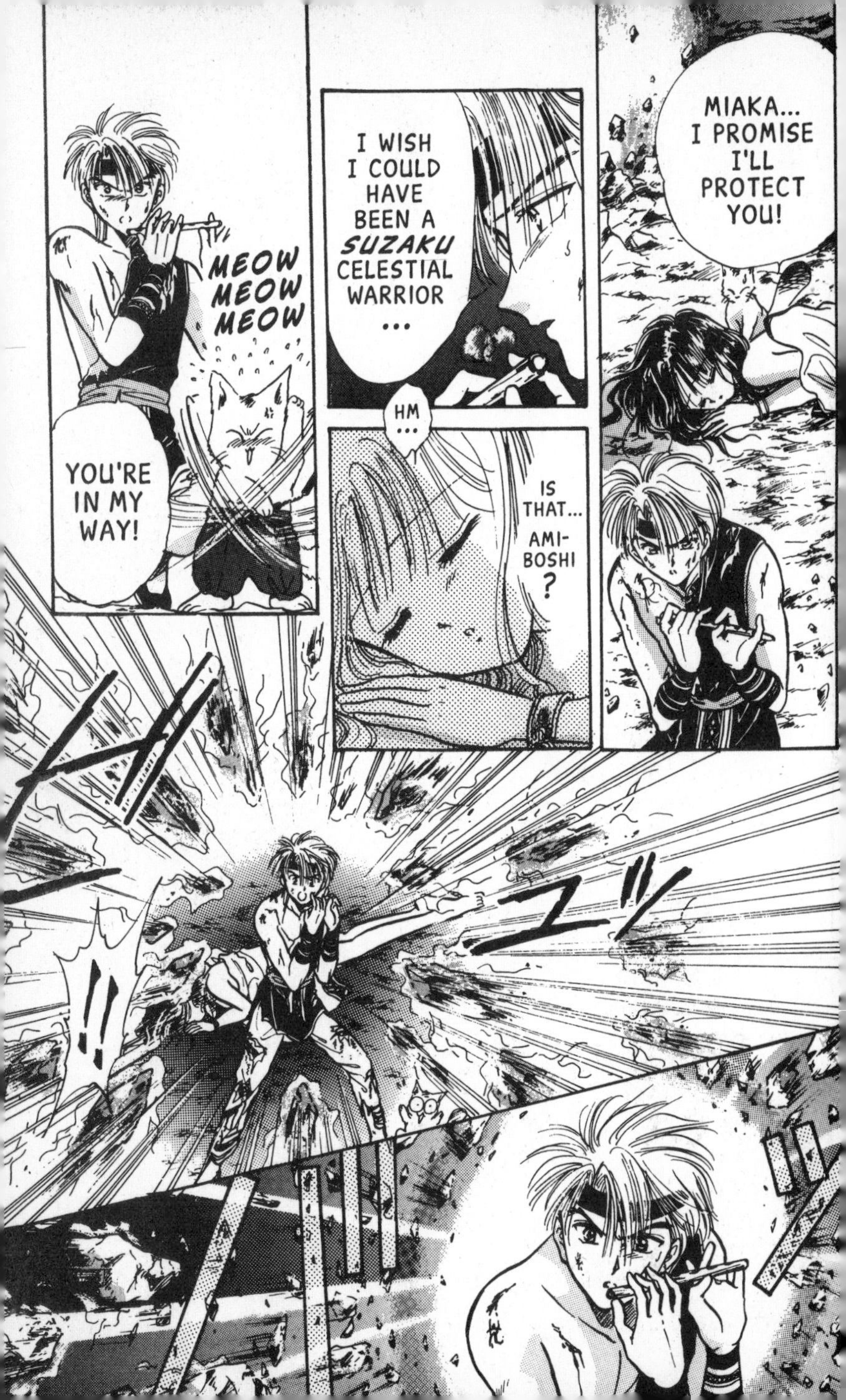

MIAKA... I PROMISE I'LL PROTECT YOU!
I WISH I COULD HAVE BEEN A *SUZAKU* CELESTIAL WARRIOR ...
HM ...
IS THAT... AMI-BOSHI ?
MEOW MEOW MEOW
YOU'RE IN MY WAY!
!!

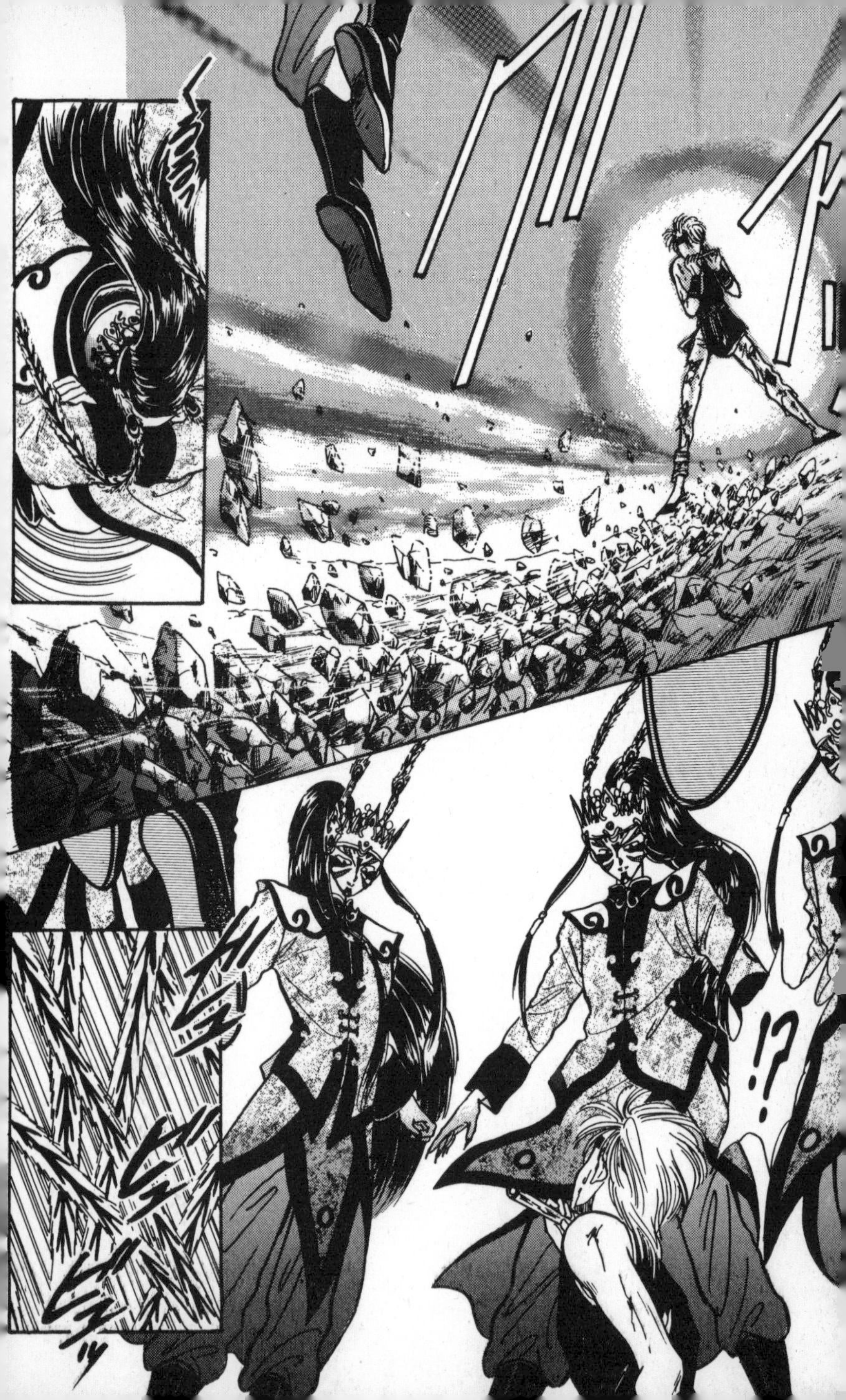

!?

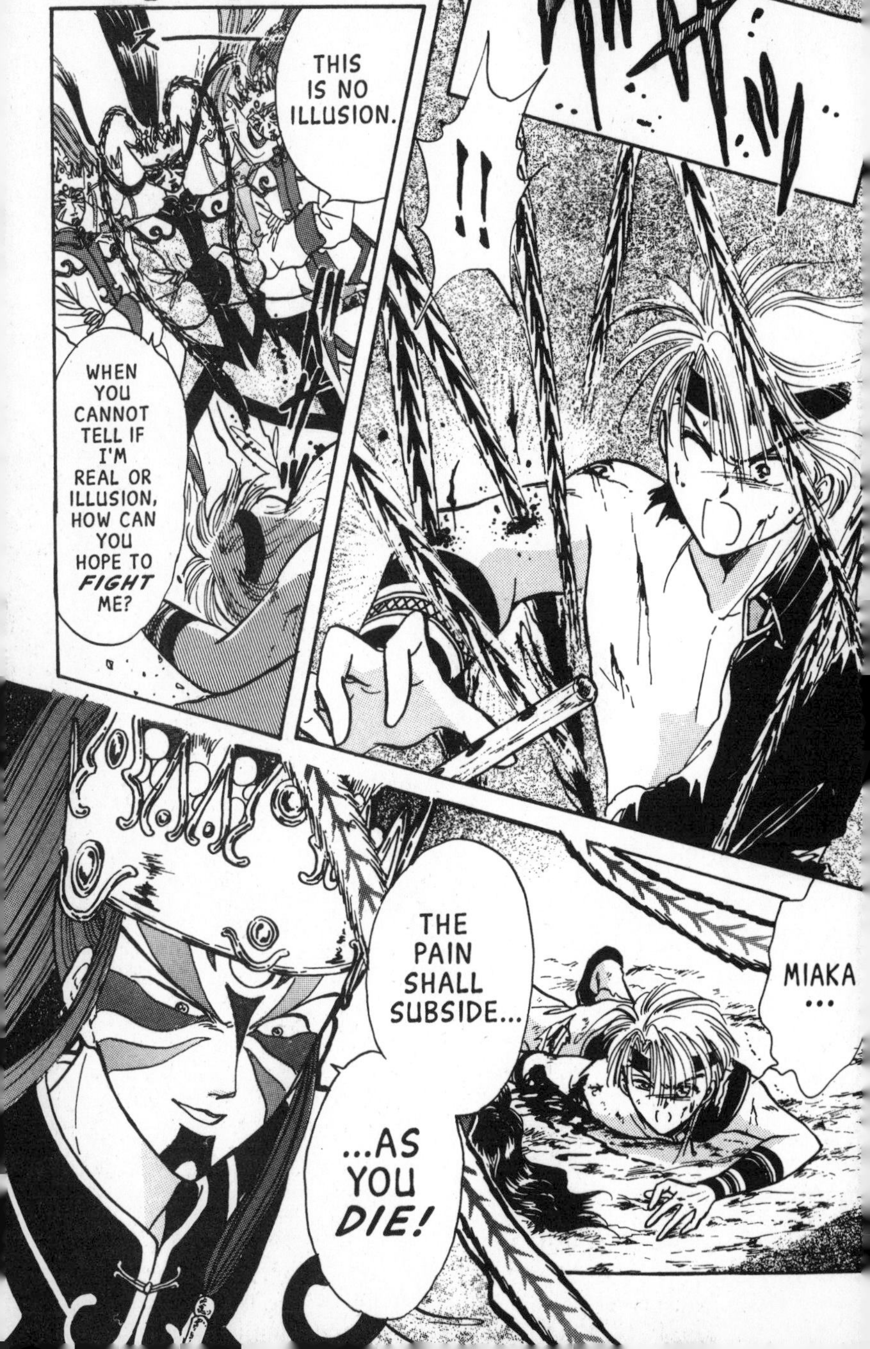
!!
THIS IS NO ILLUSION.
WHEN YOU CANNOT TELL IF I'M REAL OR ILLUSION, HOW CAN YOU HOPE TO *FIGHT* ME?
MIAKA...
THE PAIN SHALL SUBSIDE...
...AS YOU *DIE!*

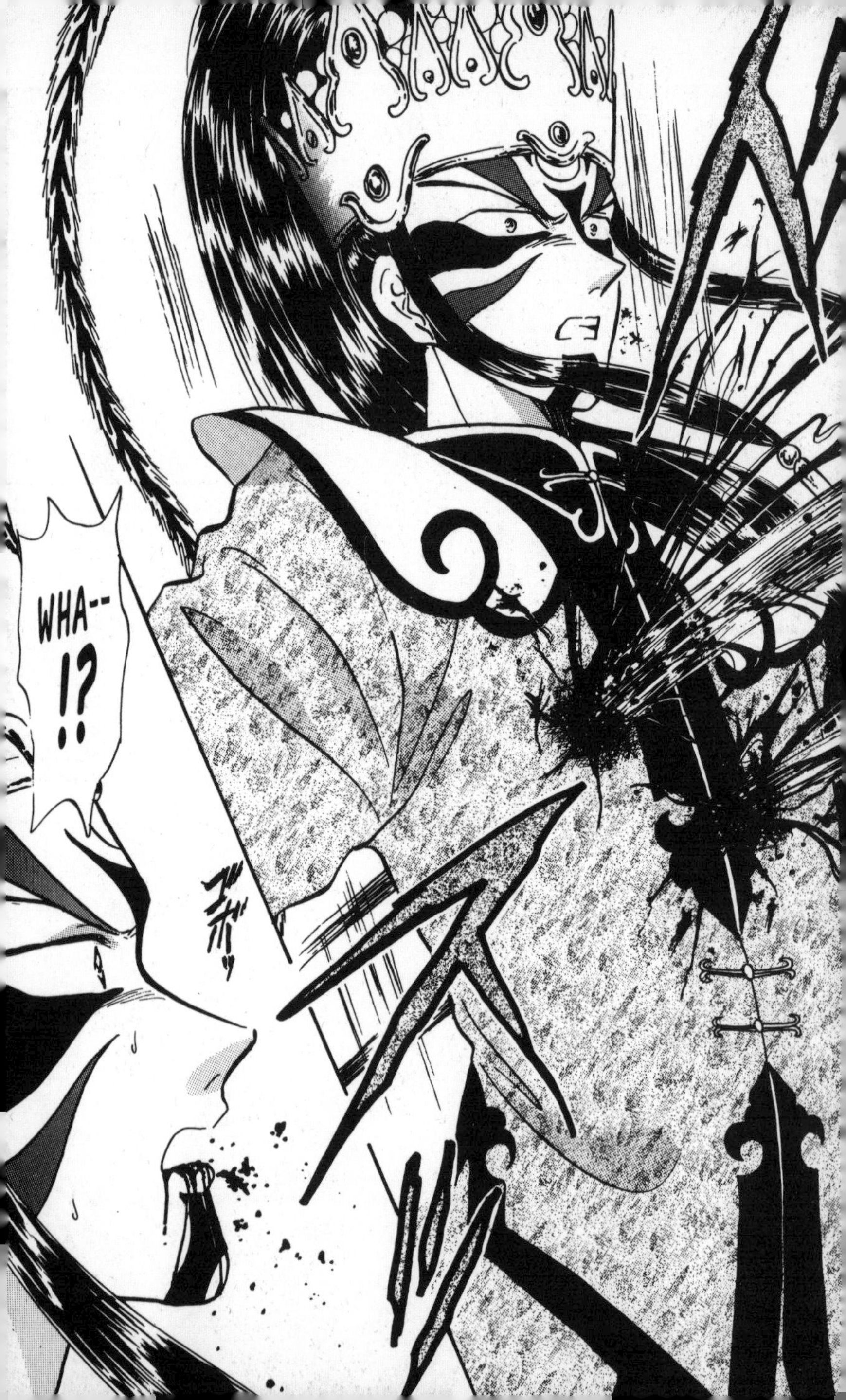
WHA-- !?

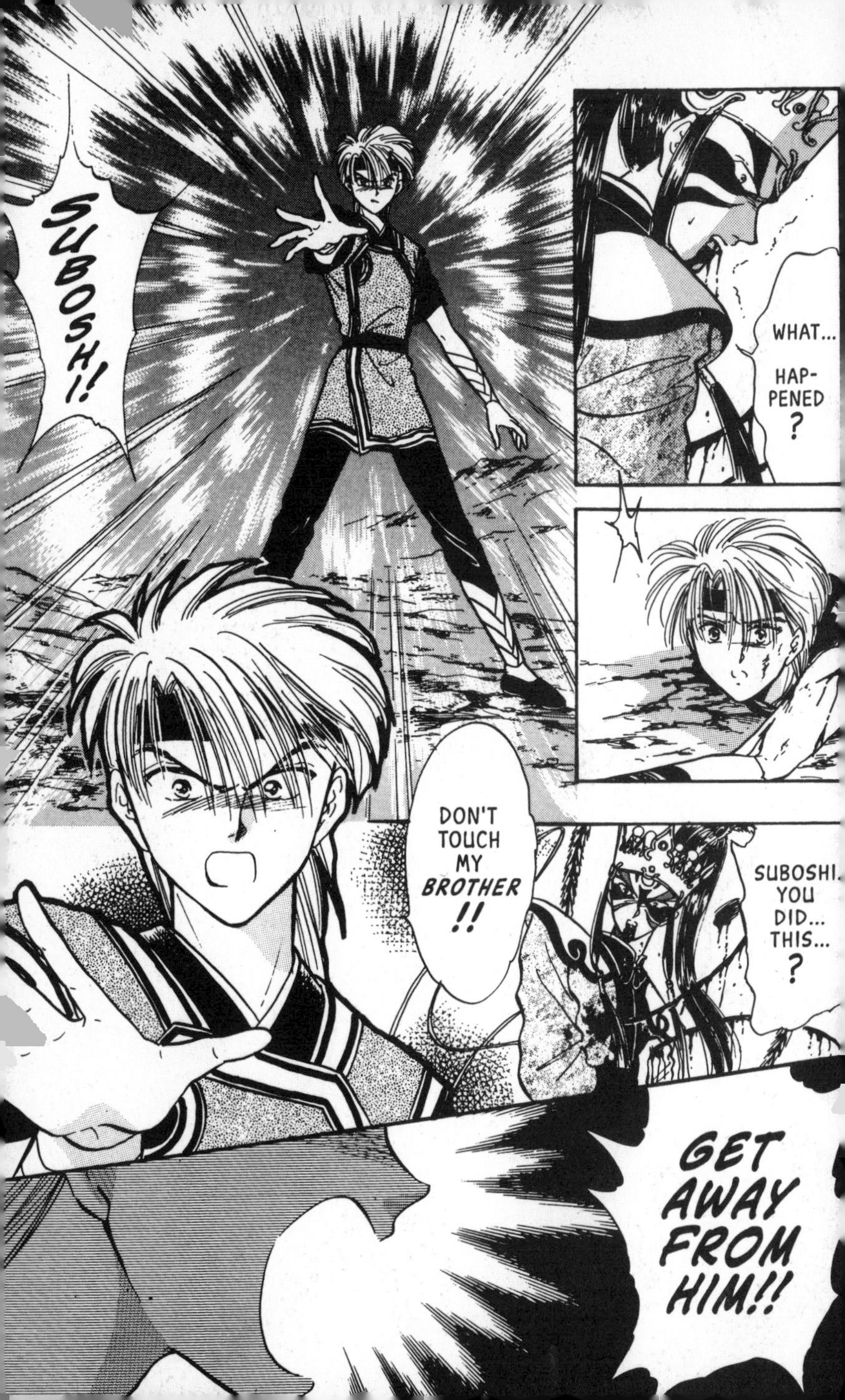
WHAT... HAPPENED?
SUBOSHI!!
SUBOSHI. YOU DID... THIS...?
DON'T TOUCH MY BROTHER!!
GET AWAY FROM HIM!!

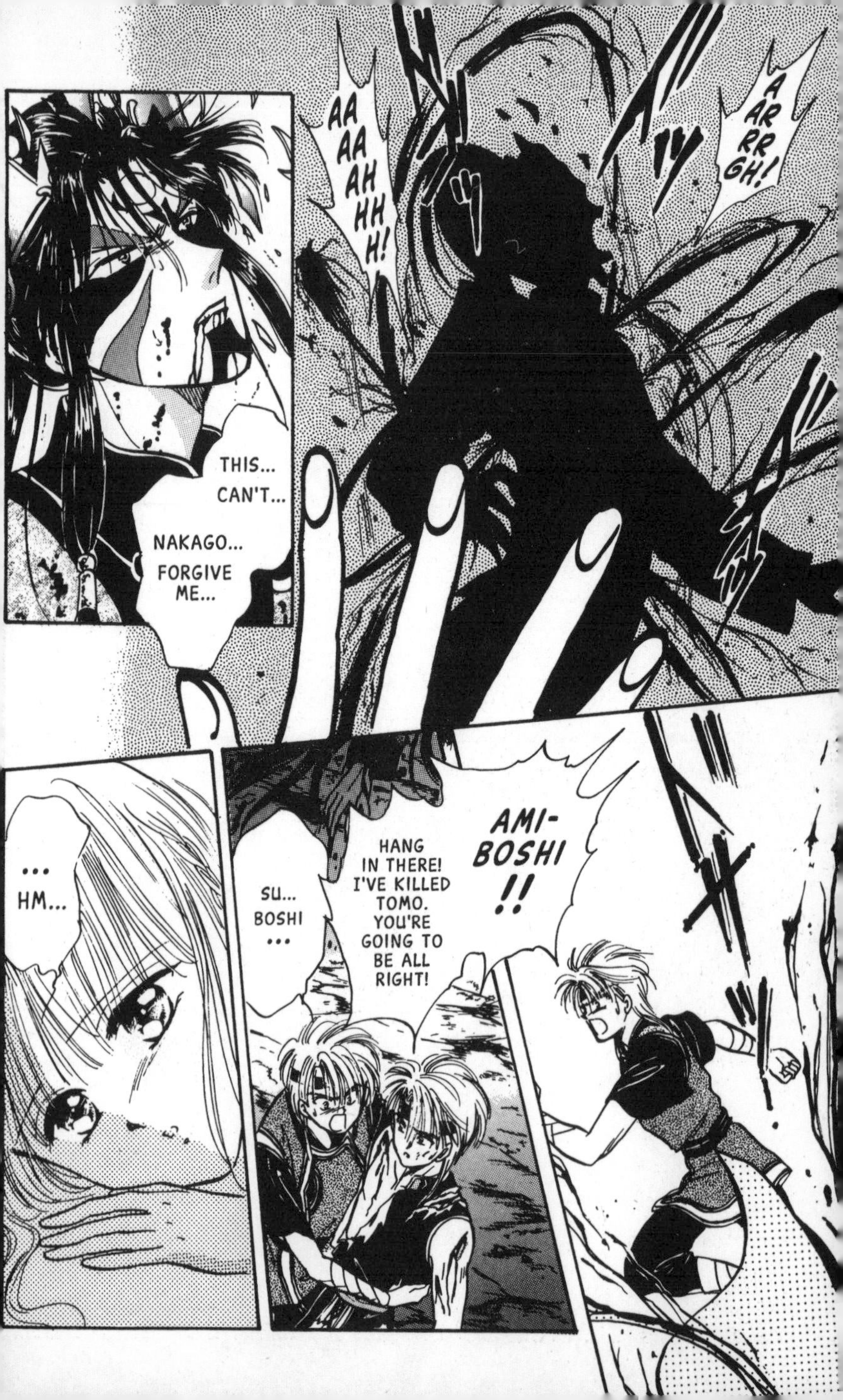

AARRRGH!
AAAAAHHHHH!
THIS... CAN'T...
NAKAGO... FORGIVE ME...
AMI-BOSHI!!
HANG IN THERE! I'VE KILLED TOMO. YOU'RE GOING TO BE ALL RIGHT!
SU... BOSHI...
... HM...

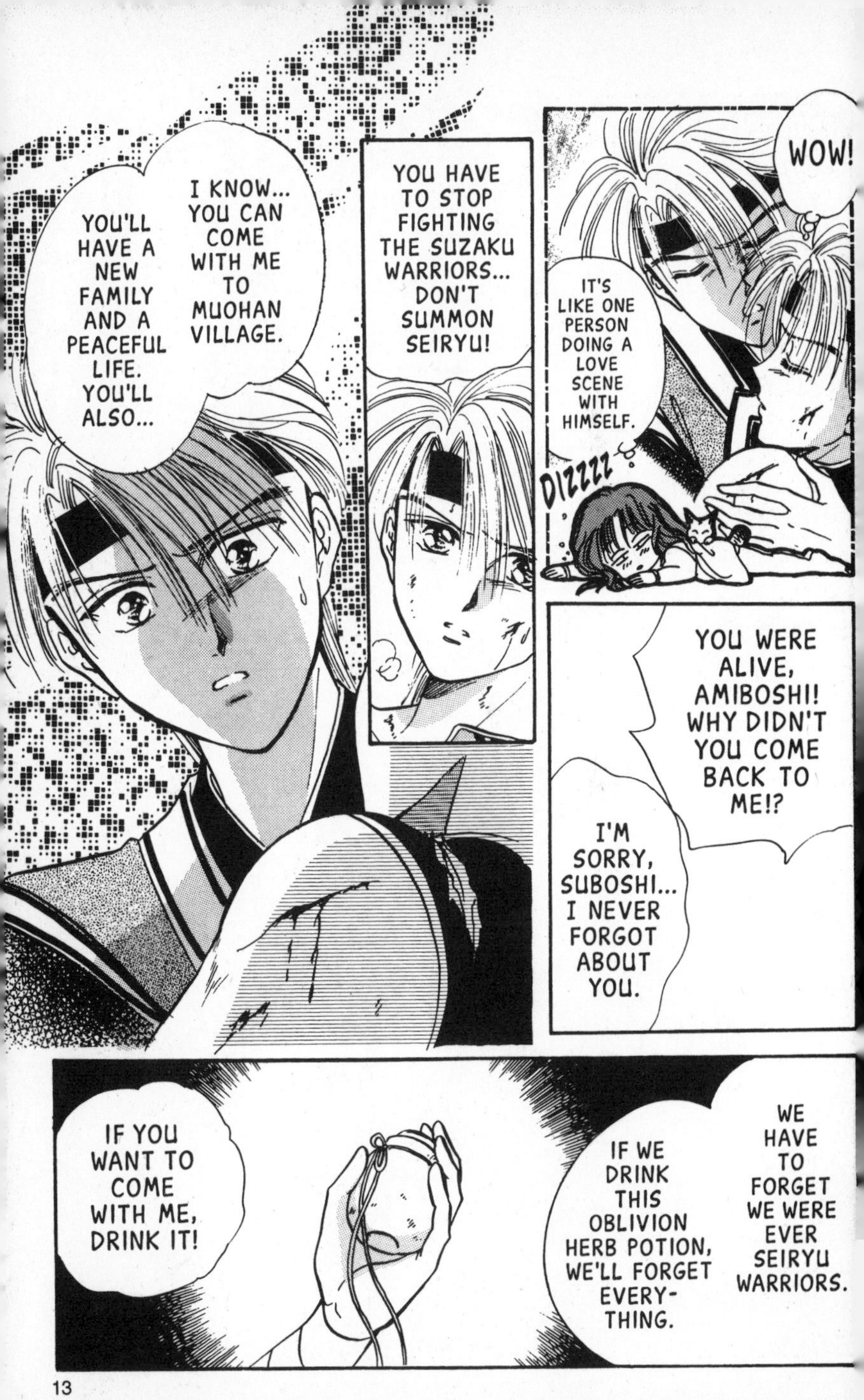
WOW!
IT'S LIKE ONE PERSON DOING A LOVE SCENE WITH HIMSELF.
DIZZZZ
YOU WERE ALIVE, AMIBOSHI! WHY DIDN'T YOU COME BACK TO ME!?
I'M SORRY, SUBOSHI... I NEVER FORGOT ABOUT YOU.
YOU HAVE TO STOP FIGHTING THE SUZAKU WARRIORS... DON'T SUMMON SEIRYU!
I KNOW... YOU CAN COME WITH ME TO MUOHAN VILLAGE.
YOU'LL HAVE A NEW FAMILY AND A PEACEFUL LIFE. YOU'LL ALSO...
WE HAVE TO FORGET WE WERE EVER SEIRYU WARRIORS.
IF WE DRINK THIS OBLIVION HERB POTION, WE'LL FORGET EVERY-THING.
IF YOU WANT TO COME WITH ME, DRINK IT!

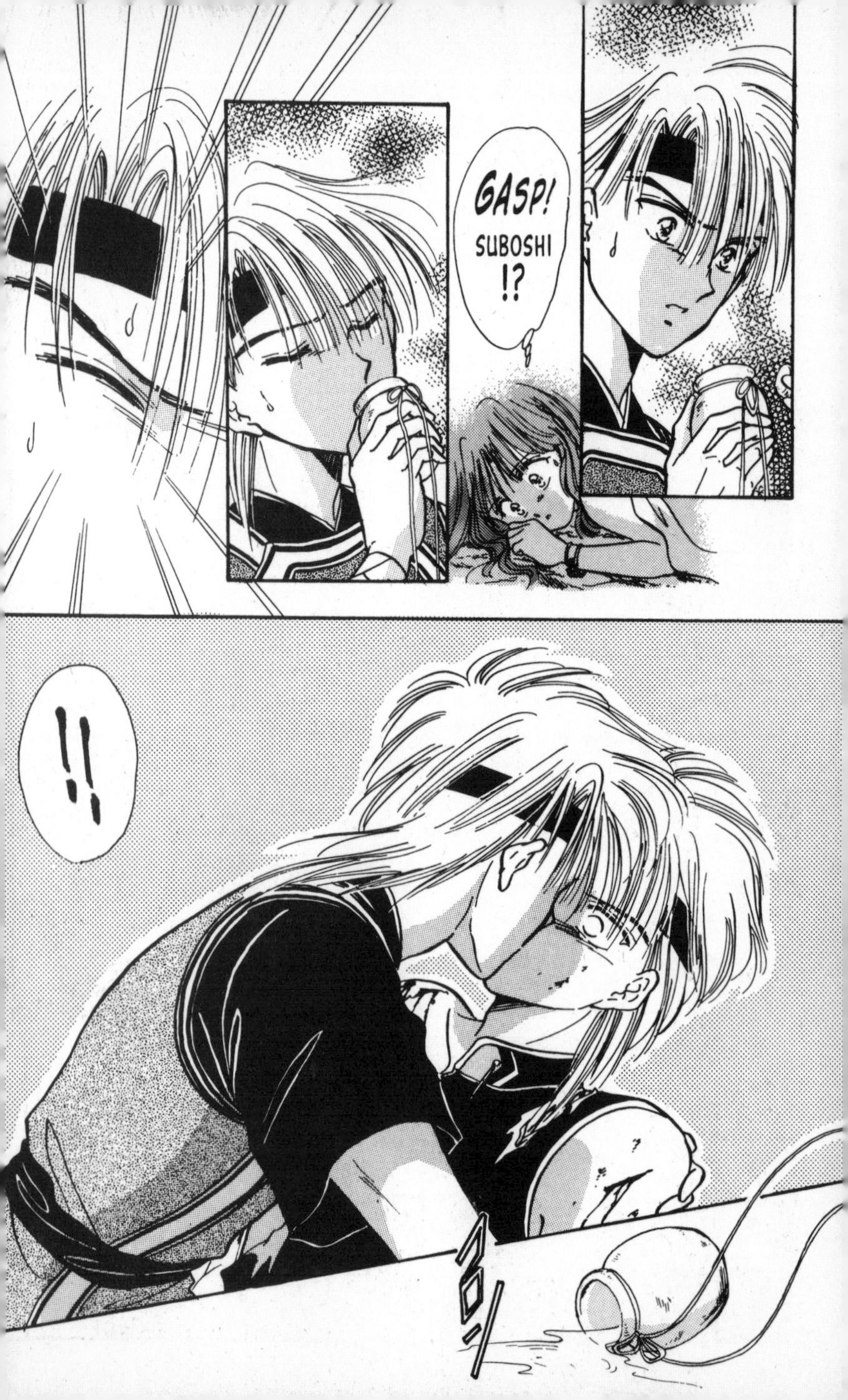
GASP! SUBOSHI !?
!!

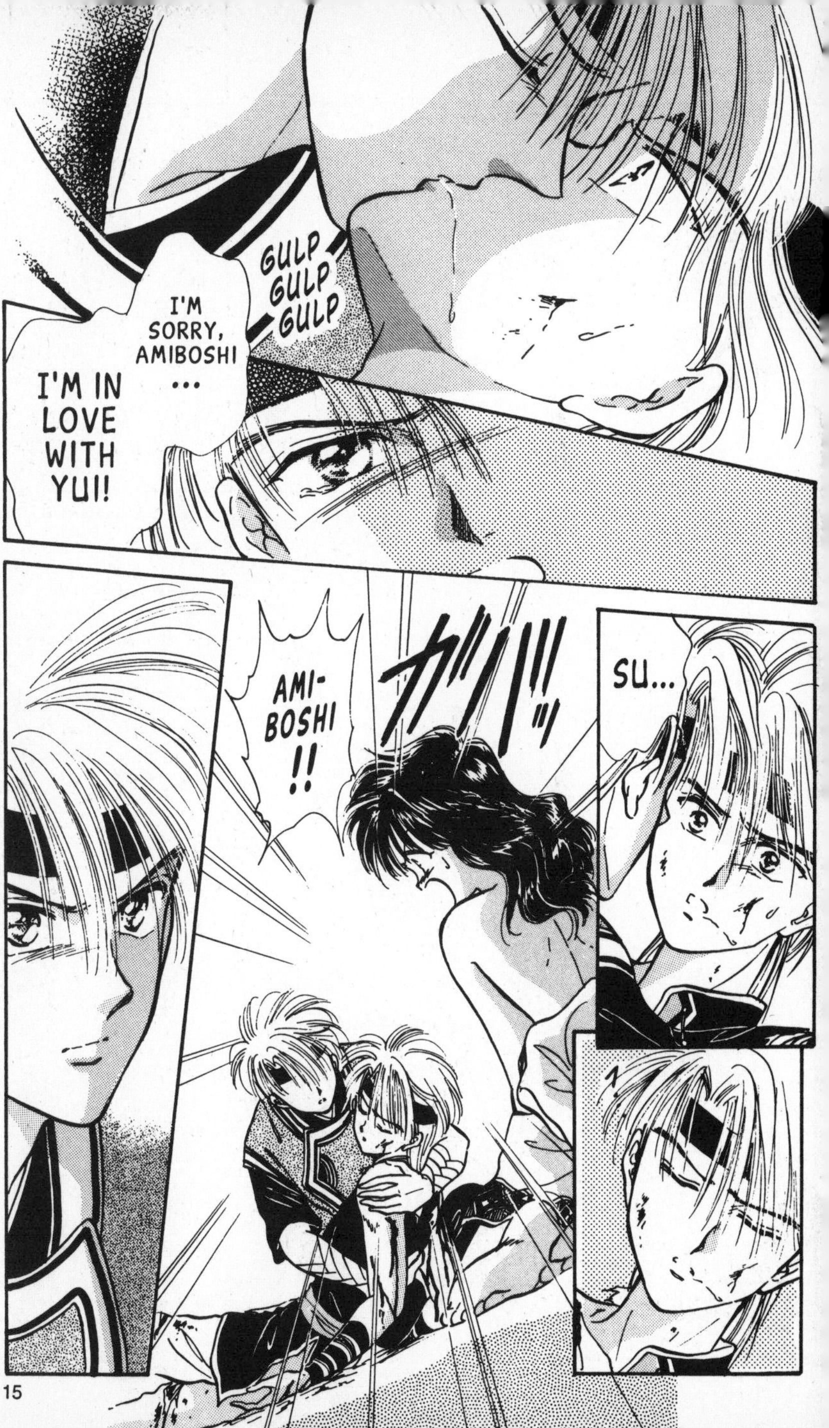
GULP GULP GULP
I'M SORRY, AMIBOSHI...
I'M IN LOVE WITH YUI!
SU...
AMI-BOSHI!!

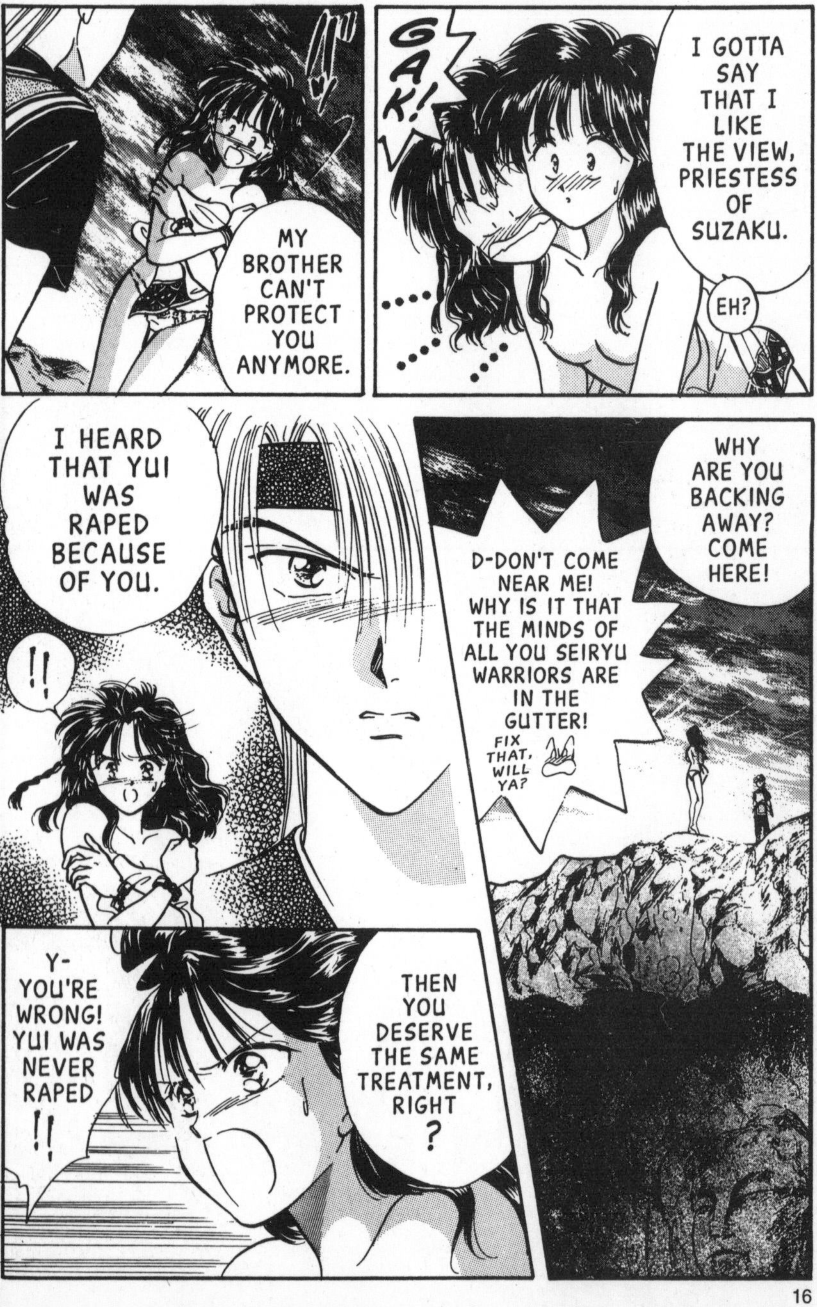
I GOTTA SAY THAT I LIKE THE VIEW, PRIESTESS OF SUZAKU.
GAK!
EH?
MY BROTHER CAN'T PROTECT YOU ANYMORE.
WHY ARE YOU BACKING AWAY? COME HERE!
D-DON'T COME NEAR ME! WHY IS IT THAT THE MINDS OF ALL YOU SEIRYU WARRIORS ARE IN THE GUTTER!
FIX THAT, WILL YA?
I HEARD THAT YUI WAS RAPED BECAUSE OF YOU.
!!
THEN YOU DESERVE THE SAME TREATMENT, RIGHT?
Y-YOU'RE WRONG! YUI WAS NEVER RAPED!!

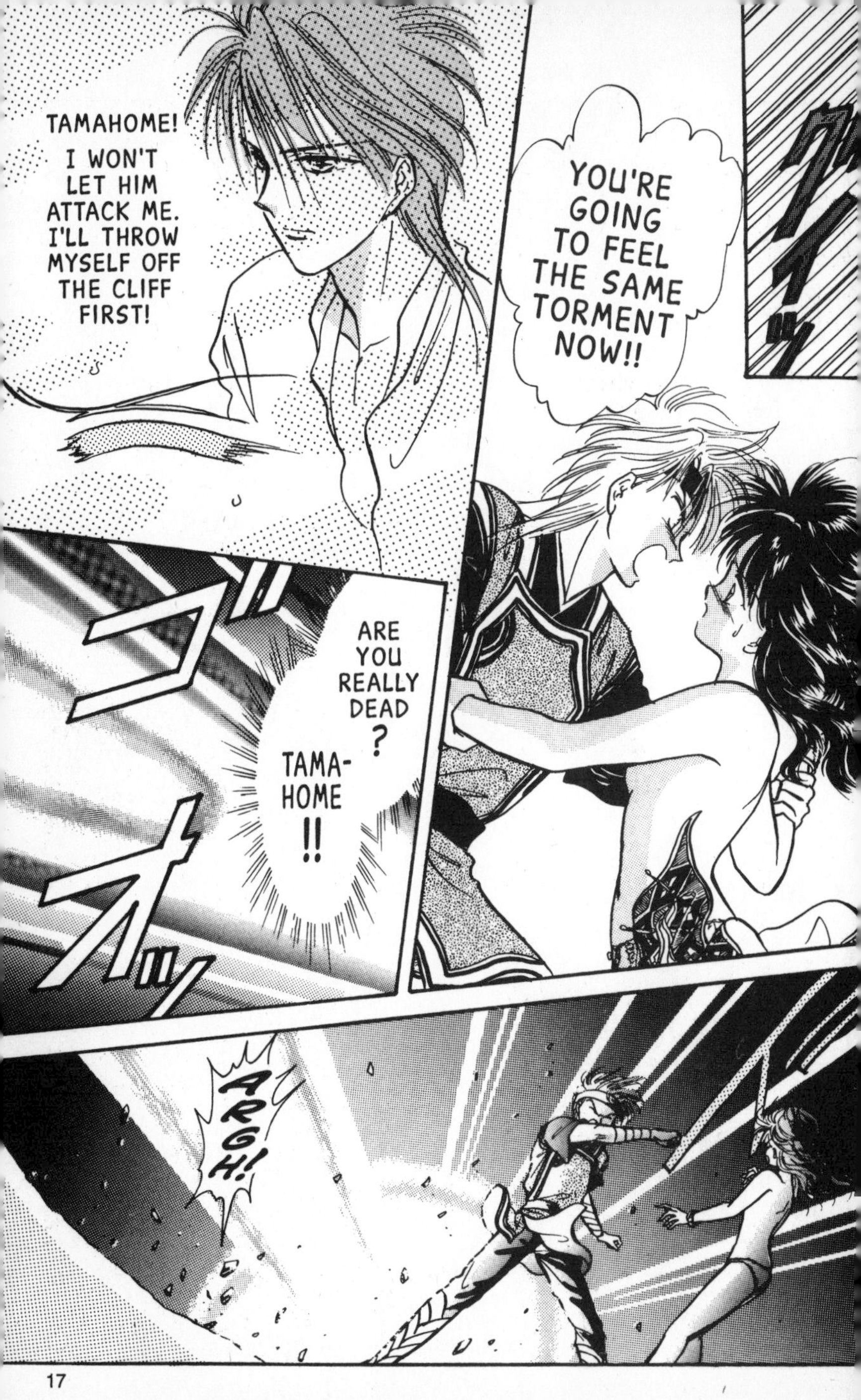
YOU'RE GOING TO FEEL THE SAME TORMENT NOW!!
TAMAHOME!
I WON'T LET HIM ATTACK ME. I'LL THROW MYSELF OFF THE CLIFF FIRST!
ARE YOU REALLY DEAD?
TAMA-HOME!!
ARGH!

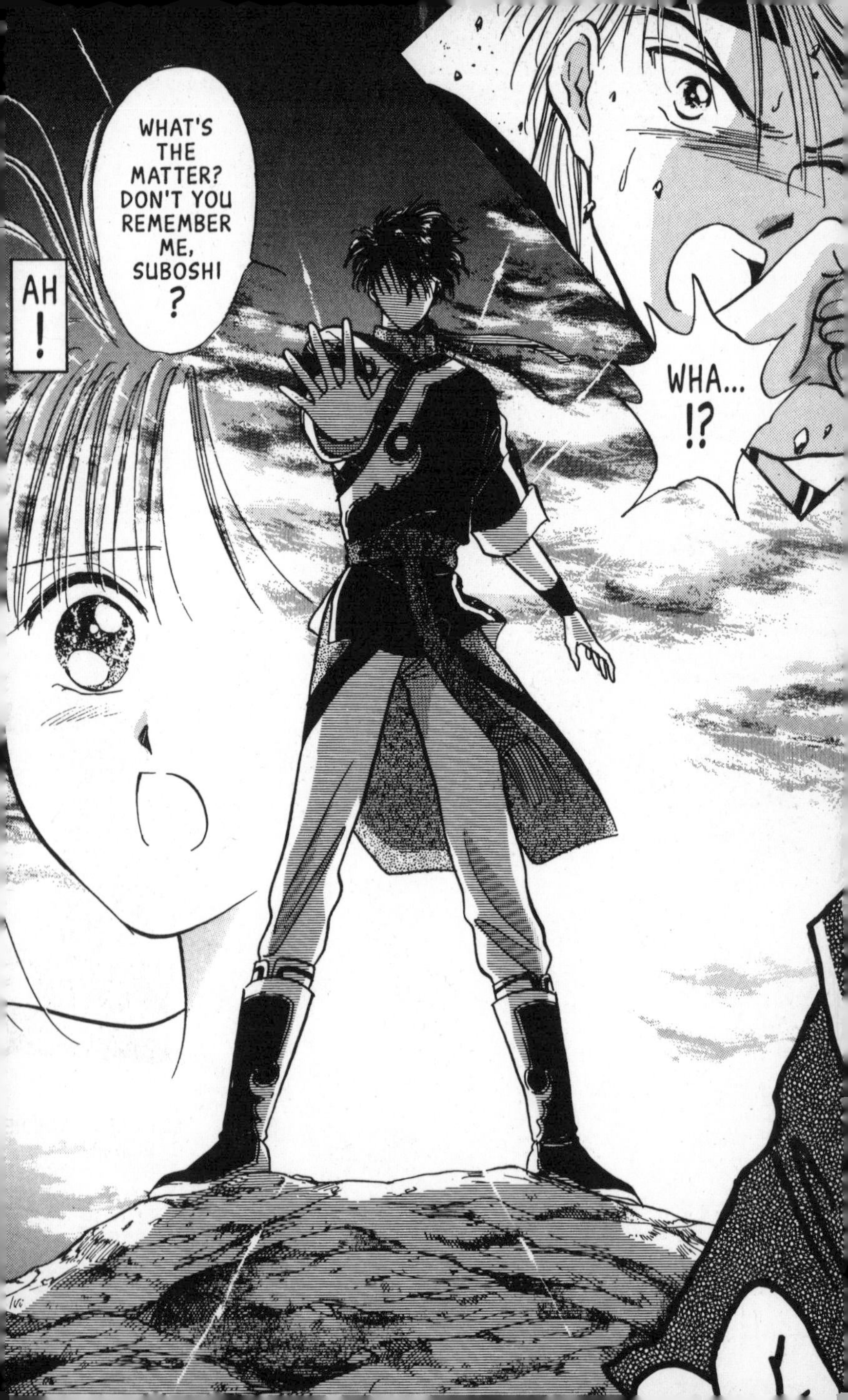
WHA... !?
WHAT'S THE MATTER? DON'T YOU REMEMBER ME, SUBOSHI ?
AH !

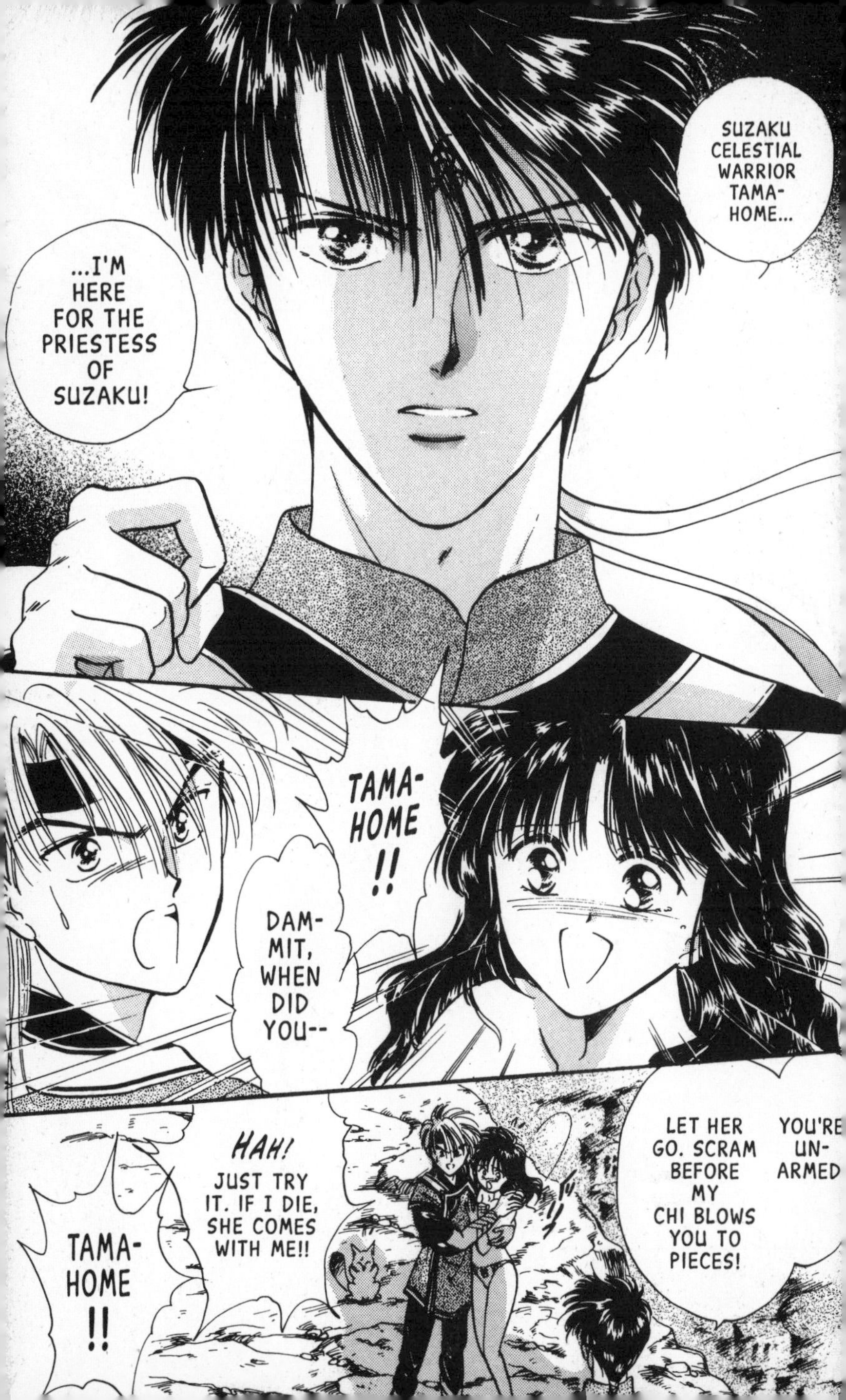
SUZAKU CELESTIAL WARRIOR TAMA-HOME...
...I'M HERE FOR THE PRIESTESS OF SUZAKU!
TAMA-HOME!!
DAM-MIT, WHEN DID YOU--
YOU'RE UN-ARMED
LET HER GO. SCRAM BEFORE MY CHI BLOWS YOU TO PIECES!
HAH! JUST TRY IT. IF I DIE, SHE COMES WITH ME!!
TAMA-HOME!!

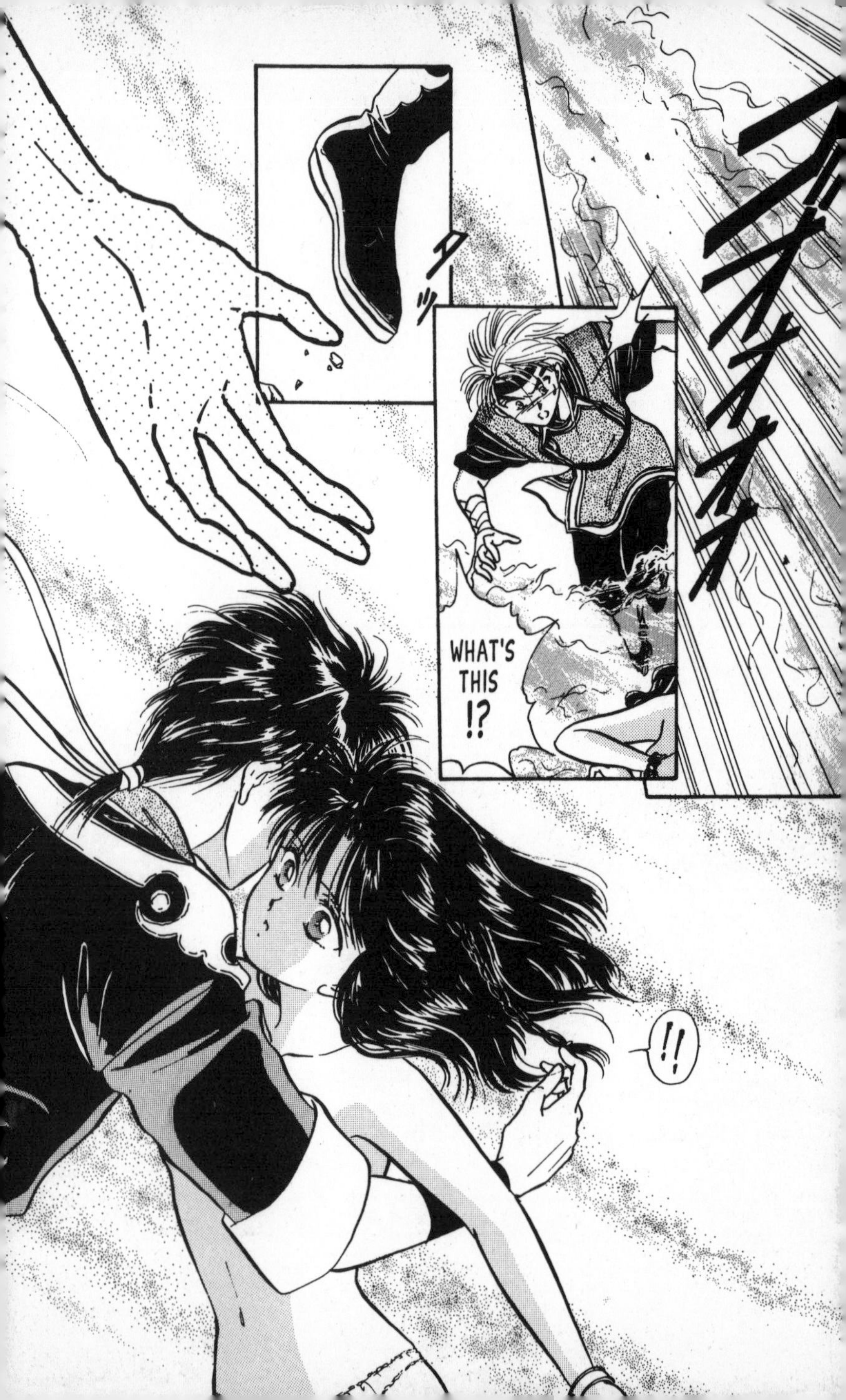
WHAT'S THIS !?
!!

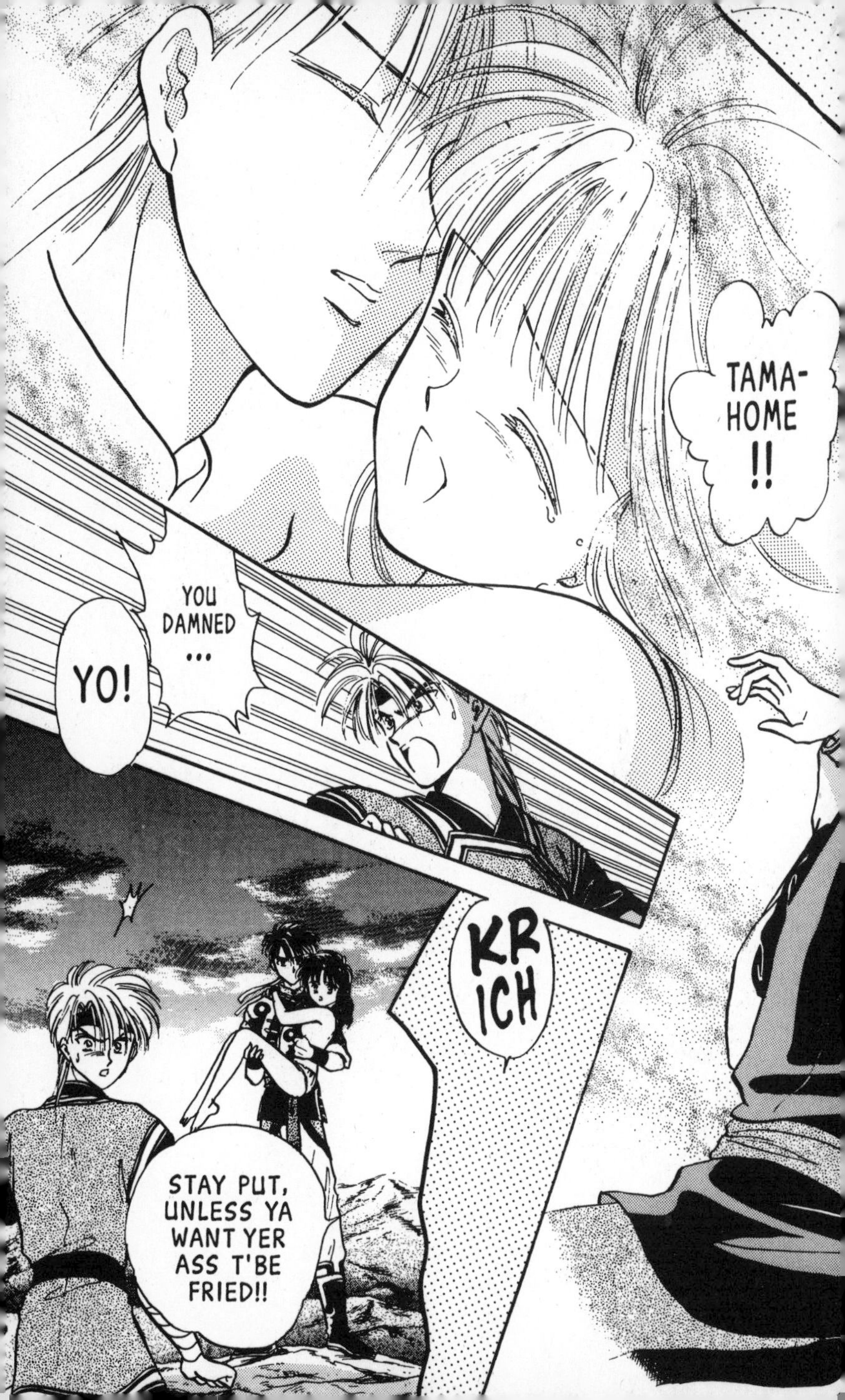
TAMA-HOME!!
YOU DAMNED ...
YO!
KRICH
STAY PUT, UNLESS YA WANT YER ASS T'BE FRIED!!

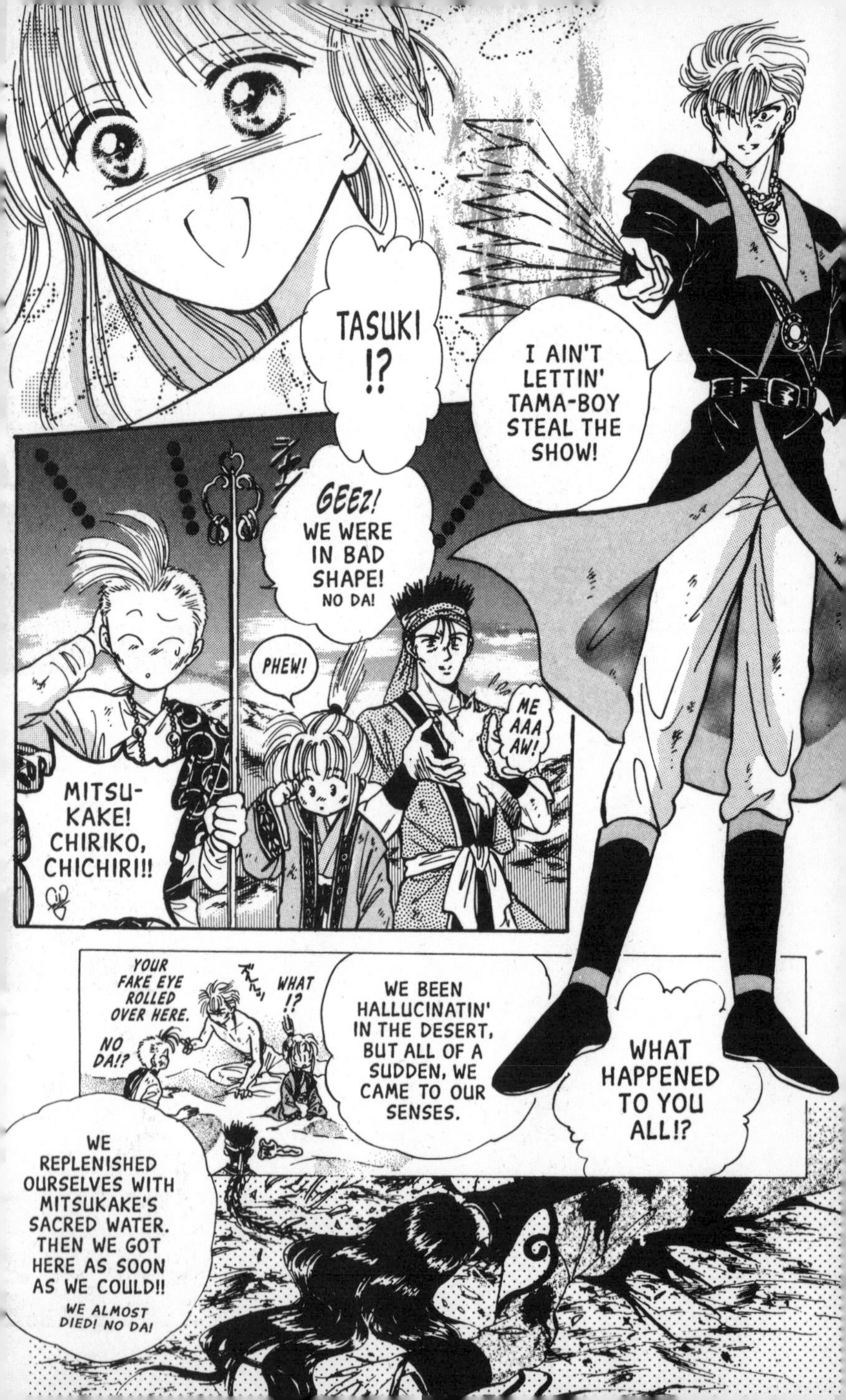
I AIN'T LETTIN' TAMA-BOY STEAL THE SHOW!
TASUKI !?
GEEZ! WE WERE IN BAD SHAPE! NO DA!
ME AAA AW!
PHEW!
MITSU-KAKE! CHIRIKO, CHICHIRI!!
WHAT HAPPENED TO YOU ALL!?
WE BEEN HALLUCINATIN' IN THE DESERT, BUT ALL OF A SUDDEN, WE CAME TO OUR SENSES.
WHAT !?
YOUR FAKE EYE ROLLED OVER HERE.
NO DA!?
WE REPLENISHED OURSELVES WITH MITSUKAKE'S SACRED WATER. THEN WE GOT HERE AS SOON AS WE COULD!!
WE ALMOST DIED! NO DA!

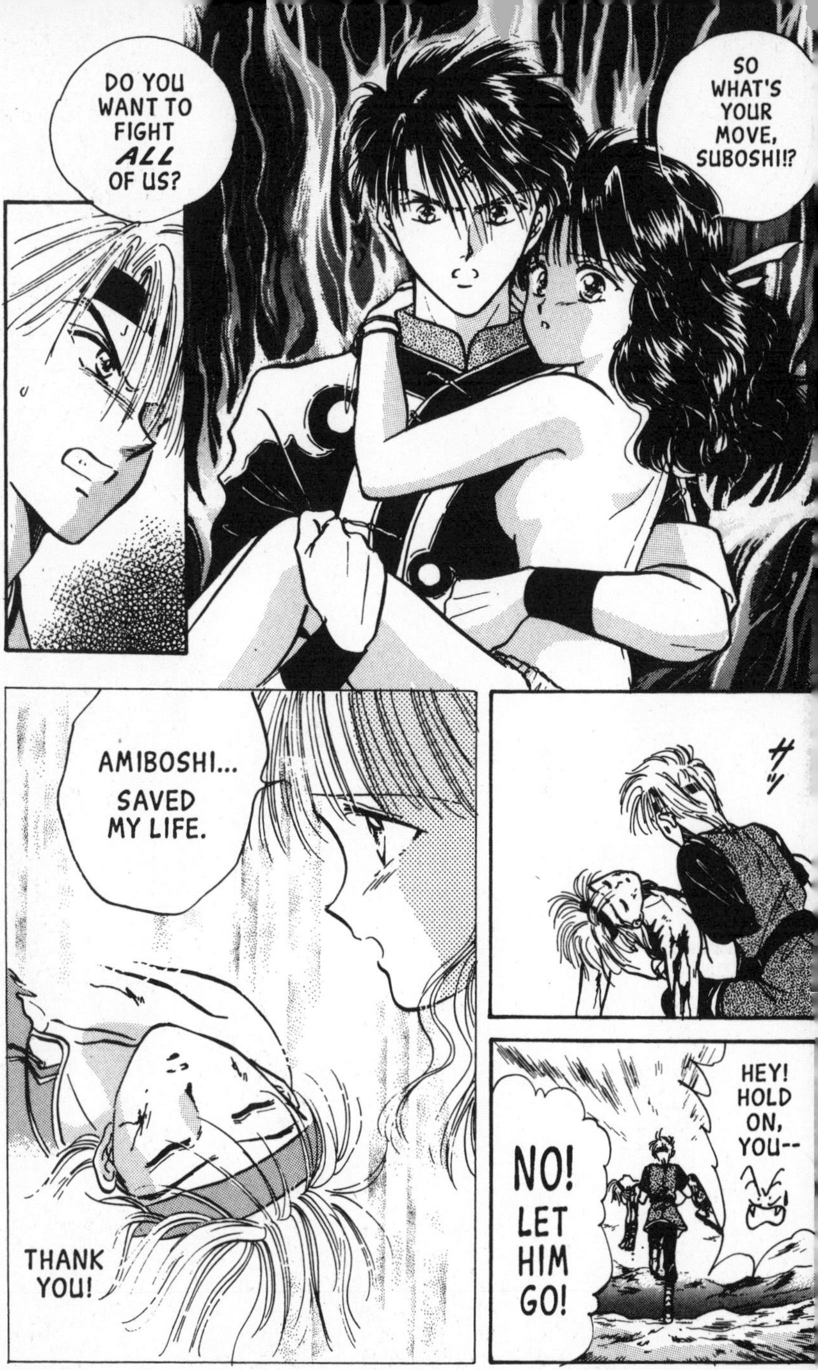
SO WHAT'S YOUR MOVE, SUBOSHI!?
DO YOU WANT TO FIGHT ALL OF US?
ザッ
HEY! HOLD ON, YOU--
NO! LET HIM GO!
AMIBOSHI... SAVED MY LIFE.
THANK YOU!

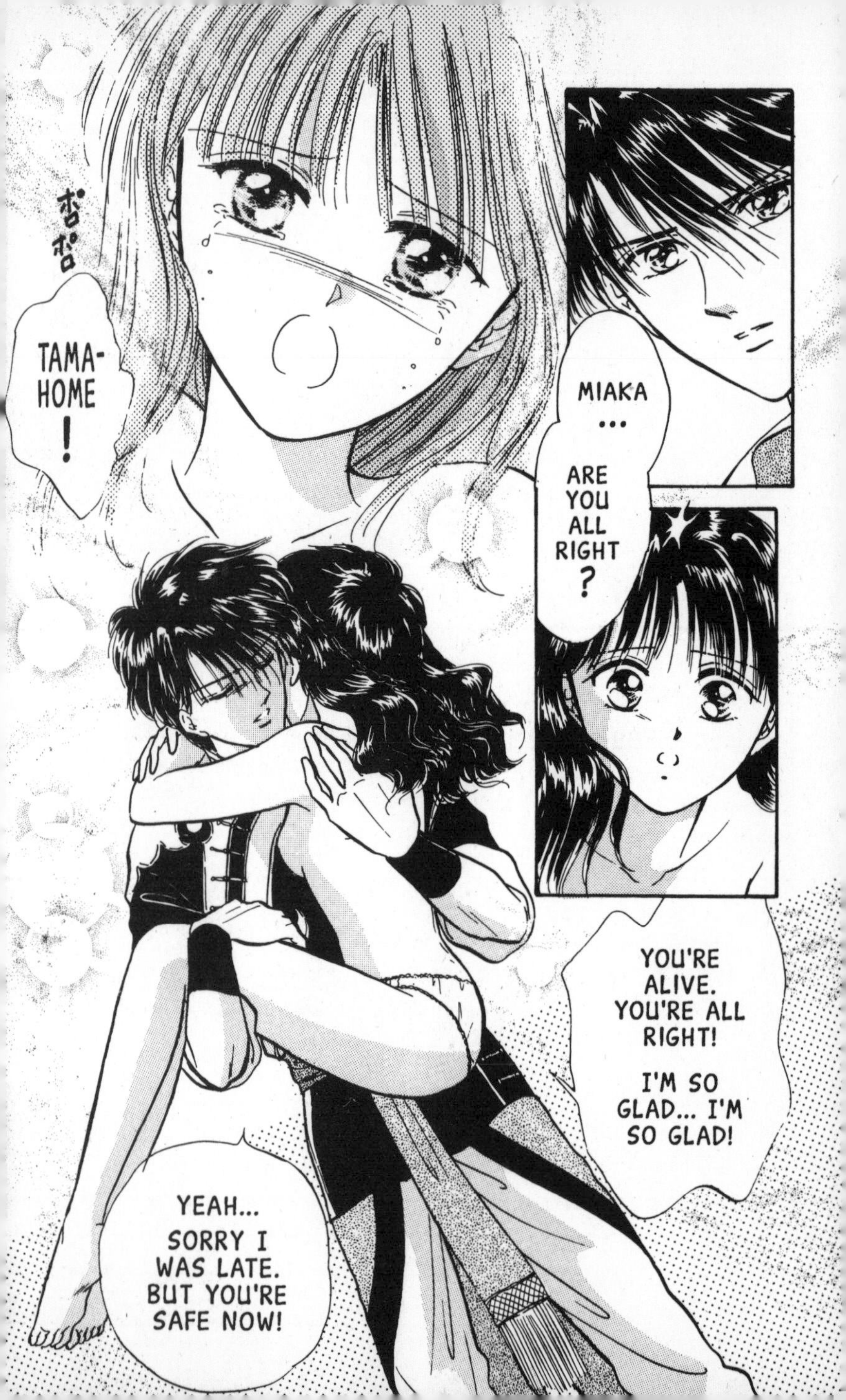
MIAKA... ARE YOU ALL RIGHT?
ポロポロ
TAMA-HOME!
YOU'RE ALIVE. YOU'RE ALL RIGHT!
I'M SO GLAD... I'M SO GLAD!
YEAH... SORRY I WAS LATE. BUT YOU'RE SAFE NOW!

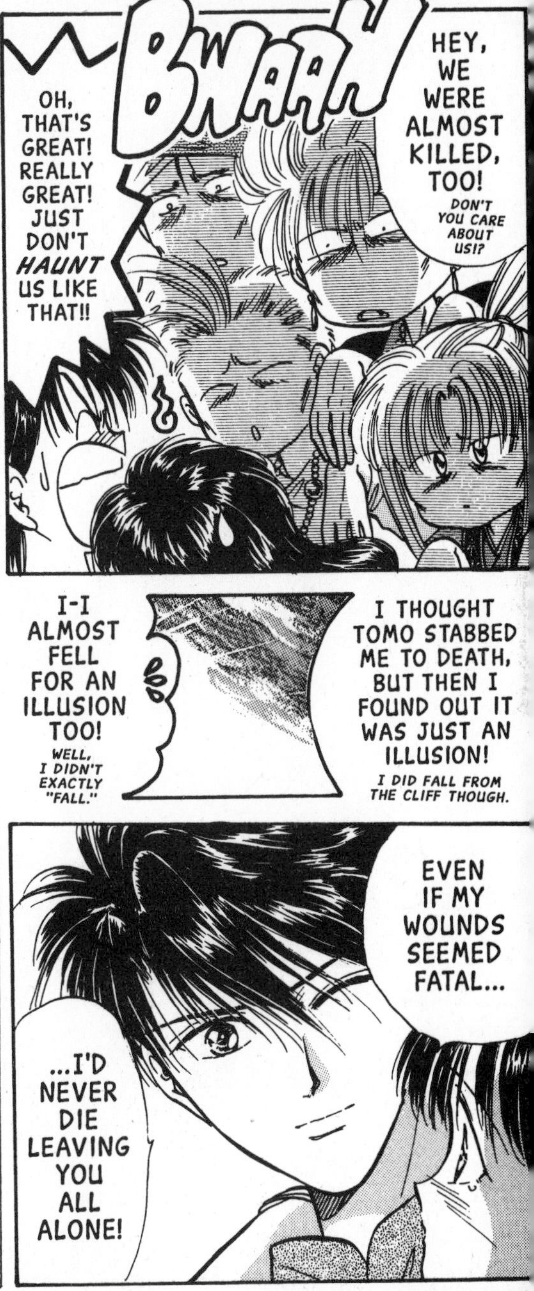
HEY, WE WERE ALMOST KILLED, TOO!
DON'T YOU CARE ABOUT US!?
BWAAH
OH, THAT'S GREAT! REALLY GREAT! JUST DON'T *HAUNT* US LIKE THAT!!
I THOUGHT TOMO STABBED ME TO DEATH, BUT THEN I FOUND OUT IT WAS JUST AN ILLUSION!
I DID FALL FROM THE CLIFF THOUGH.
I-I ALMOST FELL FOR AN ILLUSION TOO!
WELL, I DIDN'T EXACTLY "FALL."
EVEN IF MY WOUNDS SEEMED FATAL...
...I'D NEVER DIE LEAVING YOU ALL ALONE!

Veteran

Hello, hello! This is Yū Watase. Right now we're listening to Chopin. We're really into classical music these days. Speaking of music, have you had the chance to listen to CD Book 2? The first song, "Journey of Encounters," and the BGM has a Chinese sound. I'm so into it. Of course, I love all the songs! *Mr. Honda and Mr. Kajiwara from 135 are singing on the demo tape.* ♥♥♥ *How lucky can I get!!*
Nuriko's song might seem like a love song, but in fact, it's about death. Amiboshi was so sexy (his voice that is).
And Chichiri's is so cute!!
I also want to thank all of you fans who came to the signing event in Fukuoka. Thanks for all the letters and presents.
Oh, yeah! The emcee at the signing asked me whether this was my first time to Kyushu, and I was so nervous I said "Yes!" but after returning to my hotel, I realized I'd already traveled to Nagasaki with a friend of mine. I was appalled! "I'm so stupid... I've even been to Huis Ten Bosch!" I... I lied! I'm so sorry!
Oh! One more thing! I'm having a book signing in Kyoto in November (1994). So fans over there please come by.
Honest, I've never been to Kyoto! But it's been too long since I've been back to Osaka! I miss it so much!

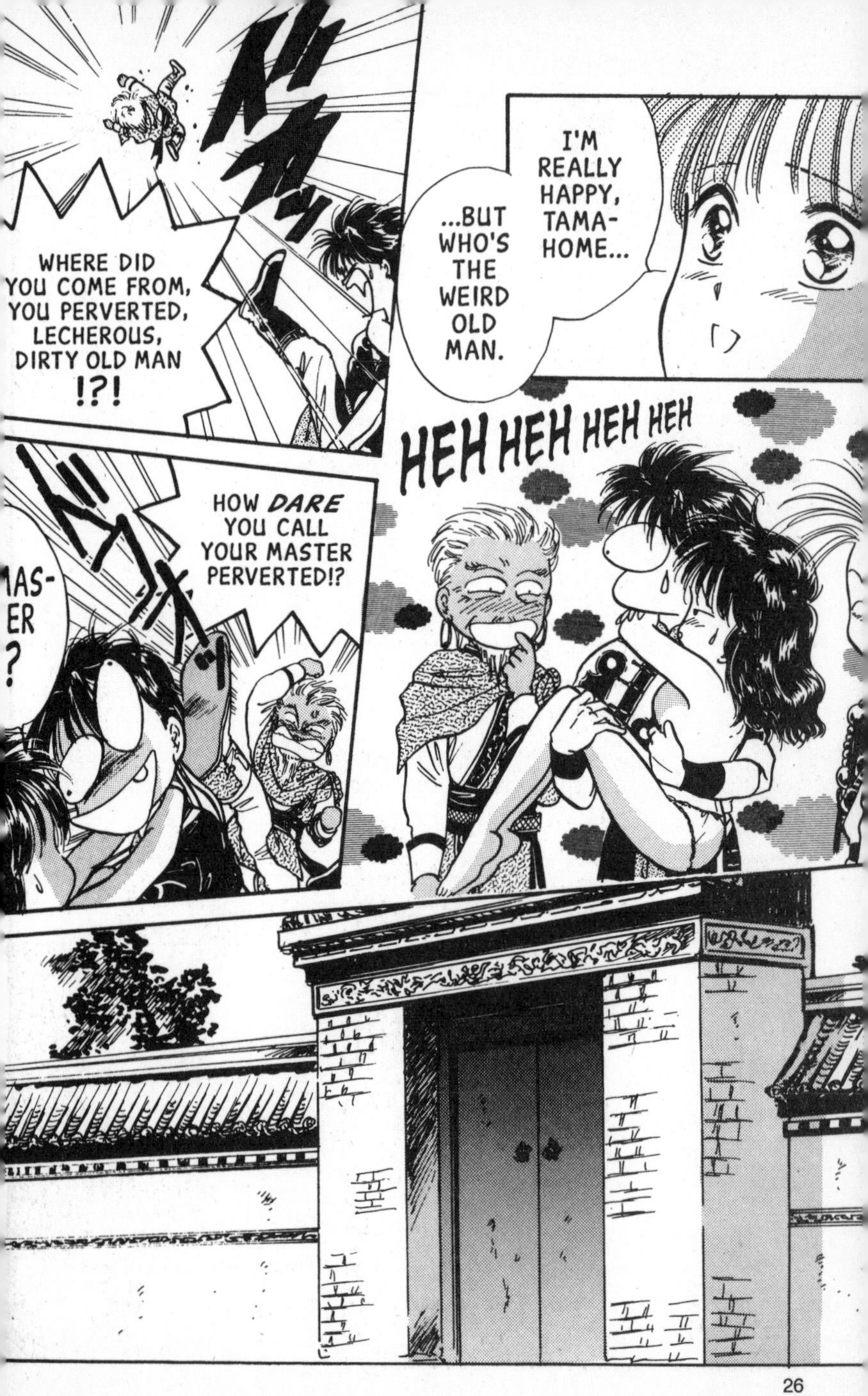
I'M REALLY HAPPY, TAMA-HOME...
...BUT WHO'S THE WEIRD OLD MAN.
WHERE DID YOU COME FROM, YOU PERVERTED, LECHEROUS, DIRTY OLD MAN !?!
HEH HEH HEH HEH
HOW *DARE* YOU CALL YOUR MASTER PERVERTED!?

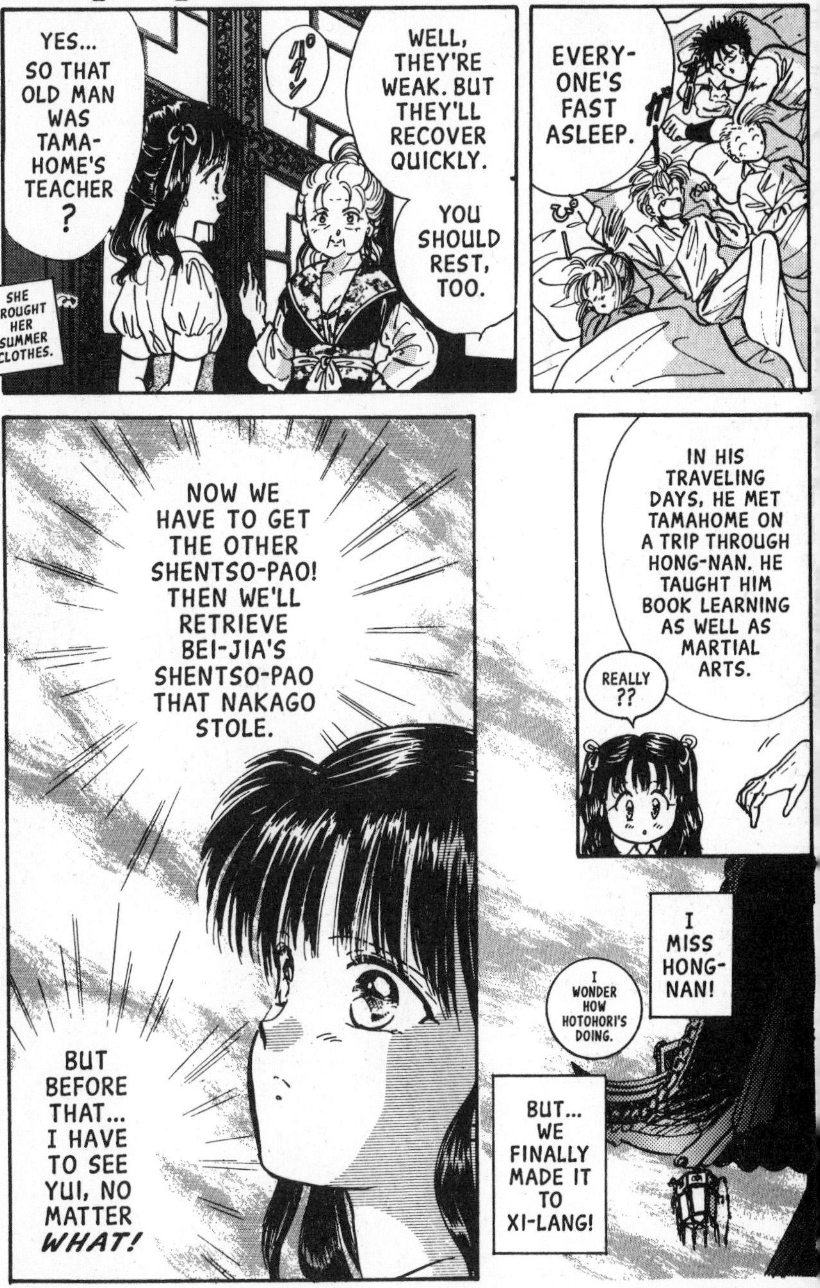
EVERY-ONE'S FAST ASLEEP.
パタン
WELL, THEY'RE WEAK. BUT THEY'LL RECOVER QUICKLY.
YOU SHOULD REST, TOO.
YES... SO THAT OLD MAN WAS TAMA-HOME'S TEACHER?
SHE BROUGHT HER SUMMER CLOTHES.
IN HIS TRAVELING DAYS, HE MET TAMAHOME ON A TRIP THROUGH HONG-NAN. HE TAUGHT HIM BOOK LEARNING AS WELL AS MARTIAL ARTS.
REALLY ??
I MISS HONG-NAN!
I WONDER HOW HOTOHORI'S DOING.
BUT... WE FINALLY MADE IT TO XI-LANG!
NOW WE HAVE TO GET THE OTHER SHENTSO-PAO! THEN WE'LL RETRIEVE BEI-JIA'S SHENTSO-PAO THAT NAKAGO STOLE.
BUT BEFORE THAT... I HAVE TO SEE YUI, NO MATTER WHAT!

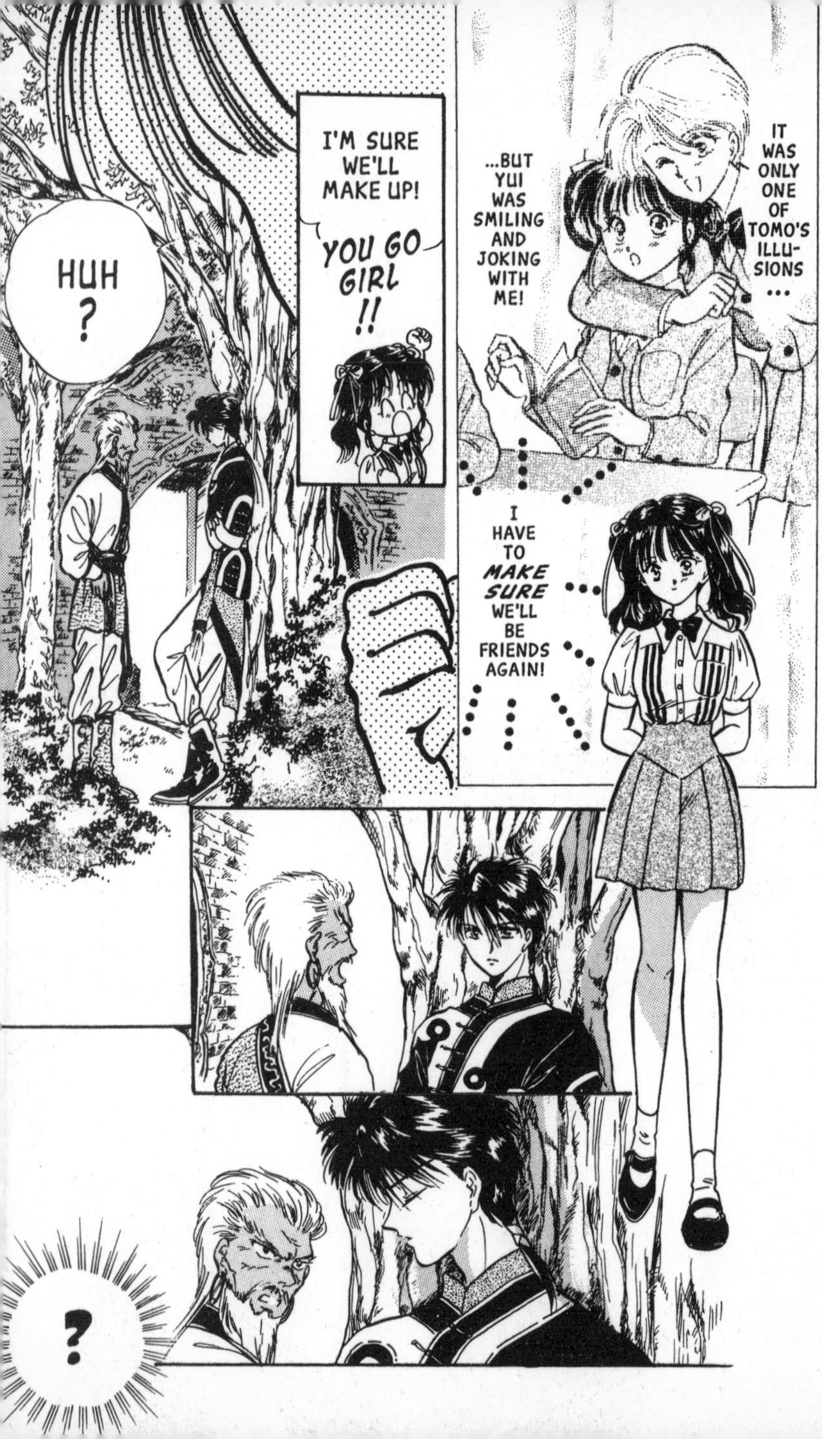
IT WAS ONLY ONE OF TOMO'S ILLUSIONS...
...BUT YUI WAS SMILING AND JOKING WITH ME!
I HAVE TO MAKE SURE WE'LL BE FRIENDS AGAIN!
I'M SURE WE'LL MAKE UP!
YOU GO GIRL !!
HUH ?
?

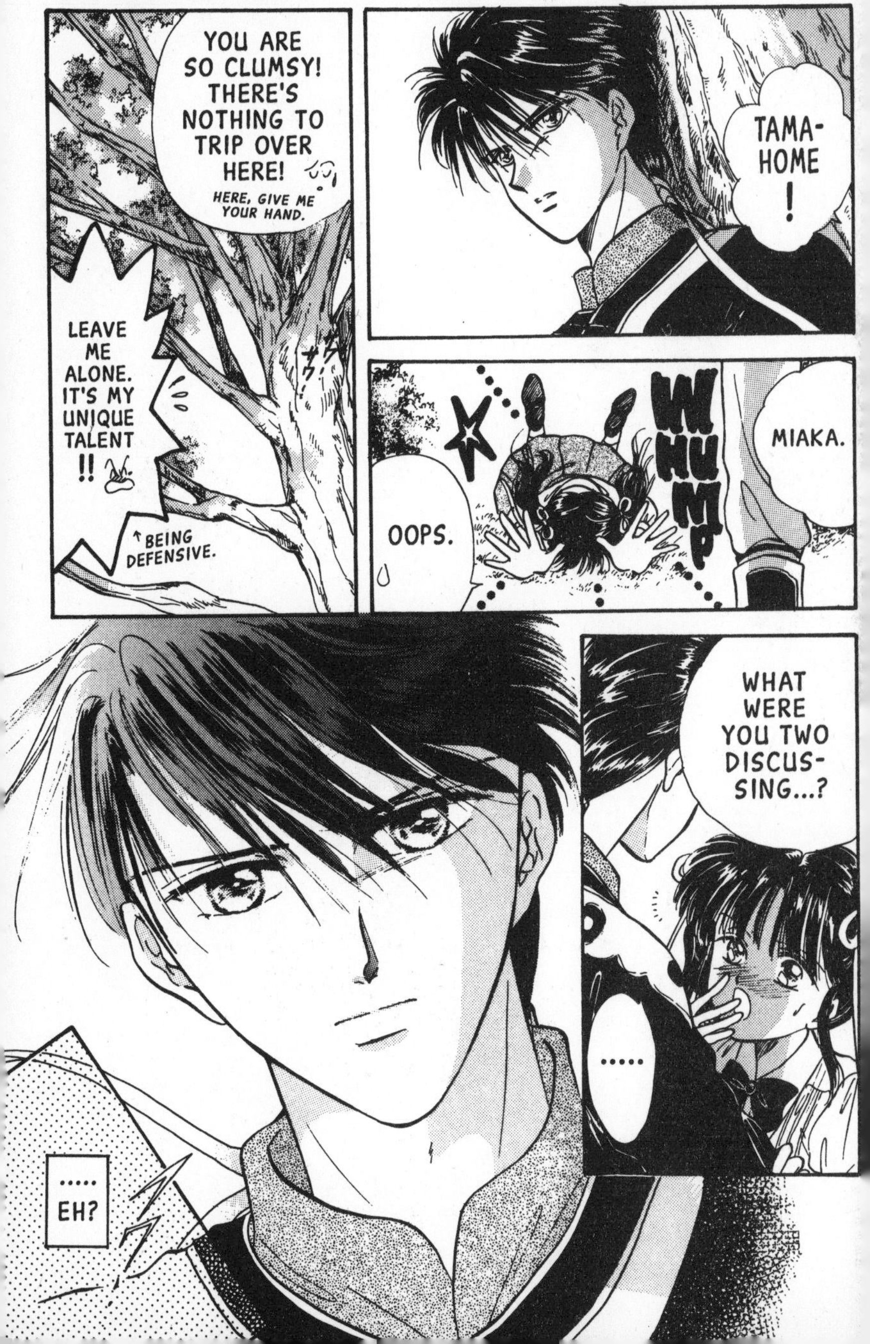
TAMA-HOME!
MIAKA.
WHUMP
OOPS.
YOU ARE SO CLUMSY! THERE'S NOTHING TO TRIP OVER HERE!
HERE, GIVE ME YOUR HAND.
LEAVE ME ALONE. IT'S MY UNIQUE TALENT!!
↑BEING DEFENSIVE.
WHAT WERE YOU TWO DISCUSSING...?
......
......EH?

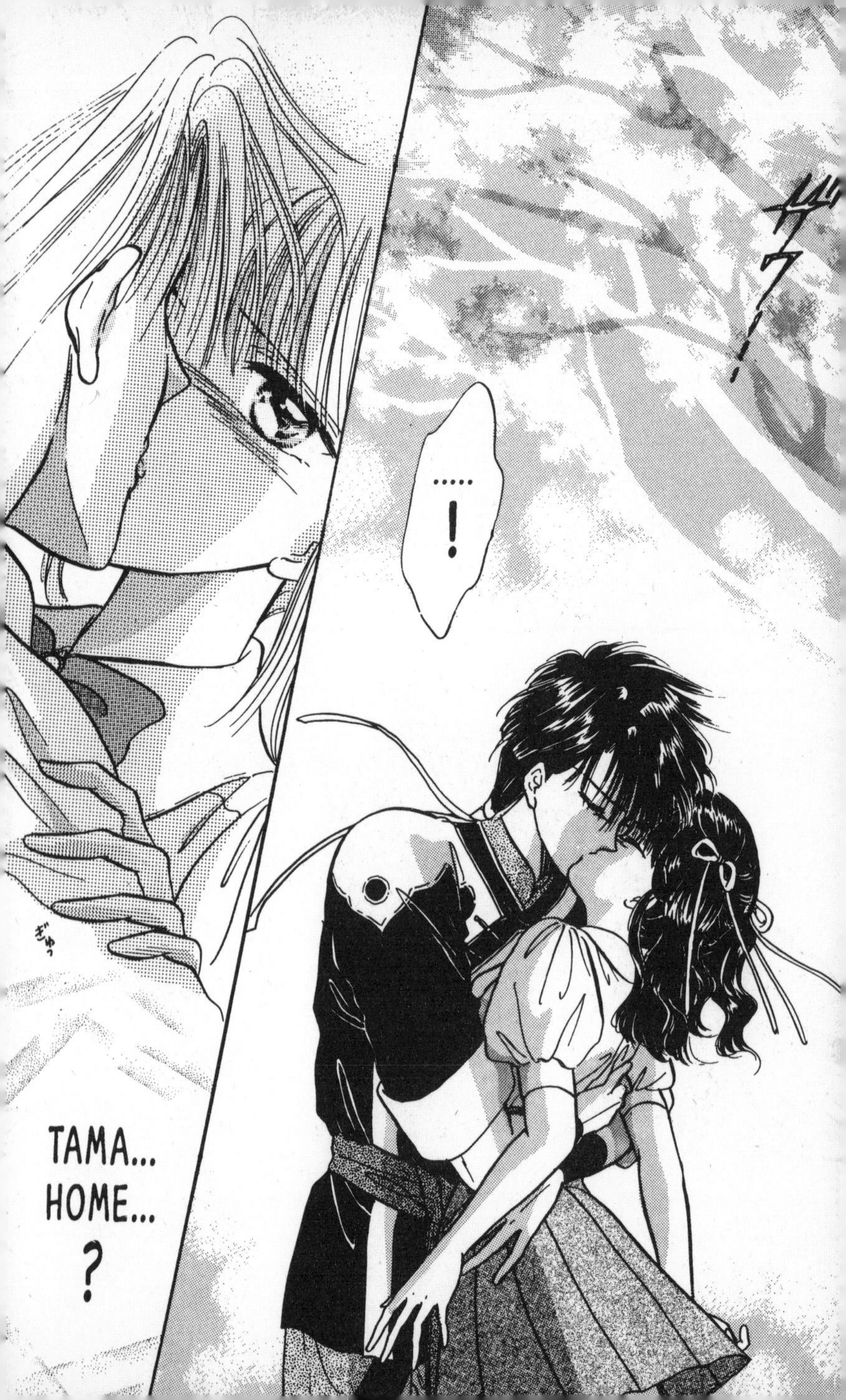
ザワー!!
....!
ぎゅっ
TAMA...
HOME...
?

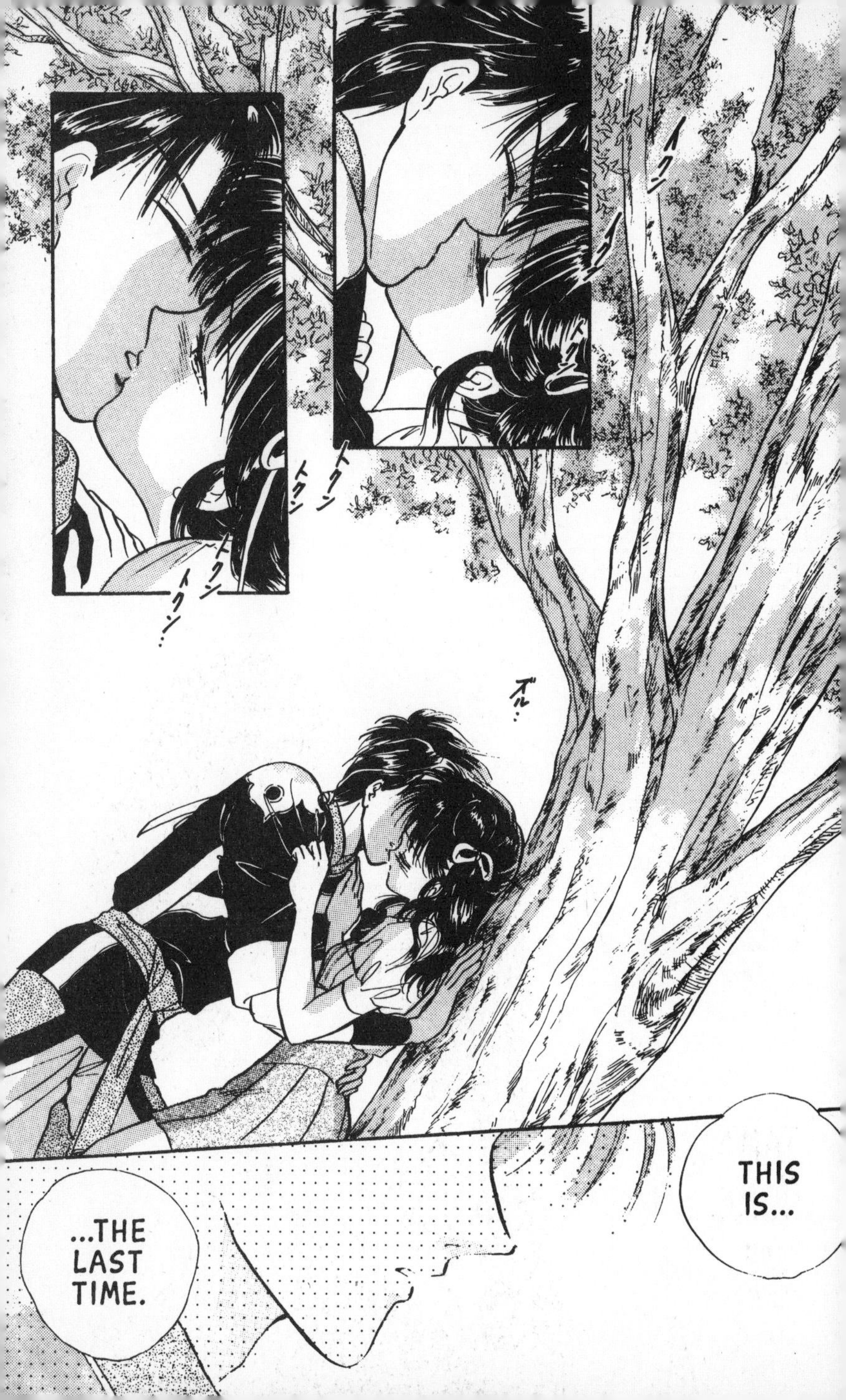
トクン トクン
トクン トクン
トクン トクン…
ズル…
THIS IS...
...THE LAST TIME.

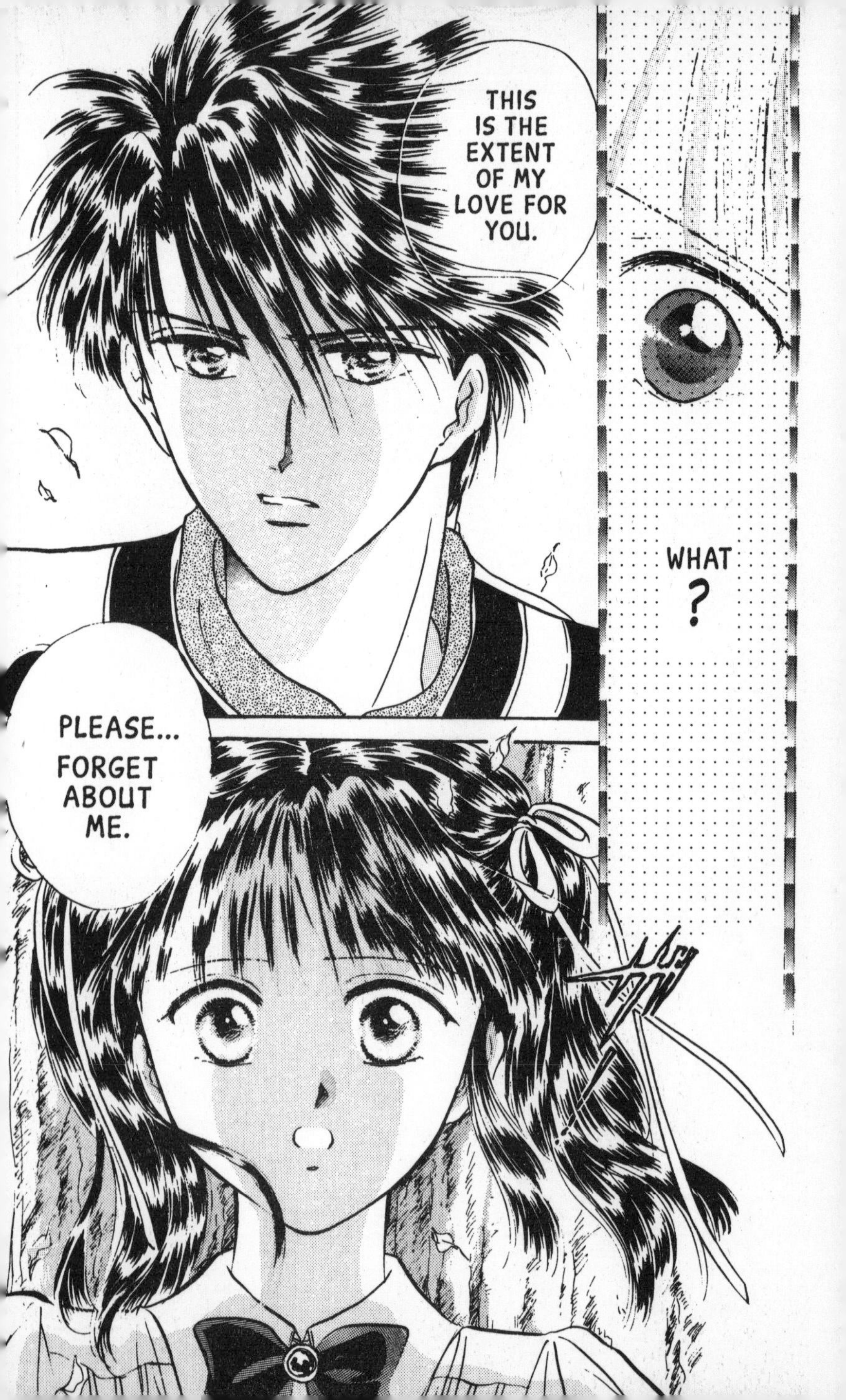
WHAT ?
THIS IS THE EXTENT OF MY LOVE FOR YOU.
PLEASE... FORGET ABOUT ME.

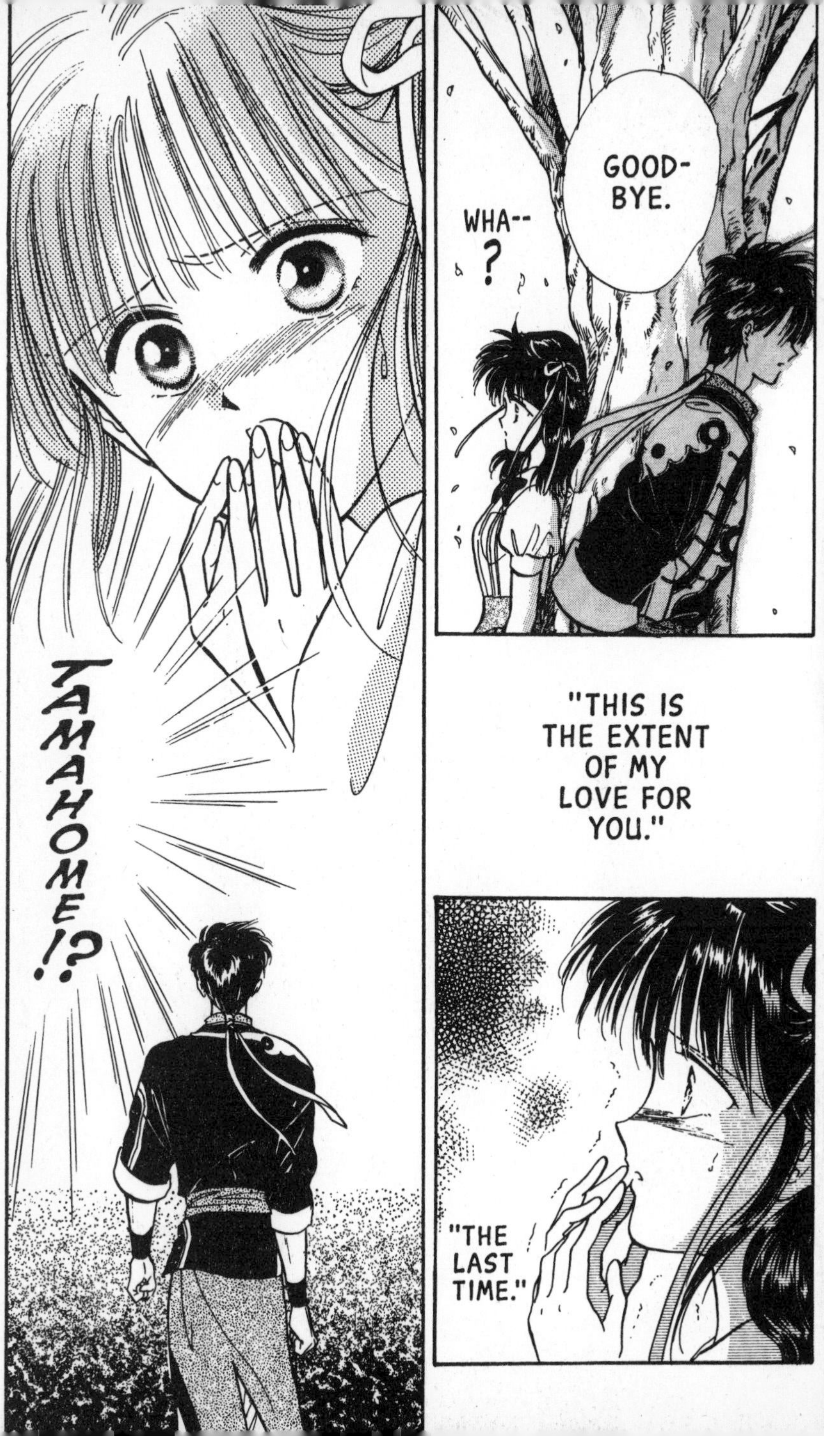
GOOD-BYE.
WHA--?
"THIS IS THE EXTENT OF MY LOVE FOR YOU."
"THE LAST TIME."
TAMAHOME!?

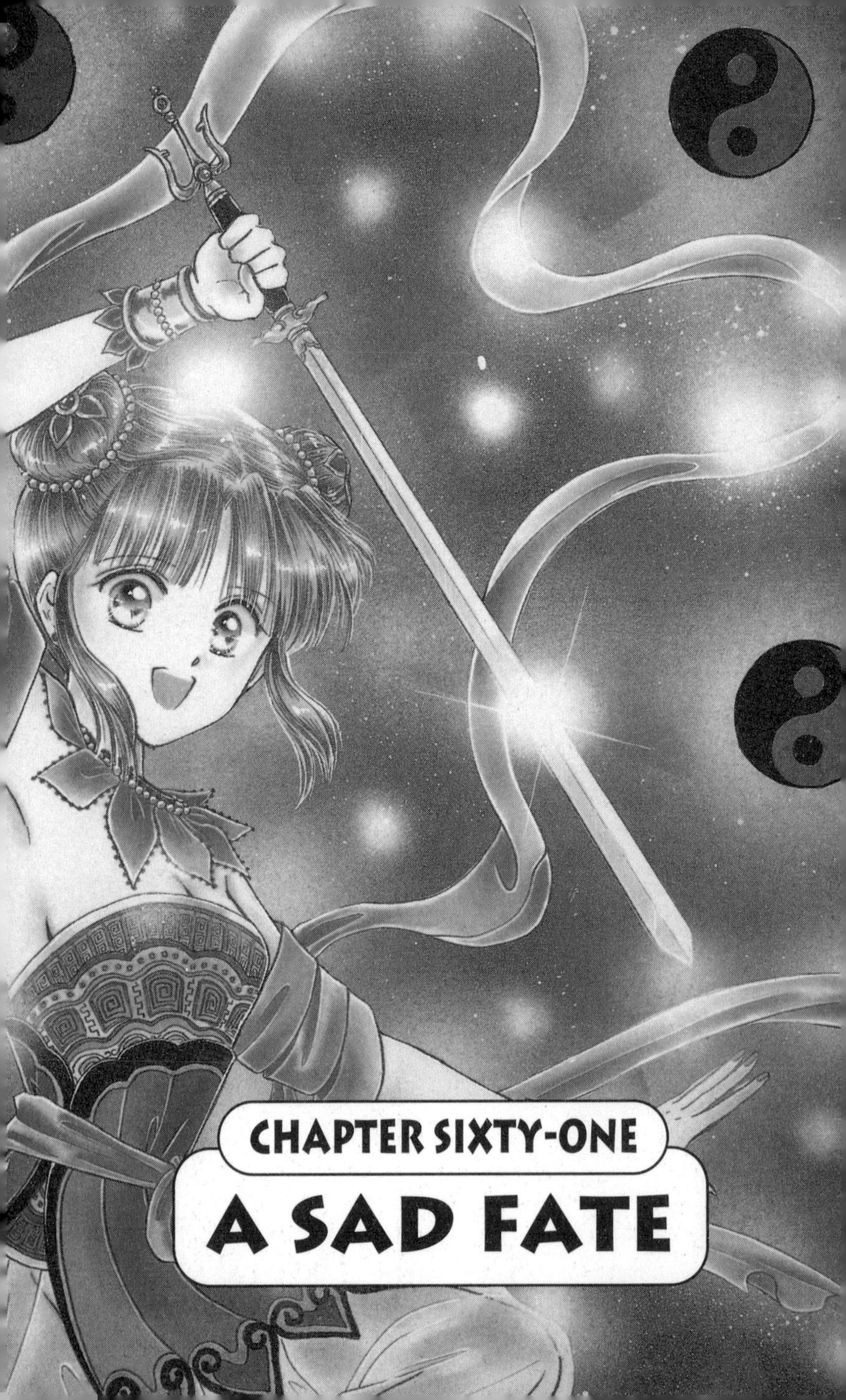
CHAPTER SIXTY-ONE
A SAD FATE

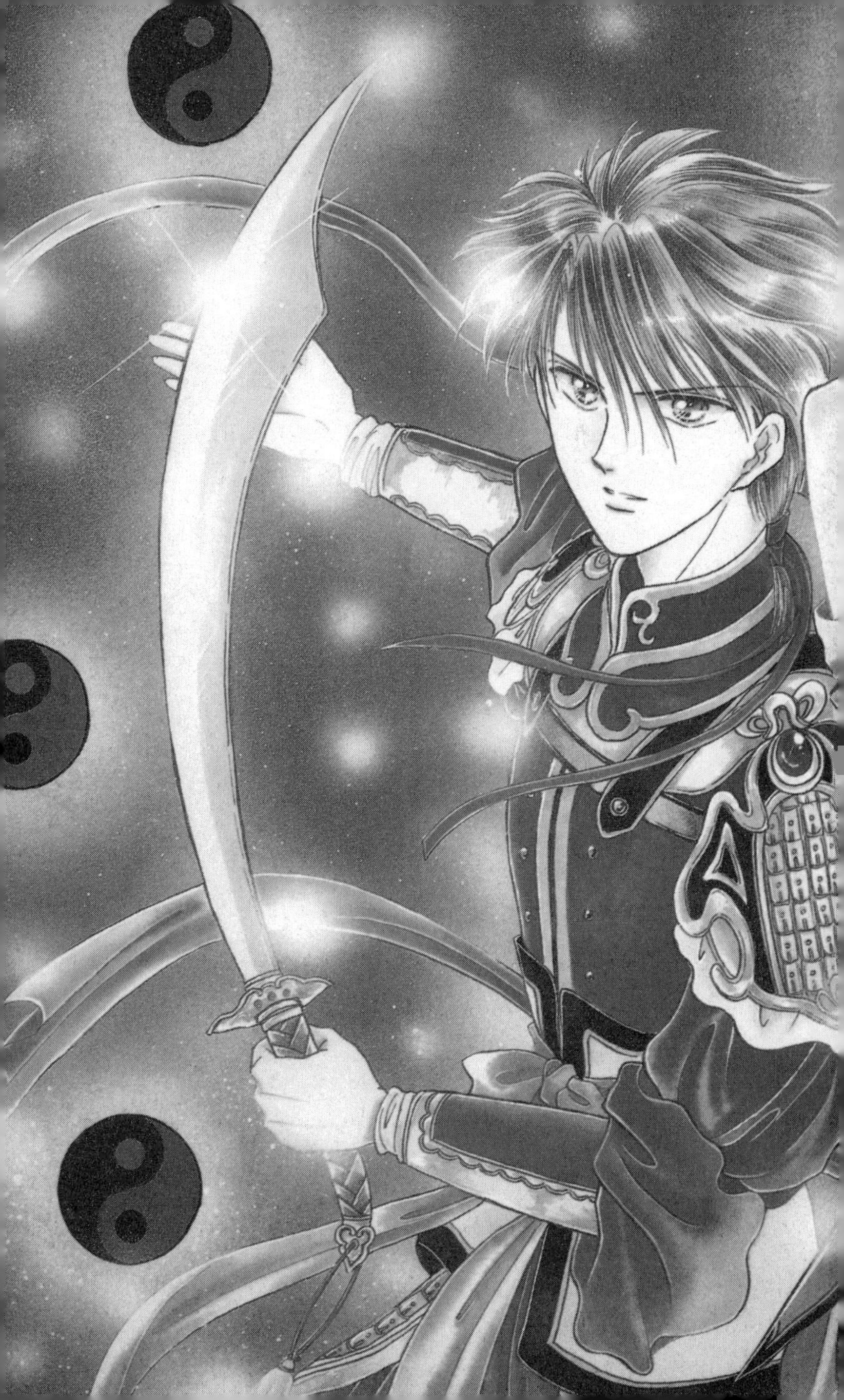

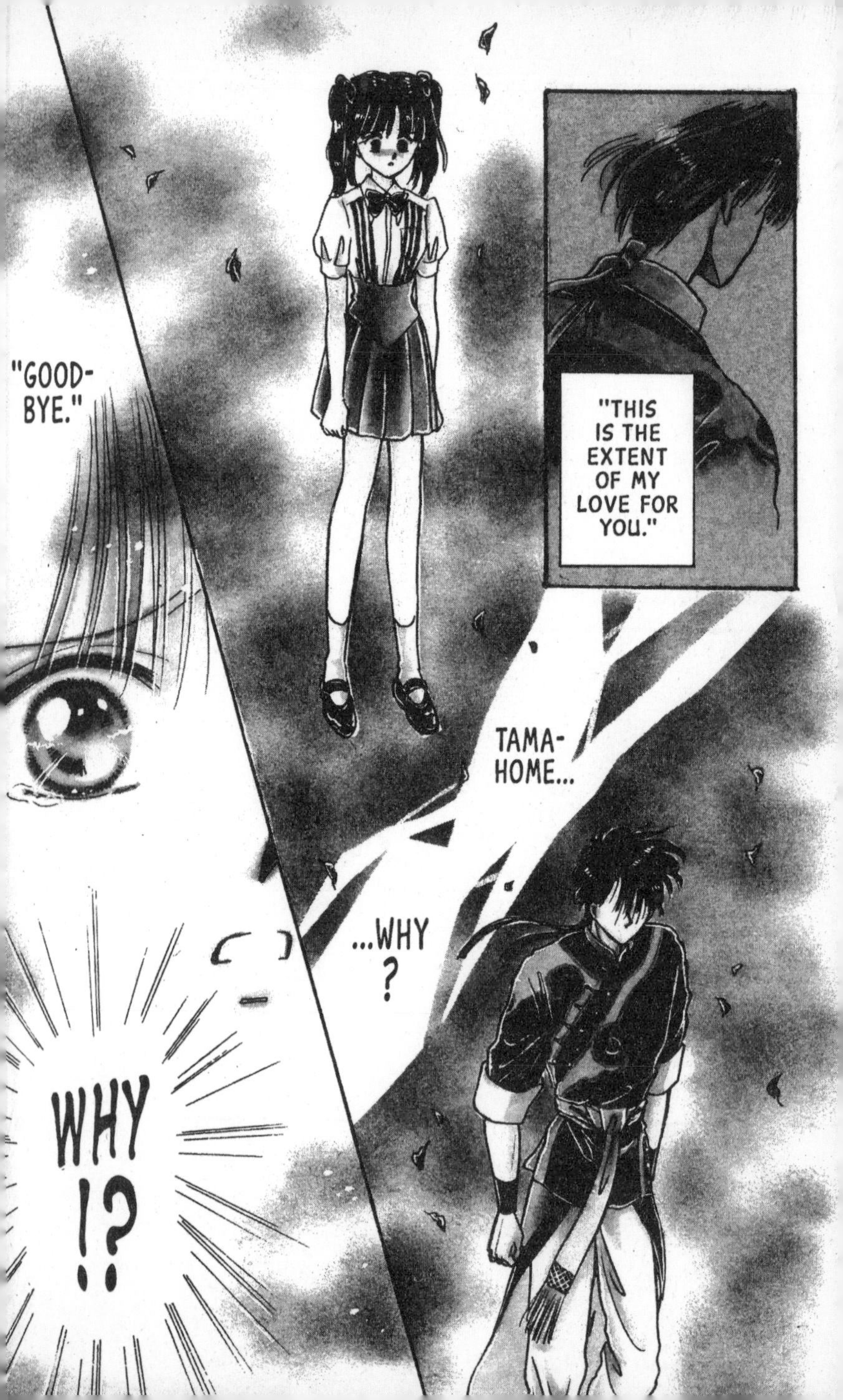
"THIS IS THE EXTENT OF MY LOVE FOR YOU."
TAMA-HOME...
...WHY ?
"GOOD-BYE."
WHY !?

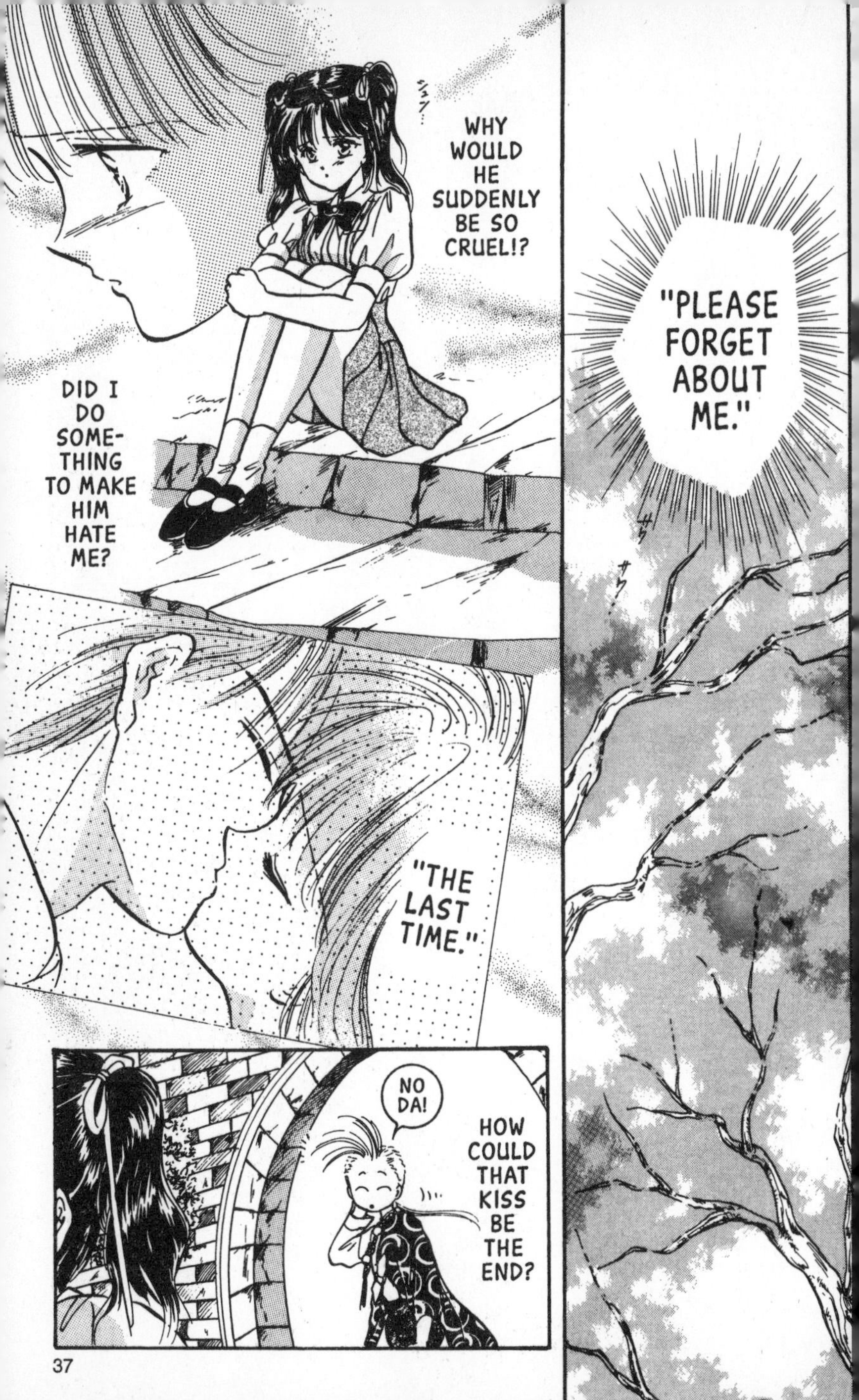
"PLEASE FORGET ABOUT ME."
WHY WOULD HE SUDDENLY BE SO CRUEL!?
DID I DO SOMETHING TO MAKE HIM HATE ME?
"THE LAST TIME."
HOW COULD THAT KISS BE THE END?
NO DA!

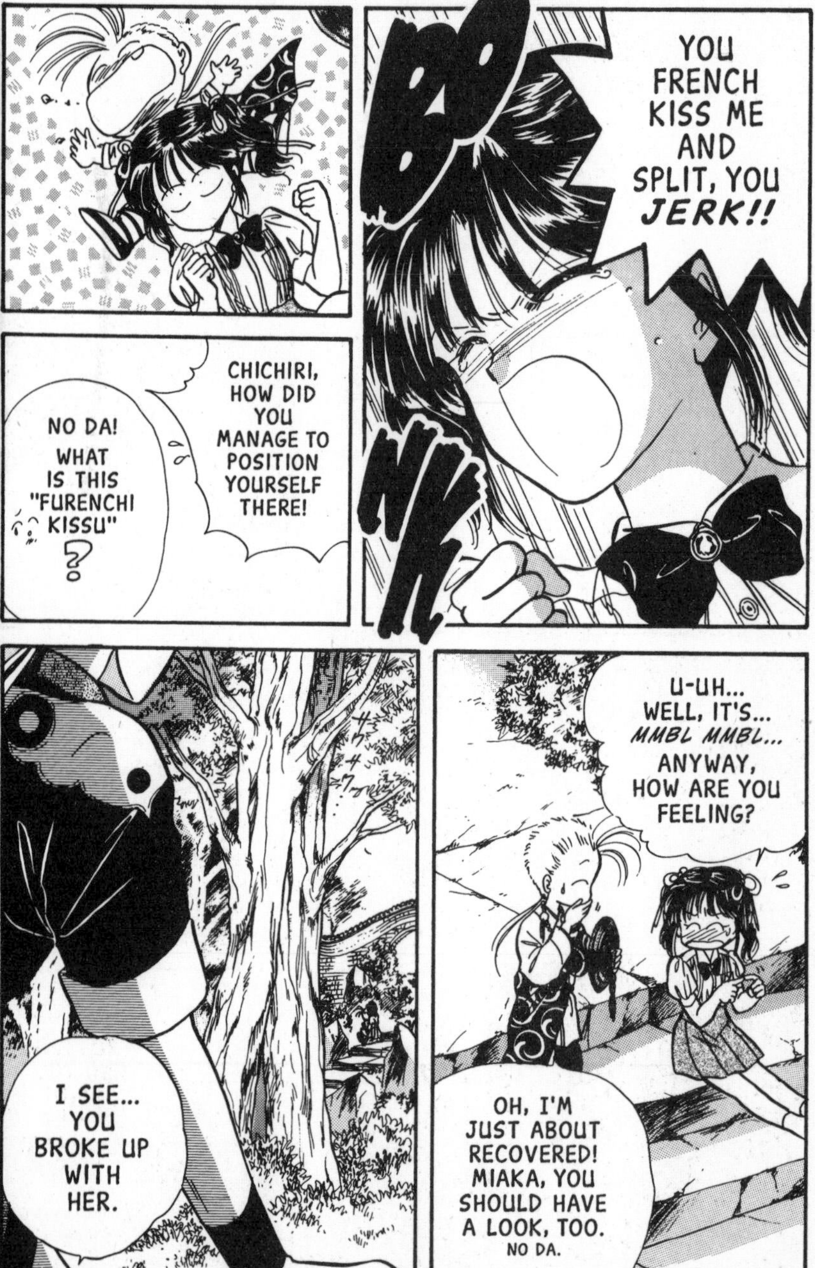
YOU FRENCH KISS ME AND SPLIT, YOU *JERK!!*
CHICHIRI, HOW DID YOU MANAGE TO POSITION YOURSELF THERE!
NO DA! WHAT IS THIS "FURENCHI KISSU" ?
U-UH... WELL, IT'S... *MMBL MMBL...* ANYWAY, HOW ARE YOU FEELING?
OH, I'M JUST ABOUT RECOVERED! MIAKA, YOU SHOULD HAVE A LOOK, TOO. NO DA.
I SEE... YOU BROKE UP WITH HER.

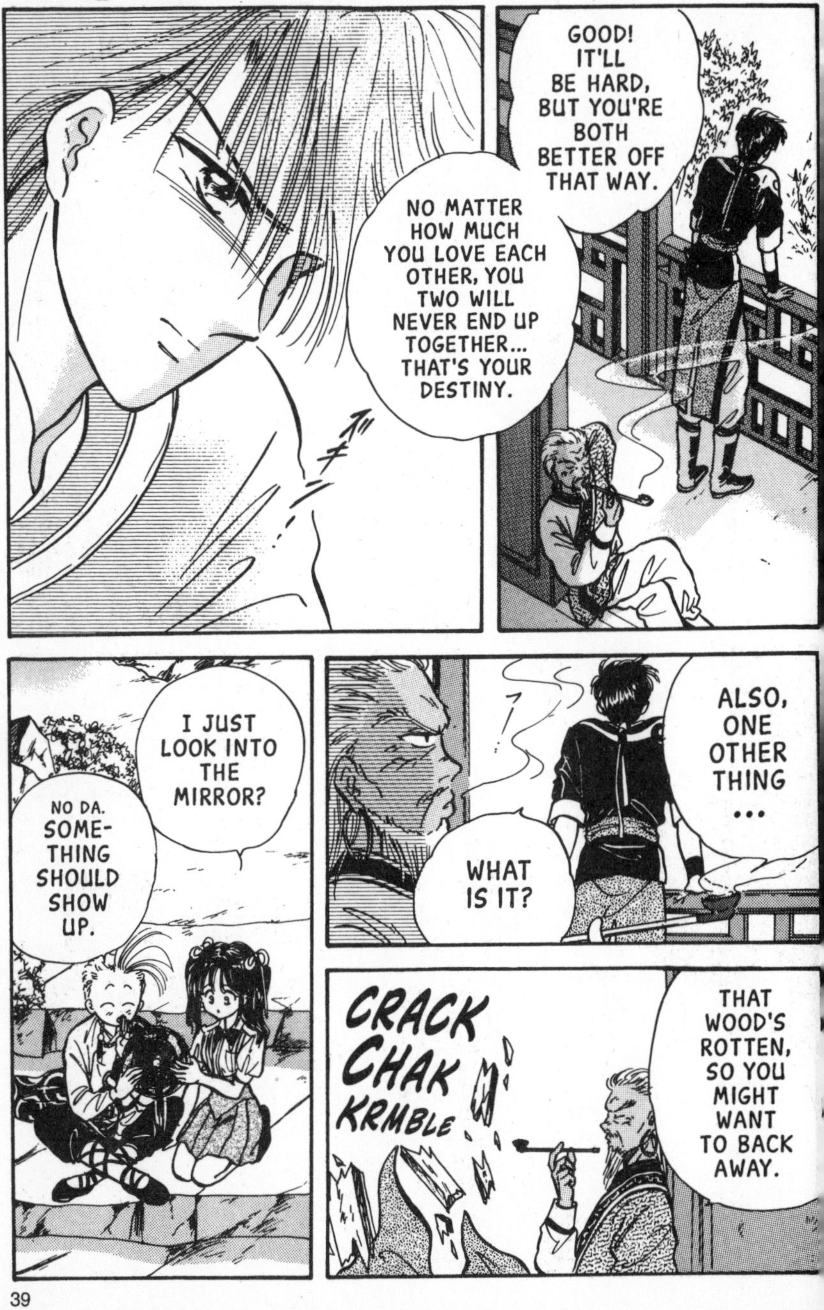
GOOD! IT'LL BE HARD, BUT YOU'RE BOTH BETTER OFF THAT WAY.
NO MATTER HOW MUCH YOU LOVE EACH OTHER, YOU TWO WILL NEVER END UP TOGETHER... THAT'S YOUR DESTINY.
ALSO, ONE OTHER THING...
WHAT IS IT?
THAT WOOD'S ROTTEN, SO YOU MIGHT WANT TO BACK AWAY.
CRACK
CHAK
KRMBLE
I JUST LOOK INTO THE MIRROR?
NO DA. SOMETHING SHOULD SHOW UP.

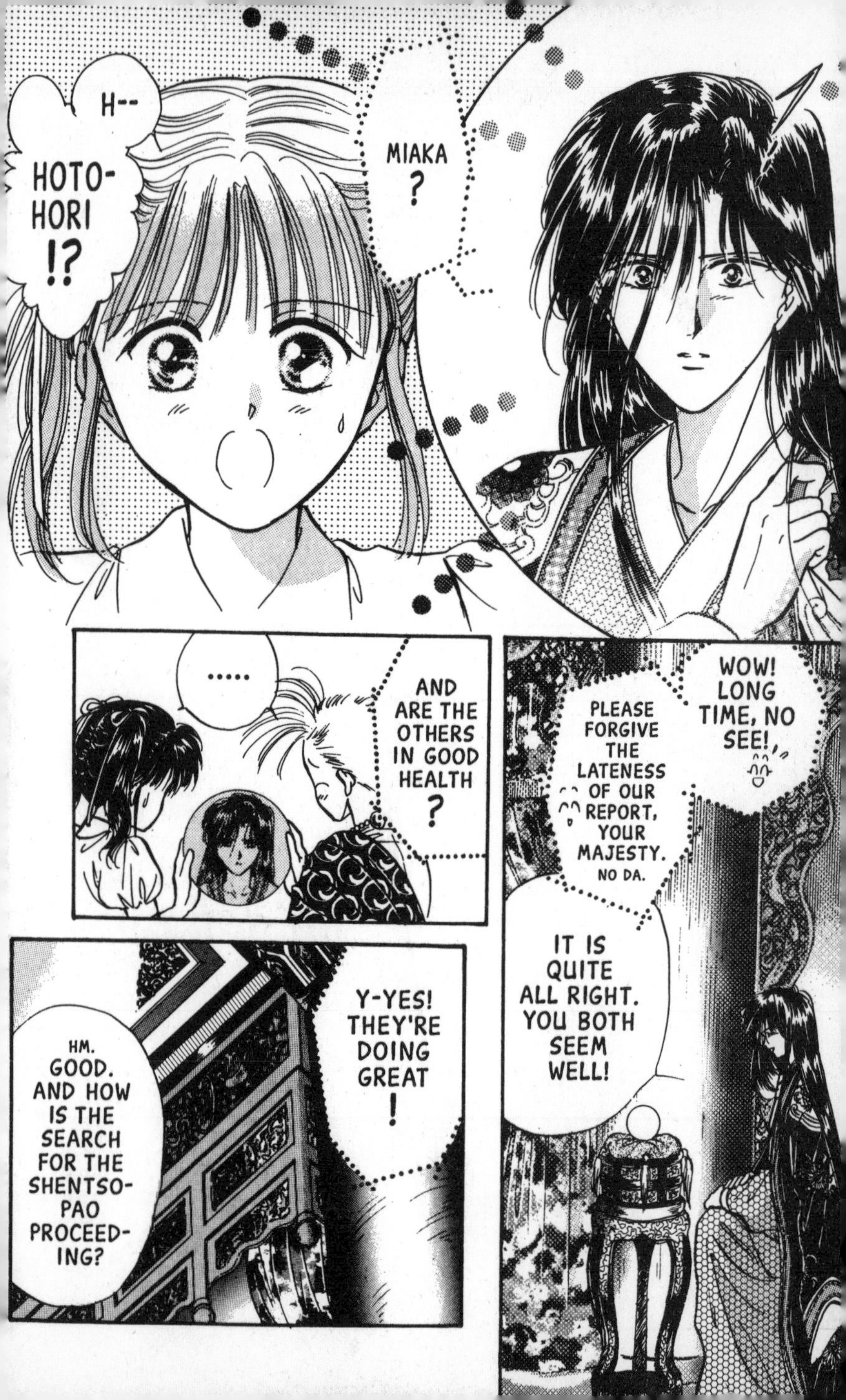
MIAKA ?
H-- HOTO-HORI !?
WOW! LONG TIME, NO SEE!
PLEASE FORGIVE THE LATENESS OF OUR REPORT, YOUR MAJESTY. NO DA.
IT IS QUITE ALL RIGHT. YOU BOTH SEEM WELL!
AND ARE THE OTHERS IN GOOD HEALTH ?
.....
Y-YES! THEY'RE DOING GREAT !
HM. GOOD. AND HOW IS THE SEARCH FOR THE SHENTSO-PAO PROCEED-ING?

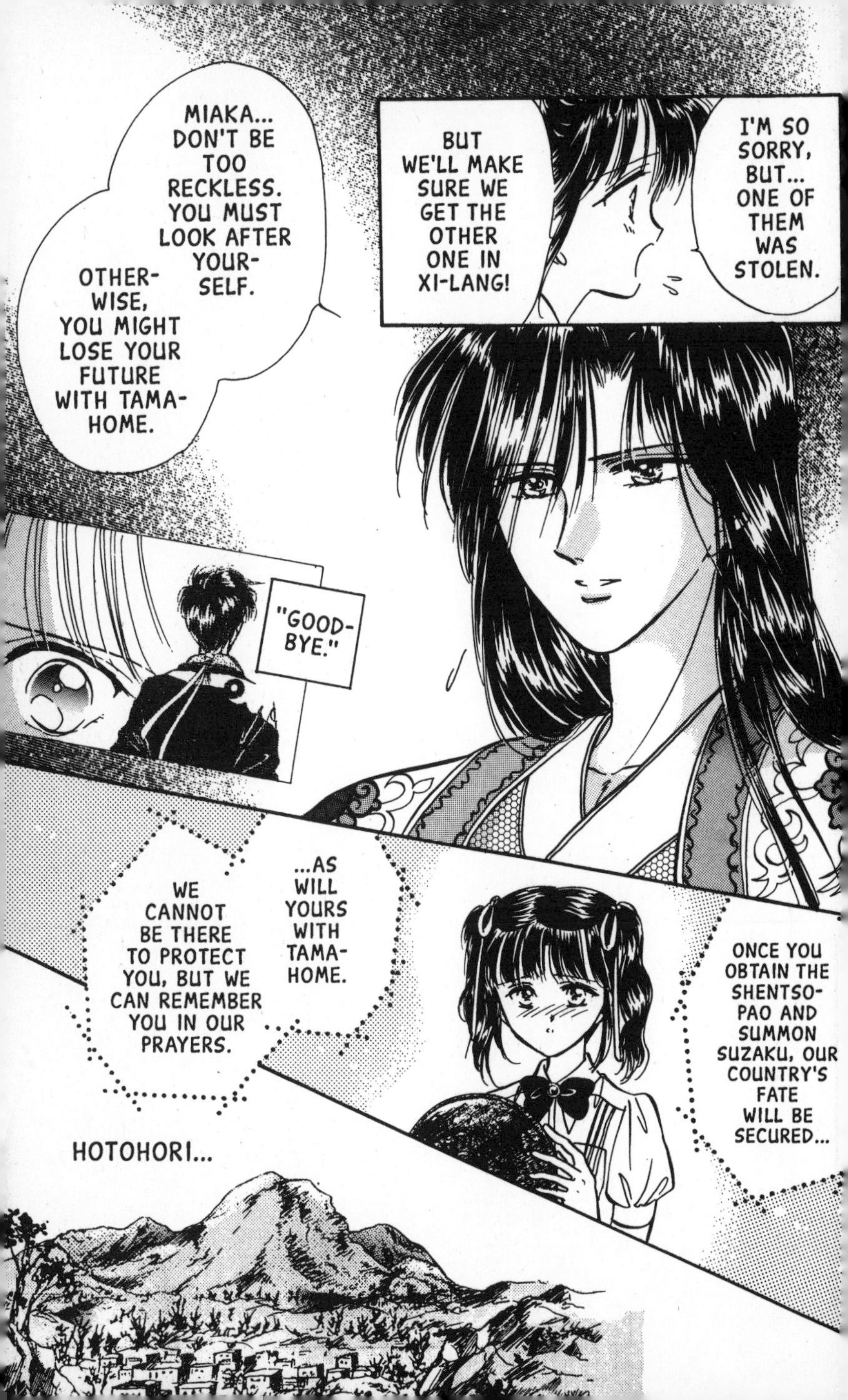
I'M SO SORRY, BUT... ONE OF THEM WAS STOLEN.
BUT WE'LL MAKE SURE WE GET THE OTHER ONE IN XI-LANG!
MIAKA... DON'T BE TOO RECKLESS. YOU MUST LOOK AFTER YOUR-SELF.
OTHER-WISE, YOU MIGHT LOSE YOUR FUTURE WITH TAMA-HOME.
"GOOD-BYE."
ONCE YOU OBTAIN THE SHENTSO-PAO AND SUMMON SUZAKU, OUR COUNTRY'S FATE WILL BE SECURED...
...AS WILL YOURS WITH TAMA-HOME.
WE CANNOT BE THERE TO PROTECT YOU, BUT WE CAN REMEMBER YOU IN OUR PRAYERS.
HOTOHORI...

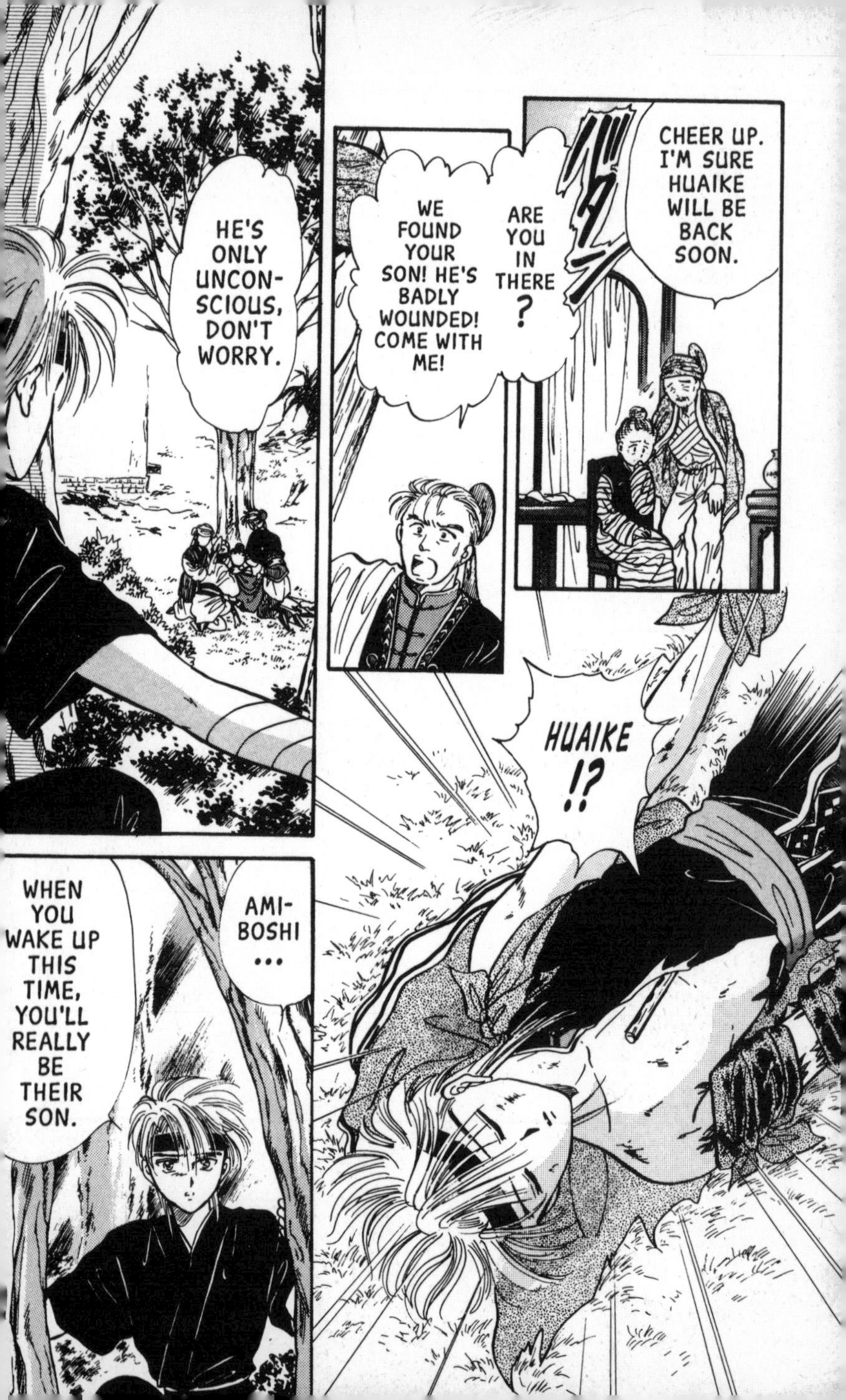
CHEER UP. I'M SURE HUAIKE WILL BE BACK SOON.
ARE YOU IN THERE?
WE FOUND YOUR SON! HE'S BADLY WOUNDED! COME WITH ME!
HE'S ONLY UNCON-SCIOUS, DON'T WORRY.
HUAIKE !?
AMI-BOSHI...
WHEN YOU WAKE UP THIS TIME, YOU'LL REALLY BE THEIR SON.

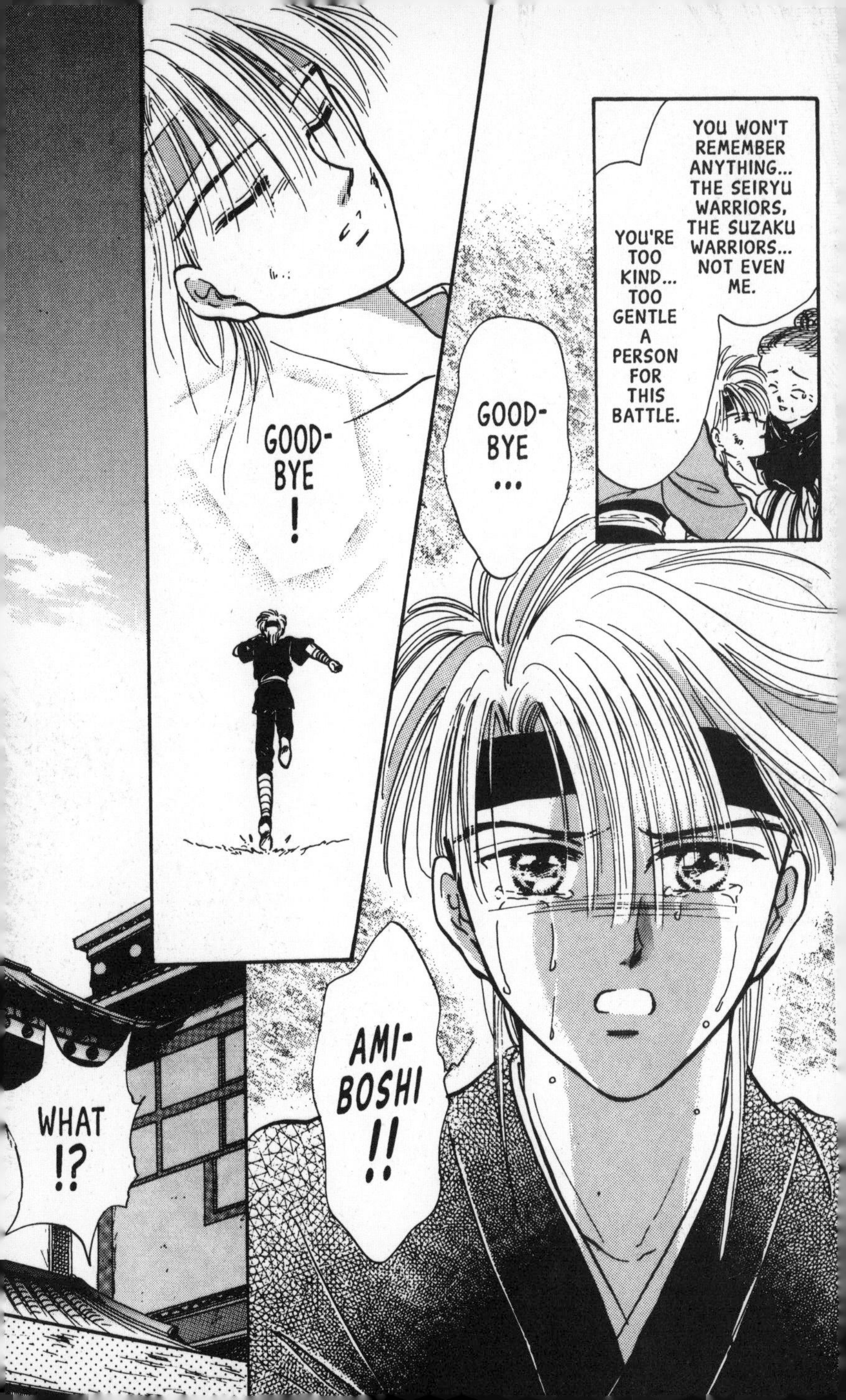
YOU WON'T REMEMBER ANYTHING... THE SEIRYU WARRIORS, THE SUZAKU WARRIORS... NOT EVEN ME.
YOU'RE TOO KIND... TOO GENTLE A PERSON FOR THIS BATTLE.
GOOD-BYE...
GOOD-BYE!
AMI-BOSHI!!
WHAT!?

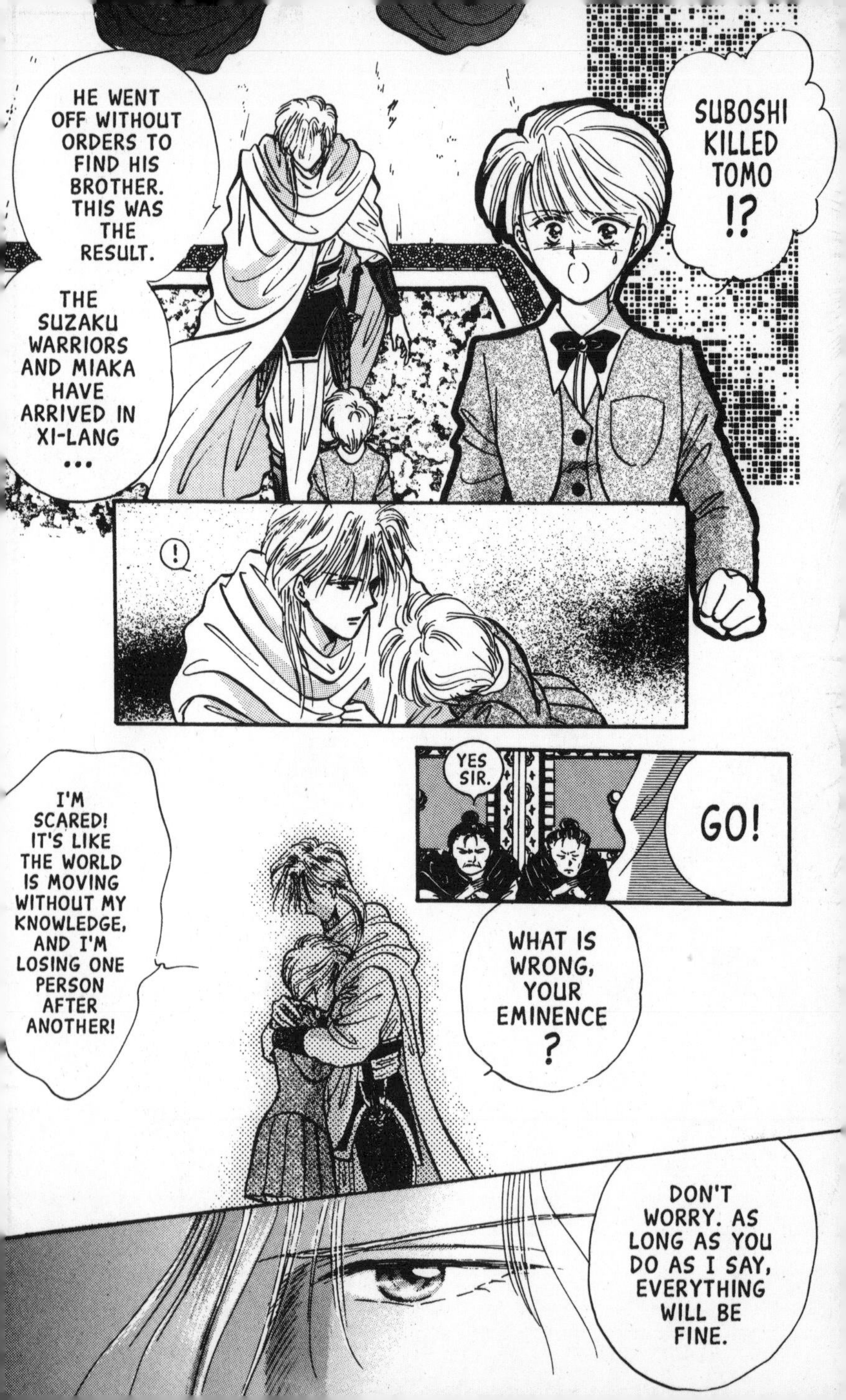
SUBOSHI KILLED TOMO !?
HE WENT OFF WITHOUT ORDERS TO FIND HIS BROTHER. THIS WAS THE RESULT.
THE SUZAKU WARRIORS AND MIAKA HAVE ARRIVED IN XI-LANG ...
!
GO!
YES SIR.
WHAT IS WRONG, YOUR EMINENCE ?
I'M SCARED! IT'S LIKE THE WORLD IS MOVING WITHOUT MY KNOWLEDGE, AND I'M LOSING ONE PERSON AFTER ANOTHER!
DON'T WORRY. AS LONG AS YOU DO AS I SAY, EVERYTHING WILL BE FINE.

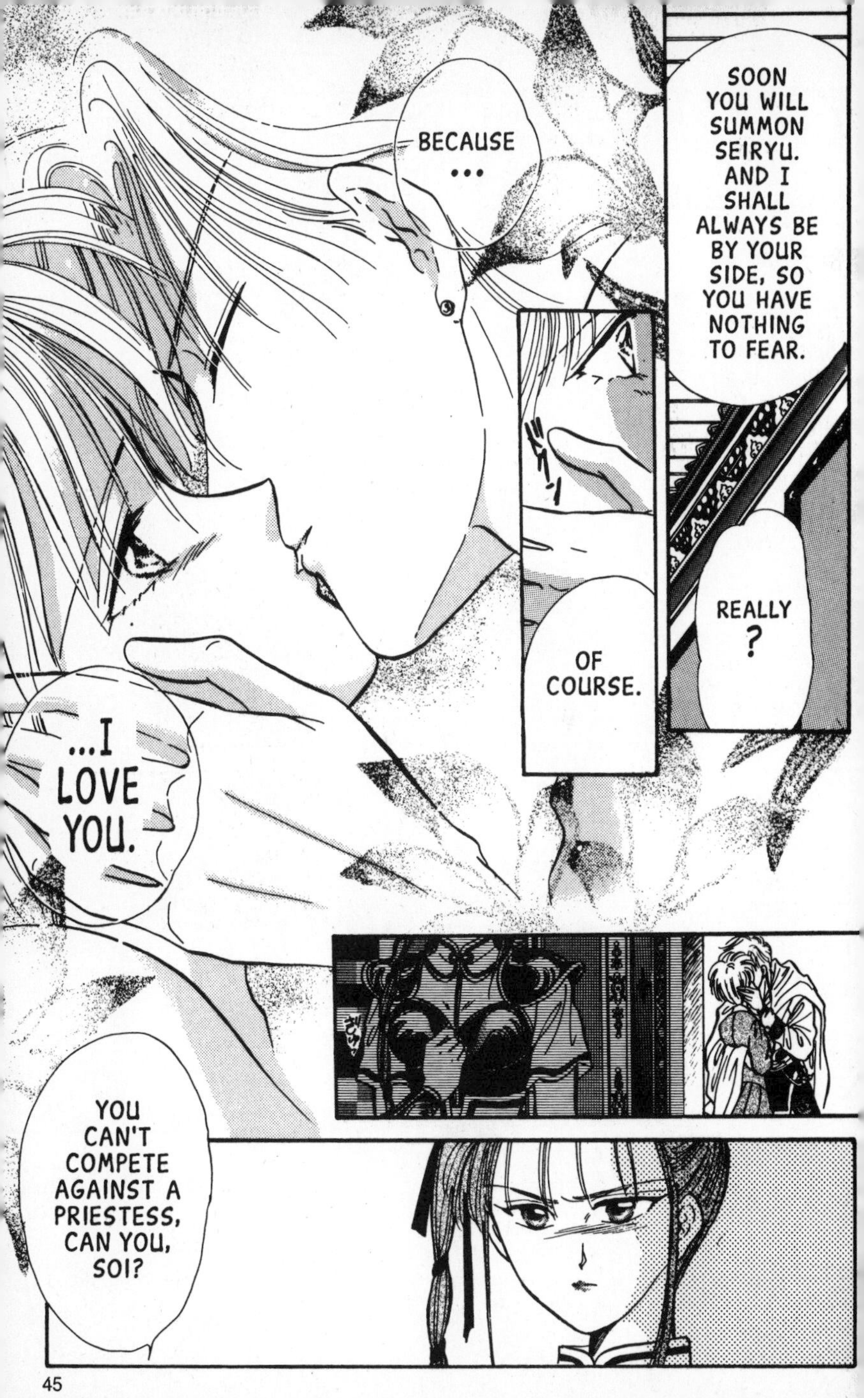
SOON YOU WILL SUMMON SEIRYU. AND I SHALL ALWAYS BE BY YOUR SIDE, SO YOU HAVE NOTHING TO FEAR.
REALLY?
OF COURSE.
BECAUSE...
...I LOVE YOU.
YOU CAN'T COMPETE AGAINST A PRIESTESS, CAN YOU, SOI?

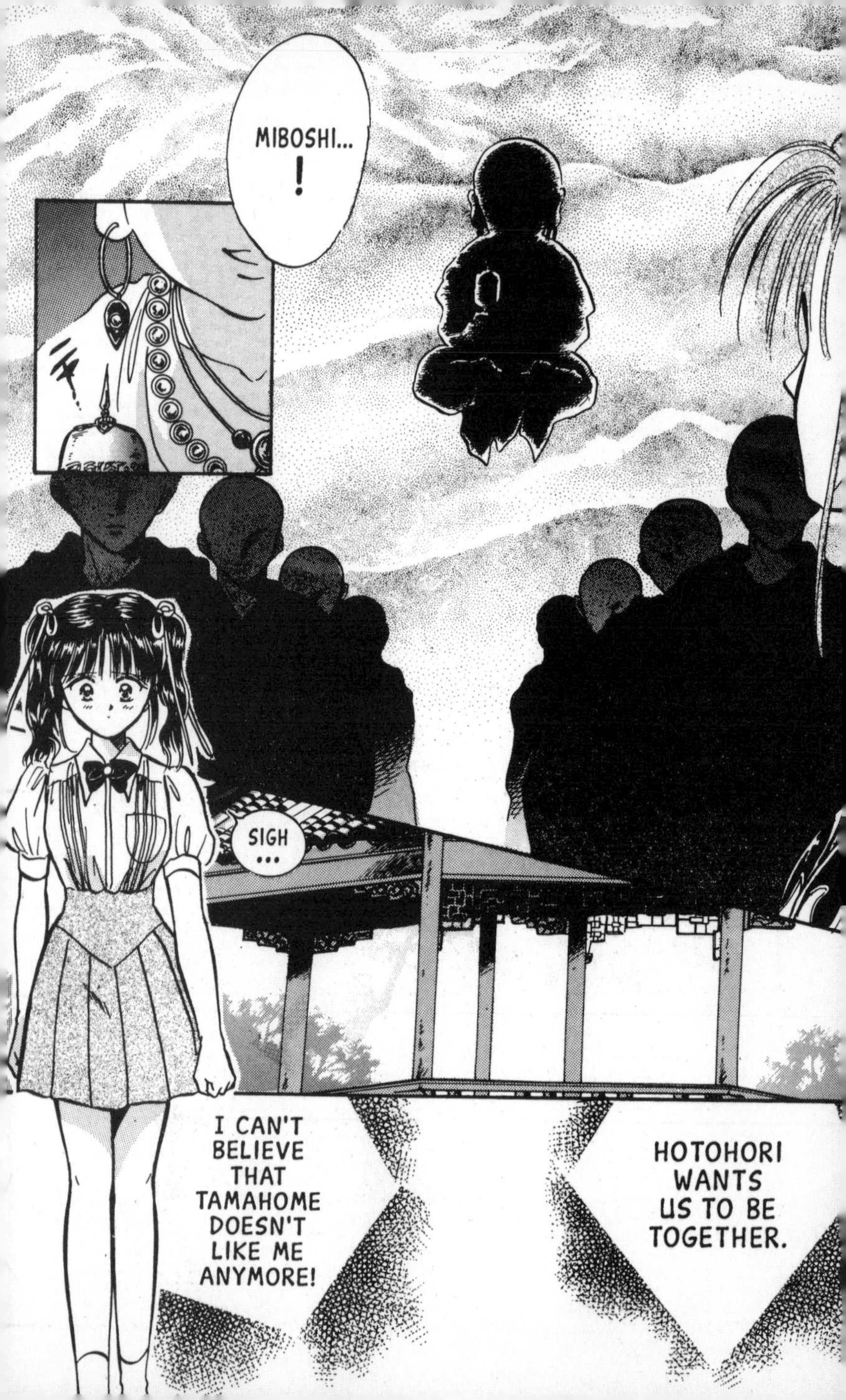
MIBOSHI... !
SIGH...
HOTOHORI WANTS US TO BE TOGETHER.
I CAN'T BELIEVE THAT TAMAHOME DOESN'T LIKE ME ANYMORE!

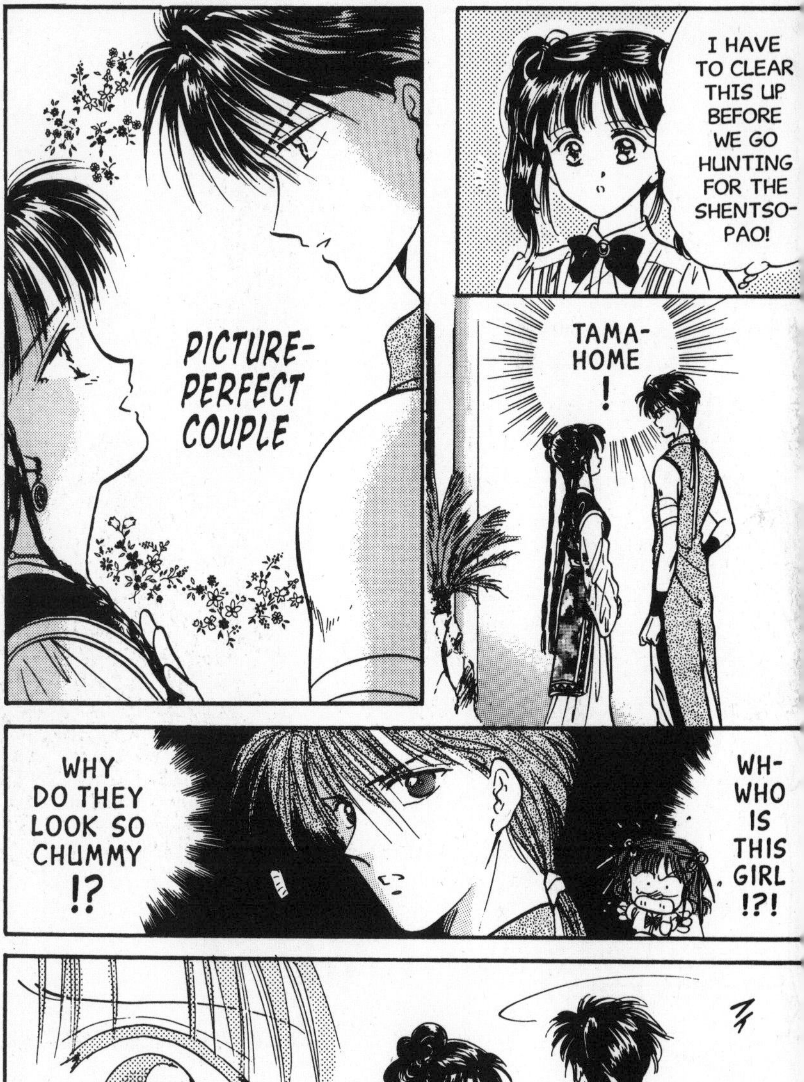
I HAVE TO CLEAR THIS UP BEFORE WE GO HUNTING FOR THE SHENTSO-PAO!
TAMA-HOME!
PICTURE-PERFECT COUPLE
WH-WHO IS THIS GIRL!?!
WHY DO THEY LOOK SO CHUMMY!?
LET'S GO!

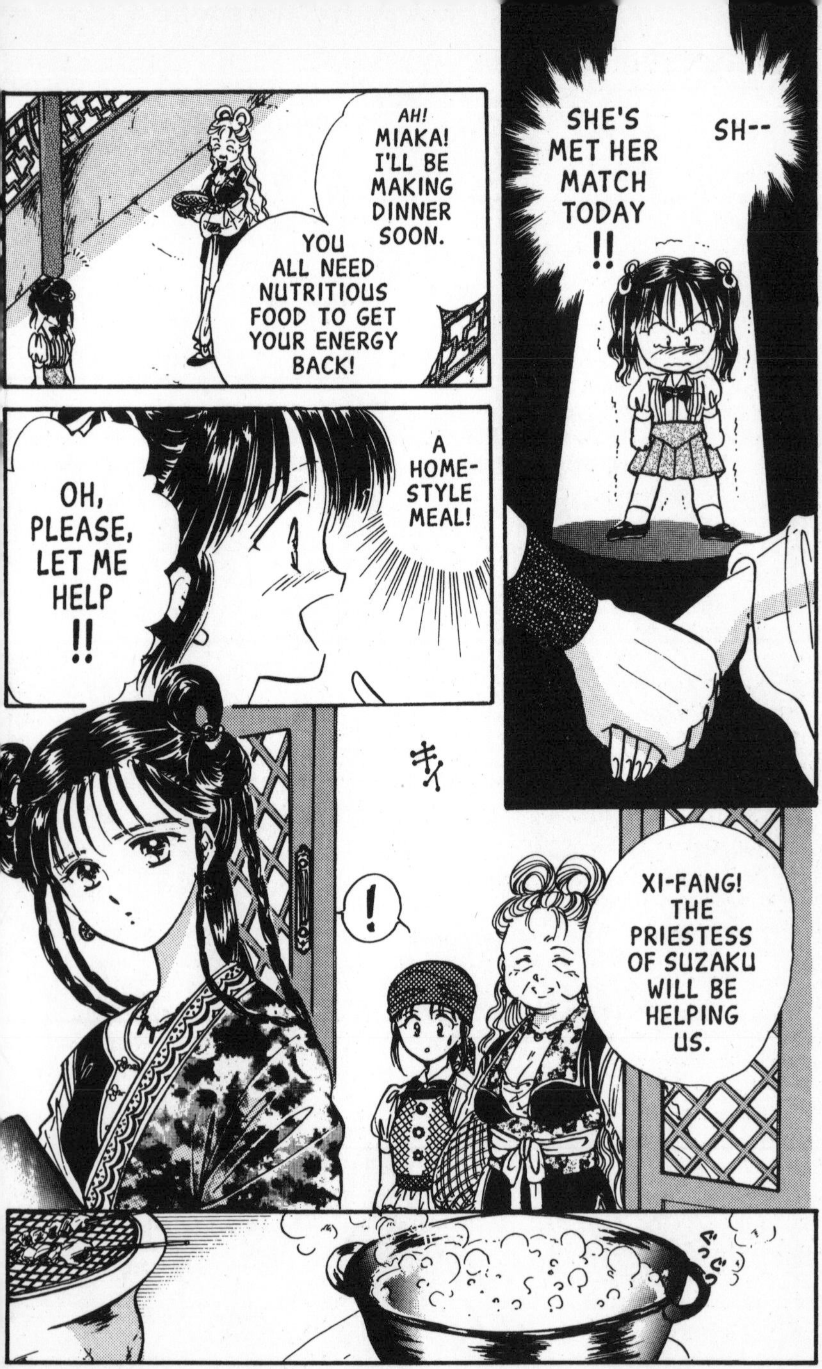
SH--
SHE'S MET HER MATCH TODAY!!
AH! MIAKA! I'LL BE MAKING DINNER SOON.
YOU ALL NEED NUTRITIOUS FOOD TO GET YOUR ENERGY BACK!
A HOME-STYLE MEAL!
OH, PLEASE, LET ME HELP!!
キイ
!
XI-FANG! THE PRIESTESS OF SUZAKU WILL BE HELPING US.

Now, what shall we talk about?
How about the stories behind how the characters developed?
First, Miaka. I think you all have your own ideas about her, but the basic color I had in mind for her was white, pure white. I wanted to depict a girl who was honest, pure and innocent. A kid that is doing her best to cope with every situation she encounters, but her naiveté can work against her too. She hesitates, and even gets self-destructive at times. Some readers have complained about this, but no one can be perfect. People feel depressed and try to run away, but in the end she says, "I'll do my best!" Watching her you might think, "Oh, no! Don't go there, Miaka!!" but she has to deal with her own obstacles and find her way back to the right path in order to make up with Yui and be with Tamahome. Yui's and Miaka's falling out might have been because of misunderstanding, but if it were me, and Yui went that far, I'd have gotten angry and cut her off! Wouldn't you? ☺ However, what is a friend but knowing the good parts and the bad parts, and loving them just the same.
Miaka loves Yui. For Miaka it's not a question of choosing love over friendship. It's way beyond that. She has such a big heart.

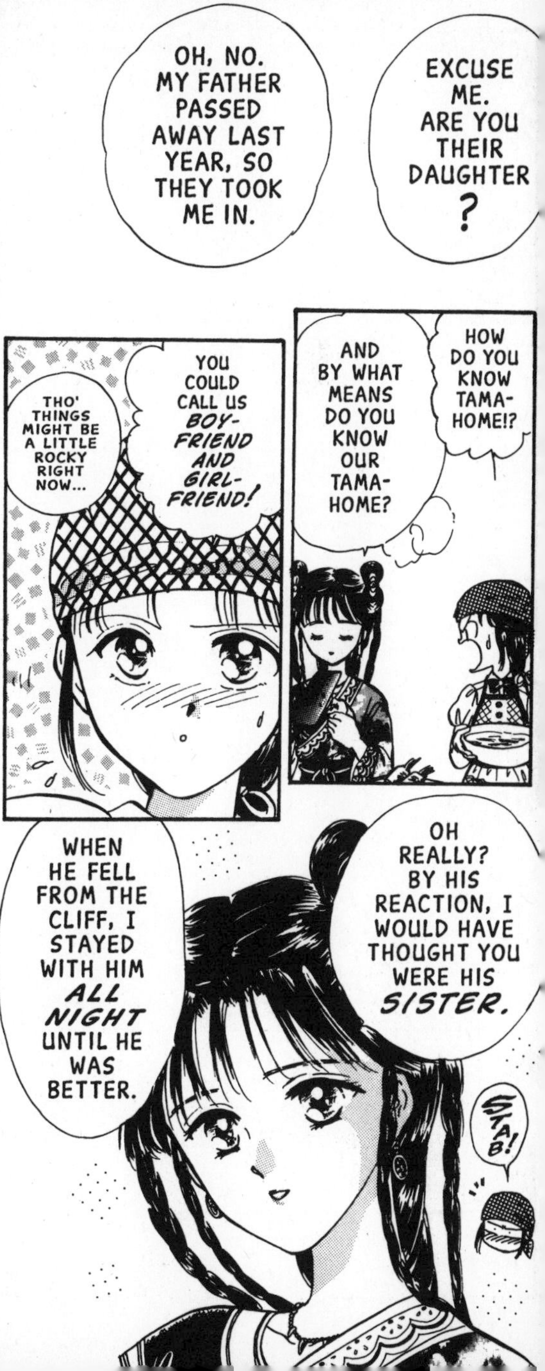
EXCUSE ME. ARE YOU THEIR DAUGHTER?
OH, NO. MY FATHER PASSED AWAY LAST YEAR, SO THEY TOOK ME IN.
HOW DO YOU KNOW TAMA-HOME!?
AND BY WHAT MEANS DO YOU KNOW OUR TAMA-HOME?
YOU COULD CALL US BOY-FRIEND AND GIRL-FRIEND!
THO' THINGS MIGHT BE A LITTLE ROCKY RIGHT NOW...
OH REALLY? BY HIS REACTION, I WOULD HAVE THOUGHT YOU WERE HIS SISTER.
WHEN HE FELL FROM THE CLIFF, I STAYED WITH HIM ALL NIGHT UNTIL HE WAS BETTER.
STAB!

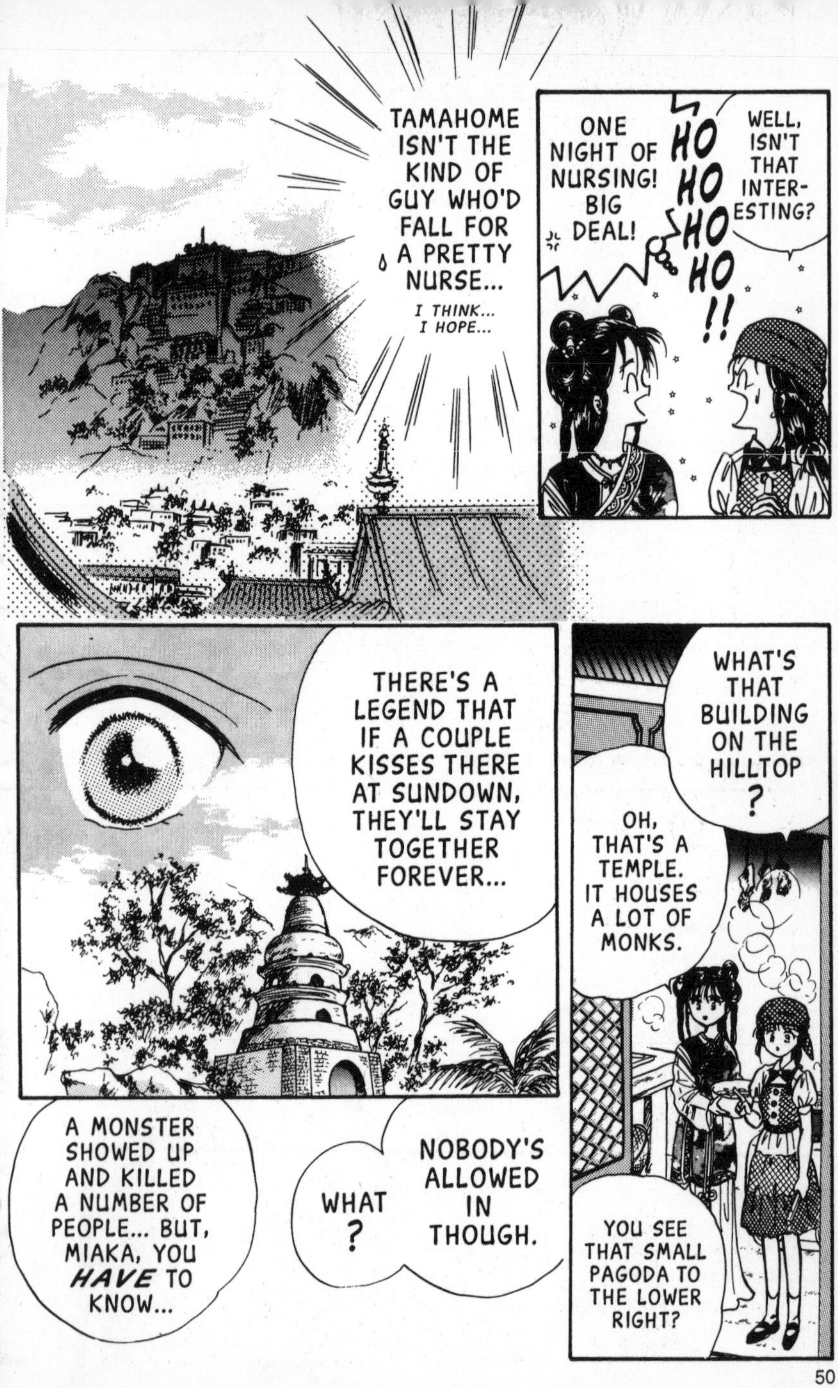
WELL, ISN'T THAT INTER-ESTING?
HO HO HO HO!!
ONE NIGHT OF NURSING! BIG DEAL!
TAMAHOME ISN'T THE KIND OF GUY WHO'D FALL FOR A PRETTY NURSE...
I THINK... I HOPE...
WHAT'S THAT BUILDING ON THE HILLTOP?
OH, THAT'S A TEMPLE. IT HOUSES A LOT OF MONKS.
YOU SEE THAT SMALL PAGODA TO THE LOWER RIGHT?
THERE'S A LEGEND THAT IF A COUPLE KISSES THERE AT SUNDOWN, THEY'LL STAY TOGETHER FOREVER...
NOBODY'S ALLOWED IN THOUGH.
WHAT?
A MONSTER SHOWED UP AND KILLED A NUMBER OF PEOPLE... BUT, MIAKA, YOU *HAVE* TO KNOW...

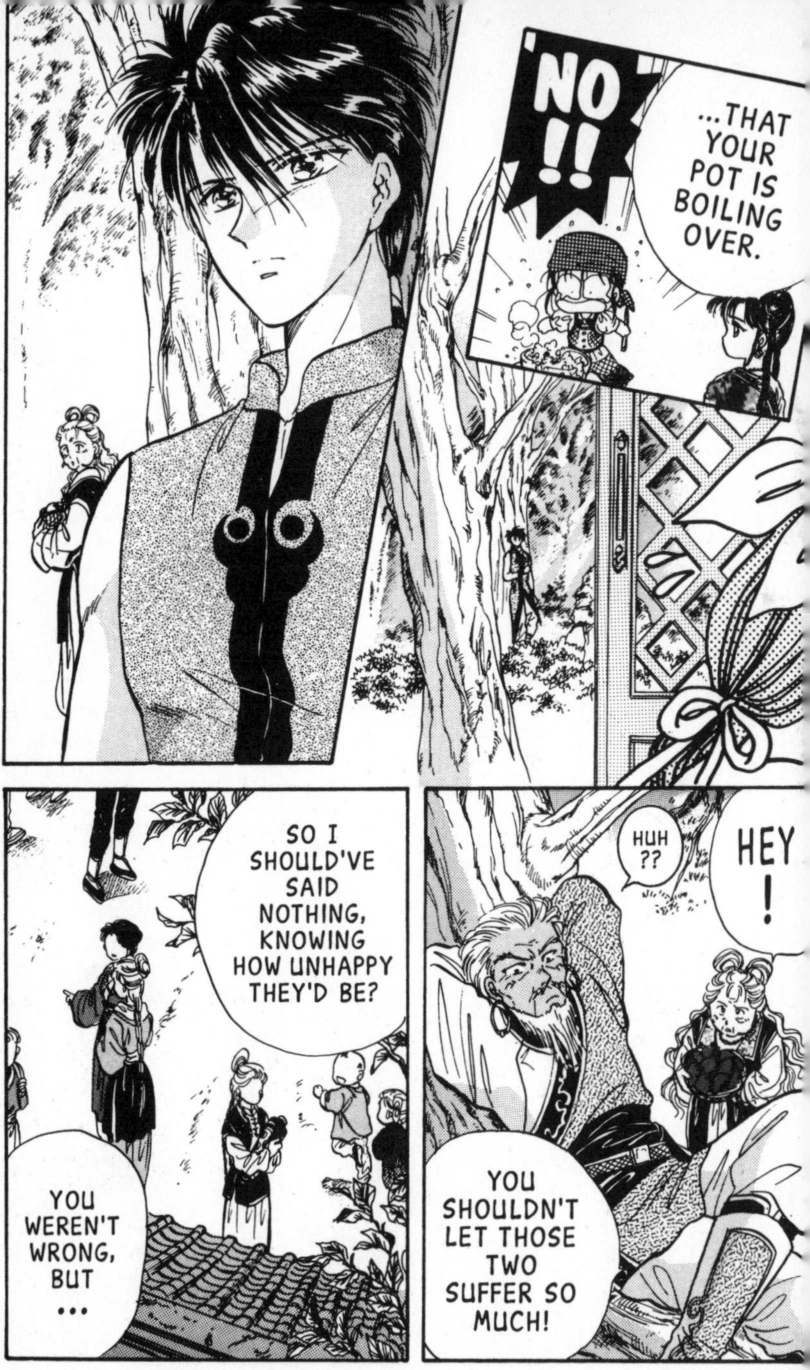

...THAT YOUR POT IS BOILING OVER.
NO!!
HEY!
HUH??
YOU SHOULDN'T LET THOSE TWO SUFFER SO MUCH!
SO I SHOULD'VE SAID NOTHING, KNOWING HOW UNHAPPY THEY'D BE?
YOU WEREN'T WRONG, BUT ...

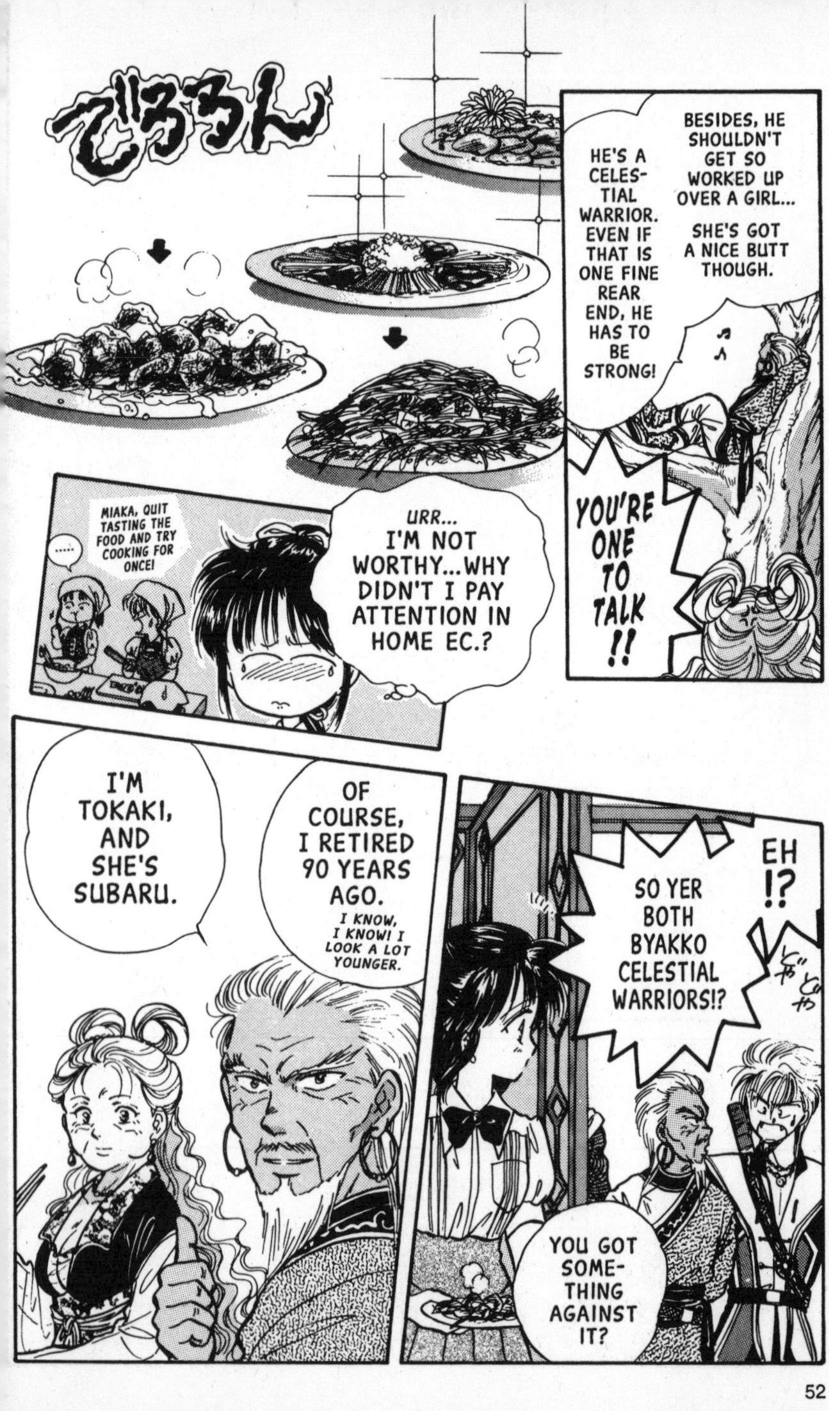
HE'S A CELESTIAL WARRIOR. EVEN IF THAT IS ONE FINE REAR END, HE HAS TO BE STRONG!
BESIDES, HE SHOULDN'T GET SO WORKED UP OVER A GIRL... SHE'S GOT A NICE BUTT THOUGH.
YOU'RE ONE TO TALK!!
でろろん
URR... I'M NOT WORTHY...WHY DIDN'T I PAY ATTENTION IN HOME EC.?
MIAKA, QUIT TASTING THE FOOD AND TRY COOKING FOR ONCE!
.....!
EH!?
SO YER BOTH BYAKKO CELESTIAL WARRIORS!?
YOU GOT SOMETHING AGAINST IT?
I'M TOKAKI, AND SHE'S SUBARU.
OF COURSE, I RETIRED 90 YEARS AGO.
I KNOW, I KNOW! I LOOK A LOT YOUNGER.

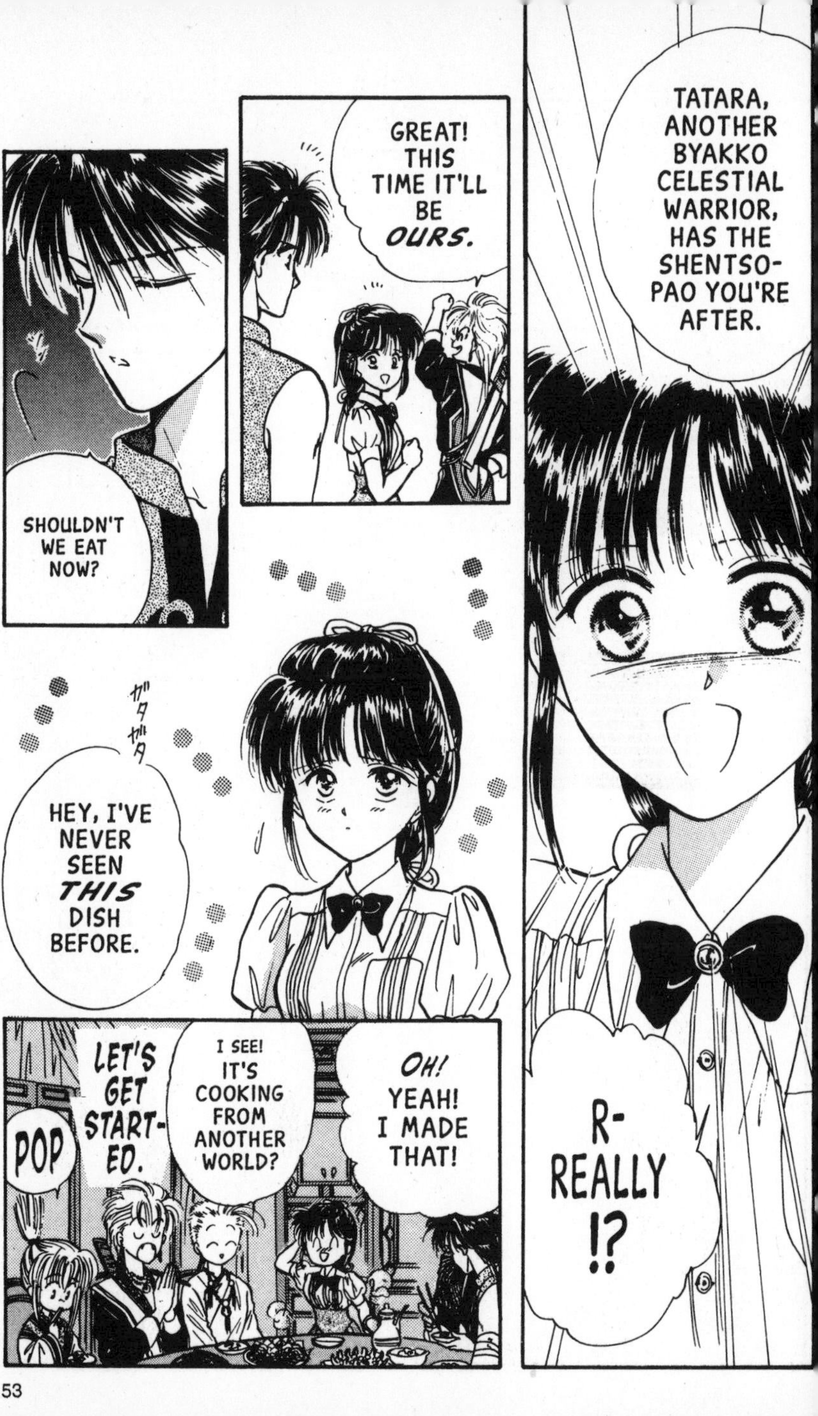
TATARA, ANOTHER BYAKKO CELESTIAL WARRIOR, HAS THE SHENTSO-PAO YOU'RE AFTER.
R-REALLY!?
GREAT! THIS TIME IT'LL BE *OURS.*
SHOULDN'T WE EAT NOW?
ガタガタ
HEY, I'VE NEVER SEEN *THIS* DISH BEFORE.
OH! YEAH! I MADE THAT!
I SEE! IT'S COOKING FROM ANOTHER WORLD?
LET'S GET START-ED.
POP

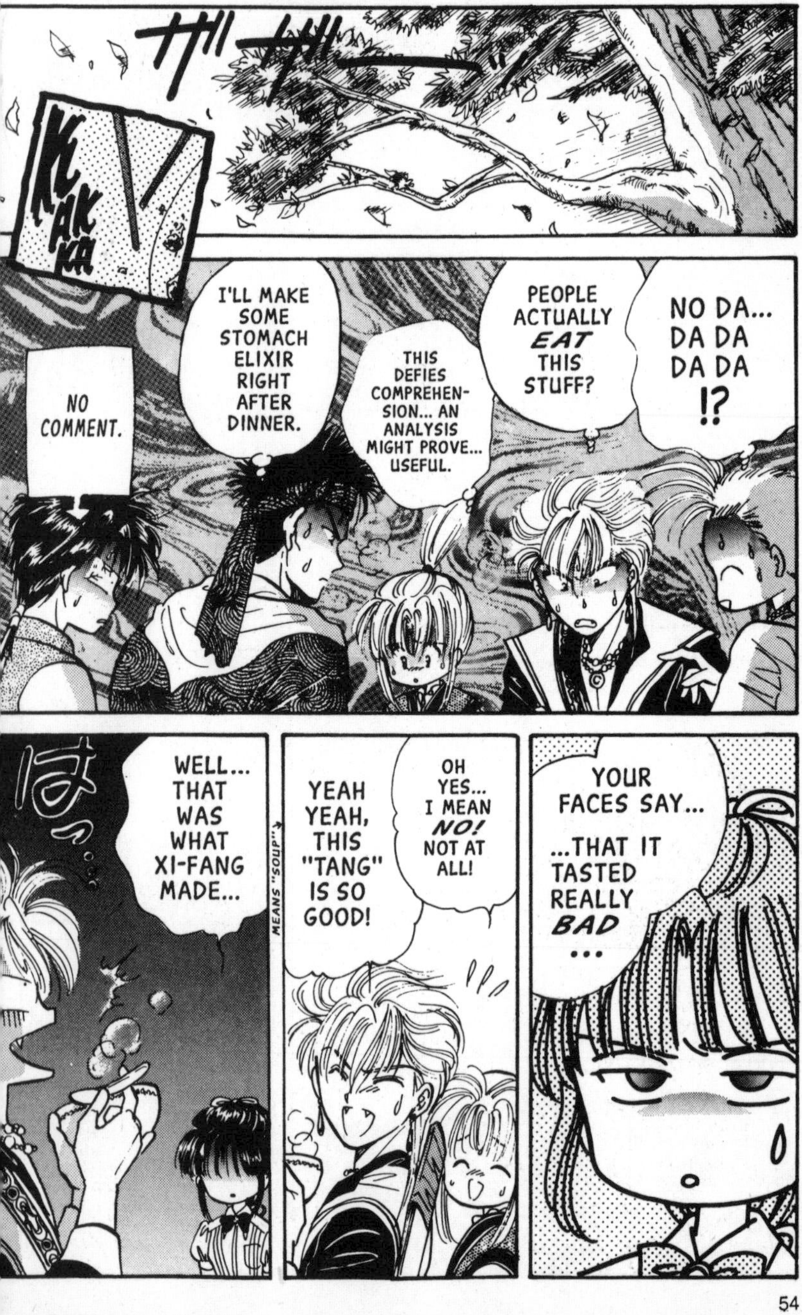
ザザーッ
KA KA KA
NO DA... DA DA DA DA !?
PEOPLE ACTUALLY EAT THIS STUFF?
THIS DEFIES COMPREHENSION... AN ANALYSIS MIGHT PROVE... USEFUL.
I'LL MAKE SOME STOMACH ELIXIR RIGHT AFTER DINNER.
NO COMMENT.
YOUR FACES SAY...
...THAT IT TASTED REALLY BAD ...
OH YES... I MEAN NO! NOT AT ALL!
YEAH YEAH, THIS "TANG" IS SO GOOD!
MEANS "SOUP"
WELL... THAT WAS WHAT XI-FANG MADE...
はっ

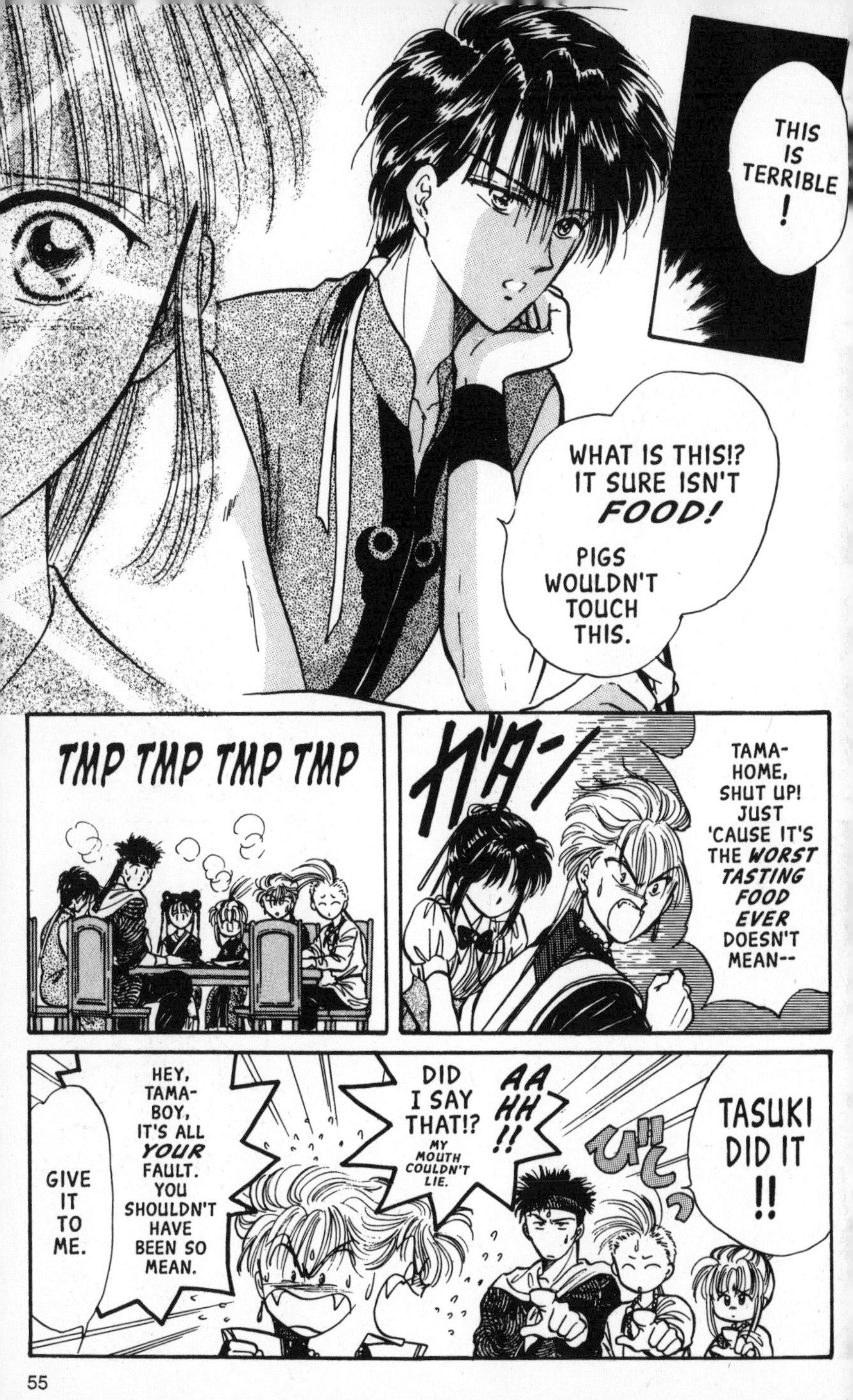
THIS IS TERRIBLE!
WHAT IS THIS!? IT SURE ISN'T FOOD!
PIGS WOULDN'T TOUCH THIS.
ガターン
TAMA-HOME, SHUT UP! JUST 'CAUSE IT'S THE WORST TASTING FOOD EVER DOESN'T MEAN--
TMP TMP TMP TMP
TASUKI DID IT!!
AAHH!!
DID I SAY THAT!?
MY MOUTH COULDN'T LIE.
HEY, TAMA-BOY, IT'S ALL YOUR FAULT. YOU SHOULDN'T HAVE BEEN SO MEAN.
GIVE IT TO ME.

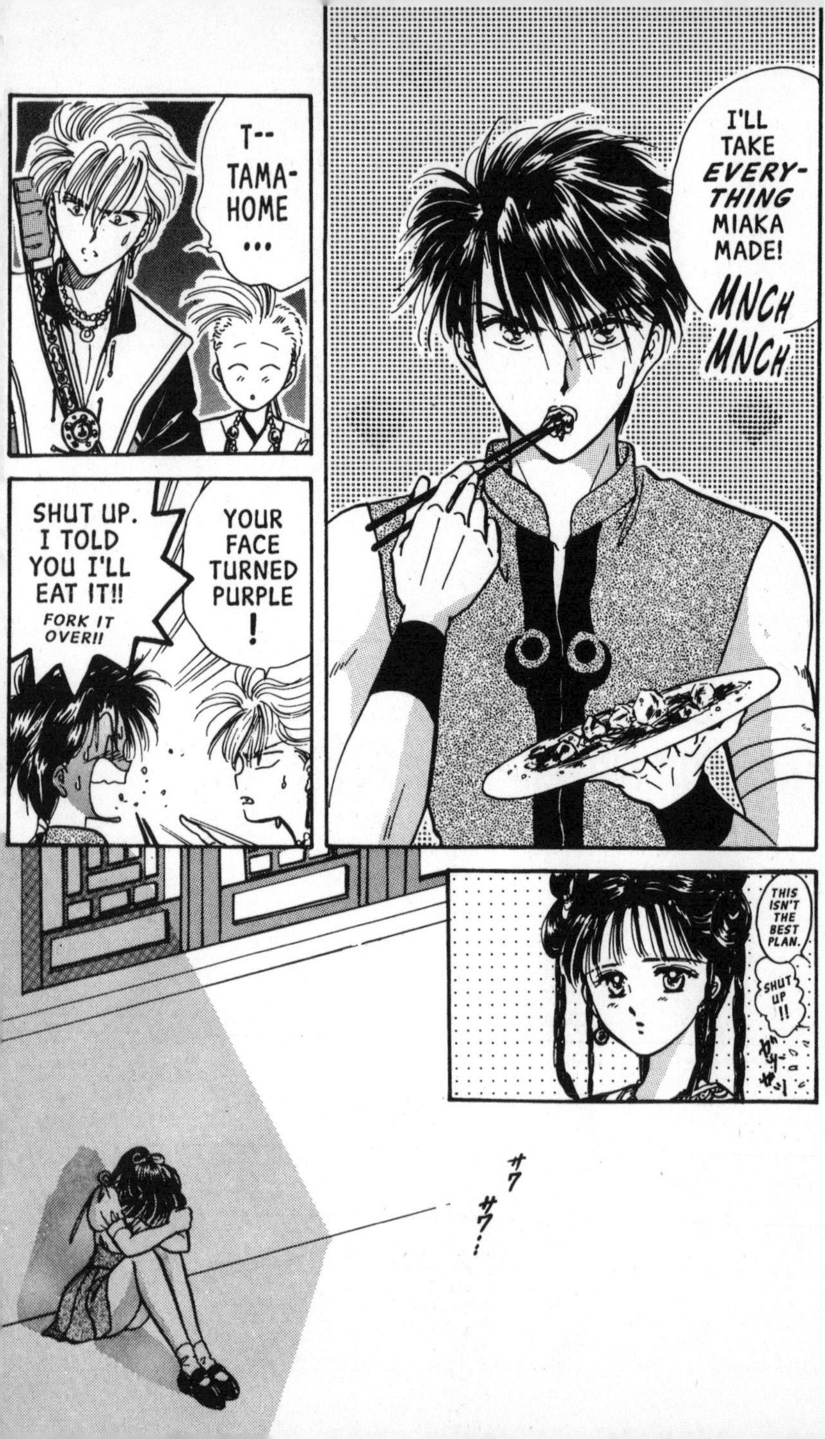
I'LL TAKE EVERYTHING MIAKA MADE!
MNCH MNCH
T-- TAMAHOME ...
YOUR FACE TURNED PURPLE!
SHUT UP. I TOLD YOU I'LL EAT IT!!
FORK IT OVER!!
THIS ISN'T THE BEST PLAN.
SHUT UP!!
サワ
サワ‥

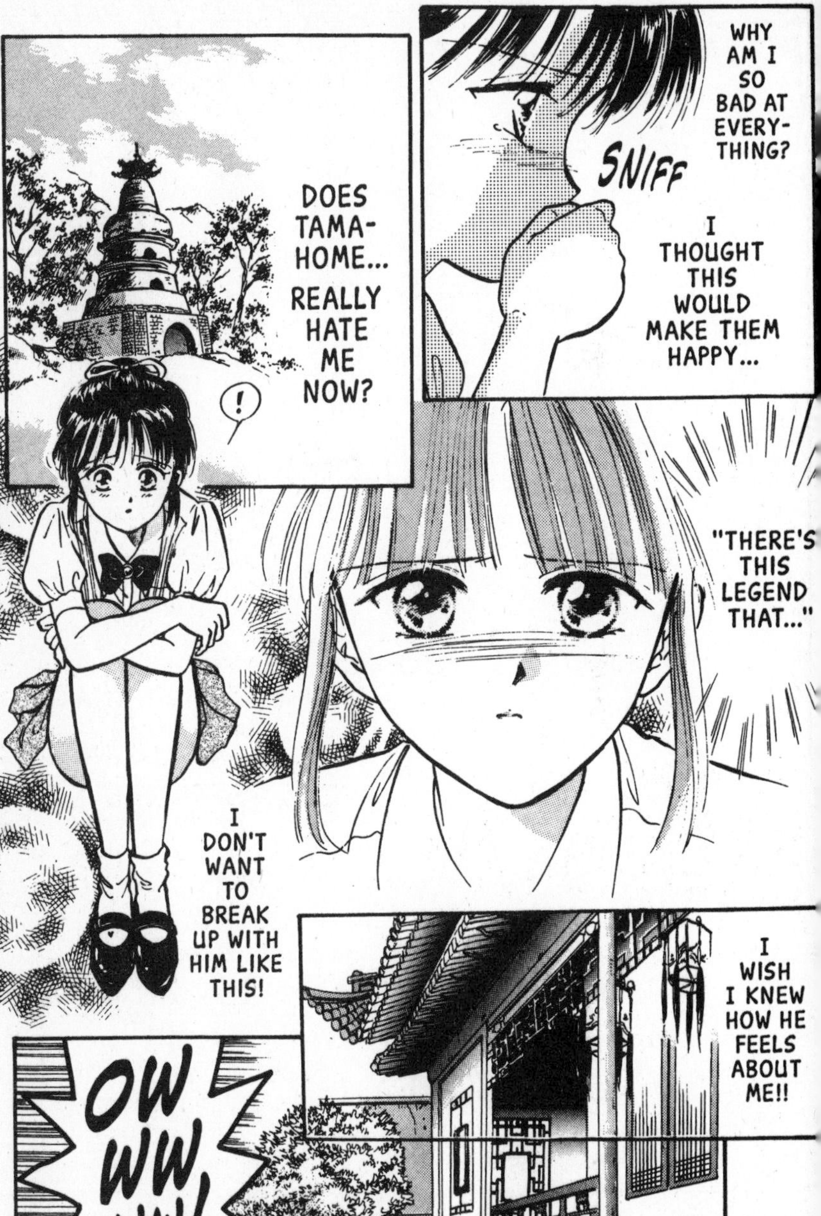
WHY AM I SO BAD AT EVERY-THING?
SNIFF
I THOUGHT THIS WOULD MAKE THEM HAPPY...
DOES TAMA-HOME...
REALLY HATE ME NOW?
"THERE'S THIS LEGEND THAT..."
!
I DON'T WANT TO BREAK UP WITH HIM LIKE THIS!
I WISH I KNEW HOW HE FEELS ABOUT ME!!
OWWWWWW!

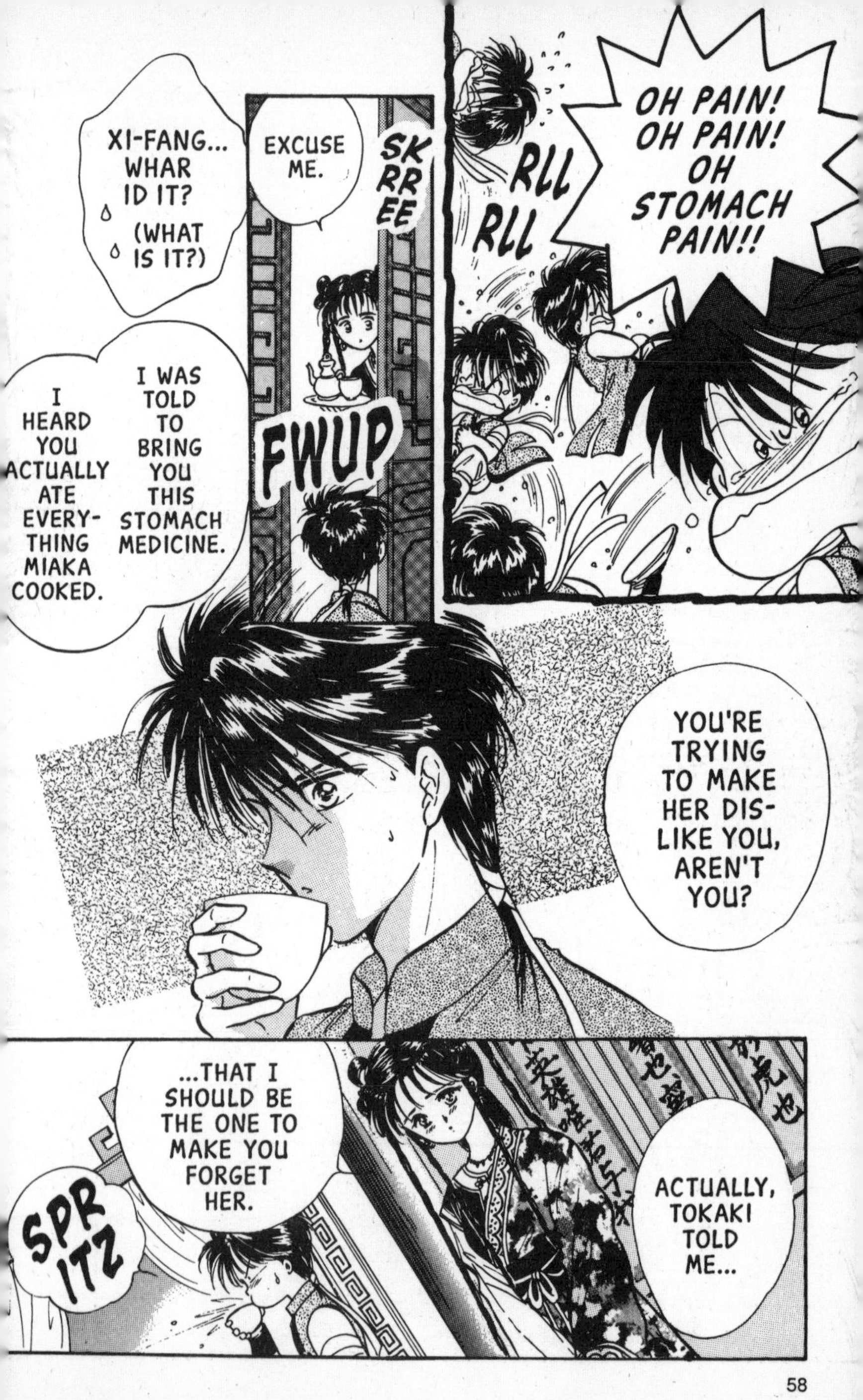
OH PAIN! OH PAIN! OH STOMACH PAIN!!
RLL RLL
EXCUSE ME.
SKRREE
XI-FANG... WHAR ID IT? (WHAT IS IT?)
FWUP
I WAS TOLD TO BRING YOU THIS STOMACH MEDICINE.
I HEARD YOU ACTUALLY ATE EVERYTHING MIAKA COOKED.
YOU'RE TRYING TO MAKE HER DIS-LIKE YOU, AREN'T YOU?
ACTUALLY, TOKAKI TOLD ME...
...THAT I SHOULD BE THE ONE TO MAKE YOU FORGET HER.
SPR ITZ

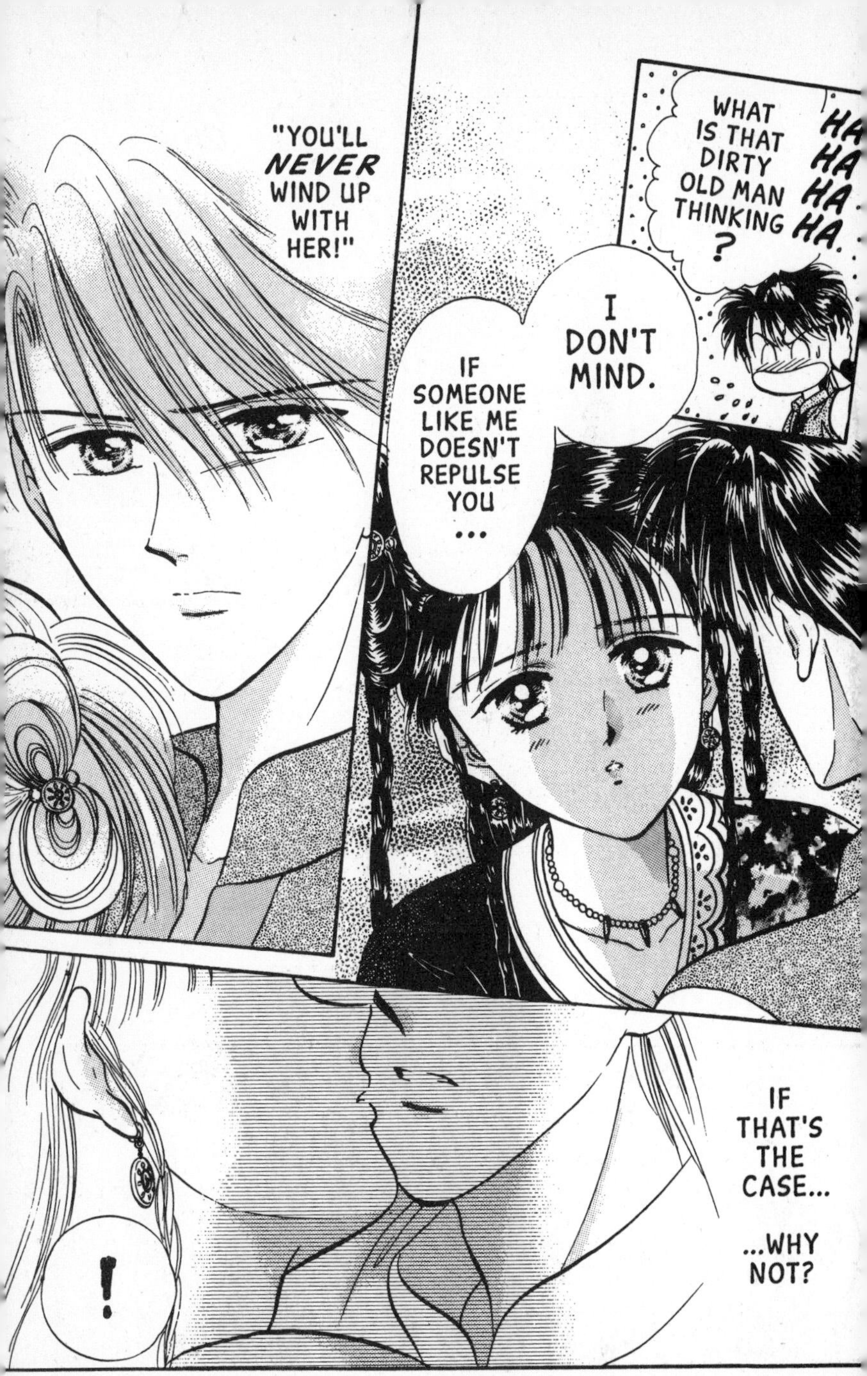

WHAT IS THAT DIRTY OLD MAN THINKING?
HA HA HA HA.
I DON'T MIND.
IF SOMEONE LIKE ME DOESN'T REPULSE YOU...
"YOU'LL *NEVER* WIND UP WITH HER!"
IF THAT'S THE CASE...
...WHY NOT?
!

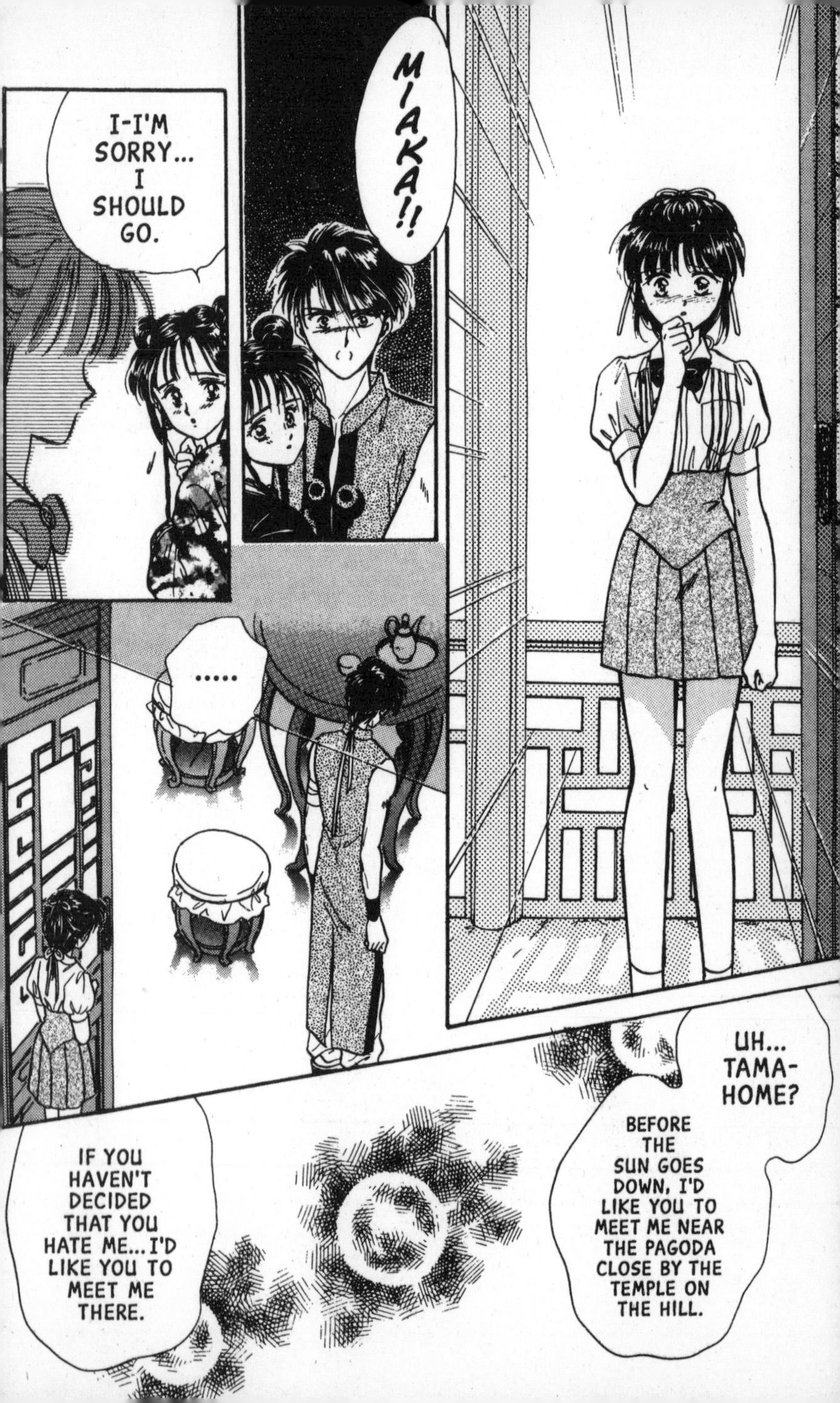
MIAKA!!
I-I'M SORRY... I SHOULD GO.
.....
UH... TAMA-HOME?
BEFORE THE SUN GOES DOWN, I'D LIKE YOU TO MEET ME NEAR THE PAGODA CLOSE BY THE TEMPLE ON THE HILL.
IF YOU HAVEN'T DECIDED THAT YOU HATE ME...I'D LIKE YOU TO MEET ME THERE.

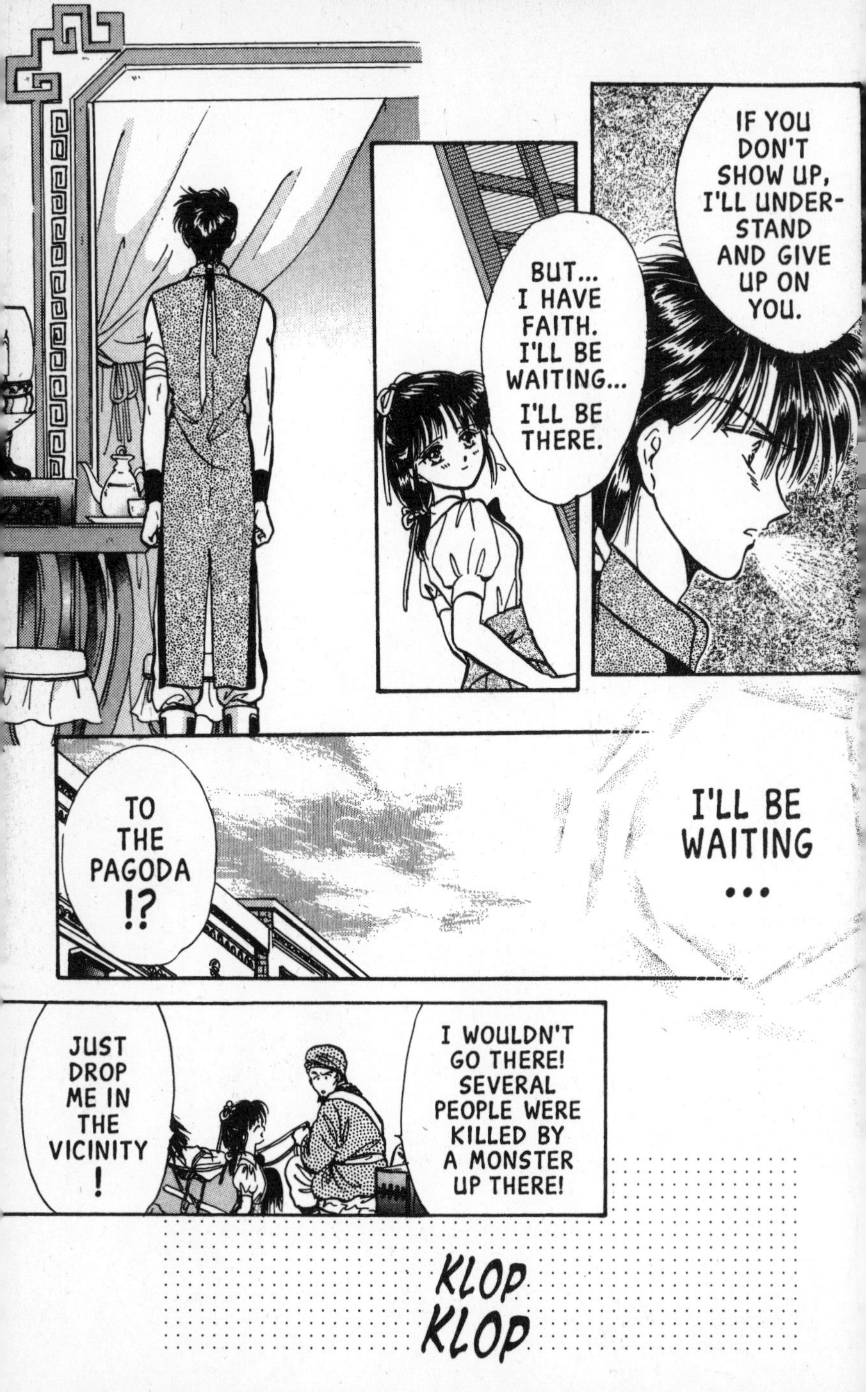
IF YOU DON'T SHOW UP, I'LL UNDER-STAND AND GIVE UP ON YOU.
BUT... I HAVE FAITH. I'LL BE WAITING...
I'LL BE THERE.
I'LL BE WAITING ...
TO THE PAGODA !?
I WOULDN'T GO THERE! SEVERAL PEOPLE WERE KILLED BY A MONSTER UP THERE!
JUST DROP ME IN THE VICINITY!
KLOP KLOP

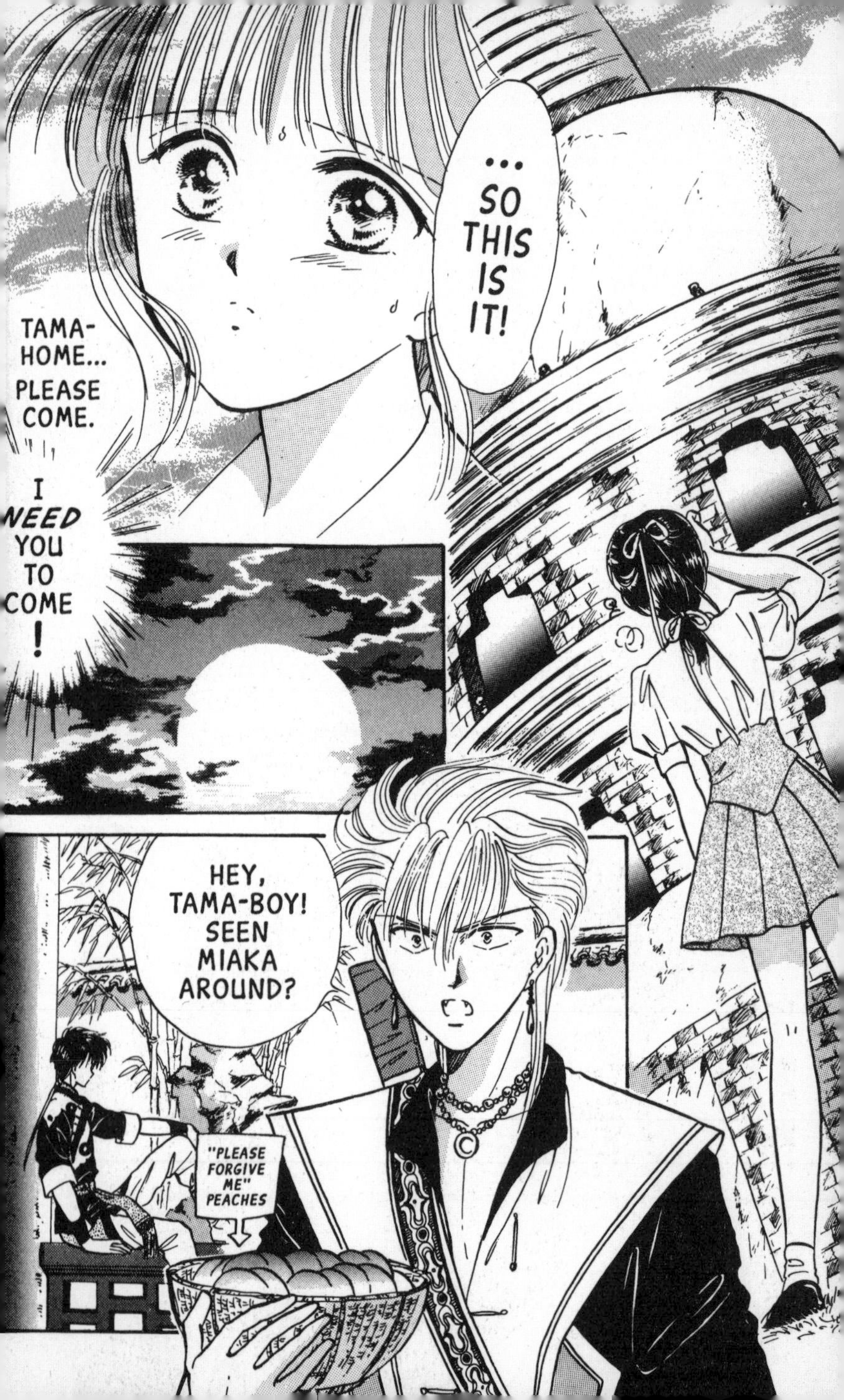
...SO THIS IS IT!
TAMA-HOME... PLEASE COME.
I *NEED* YOU TO COME!
HEY, TAMA-BOY! SEEN MIAKA AROUND?
"PLEASE FORGIVE ME" PEACHES

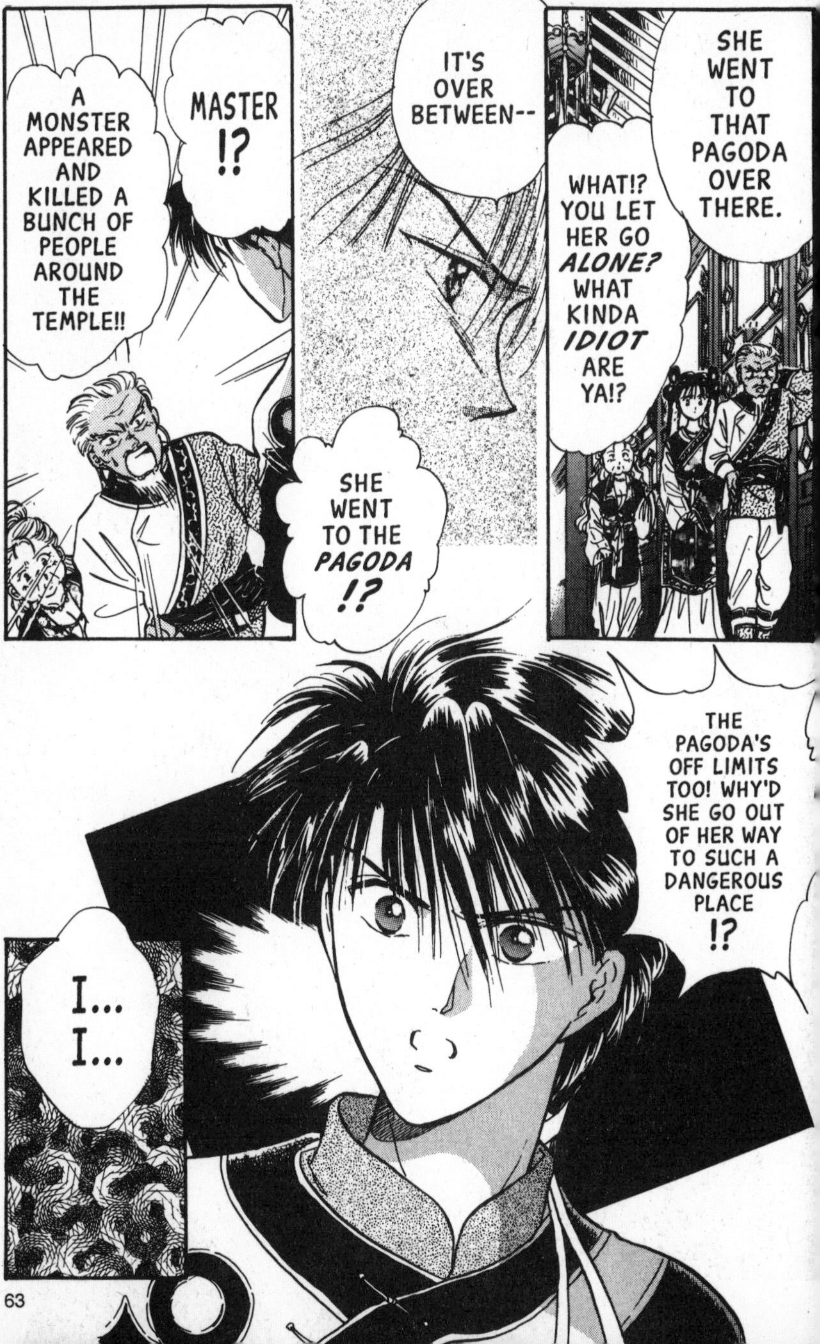
SHE WENT TO THAT PAGODA OVER THERE.
WHAT!? YOU LET HER GO *ALONE?* WHAT KINDA *IDIOT* ARE YA!?
IT'S OVER BETWEEN--
MASTER !?
A MONSTER APPEARED AND KILLED A BUNCH OF PEOPLE AROUND THE TEMPLE!!
SHE WENT TO THE *PAGODA* !?
THE PAGODA'S OFF LIMITS TOO! WHY'D SHE GO OUT OF HER WAY TO SUCH A DANGEROUS PLACE !?
I... I...

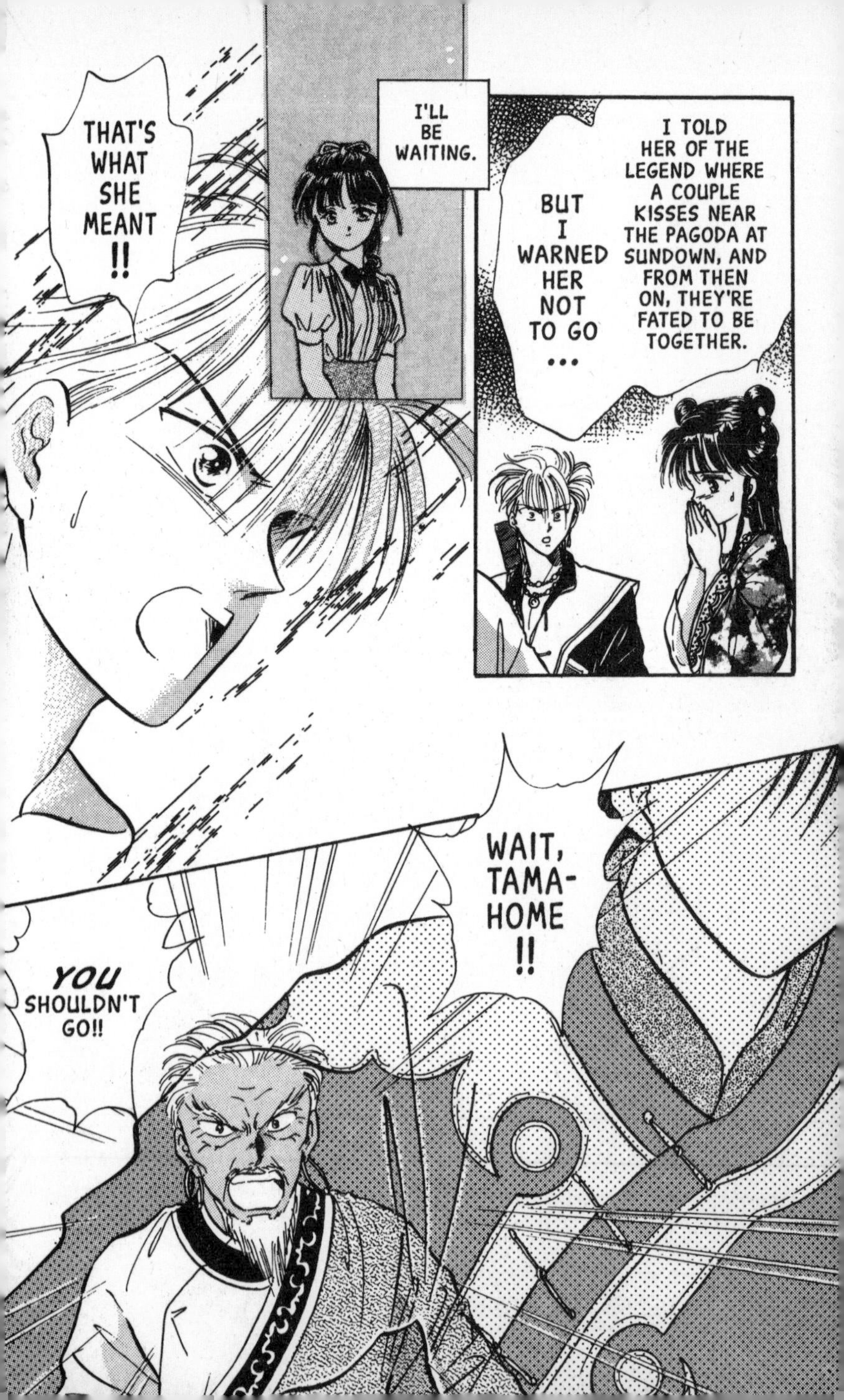
I TOLD HER OF THE LEGEND WHERE A COUPLE KISSES NEAR THE PAGODA AT SUNDOWN, AND FROM THEN ON, THEY'RE FATED TO BE TOGETHER.
BUT I WARNED HER NOT TO GO ...
I'LL BE WAITING.
THAT'S WHAT SHE MEANT !!
WAIT, TAMA-HOME !!
YOU SHOULDN'T GO!!

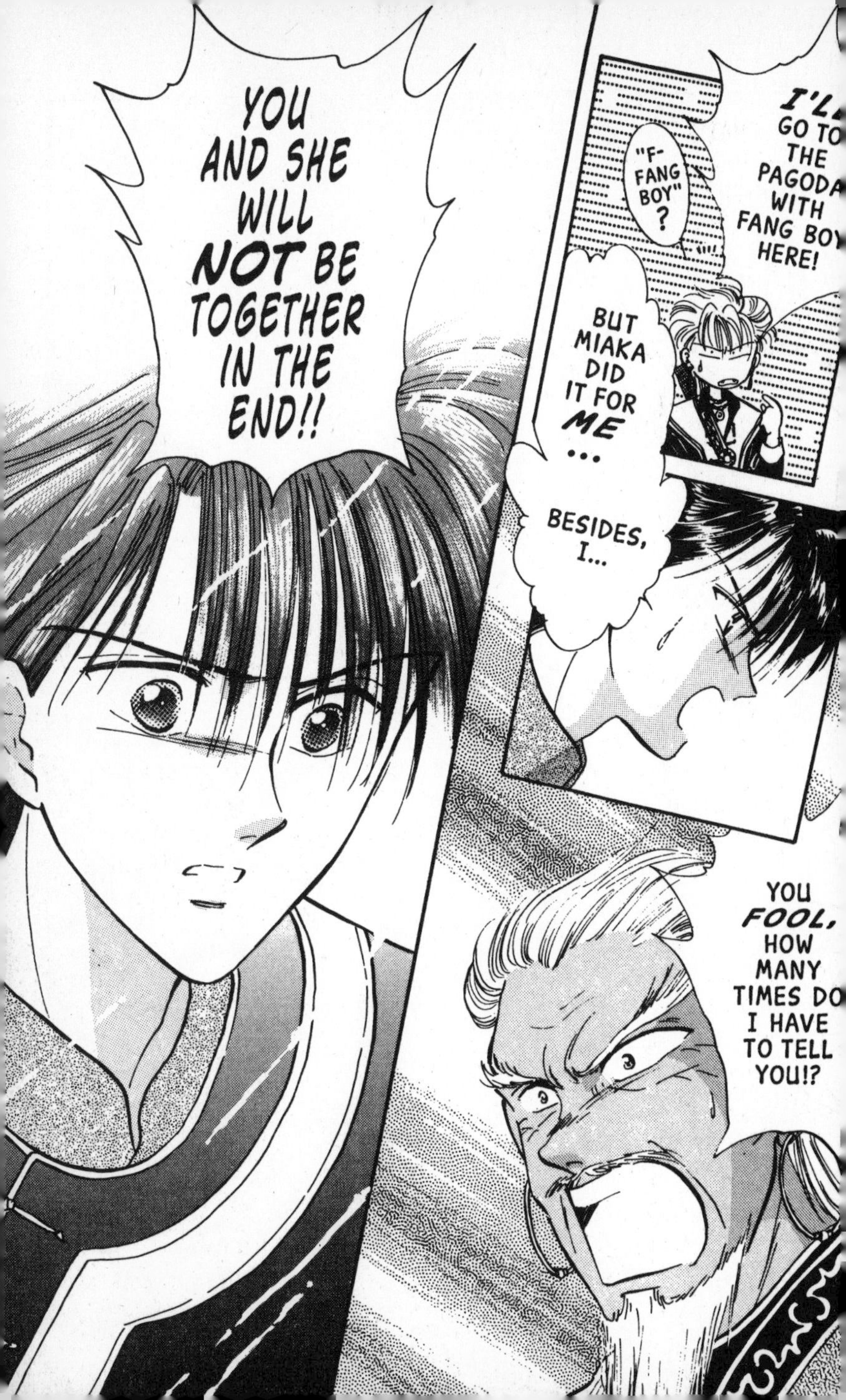
I'LL GO TO THE PAGODA WITH FANG BOY HERE!
"F-FANG BOY"?
BUT MIAKA DID IT FOR ME...
BESIDES, I...
YOU FOOL, HOW MANY TIMES DO I HAVE TO TELL YOU!?
YOU AND SHE WILL NOT BE TOGETHER IN THE END!!

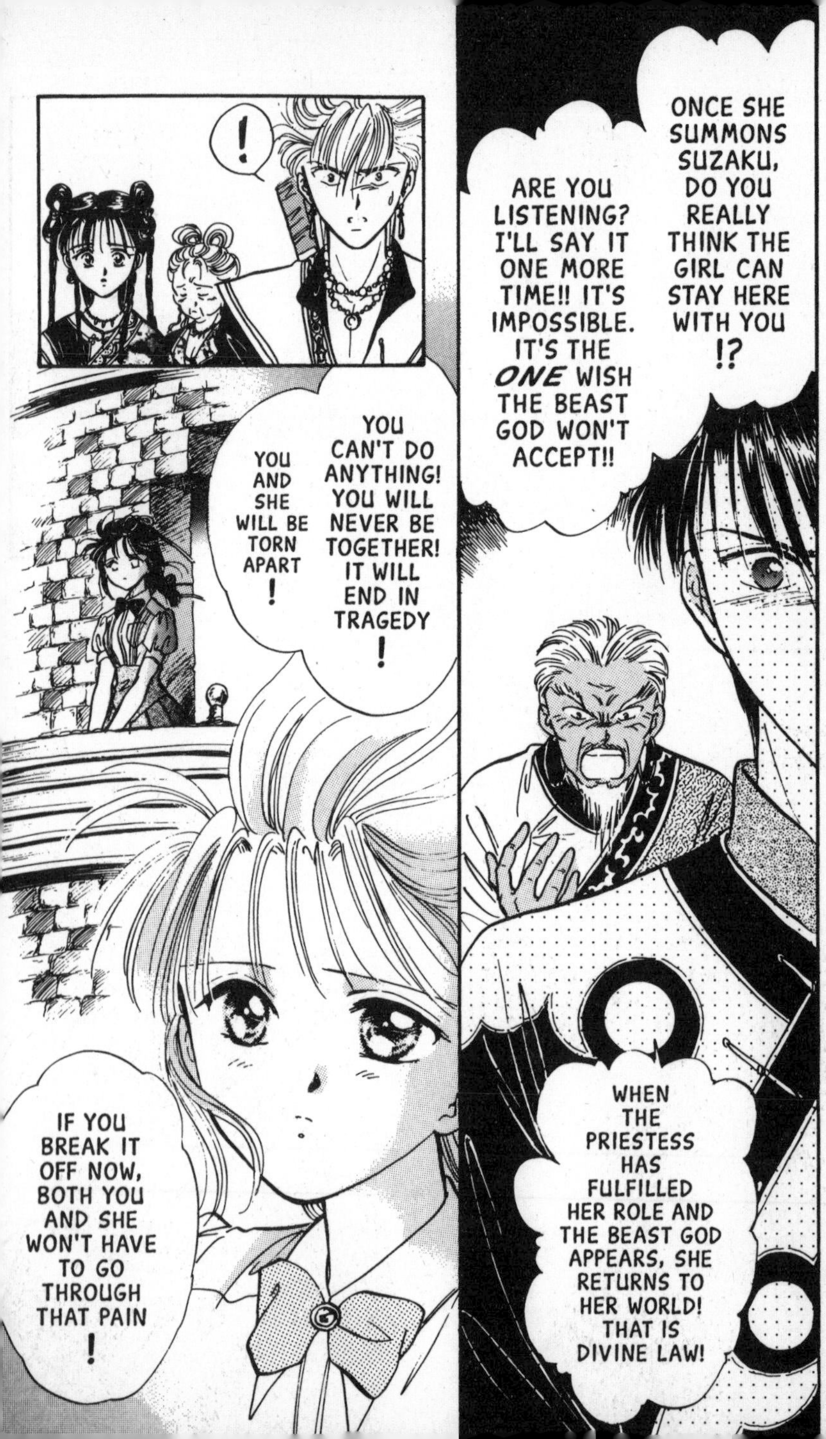
ONCE SHE SUMMONS SUZAKU, DO YOU REALLY THINK THE GIRL CAN STAY HERE WITH YOU !?
ARE YOU LISTENING? I'LL SAY IT ONE MORE TIME!! IT'S IMPOSSIBLE. IT'S THE *ONE* WISH THE BEAST GOD WON'T ACCEPT!!
WHEN THE PRIESTESS HAS FULFILLED HER ROLE AND THE BEAST GOD APPEARS, SHE RETURNS TO HER WORLD! THAT IS DIVINE LAW!
!
YOU CAN'T DO ANYTHING! YOU WILL NEVER BE TOGETHER! IT WILL END IN TRAGEDY !
YOU AND SHE WILL BE TORN APART !
IF YOU BREAK IT OFF NOW, BOTH YOU AND SHE WON'T HAVE TO GO THROUGH THAT PAIN !

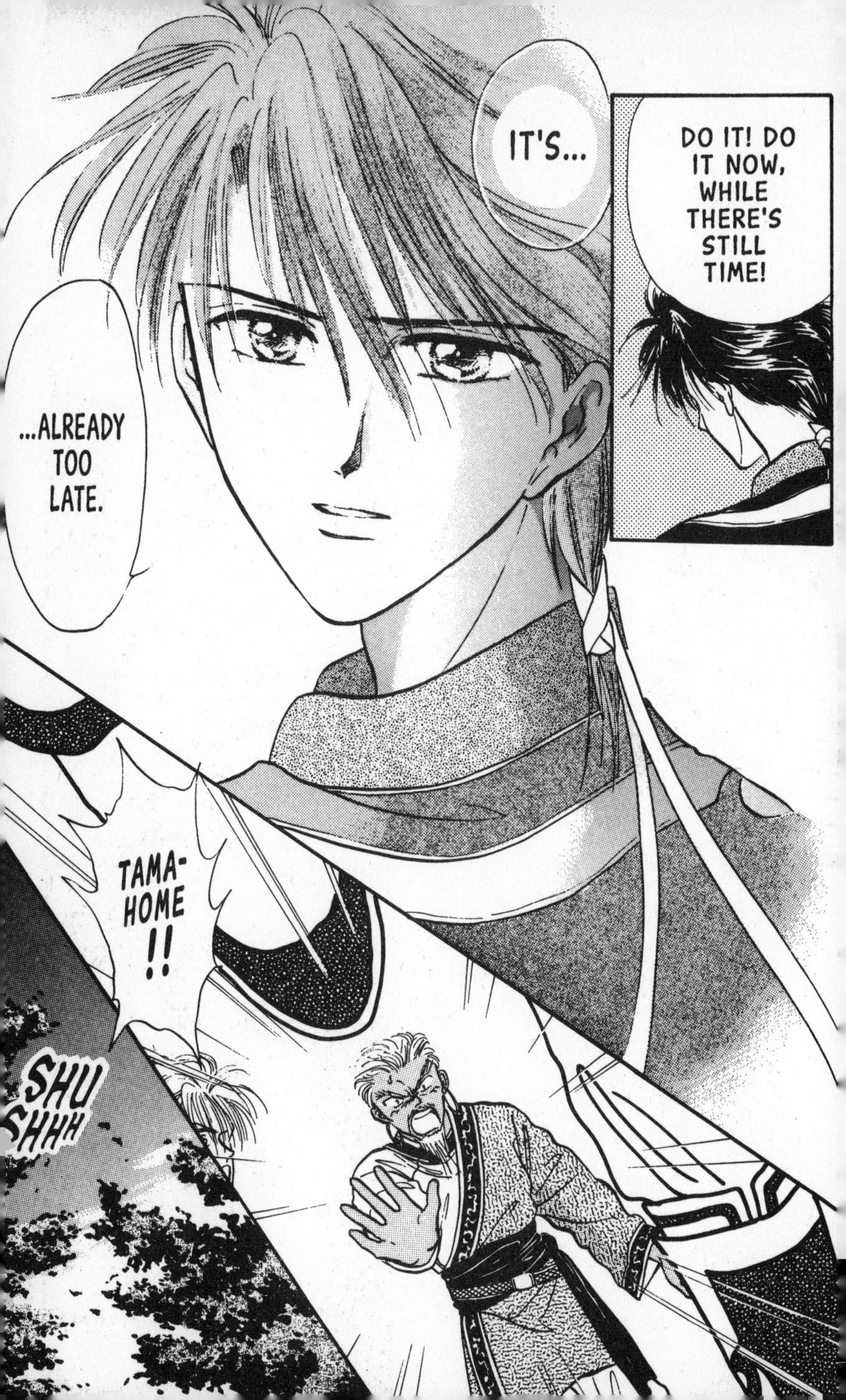
DO IT! DO IT NOW, WHILE THERE'S STILL TIME!
IT'S...
...ALREADY TOO LATE.
TAMA-HOME !!
SHU SHHH

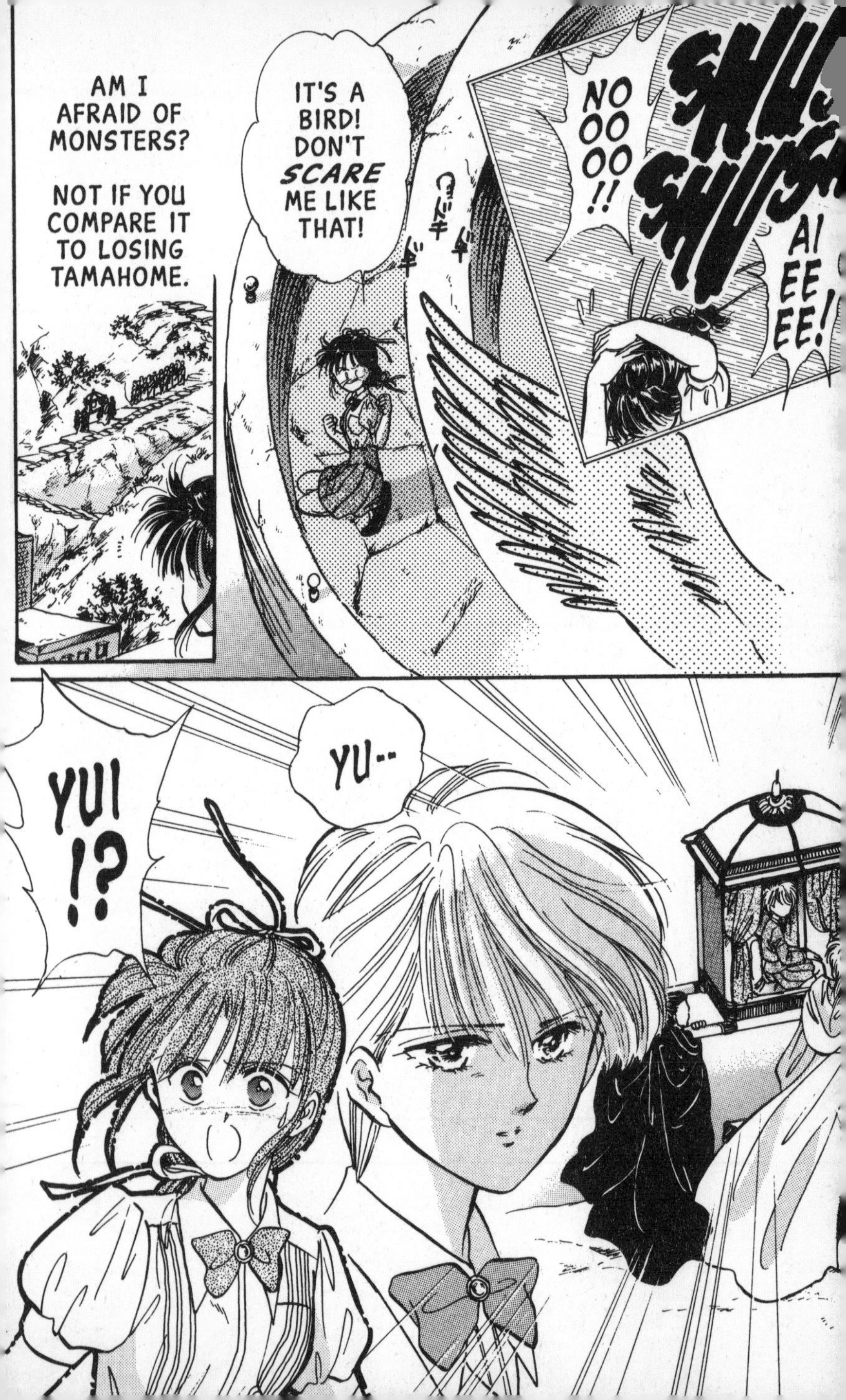
NOOOOO!!
AIEEE!
IT'S A BIRD! DON'T *SCARE* ME LIKE THAT!
AM I AFRAID OF MONSTERS?
NOT IF YOU COMPARE IT TO LOSING TAMAHOME.
YU--
YUI !?

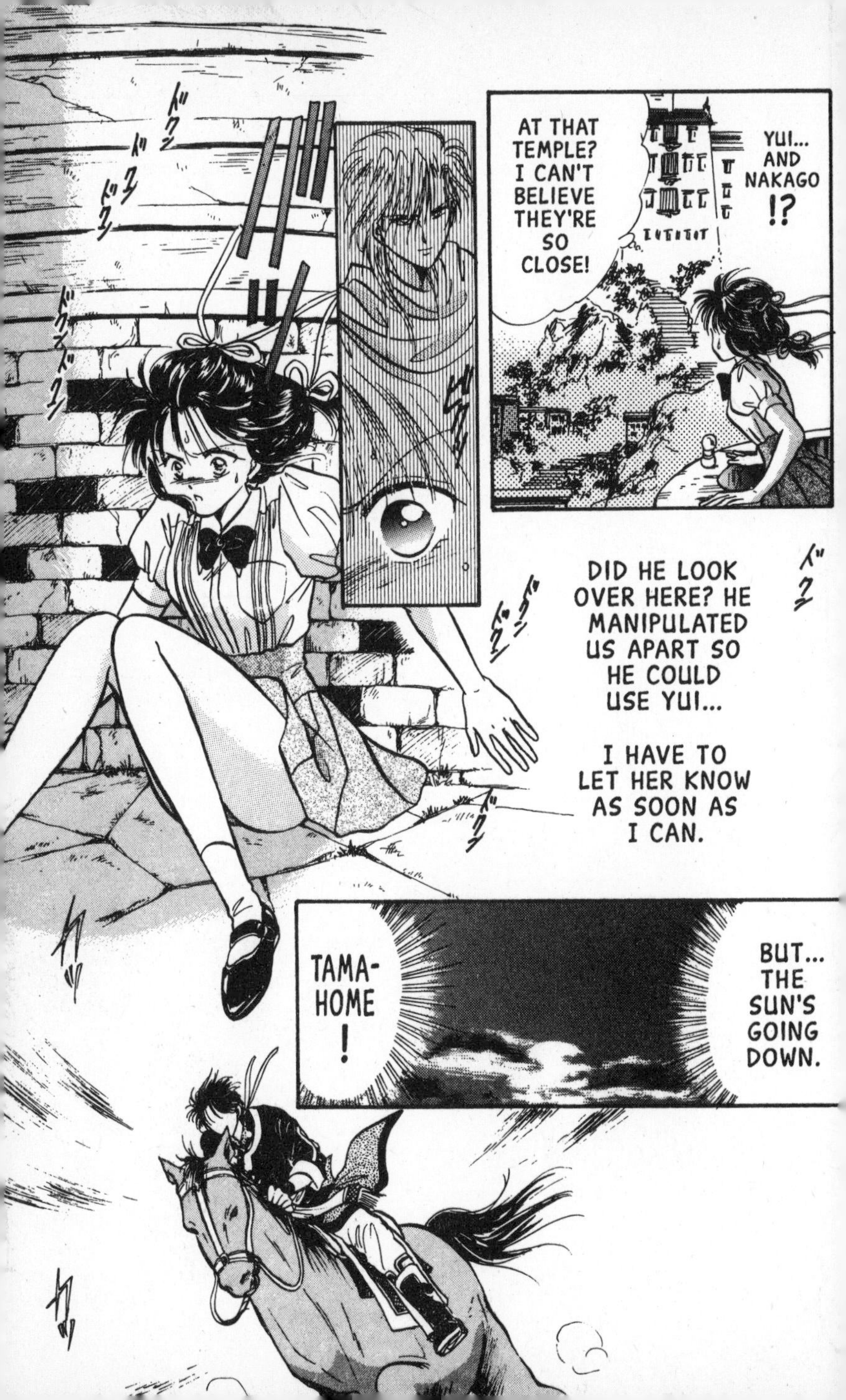
YUI... AND NAKAGO !?
AT THAT TEMPLE? I CAN'T BELIEVE THEY'RE SO CLOSE!
DID HE LOOK OVER HERE? HE MANIPULATED US APART SO HE COULD USE YUI...
I HAVE TO LET HER KNOW AS SOON AS I CAN.
BUT... THE SUN'S GOING DOWN.
TAMA-HOME !

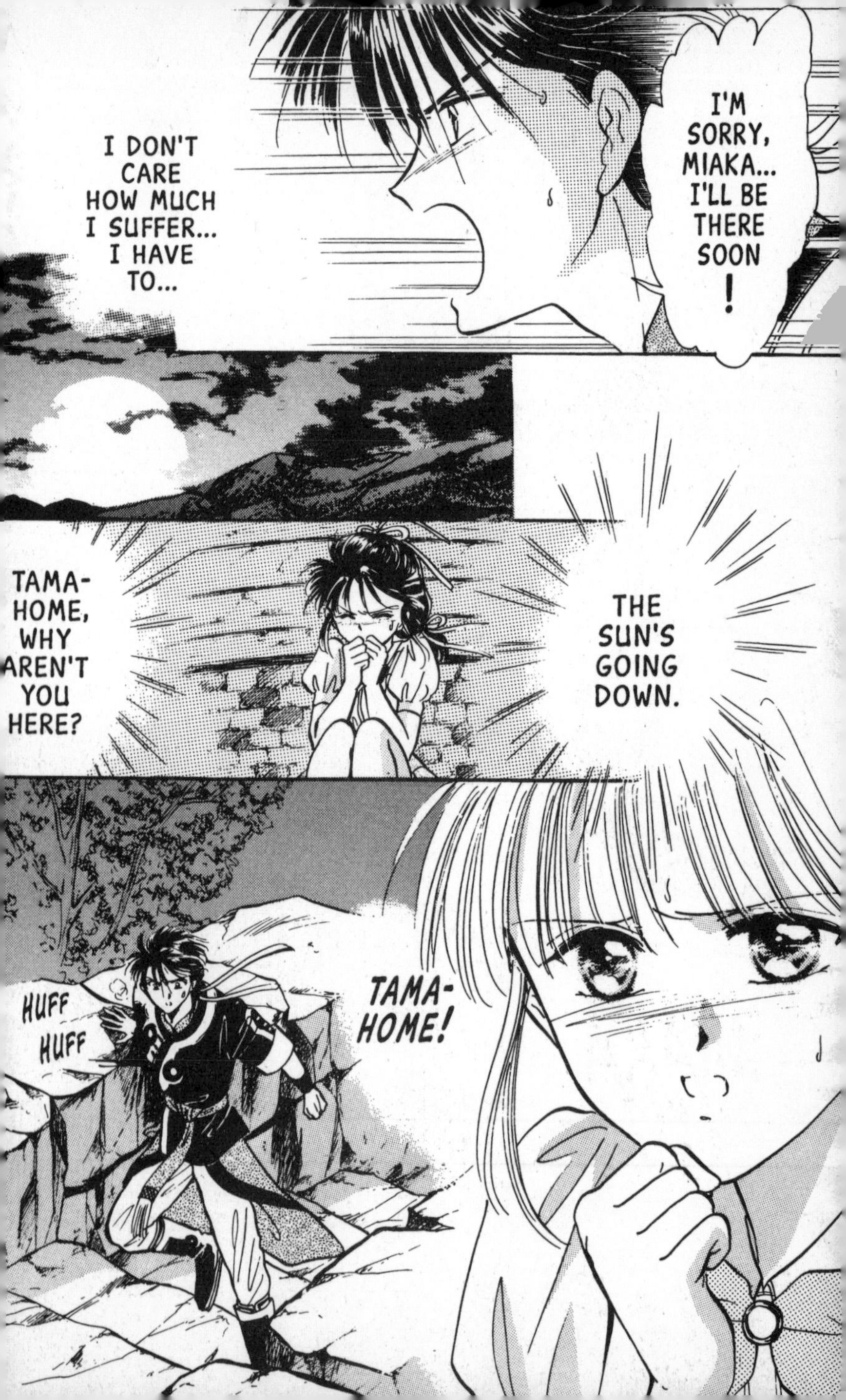
I'M SORRY, MIAKA... I'LL BE THERE SOON!
I DON'T CARE HOW MUCH I SUFFER... I HAVE TO...
THE SUN'S GOING DOWN.
TAMA-HOME, WHY AREN'T YOU HERE?
TAMA-HOME!
HUFF HUFF

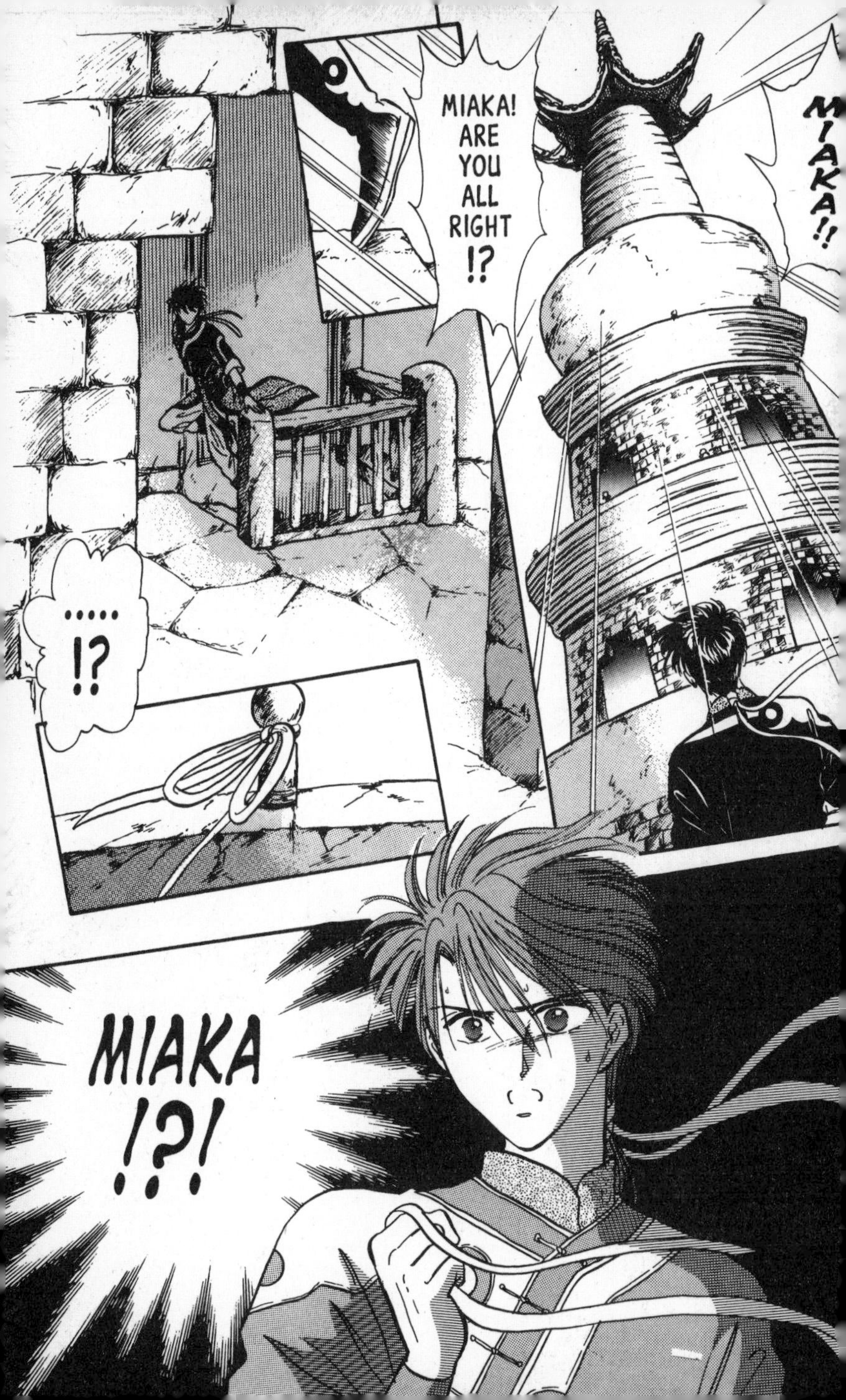
MIAKA!!
MIAKA! ARE YOU ALL RIGHT !?
..... !?
MIAKA !?!

(VIRGO)※

(VIRGO)※

WU JUN-JIA
武俊角

WU GANG-DE
武亢徳

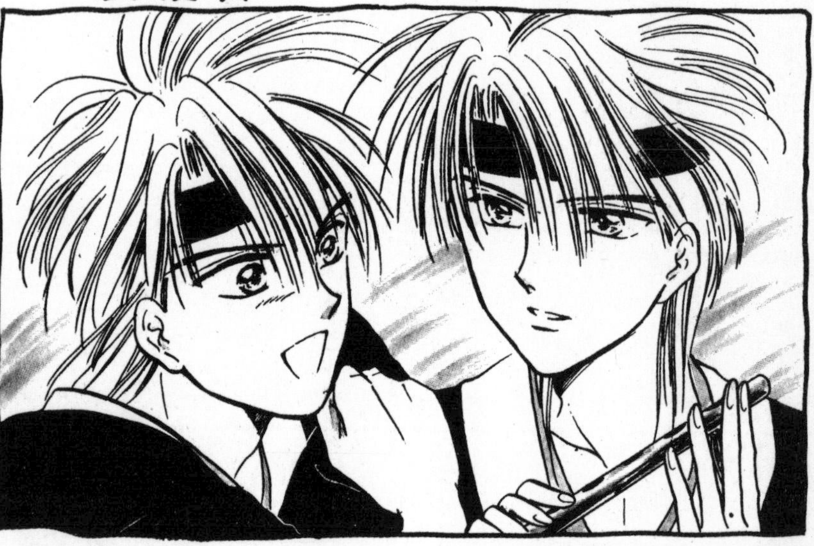

SUBOSHI

- Birthplace: Same as right side.
- Age: Same as right side.
- Family: Younger of the twins.
- Height: Same as right side.
- Blood Type: Same as right side.
- Talents: He can use a secret weapon (a weapon that doesn't look like a weapon) called the Ryusei-Sui, and control it with his will (actually there is no other way that it can be a weapon).
- The exact opposite of his brother, he's fierce, and if he gets an idea stuck in his head, he won't listen to reason--he'll just rush in like a madman. They lost their parents at a very young age and had a very tough childhood, so he's very much bonded with his brother (to the point where it goes too far). The bond is so strong that he would not hesitate to kill for his brother. Yui was the first person besides his brother to show him any tenderness and he quickly fell in love (first love) with her. It's because of Yui that he feels anger toward Miaka and jealousy toward Tamahome.

AMIBOSHI

- Birthplace: The village of Tian-Ling in the Shan-Yun province of Qu-Dong.
- Age: 15
- Family: Elder of twin brothers who lost their parents in a civil war.
- Height: 168 cm (5' 6")
- Blood Type: A
- Talents: Can emit chi through his mouth and channel it through a flute to control people's will.
- Tranquil and reserved, but at times he can be single-minded and merciless. Before the events of the book, he was a kind young man determined to judiciously protect his younger brother. And for that reason, he was faced with a dilemma and the pain of choosing between the Seiryu warriors and the Suzaku warriors.

I forgot to put in Nakago's constellation in the last volume!

⇦ HERE IT IS.

(SCORPIO)

※ The constellations for Amiboshi and Suboshi combined to make Virgo.

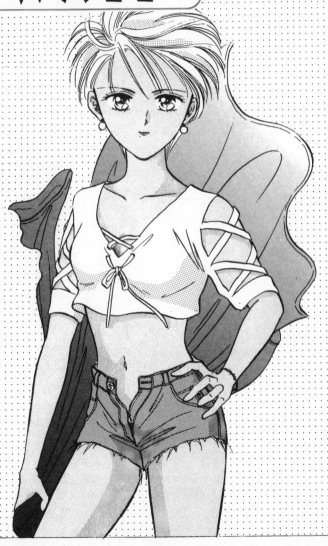

CHAPTER SIXTY-TWO
THE UNBREAKABLE
WALL

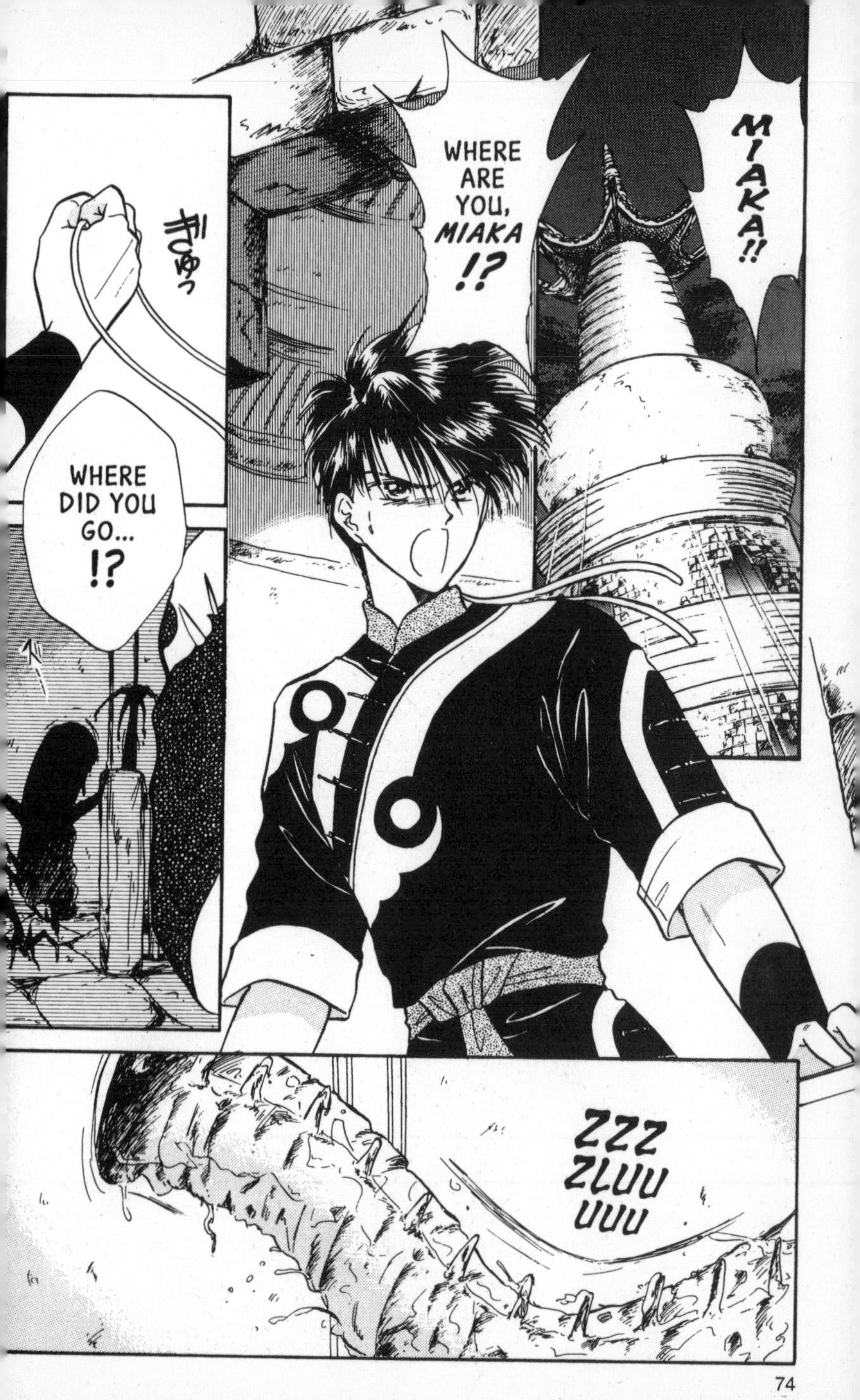
MIAKA!!
WHERE ARE YOU, MIAKA !?
ぎゅっ
WHERE DID YOU GO... !?
ZZZ ZLUU UUU

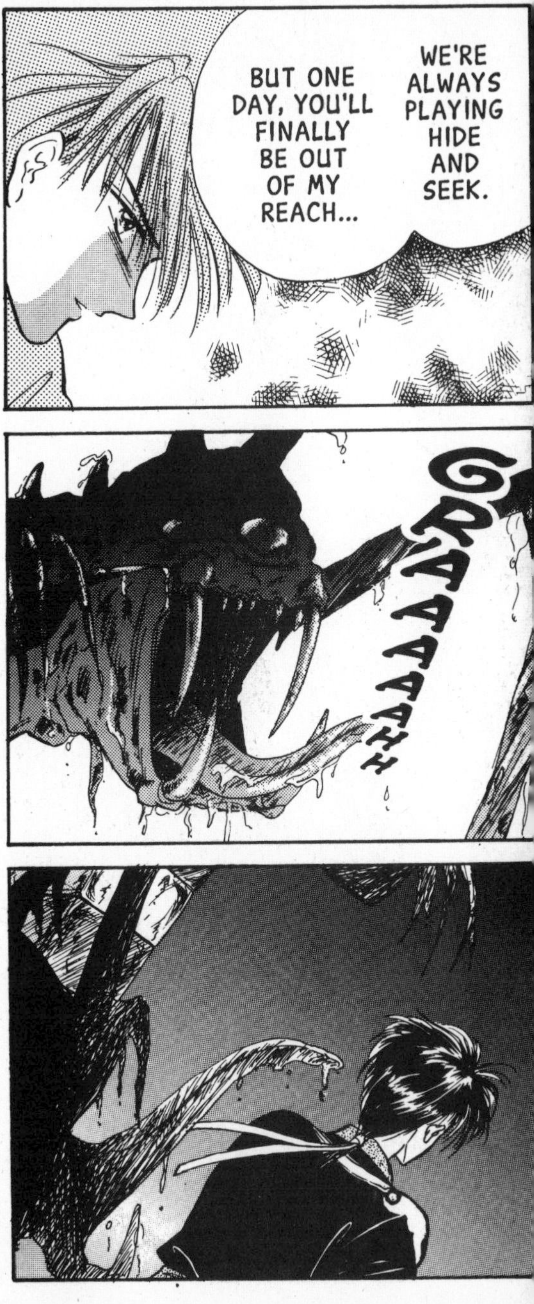
WE'RE ALWAYS PLAYING HIDE AND SEEK.
BUT ONE DAY, YOU'LL FINALLY BE OUT OF MY REACH...
GRAAAAAHH

Next is Tamahome. His character has changed significantly since before I started drawing the manga. Unaware of love, he discovers it for the first time in his life upon meeting Miaka. S-so, she's his first love! I drew Tamahome when I was 18 (before I was published), and when I worked on the short story Heart ni Jewel ("A Jewel for the Heart"), I found my old sketches for him. So he goes way back! (Oh, so does Hotohori!)
He can be a clown, but at the same time he has a dark side. So he's a little complicated. (I thought he was completely different from Manato in "Prepubescence" which I was working on at the time.) He's strong yet vulnerable. He protects himself by protecting others. That's about it. According to the CD booklet listener-response surveys, he was ranked No. 1 in the favorite-character category. (Although these were just the initial results. Miaka ranked No. 4, but in the Shōjo Comic survey she was No. 1!!) I'm not saying he's my personal type, but he's someone you want to hug and pat on the head. I wonder why!?

Hotohori! Readers go to both extremes over him. The younger readers don't seem to like him. I wonder if they relate more to Tamahome. But the ones who really like Hotohori send in letters that ramble on about him and nothing else. I mean, he's a nice guy. He's dedicated. He graciously withdrew from pursuing Miaka. Some might accuse him of going after her in Volume 6, but that's not a fair interpretation... Of course I have to defend him! I'm so sorry for him!

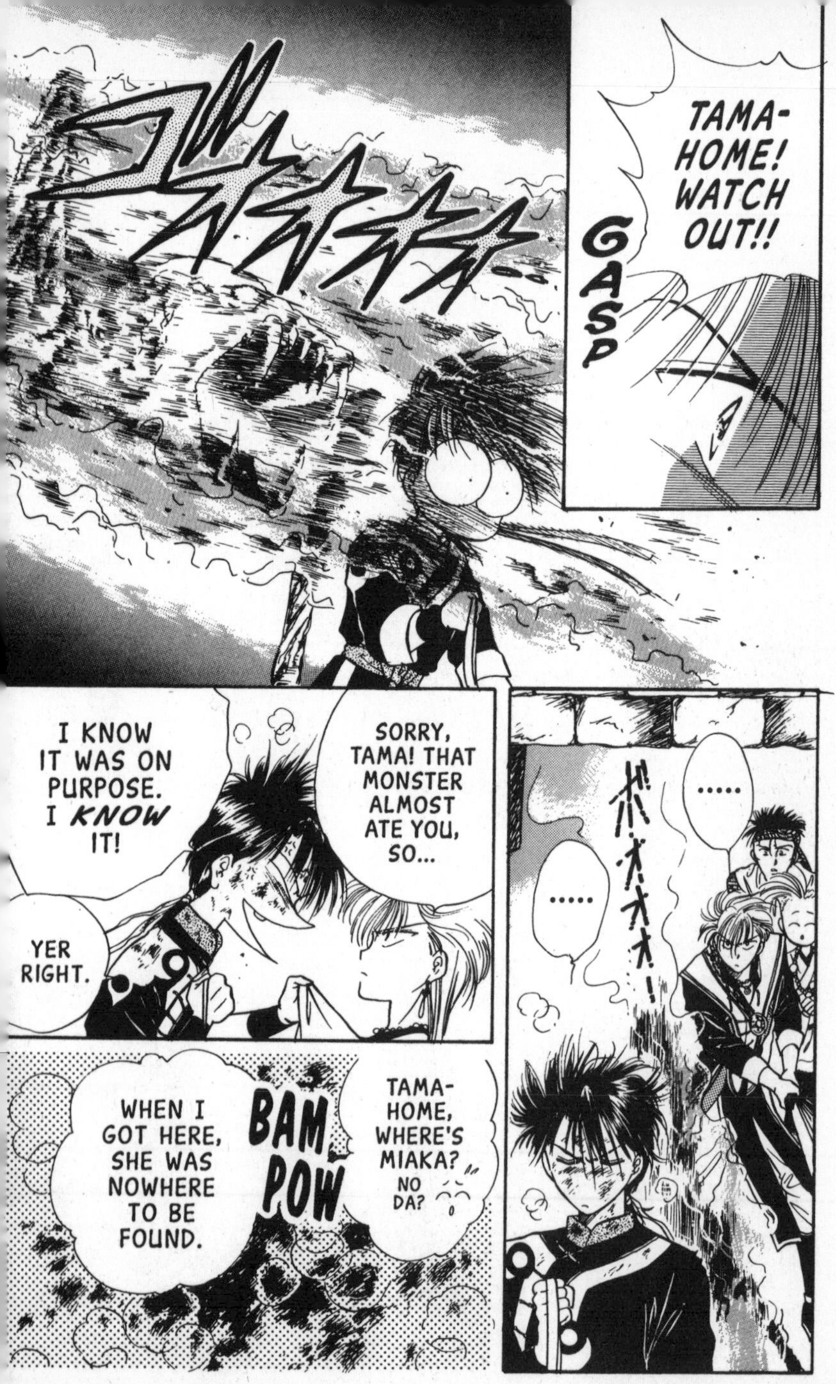
TAMA-HOME! WATCH OUT!!
GASP
.....
.....
ボォォォ!!
SORRY, TAMA! THAT MONSTER ALMOST ATE YOU, SO...
I KNOW IT WAS ON PURPOSE. I *KNOW* IT!
YER RIGHT.
TAMA-HOME, WHERE'S MIAKA?
NO DA?
BAM
POW
WHEN I GOT HERE, SHE WAS NOWHERE TO BE FOUND.

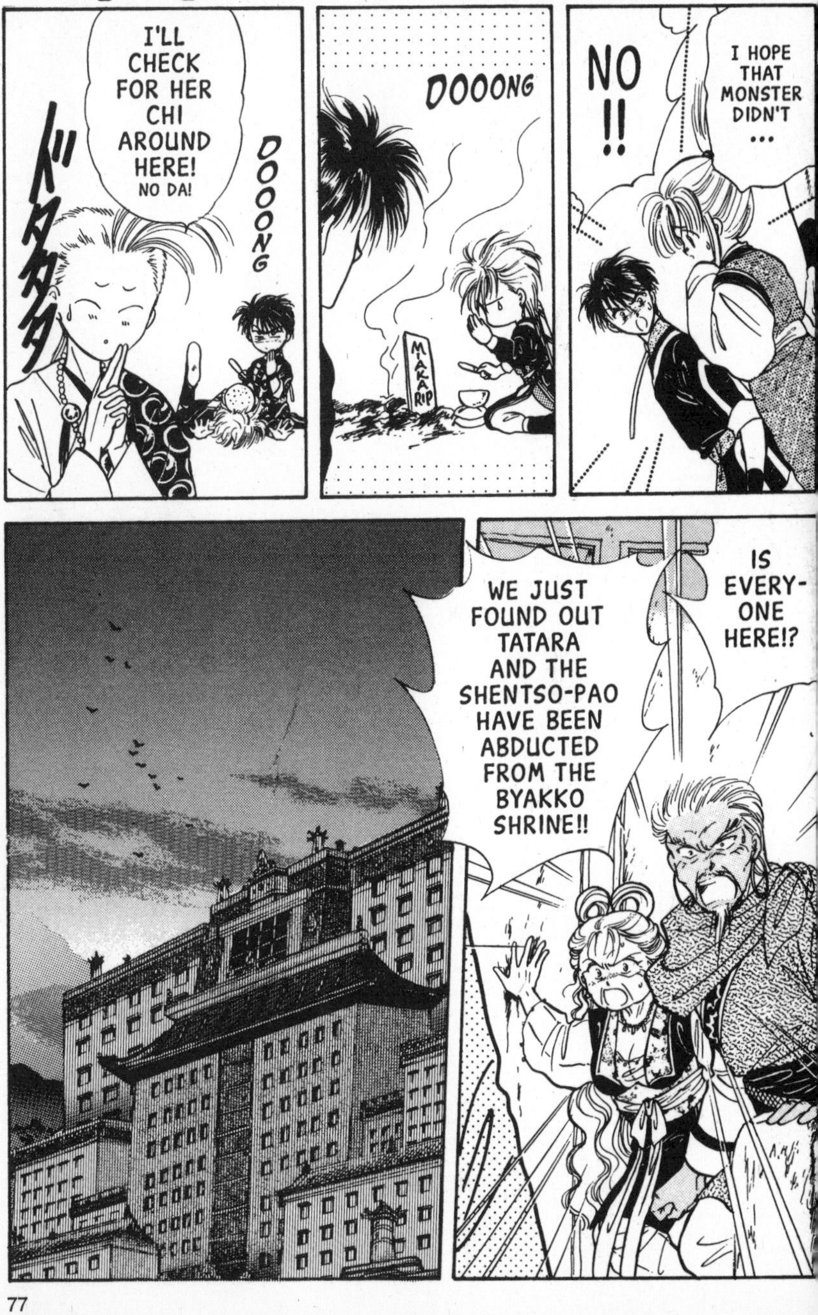
I HOPE THAT MONSTER DIDN'T ...
NO !!
DOOONG
MIAKA RIP
I'LL CHECK FOR HER CHI AROUND HERE! NO DA!
DOOOOONG
ドタタタタ
IS EVERY-ONE HERE!?
WE JUST FOUND OUT TATARA AND THE SHENTSO-PAO HAVE BEEN ABDUCTED FROM THE BYAKKO SHRINE!!

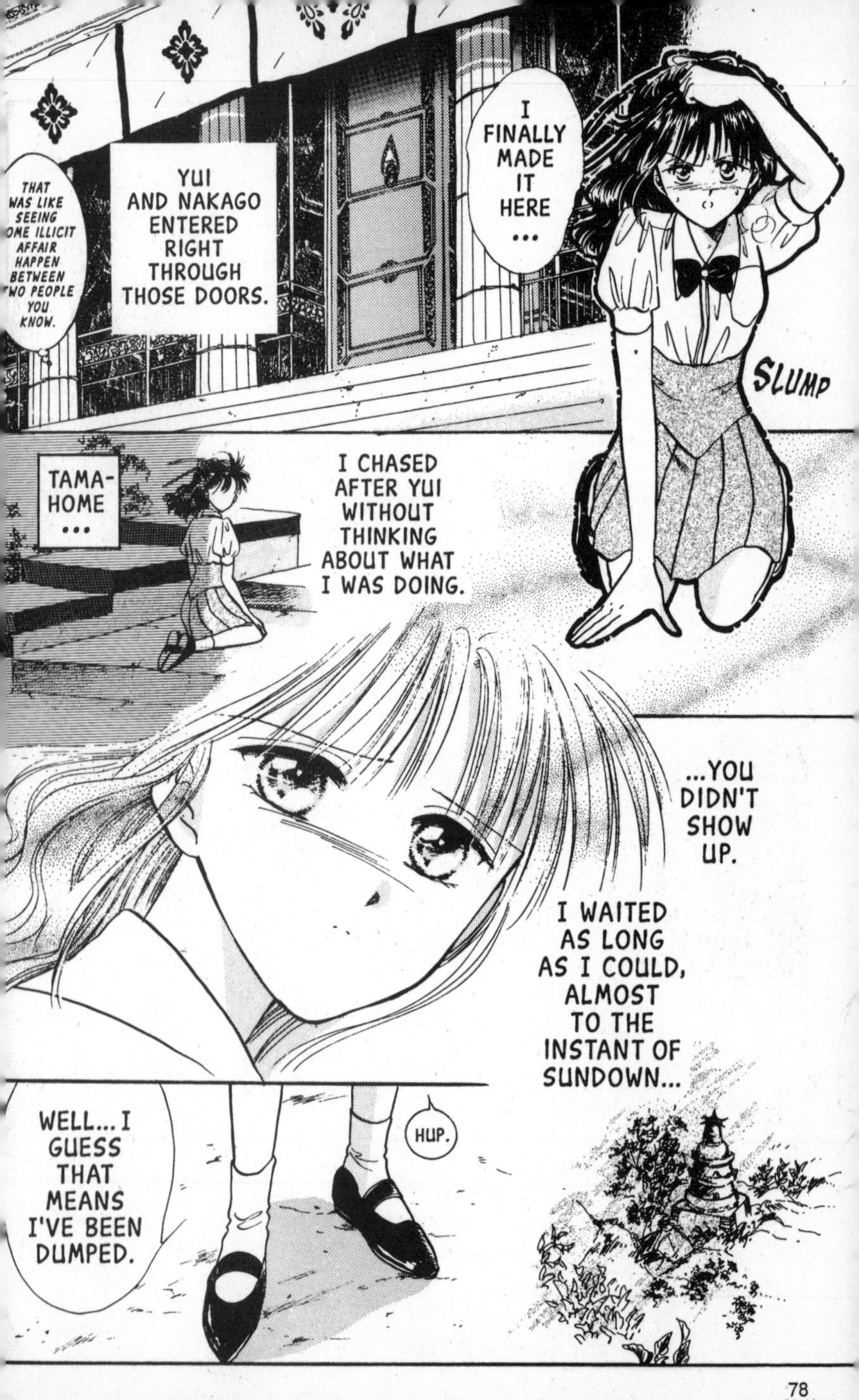
I FINALLY MADE IT HERE...
SLUMP
YUI AND NAKAGO ENTERED RIGHT THROUGH THOSE DOORS.
THAT WAS LIKE SEEING OME ILLICIT AFFAIR HAPPEN BETWEEN WO PEOPLE YOU KNOW.
I CHASED AFTER YUI WITHOUT THINKING ABOUT WHAT I WAS DOING.
TAMA-HOME...
...YOU DIDN'T SHOW UP.
I WAITED AS LONG AS I COULD, ALMOST TO THE INSTANT OF SUNDOWN...
HUP.
WELL...I GUESS THAT MEANS I'VE BEEN DUMPED.

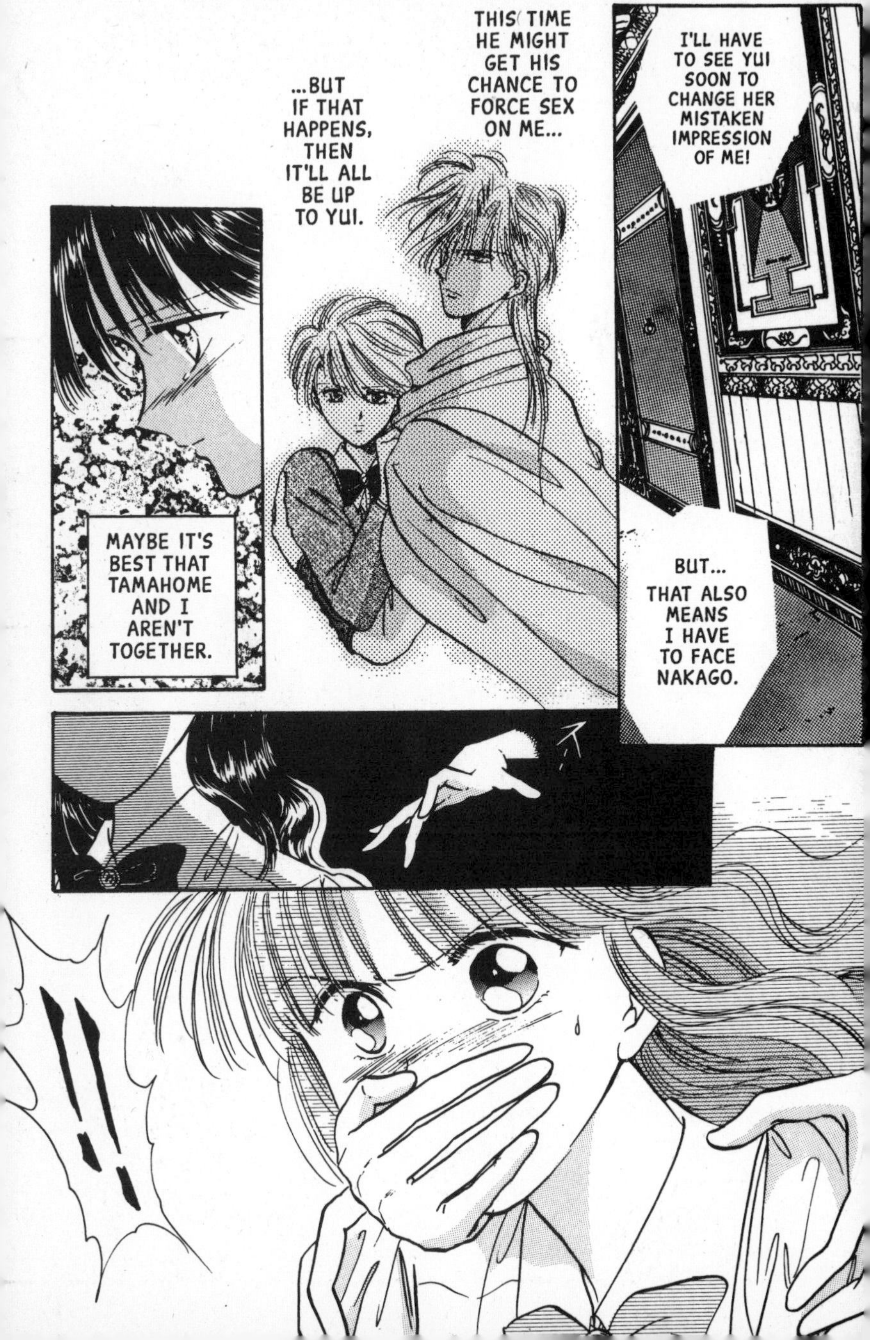
I'LL HAVE TO SEE YUI SOON TO CHANGE HER MISTAKEN IMPRESSION OF ME!
BUT... THAT ALSO MEANS I HAVE TO FACE NAKAGO.
THIS TIME HE MIGHT GET HIS CHANCE TO FORCE SEX ON ME...
...BUT IF THAT HAPPENS, THEN IT'LL ALL BE UP TO YUI.
MAYBE IT'S BEST THAT TAMAHOME AND I AREN'T TOGETHER.
!!

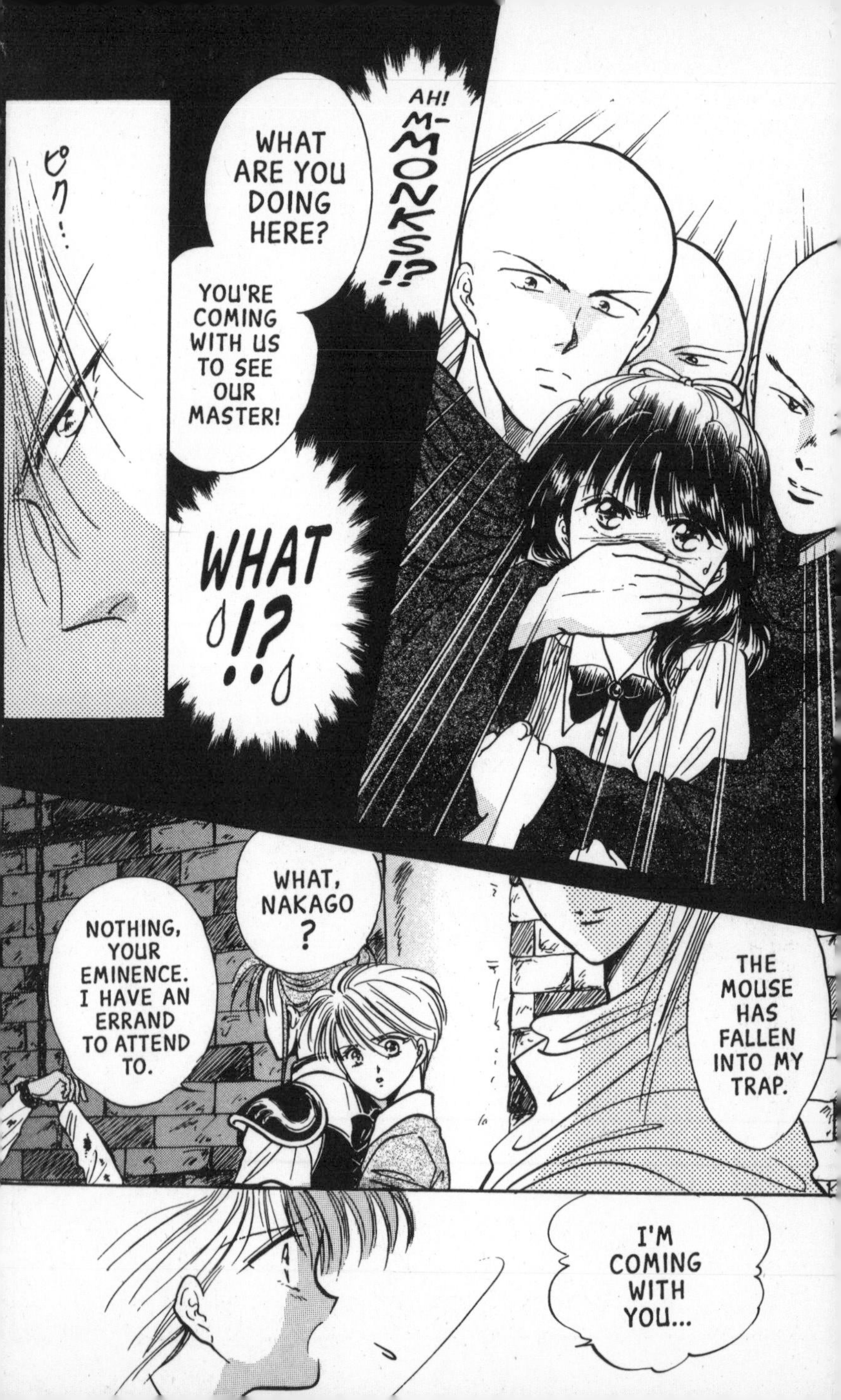
AH! M-MONKS!?
WHAT ARE YOU DOING HERE?
YOU'RE COMING WITH US TO SEE OUR MASTER!
WHAT!?
ピク…
THE MOUSE HAS FALLEN INTO MY TRAP.
WHAT, NAKAGO?
NOTHING, YOUR EMINENCE. I HAVE AN ERRAND TO ATTEND TO.
I'M COMING WITH YOU...

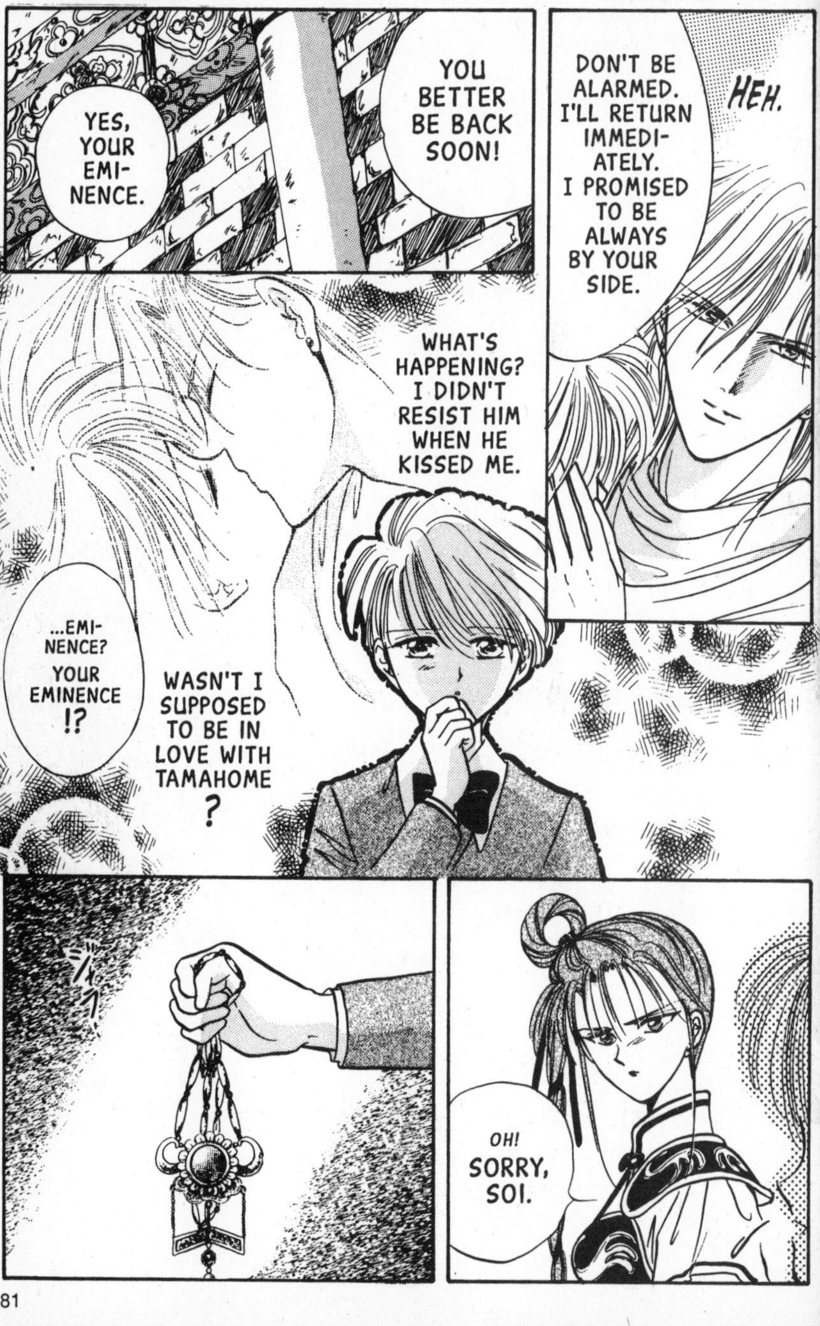
DON'T BE ALARMED. I'LL RETURN IMMEDIATELY. I PROMISED TO BE ALWAYS BY YOUR SIDE.
HEH.
YOU BETTER BE BACK SOON!
YES, YOUR EMINENCE.
WHAT'S HAPPENING? I DIDN'T RESIST HIM WHEN HE KISSED ME.
WASN'T I SUPPOSED TO BE IN LOVE WITH TAMAHOME?
...EMINENCE? YOUR EMINENCE!?
OH! SORRY, SOI.

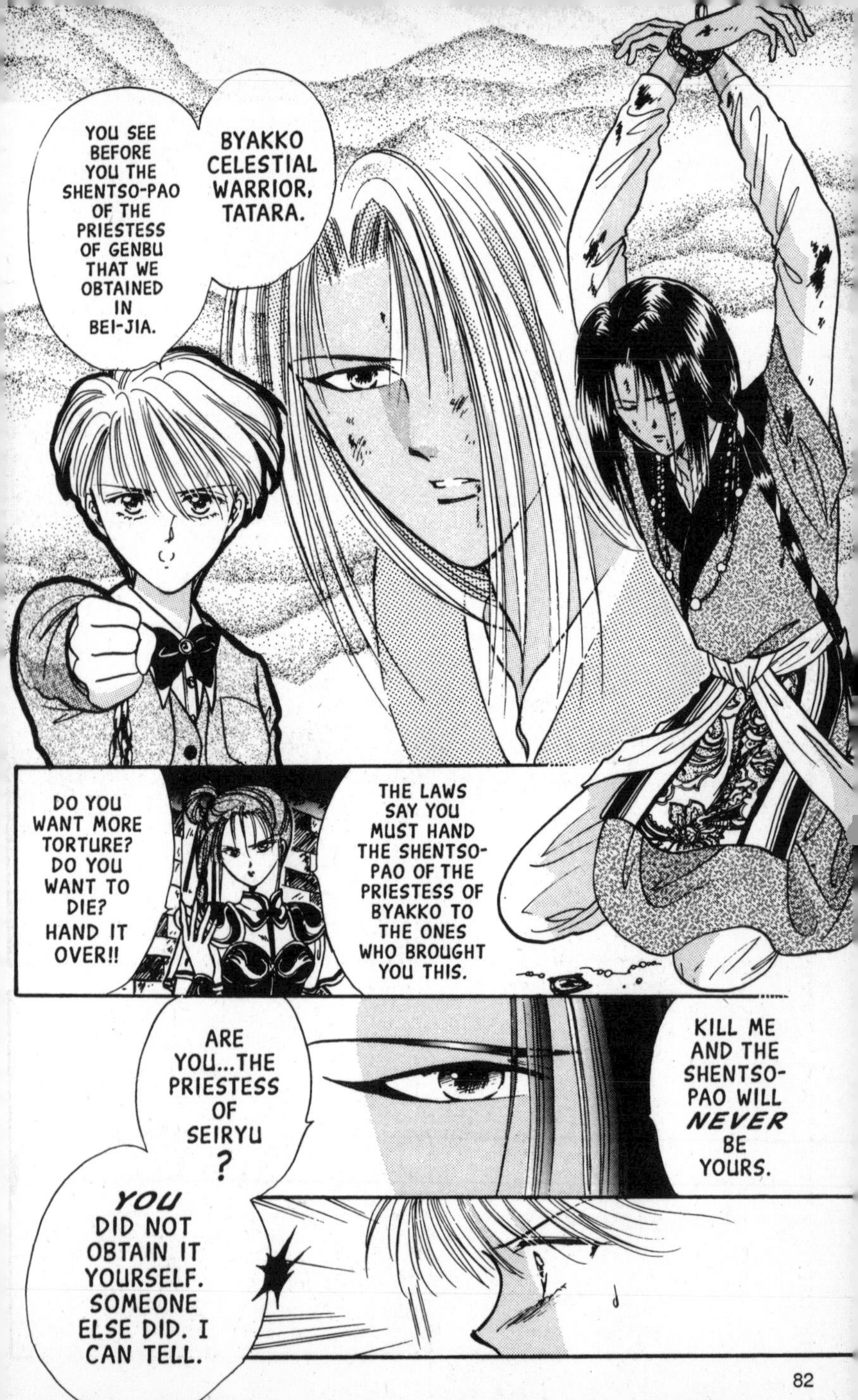

BYAKKO CELESTIAL WARRIOR, TATARA.
YOU SEE BEFORE YOU THE SHENTSO-PAO OF THE PRIESTESS OF GENBU THAT WE OBTAINED IN BEI-JIA.
THE LAWS SAY YOU MUST HAND THE SHENTSO-PAO OF THE PRIESTESS OF BYAKKO TO THE ONES WHO BROUGHT YOU THIS.
DO YOU WANT MORE TORTURE? DO YOU WANT TO DIE? HAND IT OVER!!
KILL ME AND THE SHENTSO-PAO WILL *NEVER* BE YOURS.
ARE YOU...THE PRIESTESS OF SEIRYU?
YOU DID NOT OBTAIN IT YOURSELF. SOMEONE ELSE DID. I CAN TELL.

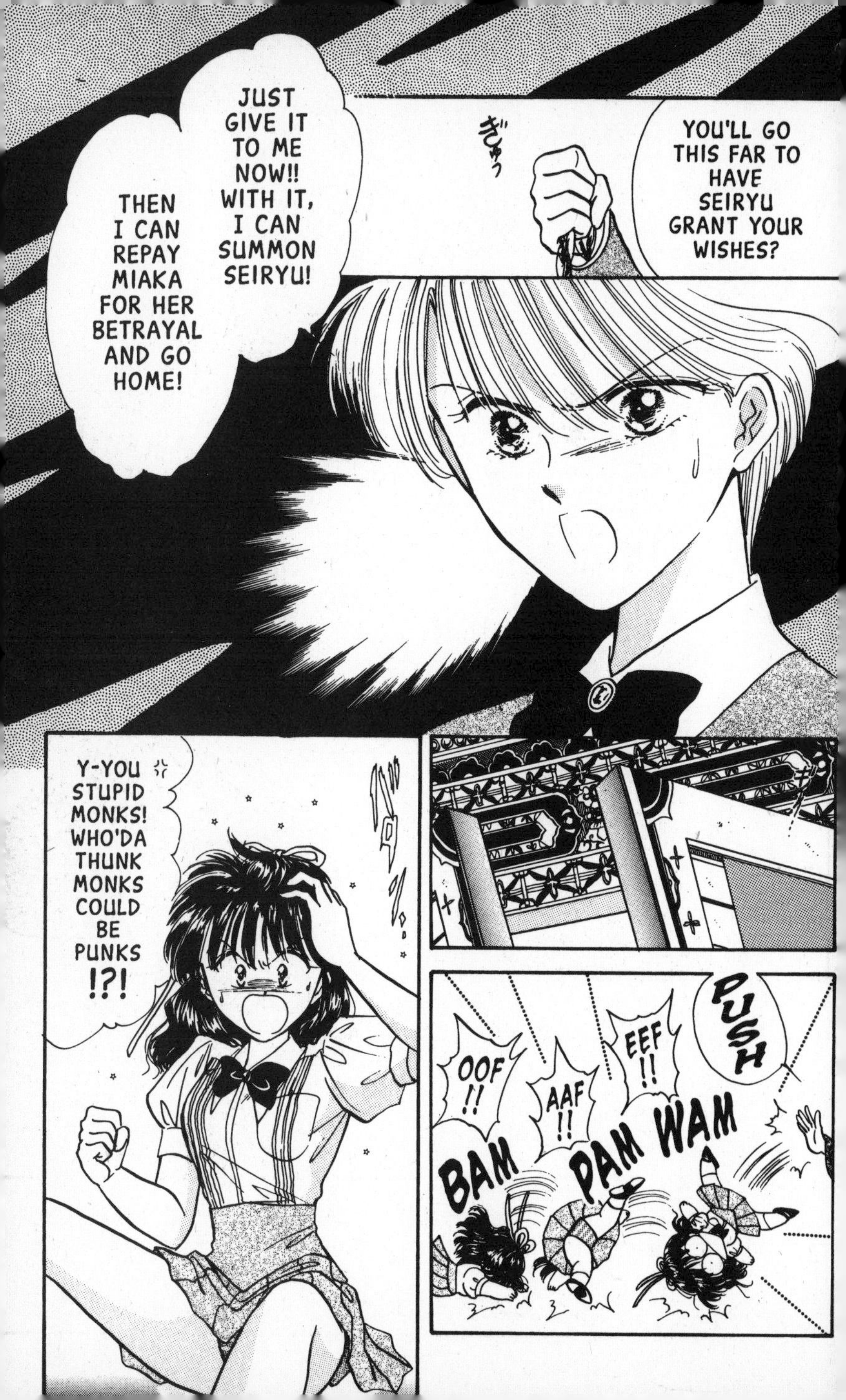
YOU'LL GO THIS FAR TO HAVE SEIRYU GRANT YOUR WISHES?
ぎゅっ
JUST GIVE IT TO ME NOW!! WITH IT, I CAN SUMMON SEIRYU!
THEN I CAN REPAY MIAKA FOR HER BETRAYAL AND GO HOME!
PUSH
EEF !!
AAF !!
OOF !!
WAM
PAM
BAM
バタン
Y-YOU STUPID MONKS! WHO'DA THUNK MONKS COULD BE PUNKS !?!

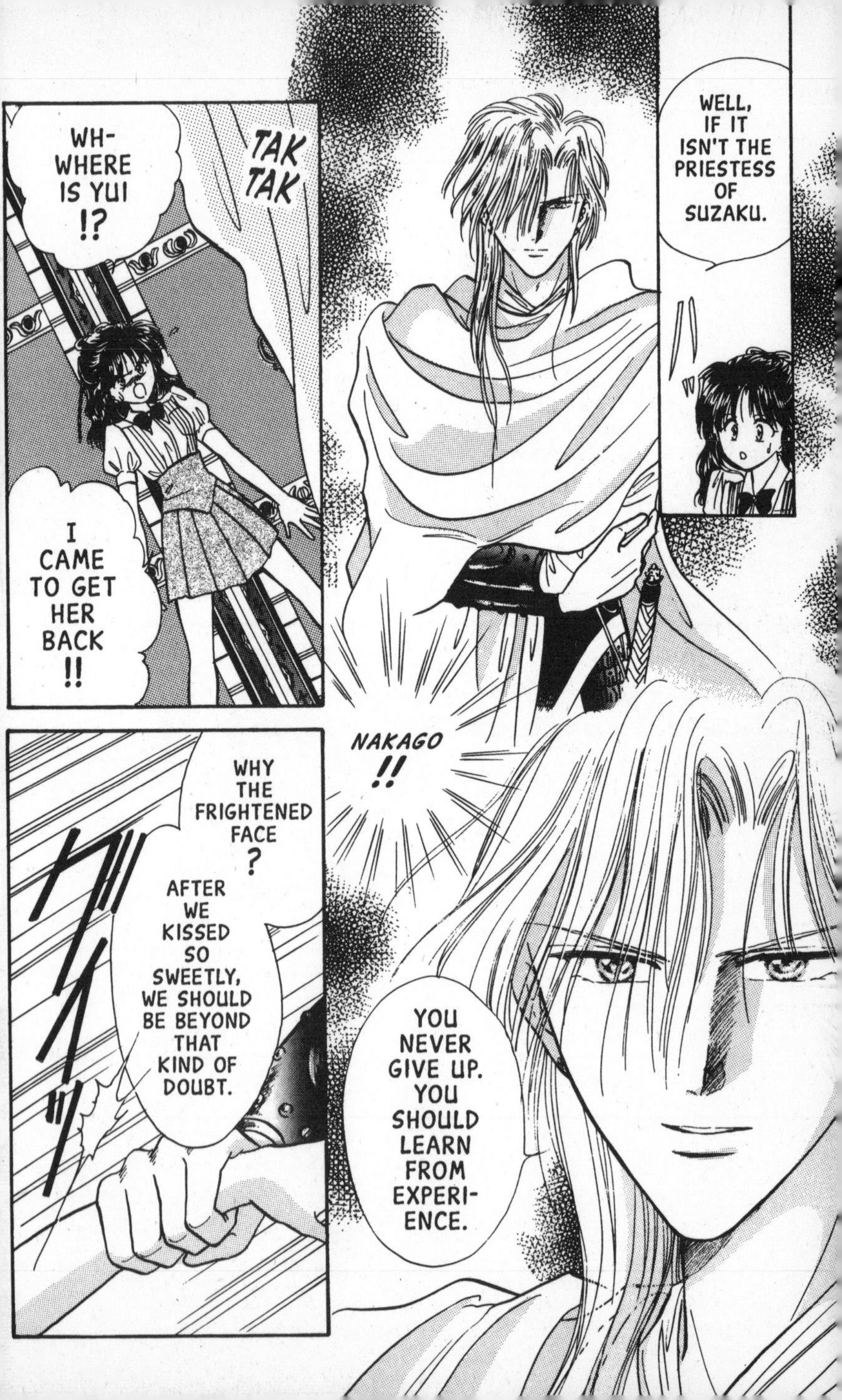
WELL, IF IT ISN'T THE PRIESTESS OF SUZAKU.
WH- WHERE IS YUI !?
TAK TAK
I CAME TO GET HER BACK !!
NAKAGO !!
YOU NEVER GIVE UP. YOU SHOULD LEARN FROM EXPERI- ENCE.
WHY THE FRIGHTENED FACE ?
AFTER WE KISSED SO SWEETLY, WE SHOULD BE BEYOND THAT KIND OF DOUBT.

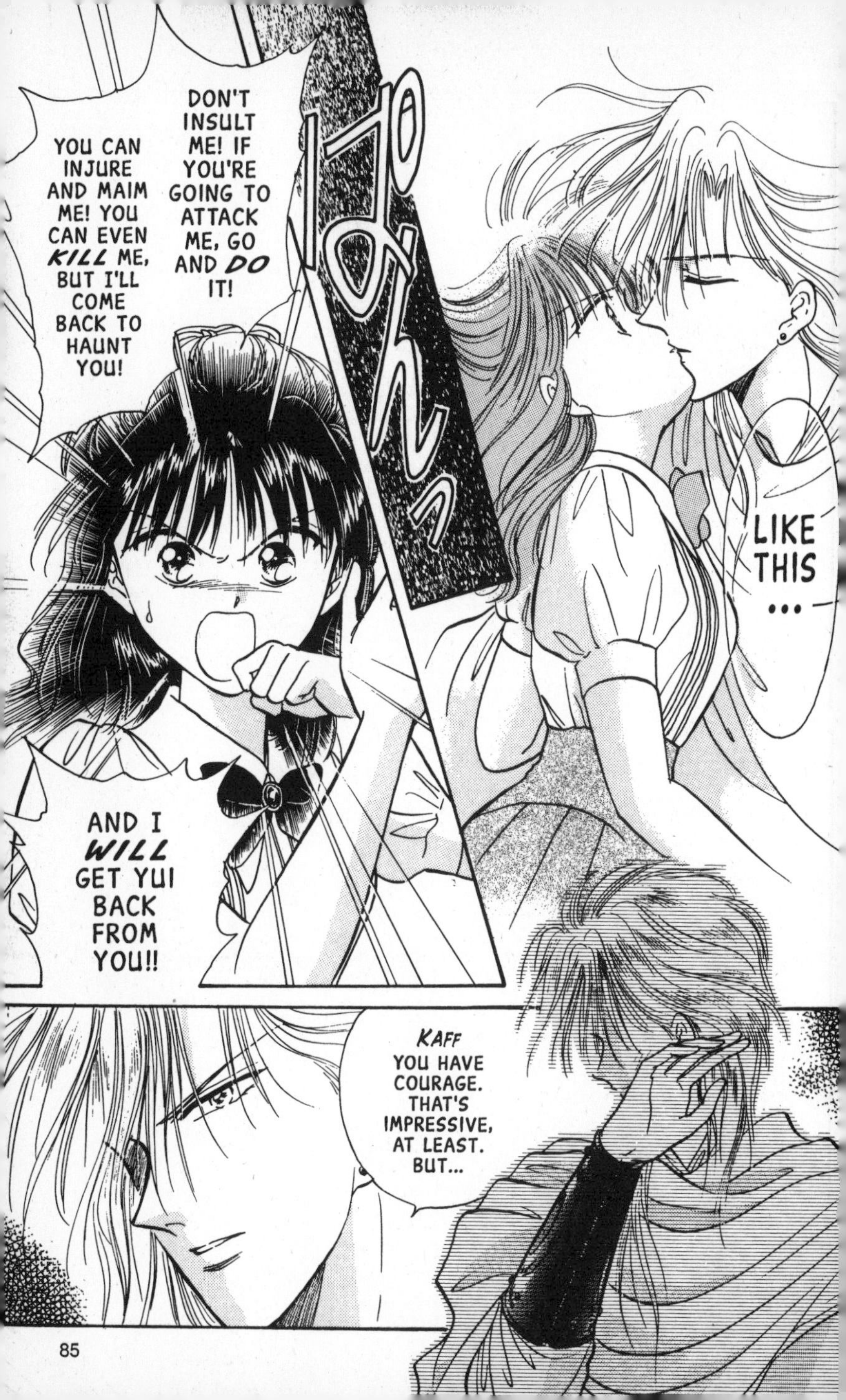
LIKE THIS...
DON'T INSULT ME! IF YOU'RE GOING TO ATTACK ME, GO AND *DO* IT!
YOU CAN INJURE AND MAIM ME! YOU CAN EVEN *KILL* ME, BUT I'LL COME BACK TO HAUNT YOU!
AND I *WILL* GET YUI BACK FROM YOU!!
KAFF
YOU HAVE COURAGE. THAT'S IMPRESSIVE, AT LEAST. BUT...

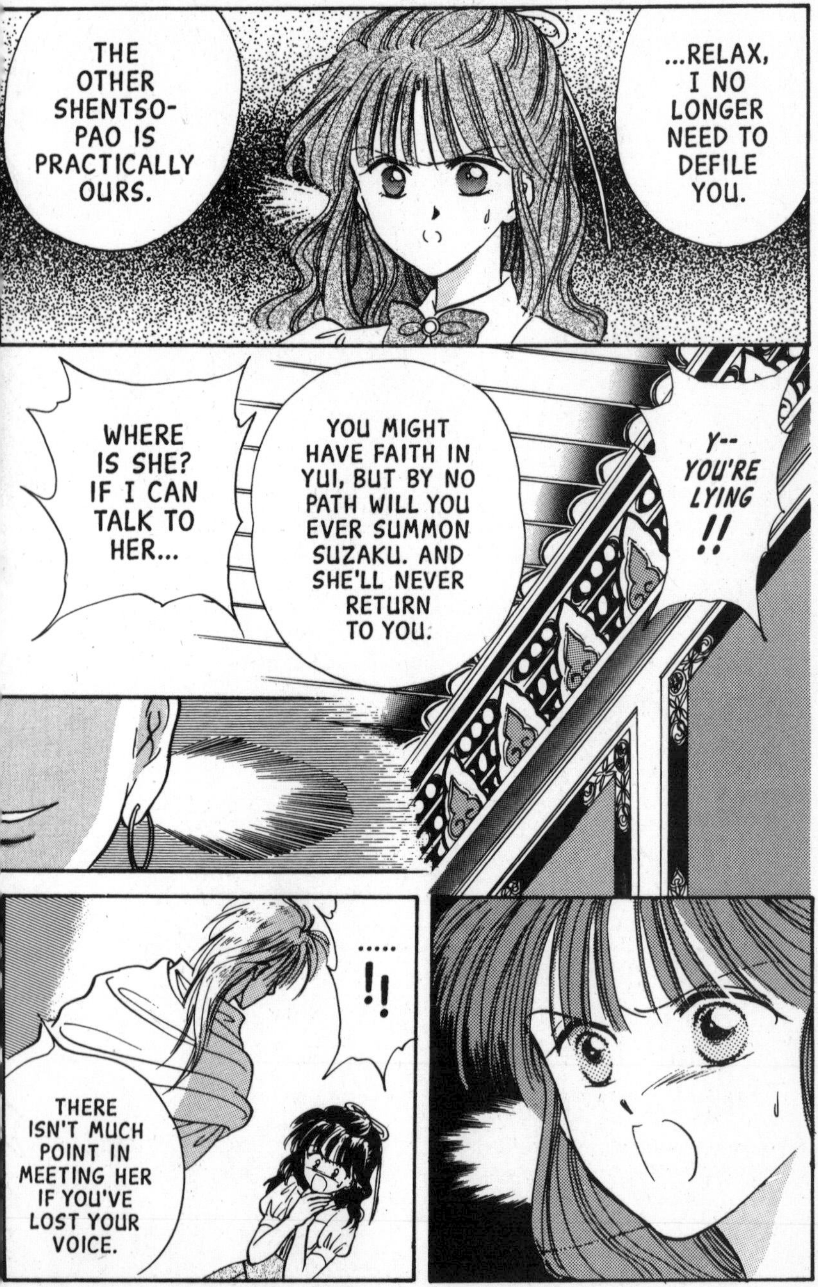
...RELAX, I NO LONGER NEED TO DEFILE YOU.
THE OTHER SHENTSO-PAO IS PRACTICALLY OURS.
Y-- YOU'RE LYING!!
YOU MIGHT HAVE FAITH IN YUI, BUT BY NO PATH WILL YOU EVER SUMMON SUZAKU. AND SHE'LL NEVER RETURN TO YOU.
WHERE IS SHE? IF I CAN TALK TO HER...
.....!!
THERE ISN'T MUCH POINT IN MEETING HER IF YOU'VE LOST YOUR VOICE.

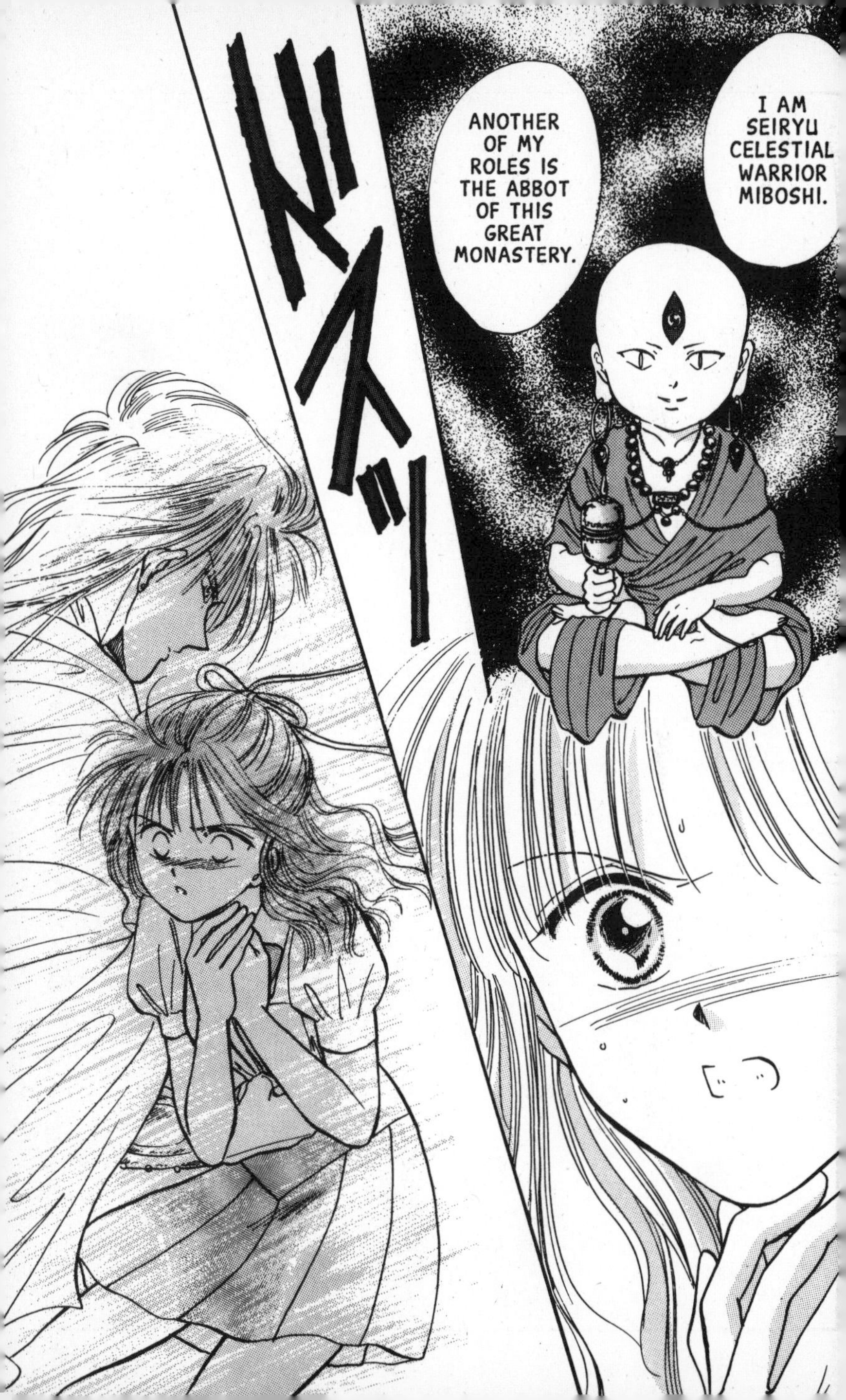
I AM SEIRYU CELESTIAL WARRIOR MIBOSHI.
ANOTHER OF MY ROLES IS THE ABBOT OF THIS GREAT MONASTERY.
ドスッ

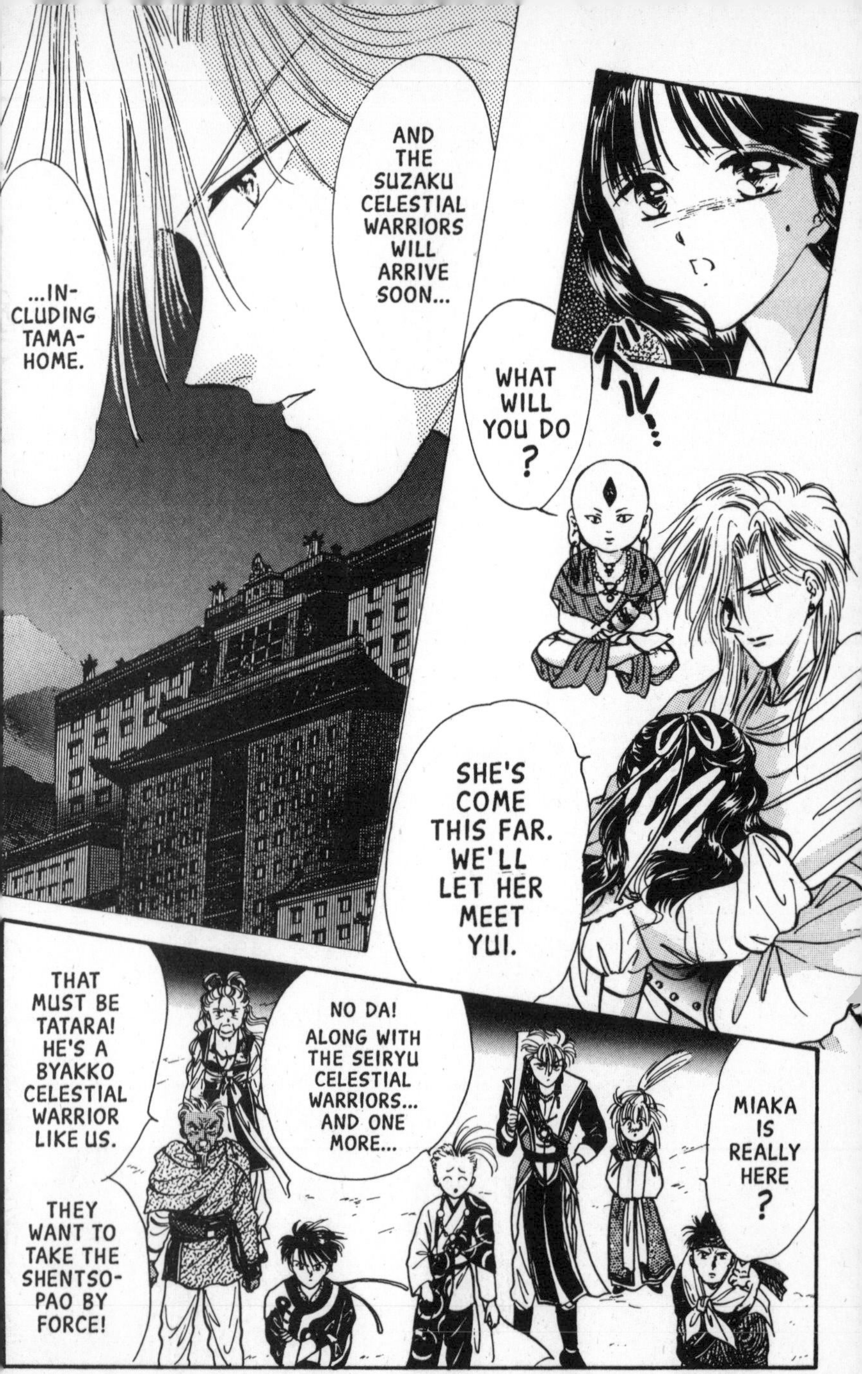
WHAT WILL YOU DO?
SHE'S COME THIS FAR. WE'LL LET HER MEET YUI.
AND THE SUZAKU CELESTIAL WARRIORS WILL ARRIVE SOON...
...IN-CLUDING TAMA-HOME.
MIAKA IS REALLY HERE?
NO DA! ALONG WITH THE SEIRYU CELESTIAL WARRIORS... AND ONE MORE...
THAT MUST BE TATARA! HE'S A BYAKKO CELESTIAL WARRIOR LIKE US.
THEY WANT TO TAKE THE SHENTSO-PAO BY FORCE!

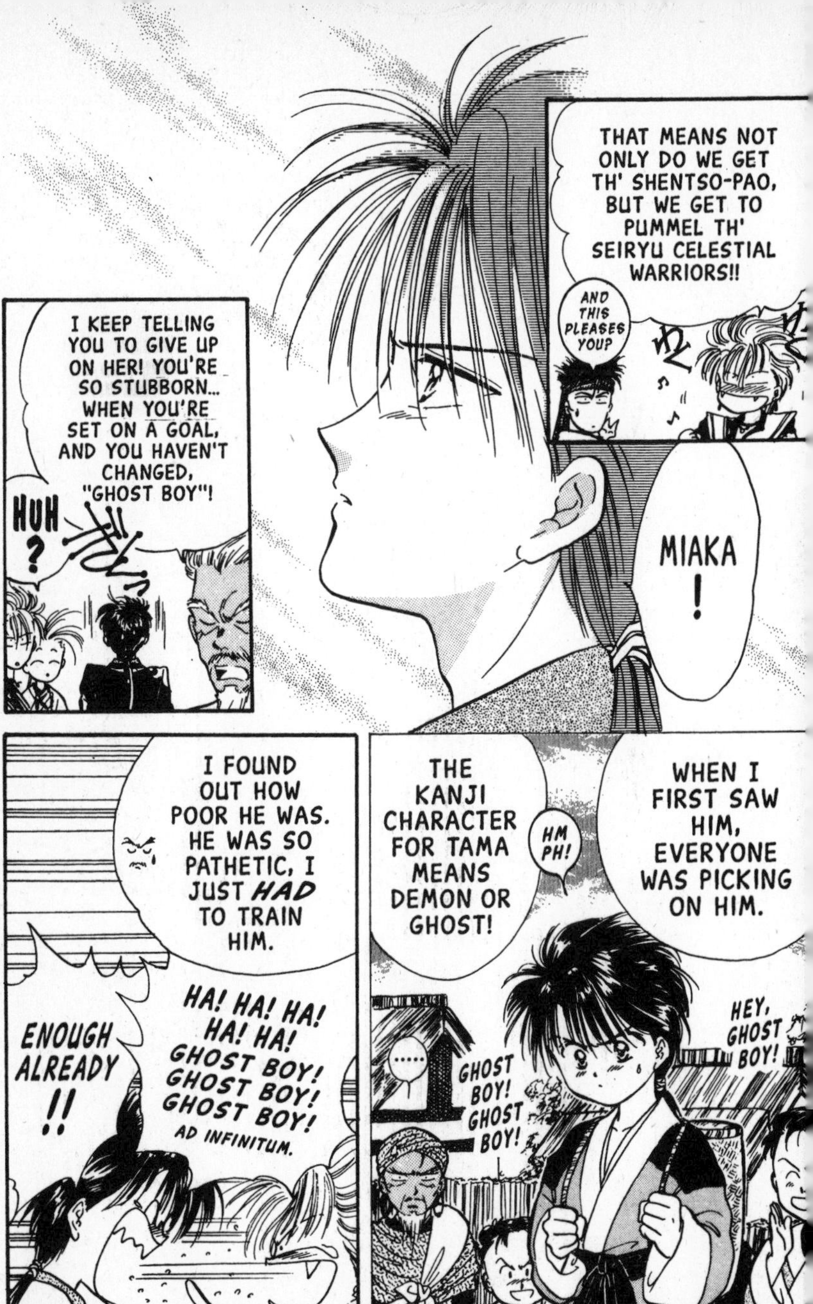
THAT MEANS NOT ONLY DO WE GET TH' SHENTSO-PAO, BUT WE GET TO PUMMEL TH' SEIRYU CELESTIAL WARRIORS!!
AND THIS PLEASES YOU?
MIAKA!
I KEEP TELLING YOU TO GIVE UP ON HER! YOU'RE SO STUBBORN... WHEN YOU'RE SET ON A GOAL, AND YOU HAVEN'T CHANGED, "GHOST BOY"!
HUH?
WHEN I FIRST SAW HIM, EVERYONE WAS PICKING ON HIM.
HEY, GHOST BOY!
GHOST BOY! GHOST BOY!
HM PH!
THE KANJI CHARACTER FOR TAMA MEANS DEMON OR GHOST!
......
I FOUND OUT HOW POOR HE WAS. HE WAS SO PATHETIC, I JUST *HAD* TO TRAIN HIM.
HA! HA! HA! HA! HA! GHOST BOY! GHOST BOY! GHOST BOY!
AD INFINITUM.
ENOUGH ALREADY!!

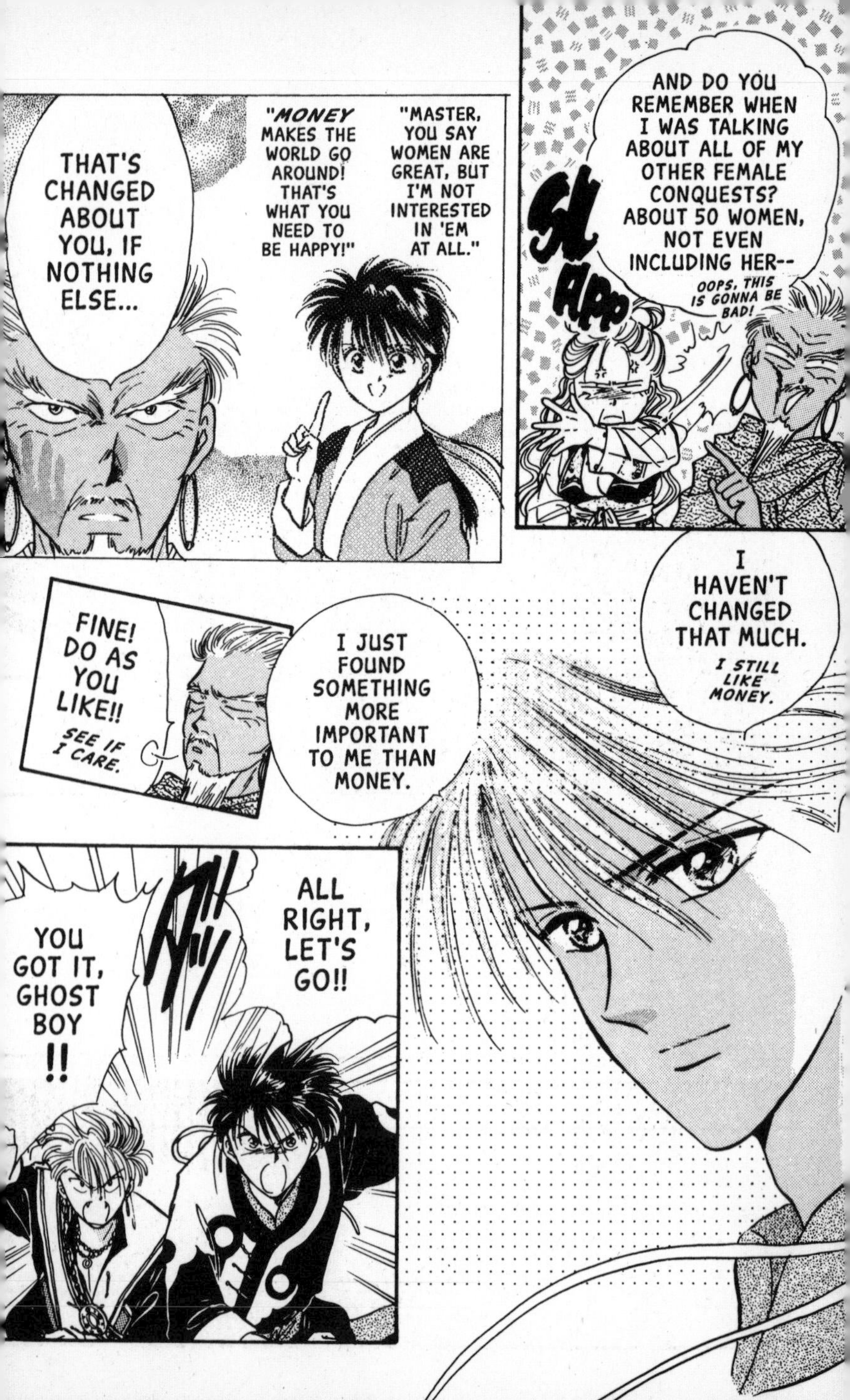
AND DO YOU REMEMBER WHEN I WAS TALKING ABOUT ALL OF MY OTHER FEMALE CONQUESTS? ABOUT 50 WOMEN, NOT EVEN INCLUDING HER--
SLAPP
OOPS, THIS IS GONNA BE BAD!
"MASTER, YOU SAY WOMEN ARE GREAT, BUT I'M NOT INTERESTED IN 'EM AT ALL."
"MONEY MAKES THE WORLD GO AROUND! THAT'S WHAT YOU NEED TO BE HAPPY!"
THAT'S CHANGED ABOUT YOU, IF NOTHING ELSE...
I HAVEN'T CHANGED THAT MUCH.
I STILL LIKE MONEY.
I JUST FOUND SOMETHING MORE IMPORTANT TO ME THAN MONEY.
FINE! DO AS YOU LIKE!!
SEE IF I CARE.
ALL RIGHT, LET'S GO!!
YOU GOT IT, GHOST BOY !!

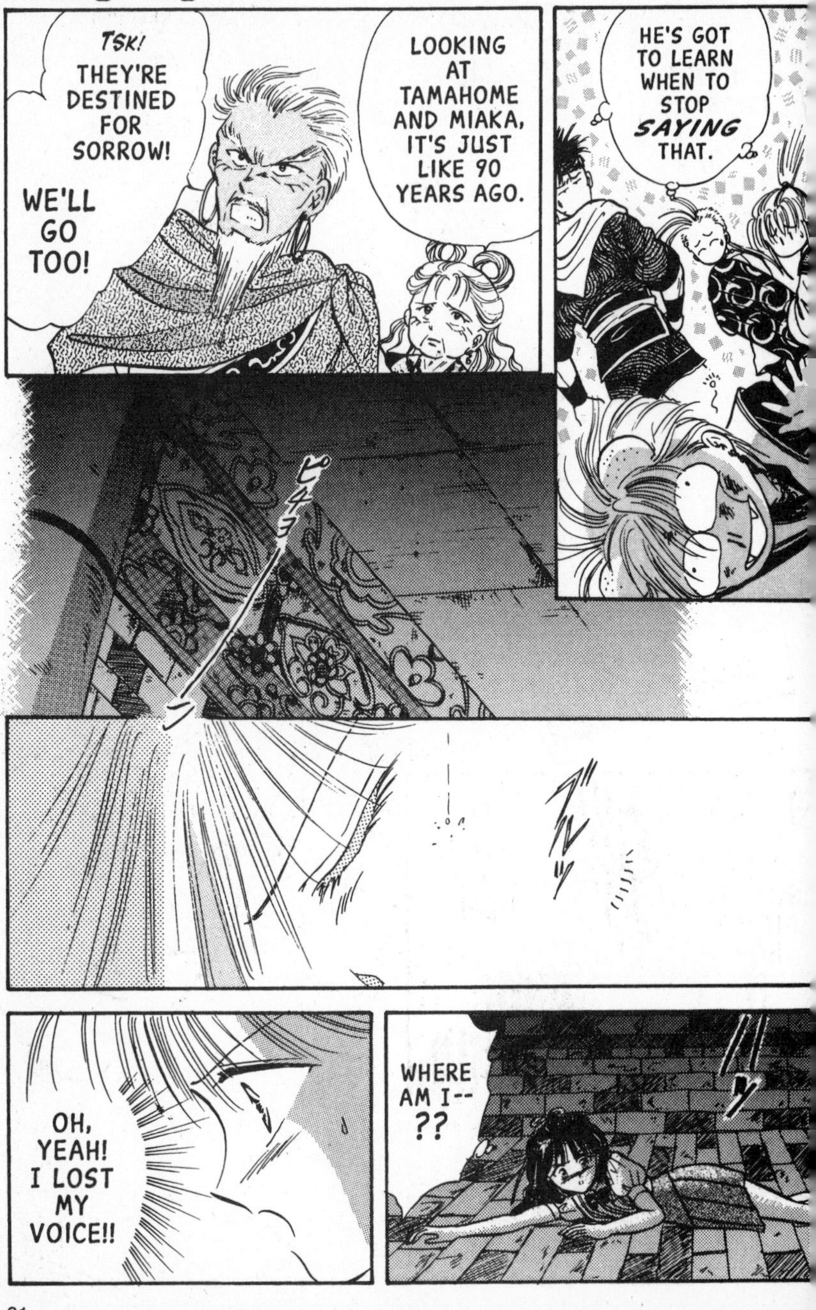
HE'S GOT TO LEARN WHEN TO STOP *SAYING* THAT.
LOOKING AT TAMAHOME AND MIAKA, IT'S JUST LIKE 90 YEARS AGO.
TSK! THEY'RE DESTINED FOR SORROW!
WE'LL GO TOO!
WHERE AM I-- ??
OH, YEAH! I LOST MY VOICE!!

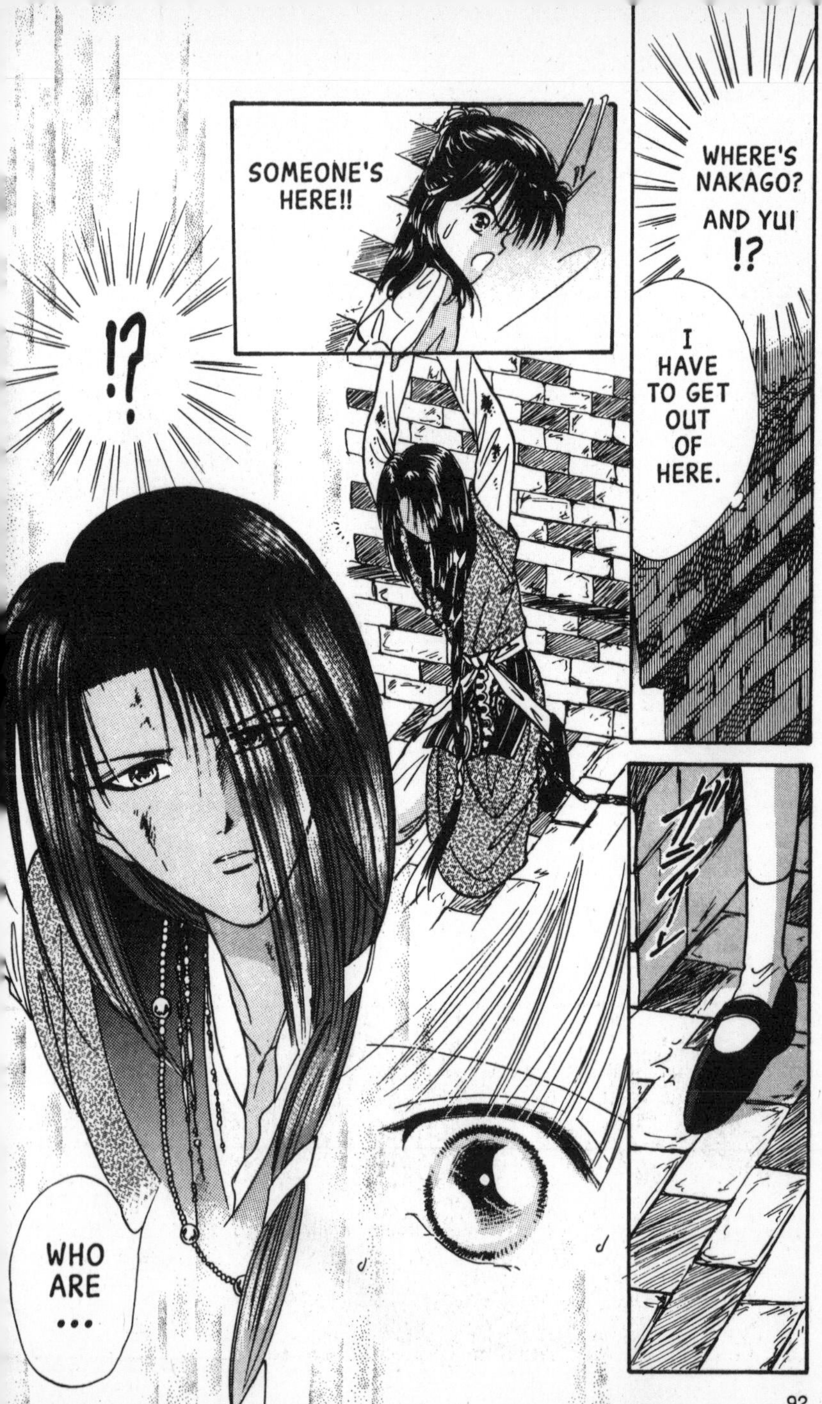

WHERE'S NAKAGO? AND YUI !?
I HAVE TO GET OUT OF HERE.
SOMEONE'S HERE!!
!?
WHO ARE ...

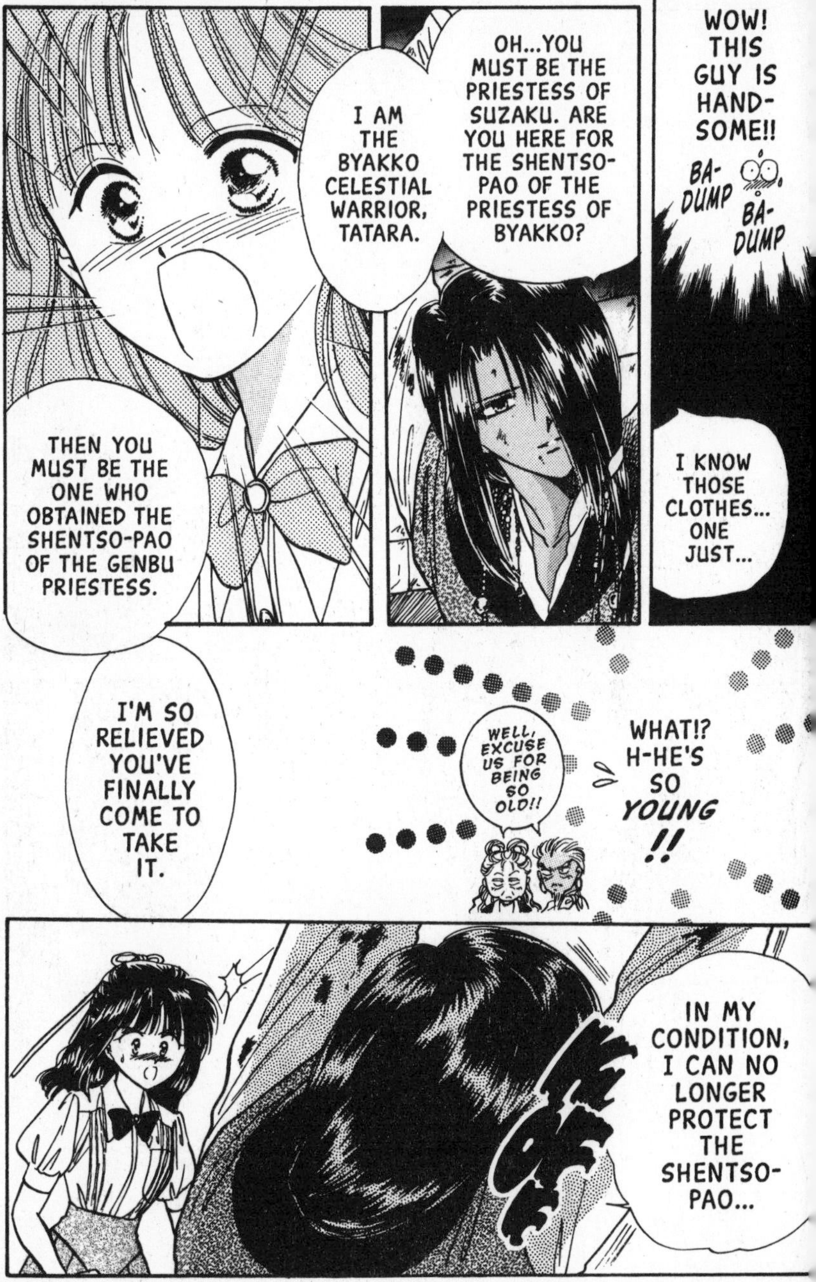
WOW! THIS GUY IS HAND-SOME!!
BA-DUMP
BA-DUMP
I KNOW THOSE CLOTHES... ONE JUST...
OH...YOU MUST BE THE PRIESTESS OF SUZAKU. ARE YOU HERE FOR THE SHENTSO-PAO OF THE PRIESTESS OF BYAKKO?
I AM THE BYAKKO CELESTIAL WARRIOR, TATARA.
THEN YOU MUST BE THE ONE WHO OBTAINED THE SHENTSO-PAO OF THE GENBU PRIESTESS.
I'M SO RELIEVED YOU'VE FINALLY COME TO TAKE IT.
WHAT!? H-HE'S SO YOUNG!!
WELL, EXCUSE US FOR BEING SO OLD!!
IN MY CONDITION, I CAN NO LONGER PROTECT THE SHENTSO-PAO...

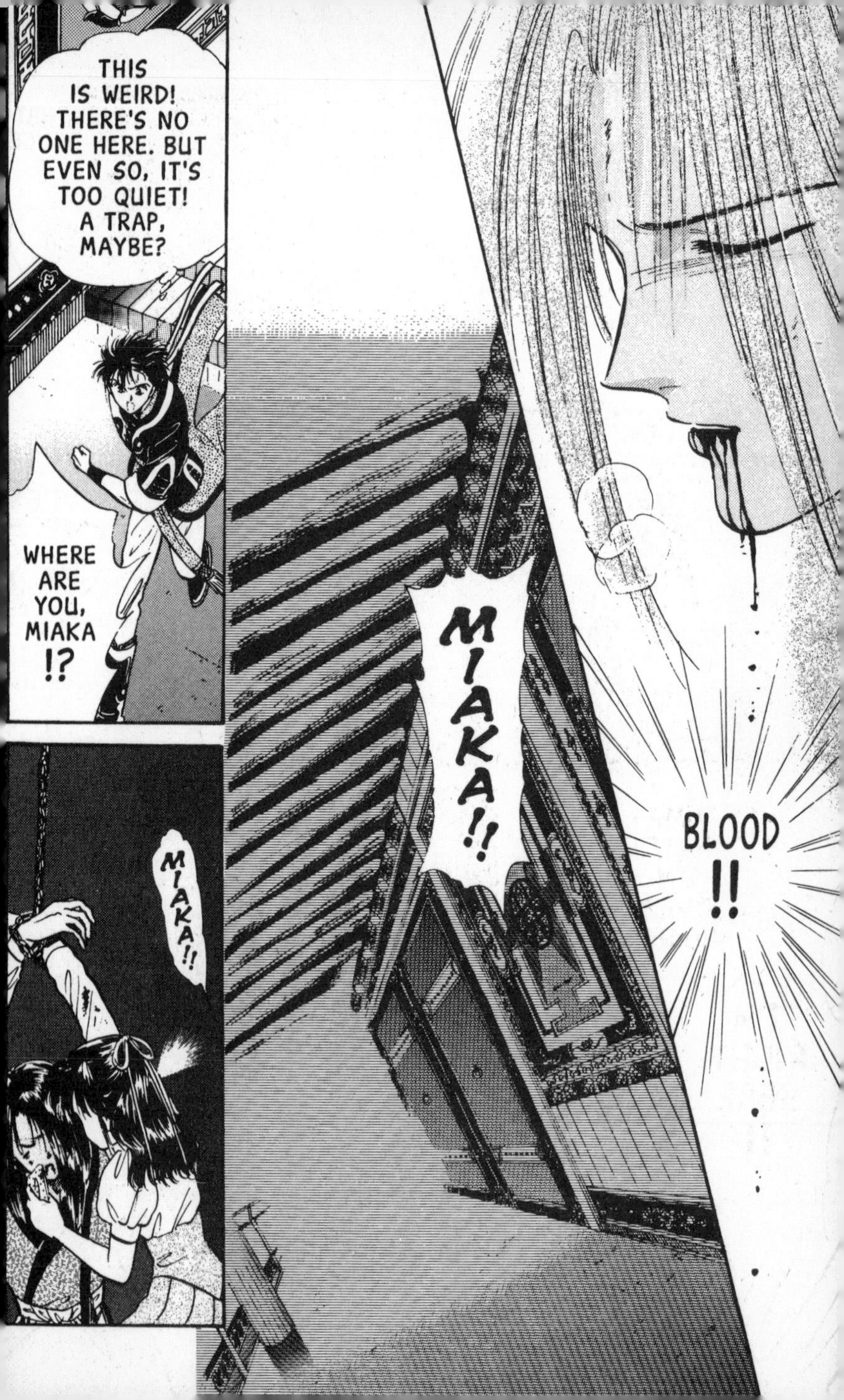

BLOOD !!
MIAKA!!
THIS IS WEIRD! THERE'S NO ONE HERE. BUT EVEN SO, IT'S TOO QUIET! A TRAP, MAYBE?
WHERE ARE YOU, MIAKA !?
MIAKA!!

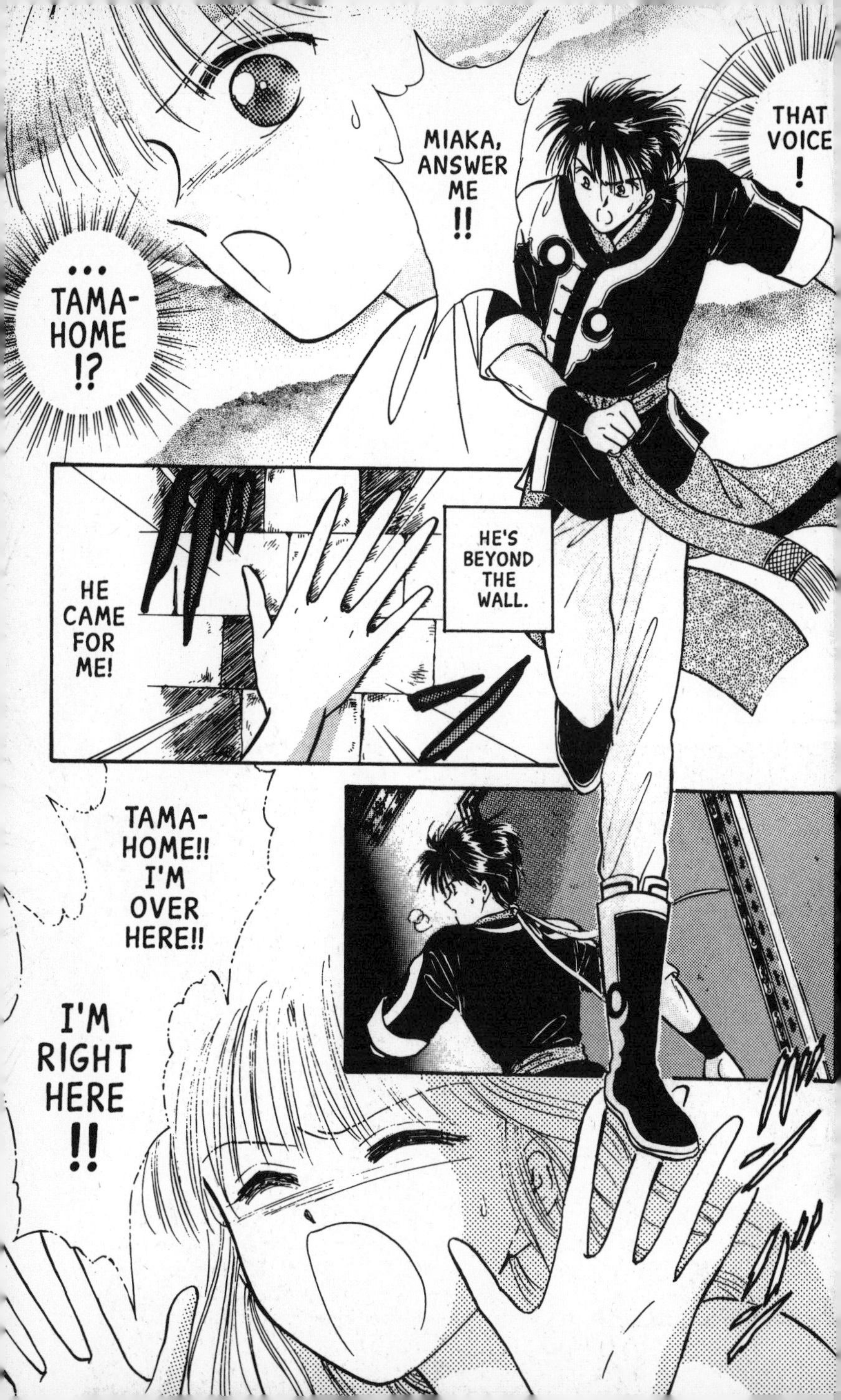
THAT VOICE!
MIAKA, ANSWER ME!!
...TAMA-HOME!?
HE'S BEYOND THE WALL.
HE CAME FOR ME!
TAMA-HOME!! I'M OVER HERE!!
I'M RIGHT HERE!!

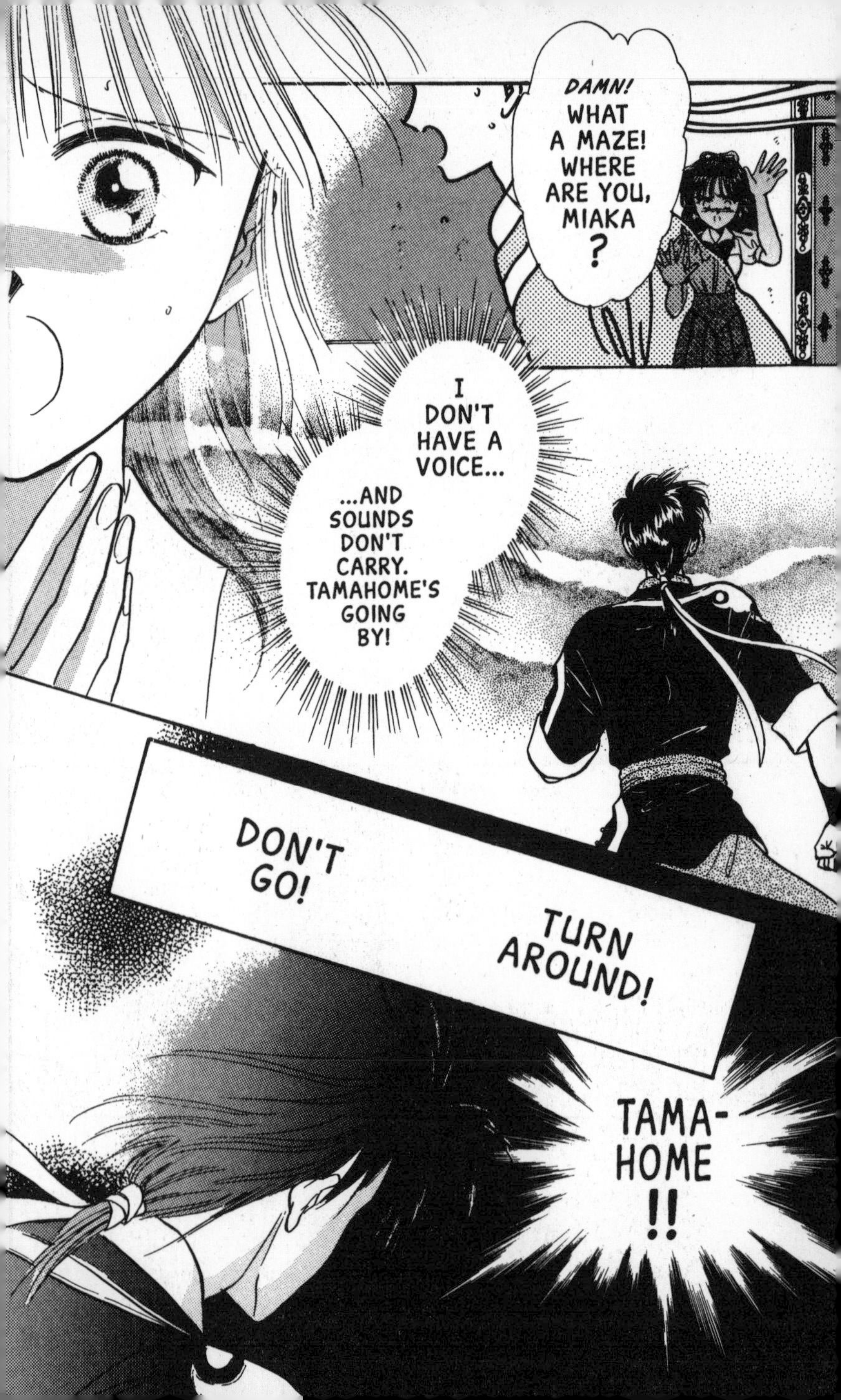
DAMN! WHAT A MAZE! WHERE ARE YOU, MIAKA ?
I DON'T HAVE A VOICE...
...AND SOUNDS DON'T CARRY. TAMAHOME'S GOING BY!
DON'T GO!
TURN AROUND!
TAMA-HOME !!

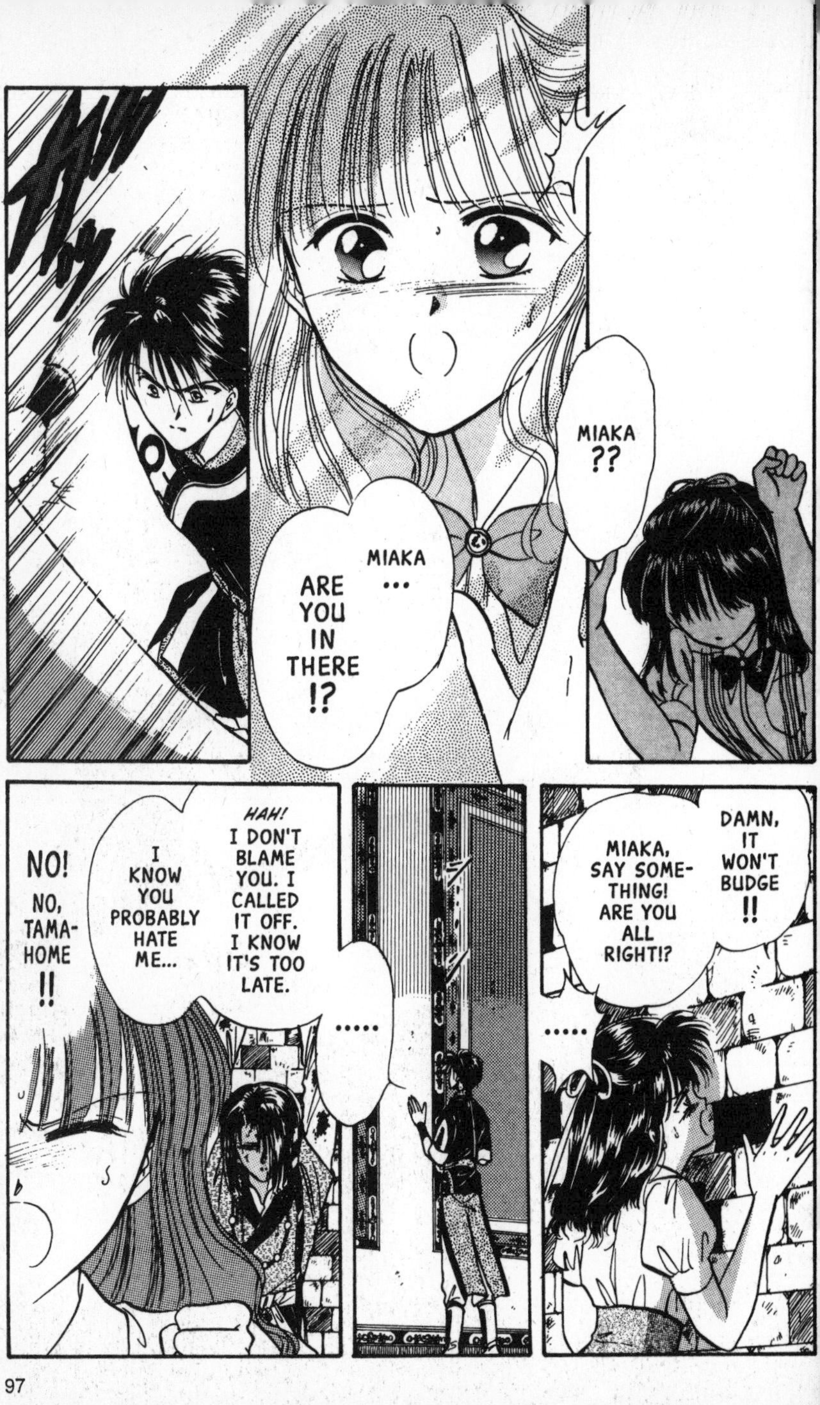
MIAKA ??
MIAKA ... ARE YOU IN THERE !?
DAMN, IT WON'T BUDGE !!
MIAKA, SAY SOME-THING! ARE YOU ALL RIGHT!?
.....
.....
HAH! I DON'T BLAME YOU. I CALLED IT OFF. I KNOW IT'S TOO LATE.
I KNOW YOU PROBABLY HATE ME...
NO! NO, TAMA-HOME !!

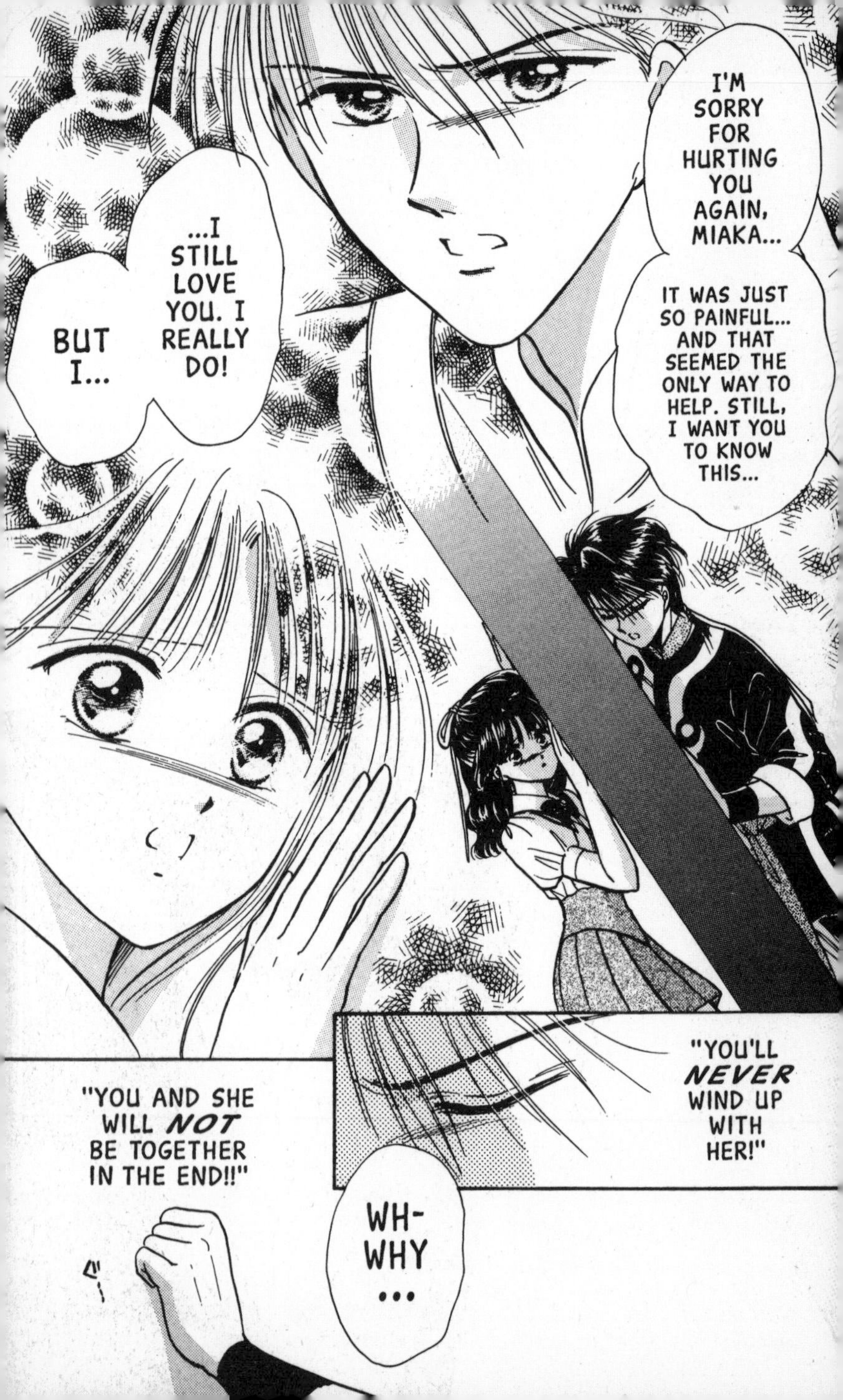
I'M SORRY FOR HURTING YOU AGAIN, MIAKA...
IT WAS JUST SO PAINFUL... AND THAT SEEMED THE ONLY WAY TO HELP. STILL, I WANT YOU TO KNOW THIS...
...I STILL LOVE YOU. I REALLY DO!
BUT I...
"YOU'LL NEVER WIND UP WITH HER!"
"YOU AND SHE WILL NOT BE TOGETHER IN THE END!!"
WH- WHY...

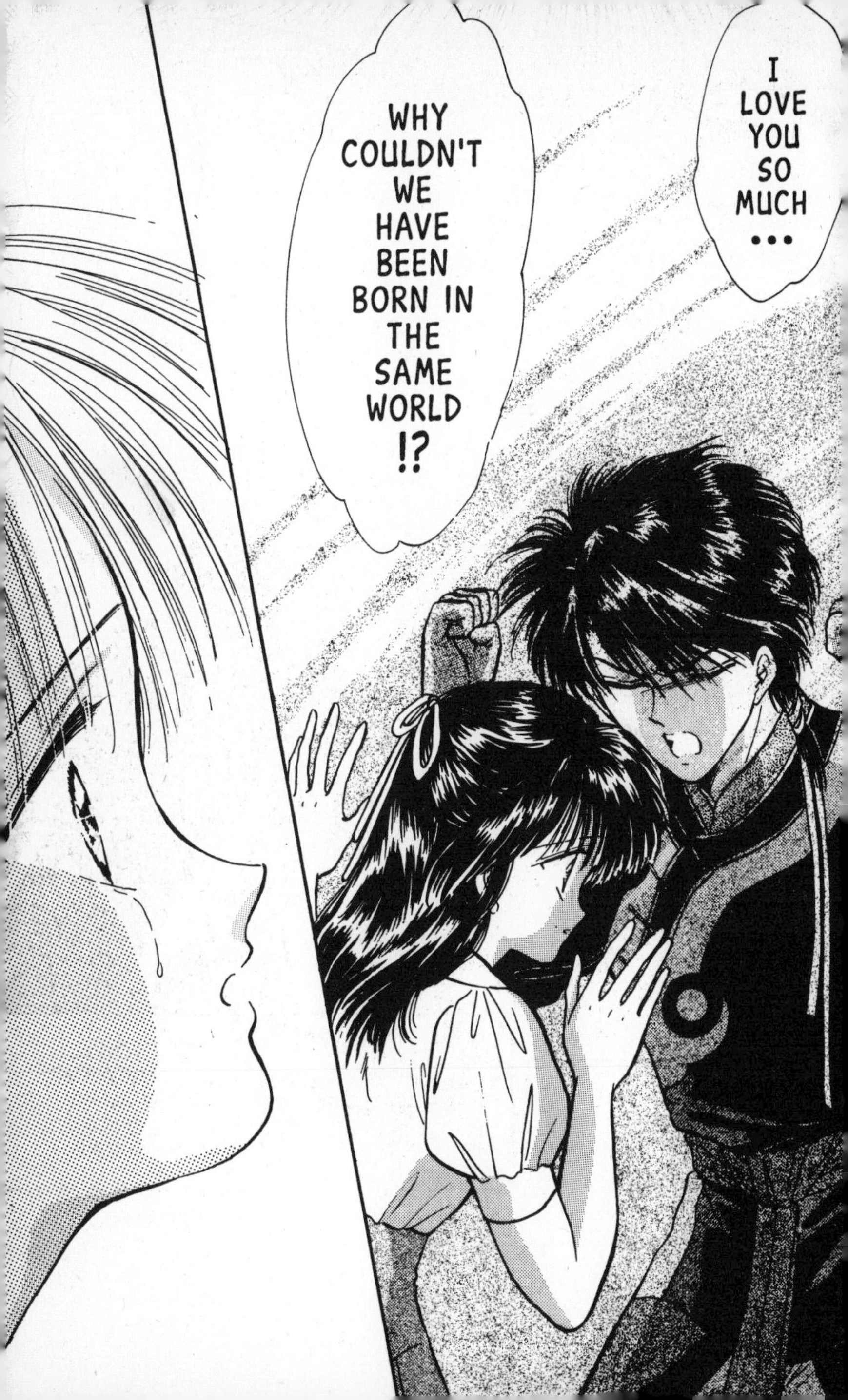
I LOVE YOU SO MUCH...
WHY COULDN'T WE HAVE BEEN BORN IN THE SAME WORLD !?

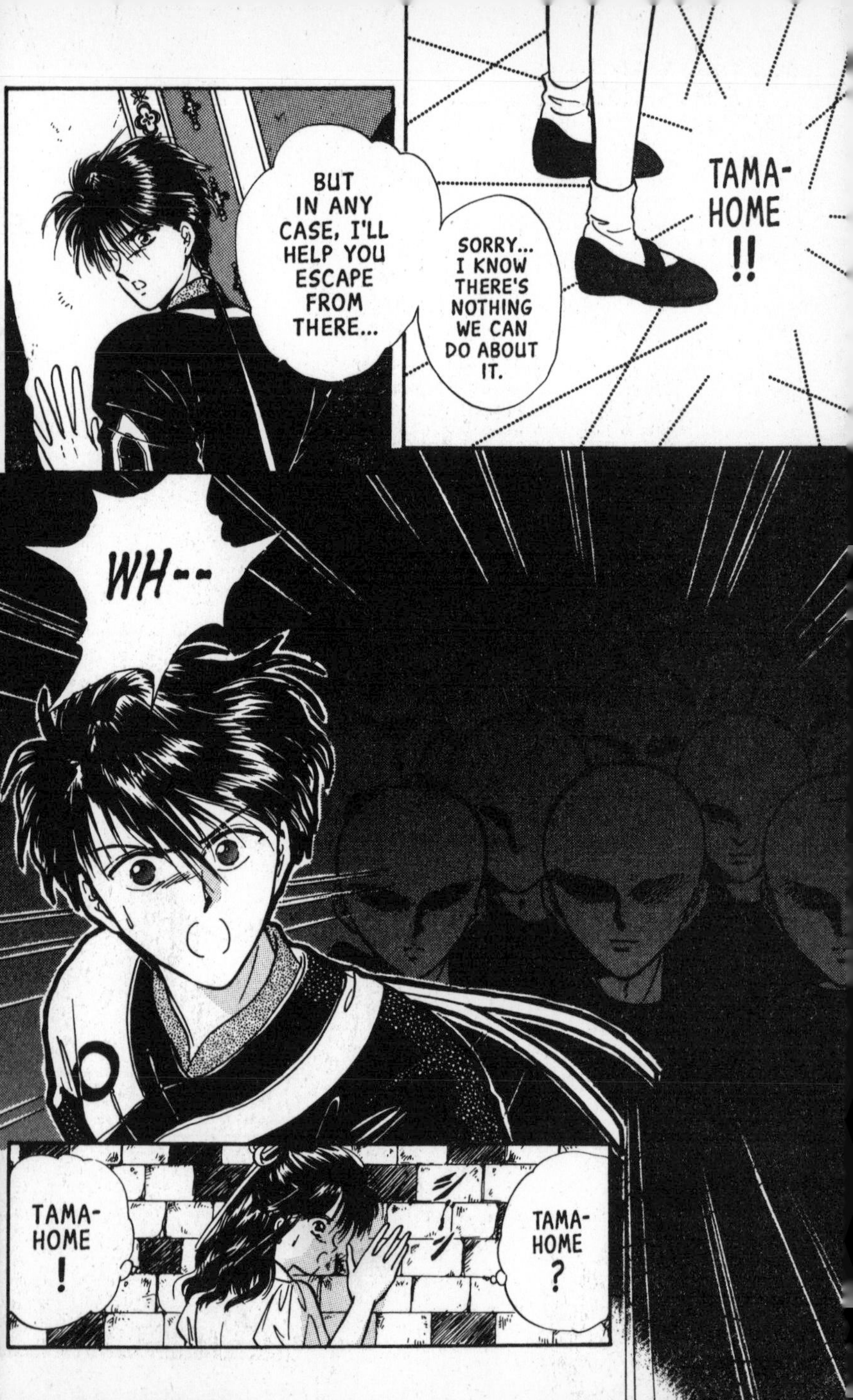
TAMA-HOME !!
SORRY... I KNOW THERE'S NOTHING WE CAN DO ABOUT IT.
BUT IN ANY CASE, I'LL HELP YOU ESCAPE FROM THERE...
WH--
TAMA-HOME ?
TAMA-HOME !

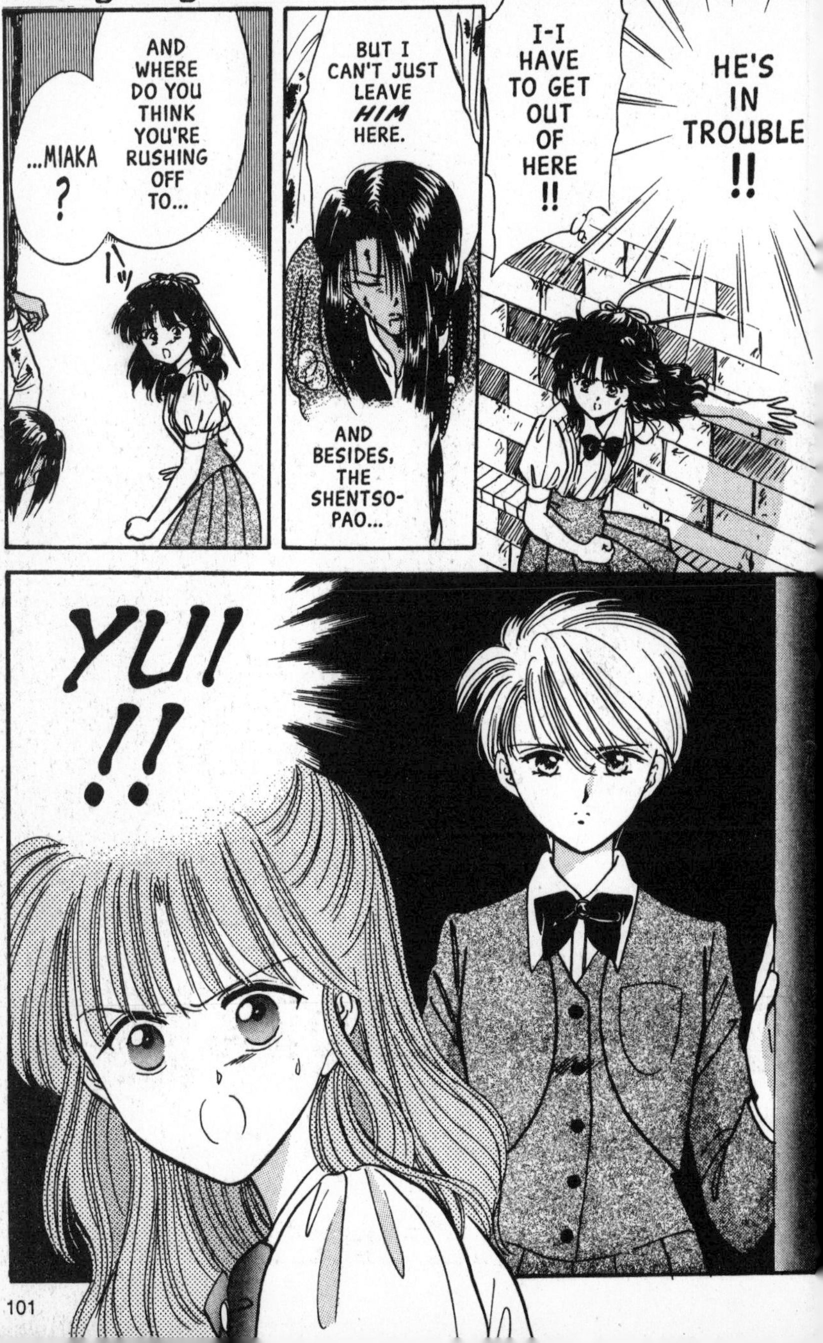
HE'S IN TROUBLE!!
I-I HAVE TO GET OUT OF HERE!!
BUT I CAN'T JUST LEAVE *HIM* HERE.
AND BESIDES, THE SHENTSO-PAO...
AND WHERE DO YOU THINK YOU'RE RUSHING OFF TO...
...MIAKA?
ハッ
YUI!!

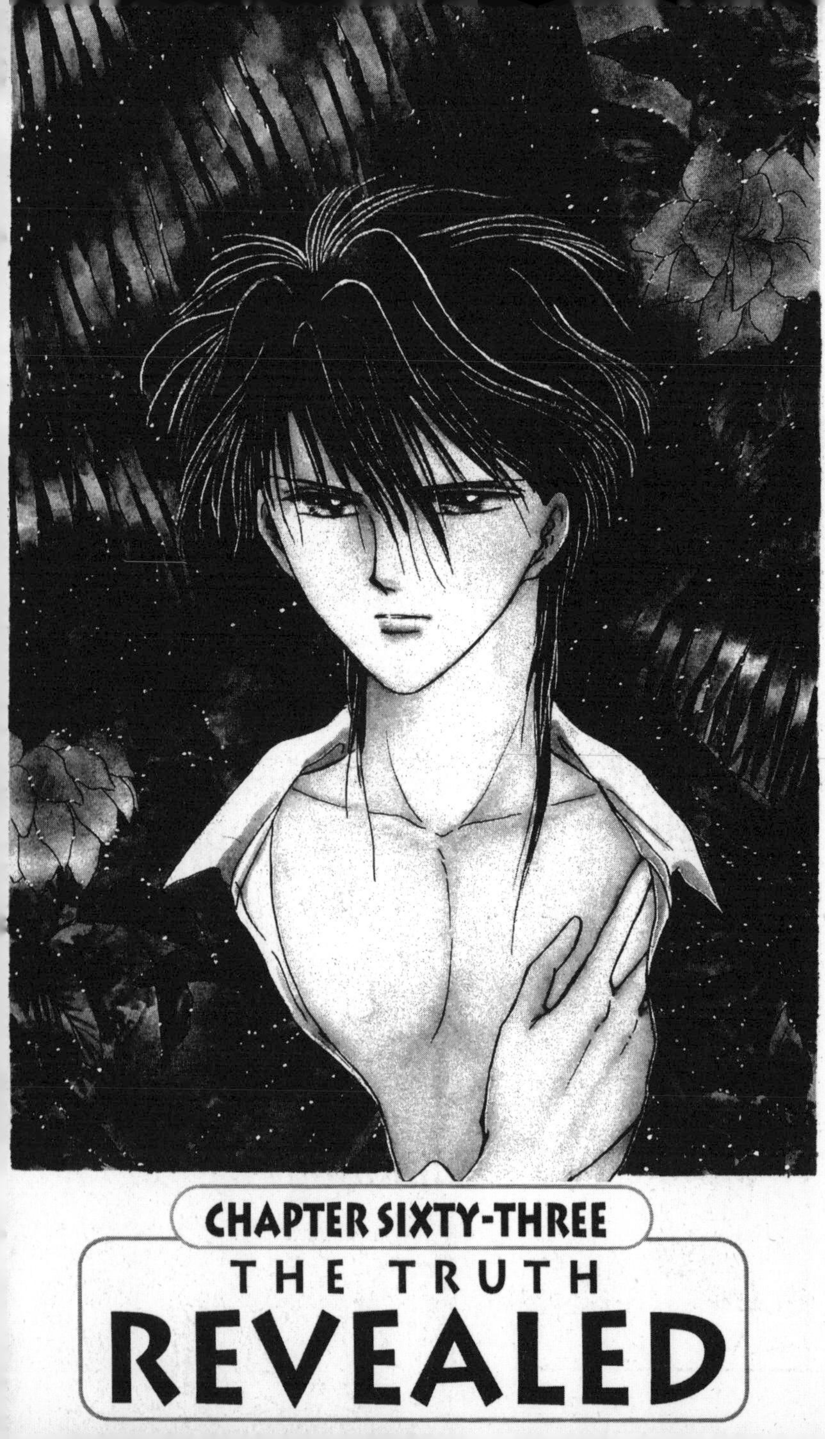

CHAPTER SIXTY-THREE

THE TRUTH REVEALED

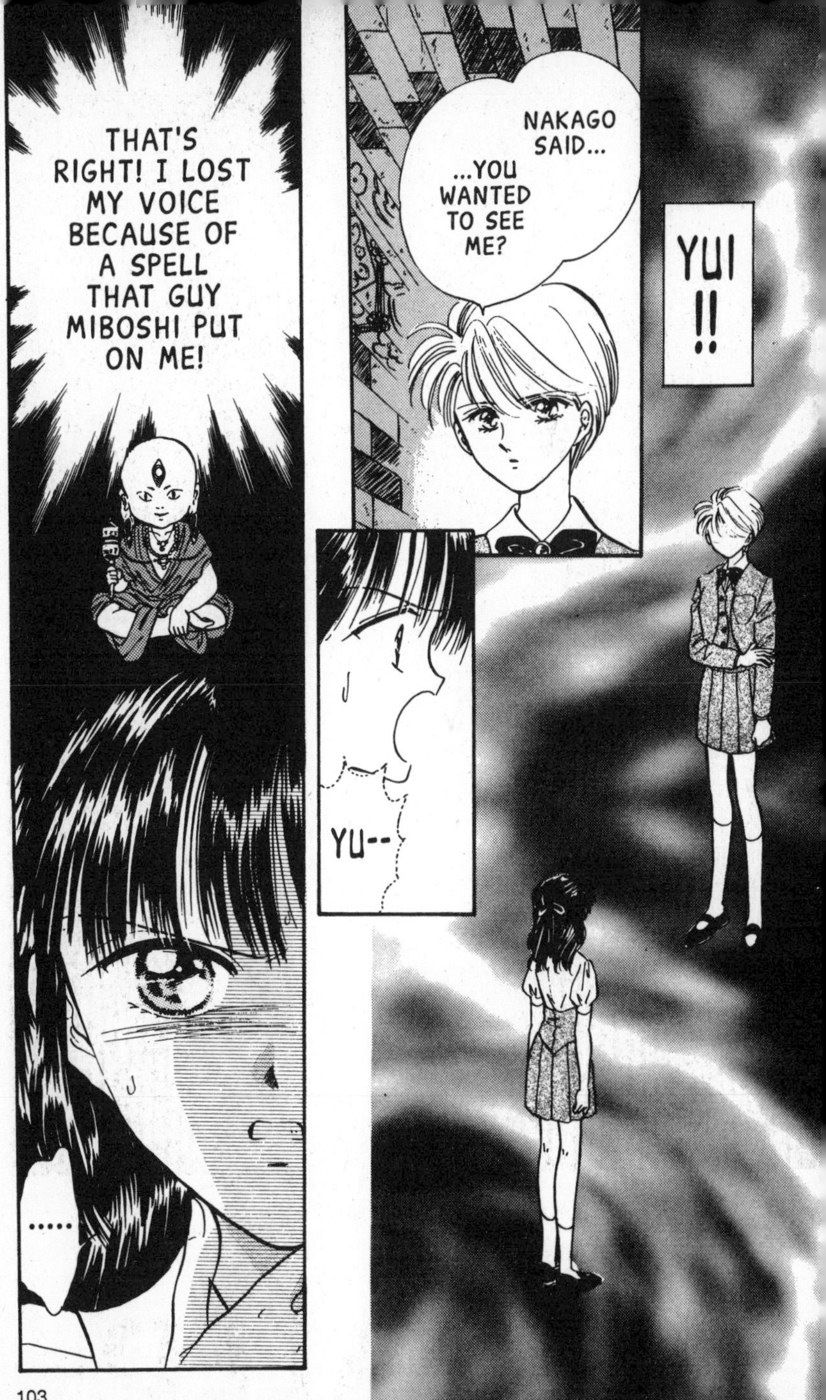
YUI !!
NAKAGO SAID...
...YOU WANTED TO SEE ME?
YU--
THAT'S RIGHT! I LOST MY VOICE BECAUSE OF A SPELL THAT GUY MIBOSHI PUT ON ME!
......

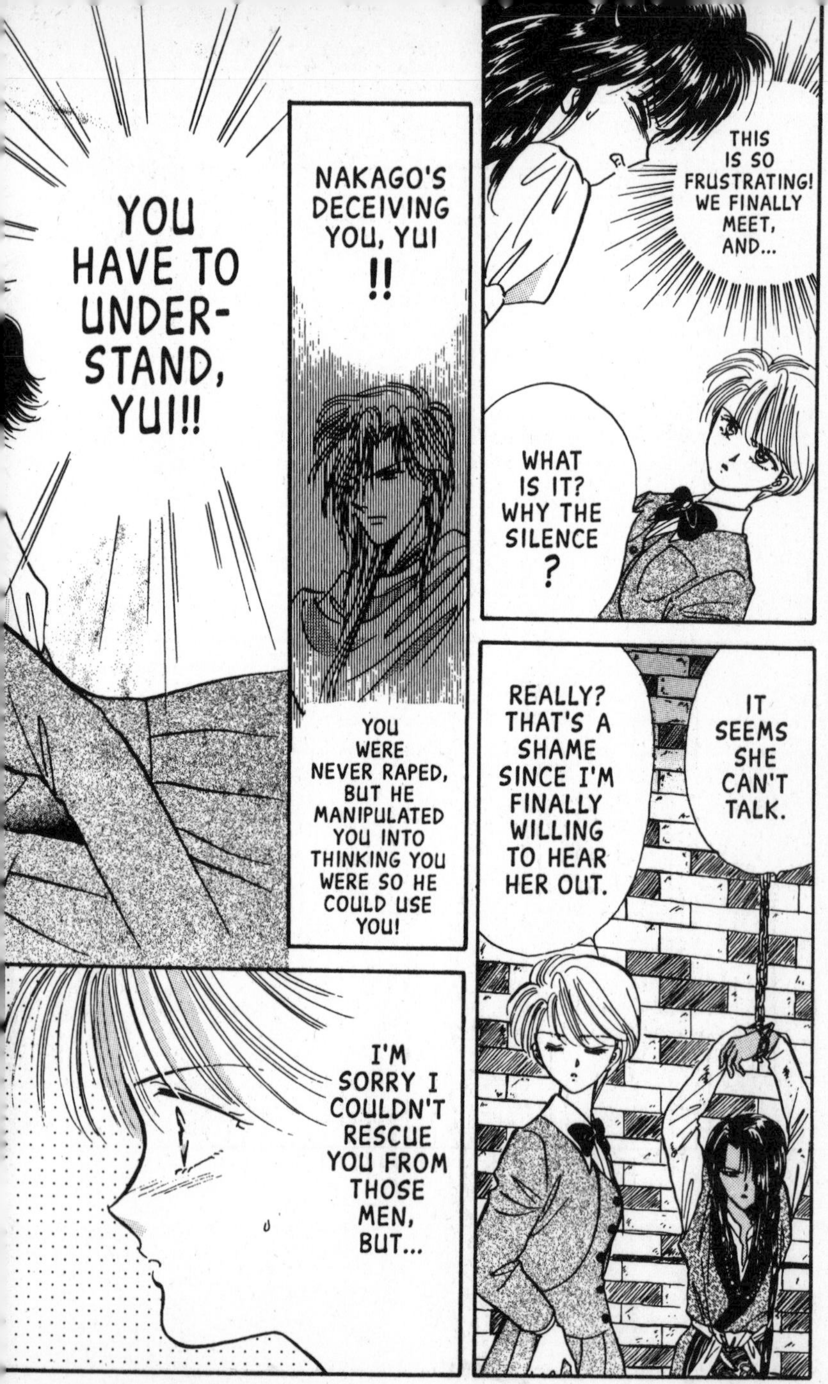
THIS IS SO FRUSTRATING! WE FINALLY MEET, AND...
WHAT IS IT? WHY THE SILENCE?
IT SEEMS SHE CAN'T TALK.
REALLY? THAT'S A SHAME SINCE I'M FINALLY WILLING TO HEAR HER OUT.
NAKAGO'S DECEIVING YOU, YUI!!
YOU WERE NEVER RAPED, BUT HE MANIPULATED YOU INTO THINKING YOU WERE SO HE COULD USE YOU!
YOU HAVE TO UNDER-STAND, YUI!!
I'M SORRY I COULDN'T RESCUE YOU FROM THOSE MEN, BUT...

Veteran

Maybe Hotohori's meant for older readers like high school students. But when Fushigi Yūgi was covered in a magazine column, they said that Hotohori was much more popular than Tamahome! (Nuriko was popular too.) Go, Hotohori! If I were to get married, he'd be my first choice!! When I first came up with him at the age of 18, I hadn't decided whether the story would be set in Japan or China. But the earliest versions had him as a prince. Then one day, when we began the serial, my editor said, "Let's just go for it and make him emperor." *That also limited his actions.*
Although Nuriko passed away a while ago, he's still popular. No. 3 in the CD booklet survey! Readers from Taiwan requested that I bring him back to life. Sorry, but...
His homosexuality was conceived for comic relief, but it ended up being a very good concept. *It added character.* With Hotohori, I had in mind a man who had the beauty of a woman, but for Nuriko, he basically is a woman... At first, I made his body totally masculine. He was tall and manly. *I have the drawings.* But that would have made him into "just another cross dresser." So I just decided, "Make him look like Hibari-kun!" (from the manga, Stop Hibari-kun) and he ended up that way. Come to think of it, if Nuriko loved Hotohori, it would seem like homosexual love, but he loved him as a woman. It's not so much gay as transsexual. In other words, he's kind of like a big sister (?) you could turn to who would understand both men's and women's feelings.

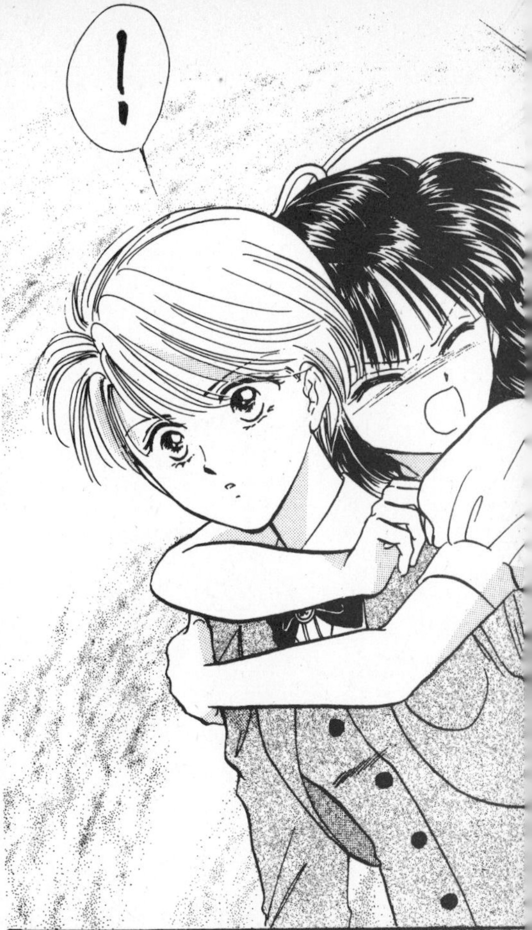
!

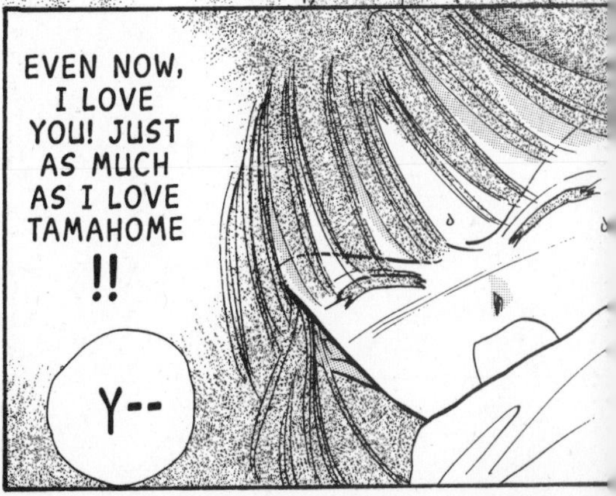
EVEN NOW, I LOVE YOU! JUST AS MUCH AS I LOVE TAMAHOME !!
Y--

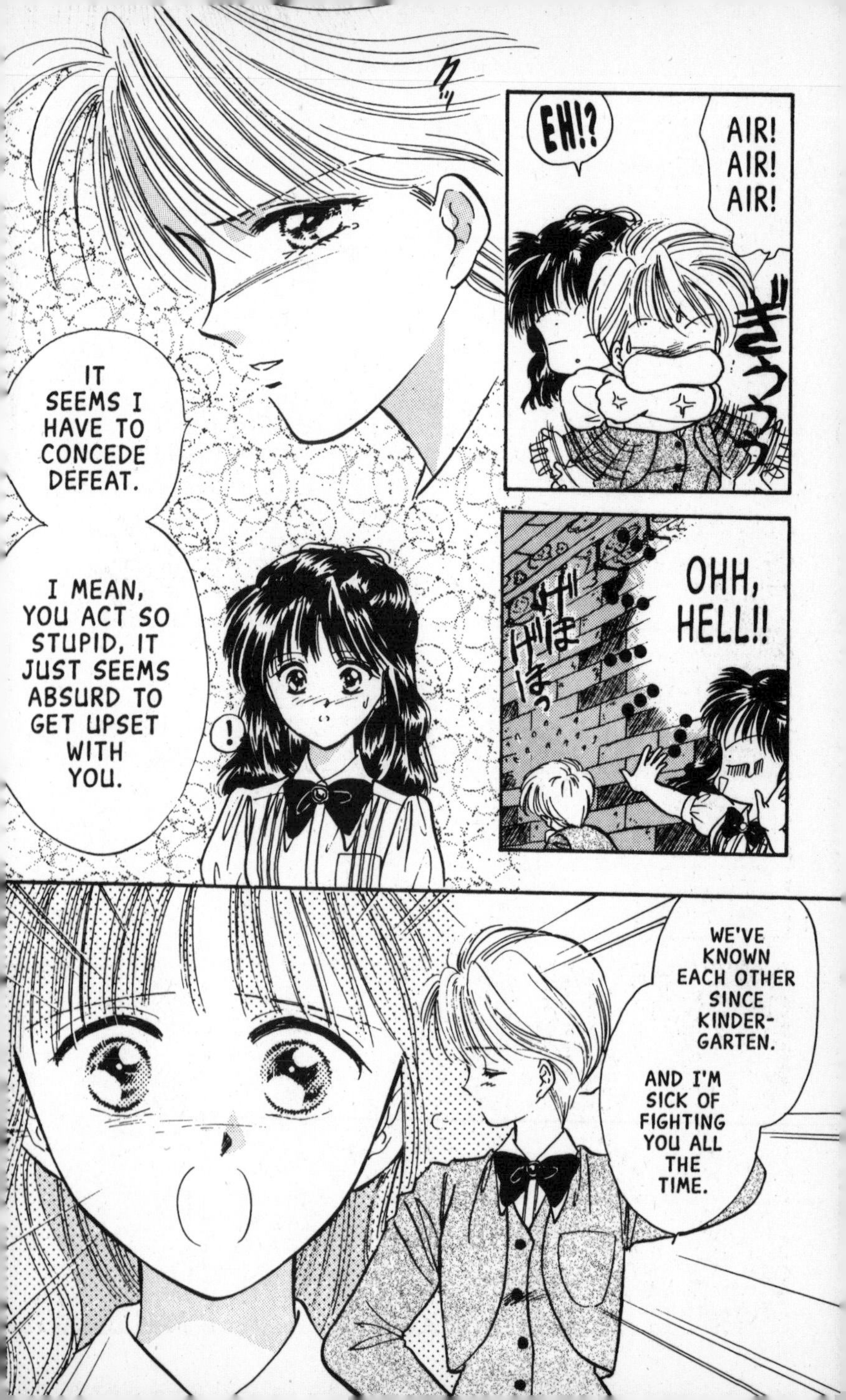
AIR! AIR! AIR!
EH!?
OHH, HELL!!
げほげほっ
IT SEEMS I HAVE TO CONCEDE DEFEAT.
I MEAN, YOU ACT SO STUPID, IT JUST SEEMS ABSURD TO GET UPSET WITH YOU.
!
WE'VE KNOWN EACH OTHER SINCE KINDER-GARTEN.
AND I'M SICK OF FIGHTING YOU ALL THE TIME.

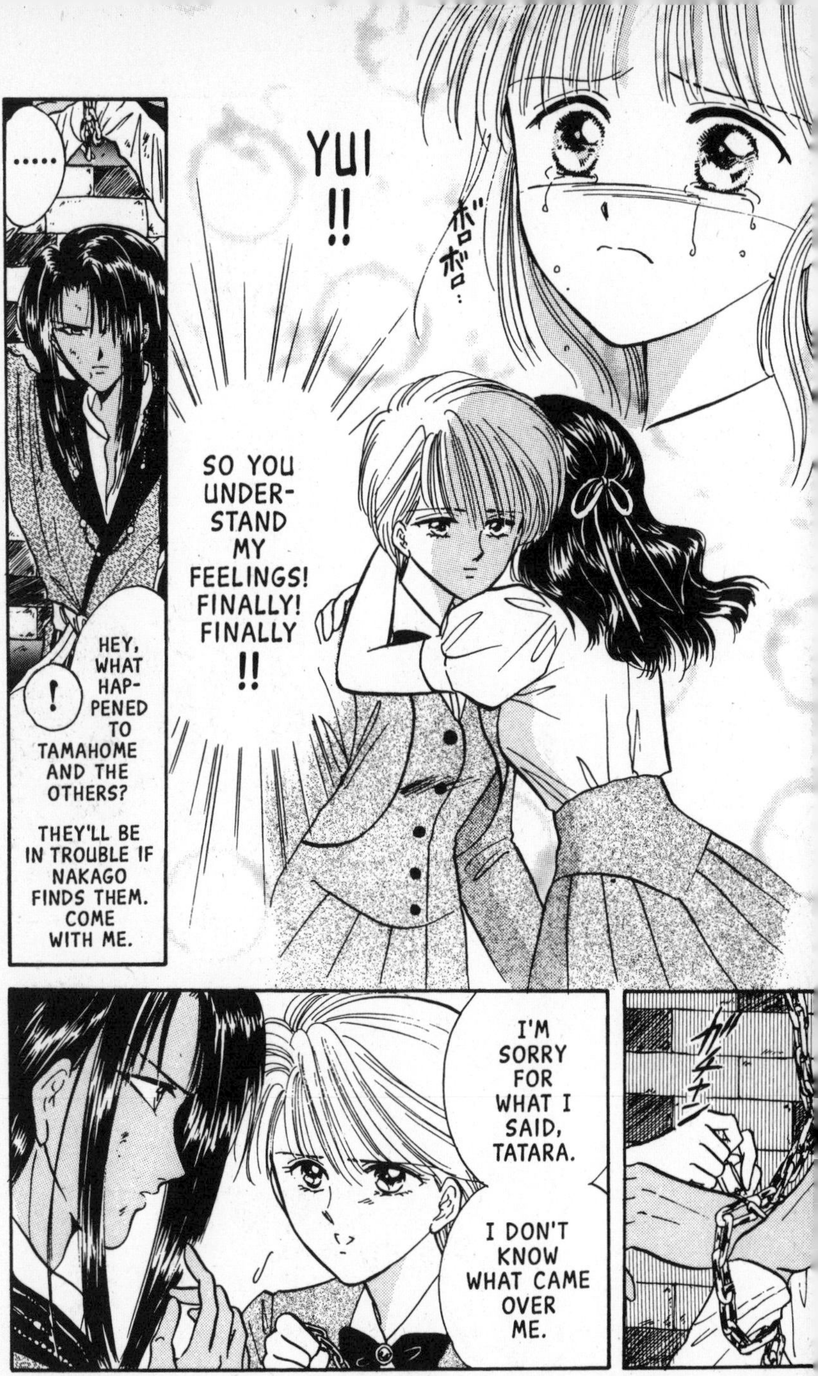

ボロボロ…
YUI !!
SO YOU UNDER-STAND MY FEELINGS! FINALLY! FINALLY !!
......
!
HEY, WHAT HAP-PENED TO TAMAHOME AND THE OTHERS?
THEY'LL BE IN TROUBLE IF NAKAGO FINDS THEM. COME WITH ME.
I'M SORRY FOR WHAT I SAID, TATARA.
I DON'T KNOW WHAT CAME OVER ME.

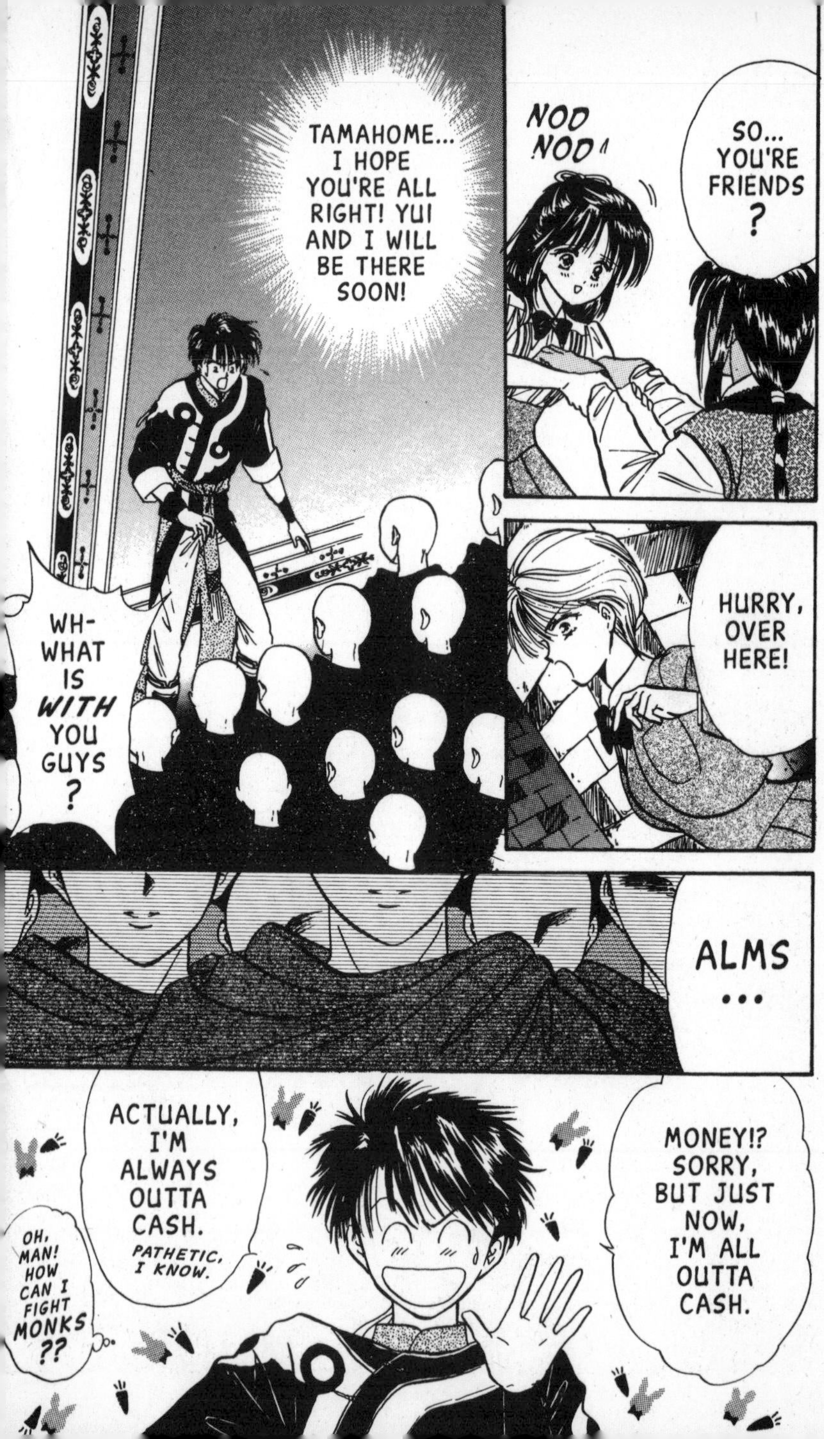
SO... YOU'RE FRIENDS?
NOD NOD
HURRY, OVER HERE!
TAMAHOME... I HOPE YOU'RE ALL RIGHT! YUI AND I WILL BE THERE SOON!
WH-WHAT IS *WITH* YOU GUYS?
ALMS...
MONEY!? SORRY, BUT JUST NOW, I'M ALL OUTTA CASH.
ACTUALLY, I'M ALWAYS OUTTA CASH.
PATHETIC, I KNOW.
OH, MAN! HOW CAN I FIGHT MONKS??

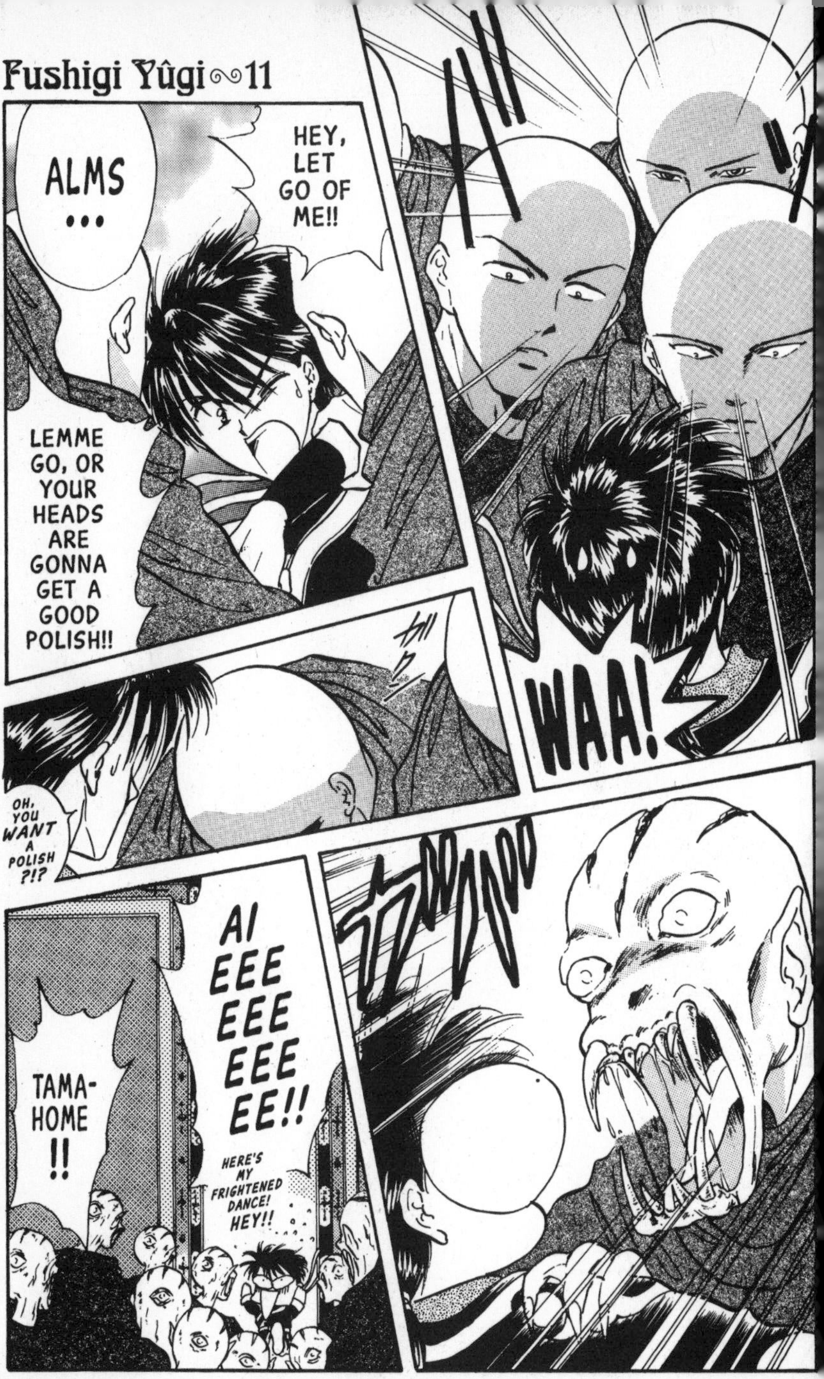
WAA!
ALMS ...
HEY, LET GO OF ME!!
LEMME GO, OR YOUR HEADS ARE GONNA GET A GOOD POLISH!!
OH, YOU WANT A POLISH ?!?
AI EEE EEE EEE EE!!
TAMA-HOME !!
HERE'S MY FRIGHTENED DANCE! HEY!!

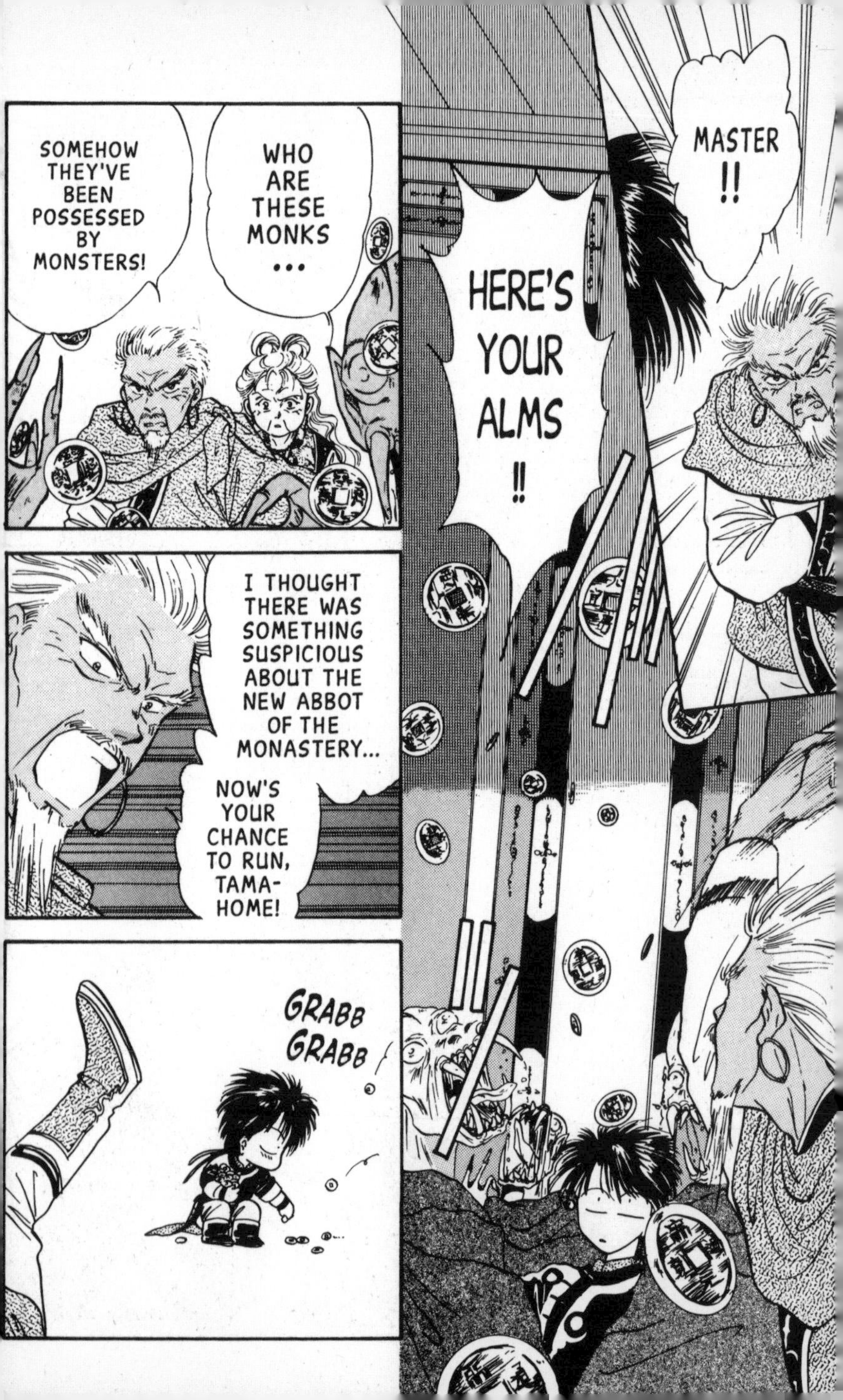
MASTER!!
HERE'S YOUR ALMS!!
WHO ARE THESE MONKS...
SOMEHOW THEY'VE BEEN POSSESSED BY MONSTERS!
I THOUGHT THERE WAS SOMETHING SUSPICIOUS ABOUT THE NEW ABBOT OF THE MONASTERY...
NOW'S YOUR CHANCE TO RUN, TAMA-HOME!
GRABB GRABB

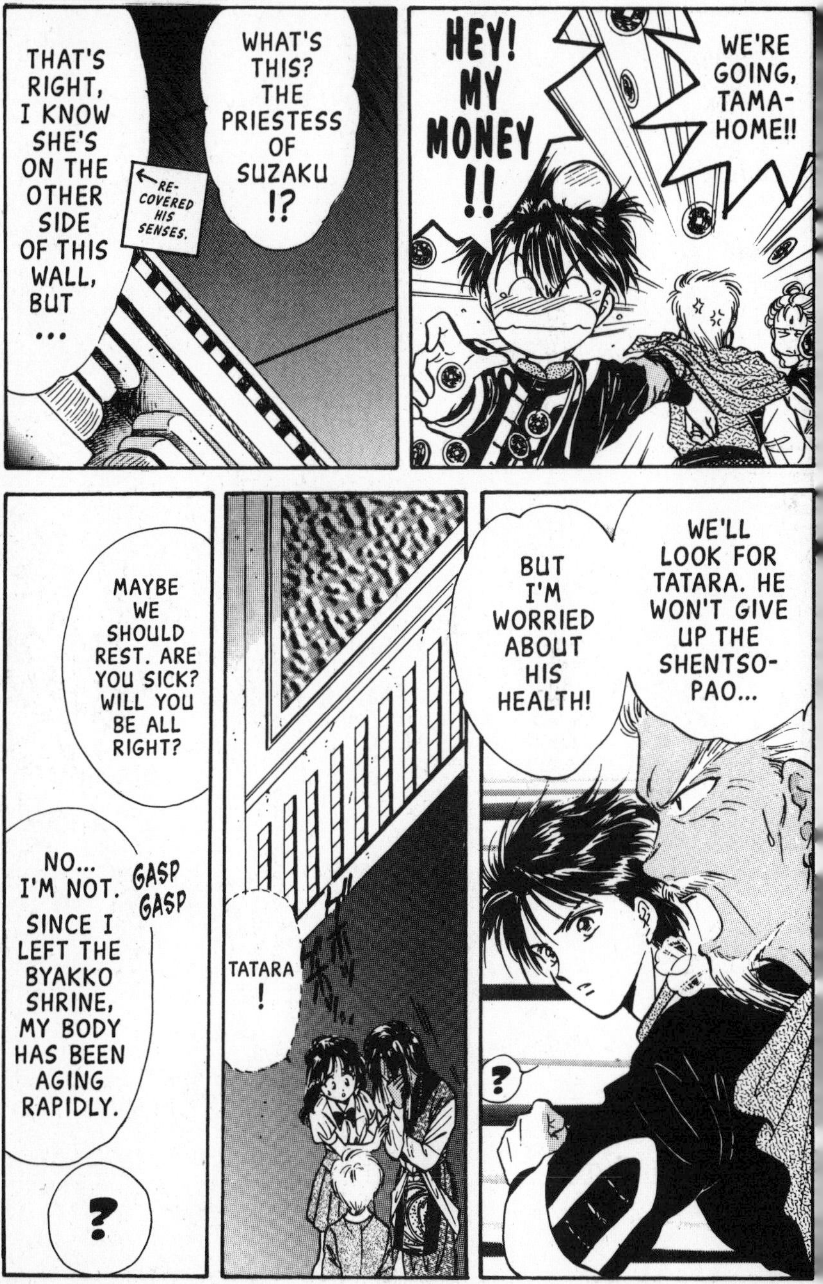
WE'RE GOING, TAMA-HOME!!
HEY! MY MONEY!!
WHAT'S THIS? THE PRIESTESS OF SUZAKU!?
THAT'S RIGHT, I KNOW SHE'S ON THE OTHER SIDE OF THIS WALL, BUT...
RE-COVERED HIS SENSES.
WE'LL LOOK FOR TATARA. HE WON'T GIVE UP THE SHENTSO-PAO...
BUT I'M WORRIED ABOUT HIS HEALTH!
?
TATARA!
MAYBE WE SHOULD REST. ARE YOU SICK? WILL YOU BE ALL RIGHT?
NO... I'M NOT.
GASP GASP
SINCE I LEFT THE BYAKKO SHRINE, MY BODY HAS BEEN AGING RAPIDLY.
?

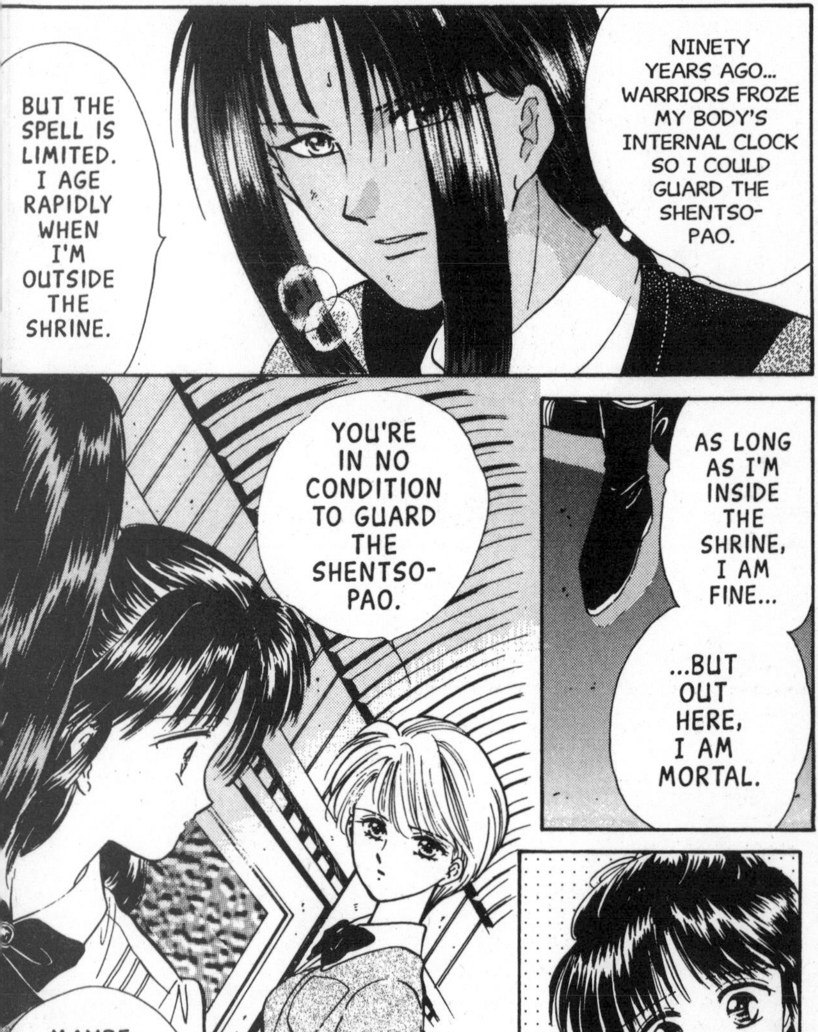
NINETY YEARS AGO... WARRIORS FROZE MY BODY'S INTERNAL CLOCK SO I COULD GUARD THE SHENTSO-PAO.
BUT THE SPELL IS LIMITED. I AGE RAPIDLY WHEN I'M OUTSIDE THE SHRINE.
AS LONG AS I'M INSIDE THE SHRINE, I AM FINE...
...BUT OUT HERE, I AM MORTAL.
HEY...
YOU'RE IN NO CONDITION TO GUARD THE SHENTSO-PAO.
MAYBE YOU SHOULD GIVE IT TO MIAKA AS SOON AS POSSIBLE.

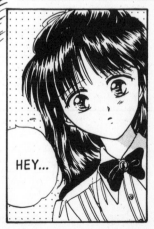

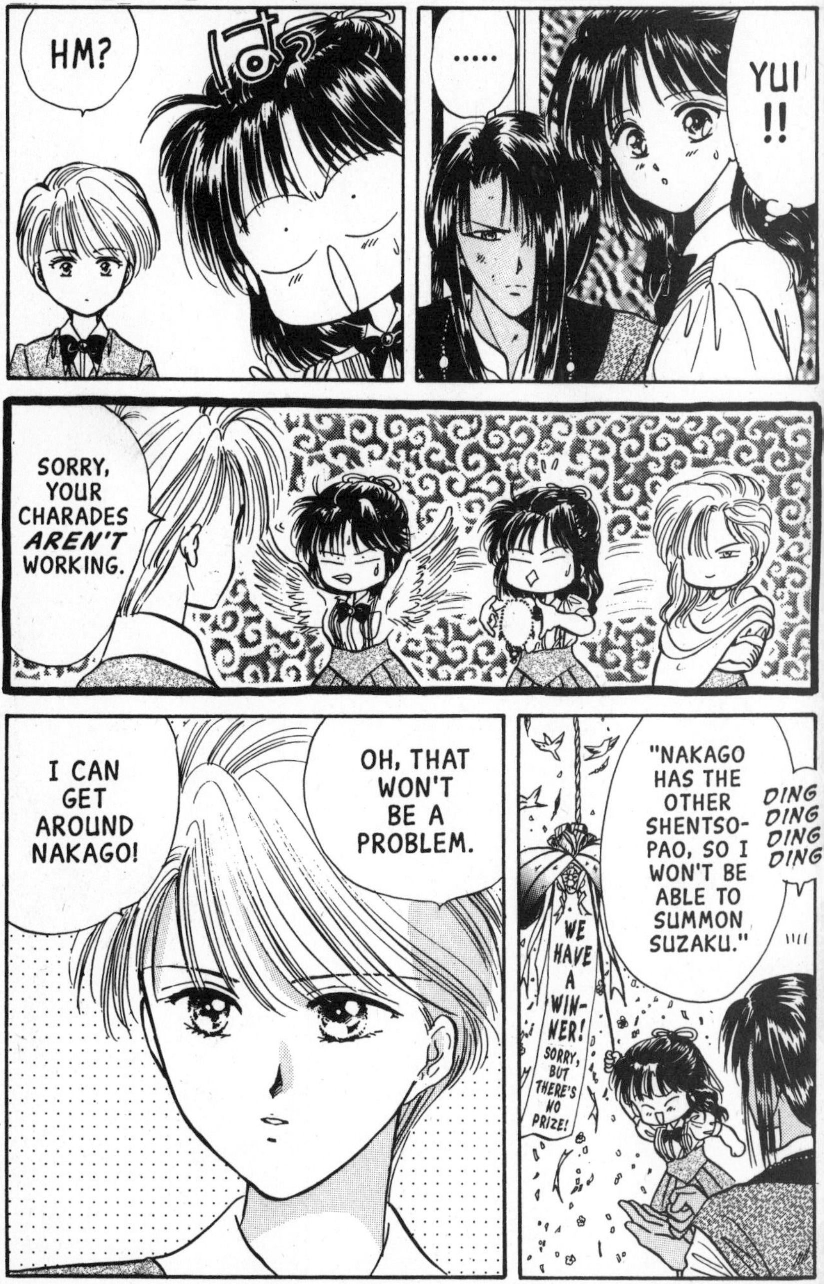
YUI !!
.....
HM?
SORRY, YOUR CHARADES *AREN'T* WORKING.
"NAKAGO HAS THE OTHER SHENTSO-PAO, SO I WON'T BE ABLE TO SUMMON SUZAKU."
DING DING DING DING
WE HAVE A WIN-NER!
SORRY, BUT THERE'S NO PRIZE!
OH, THAT WON'T BE A PROBLEM.
I CAN GET AROUND NAKAGO!

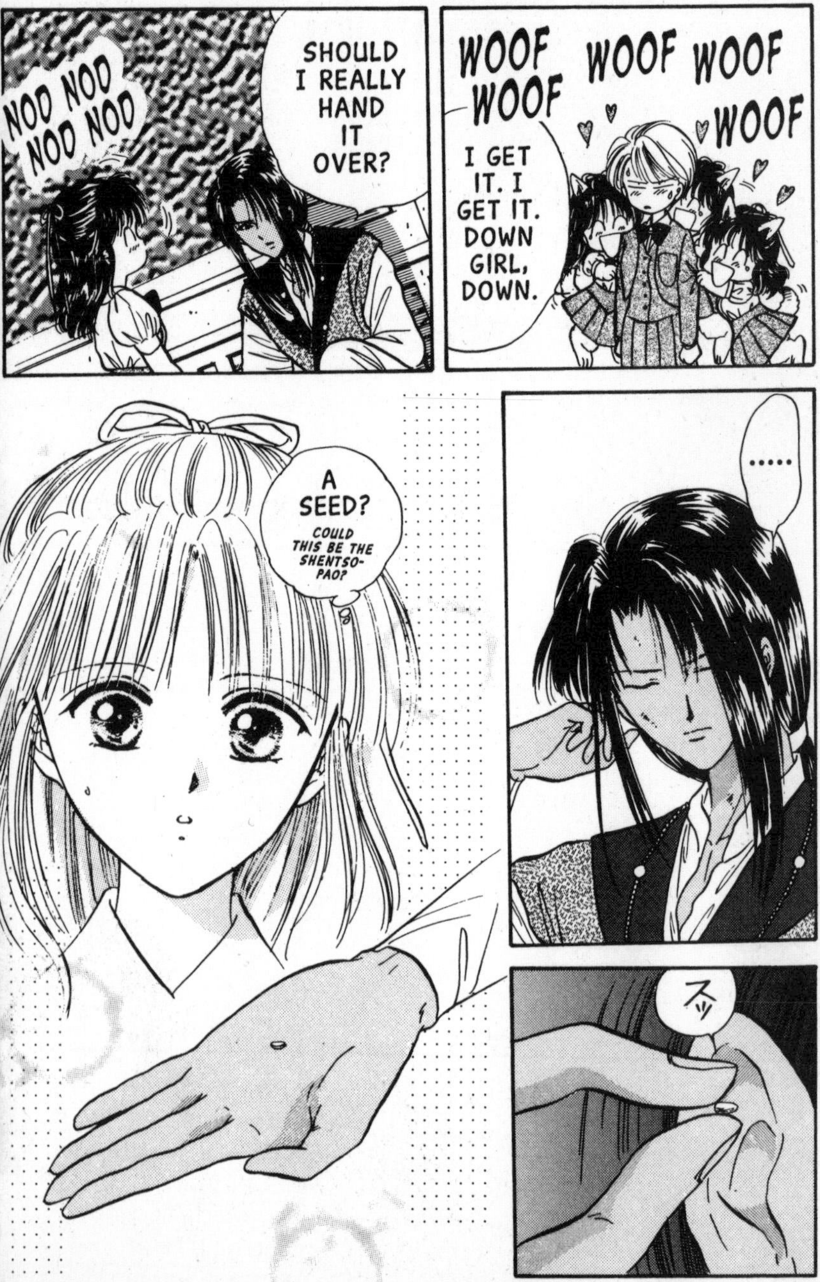
WOOF WOOF WOOF WOOF WOOF
I GET IT. I GET IT. DOWN GIRL, DOWN.
NOD NOD NOD NOD
SHOULD I REALLY HAND IT OVER?
.....
スッ
A SEED?
COULD THIS BE THE SHENTSO-PAO?

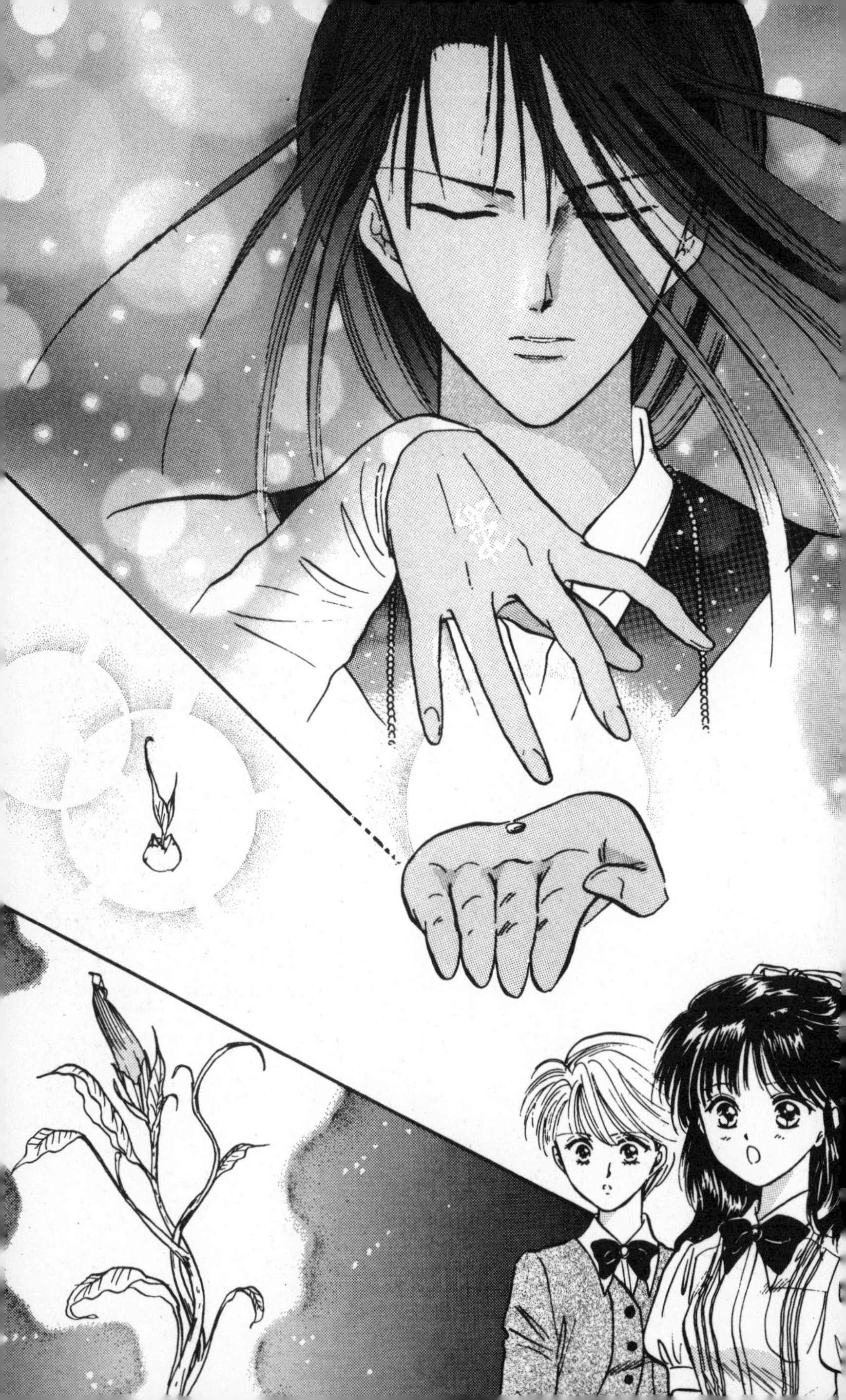

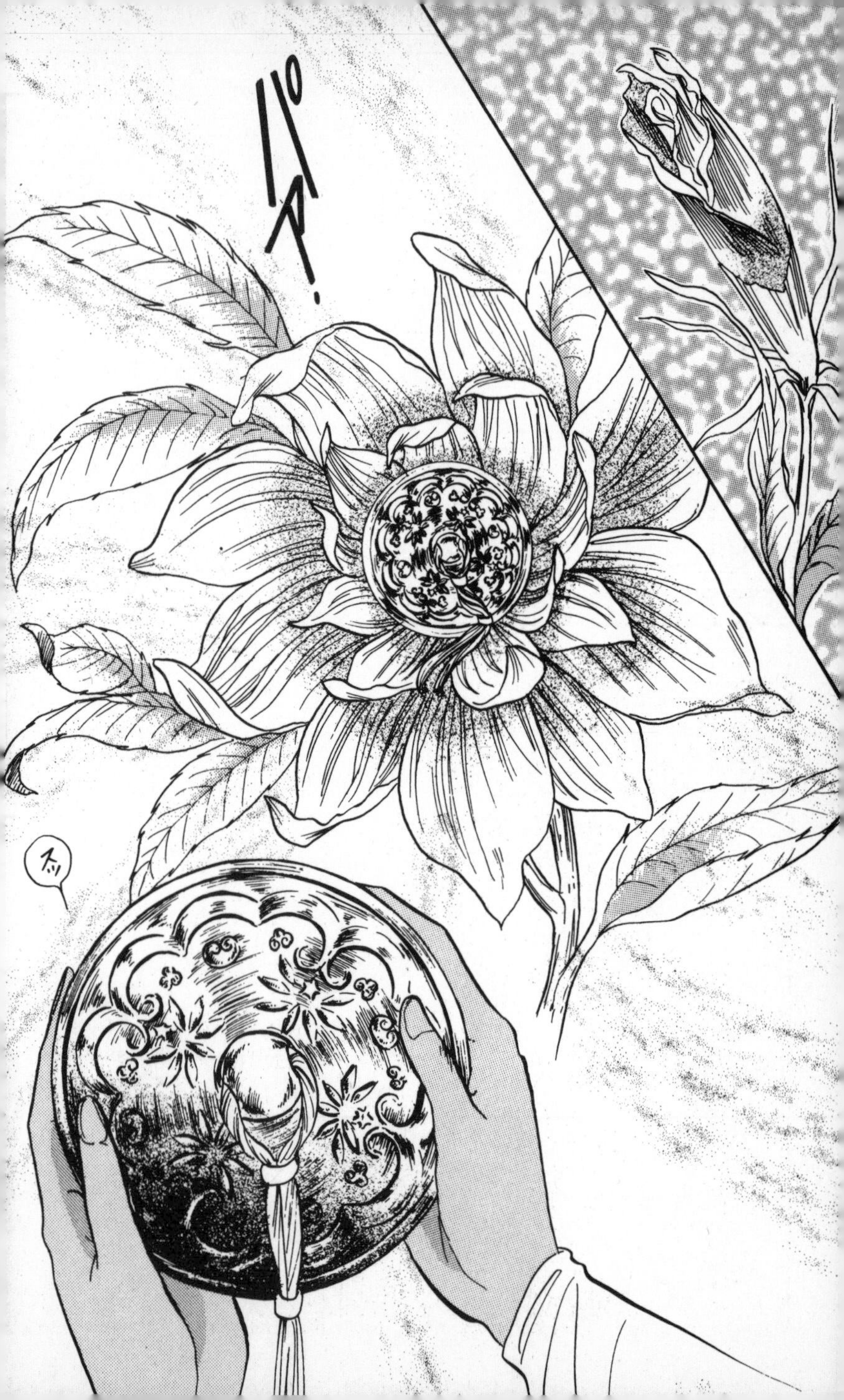
パァ!
スッ

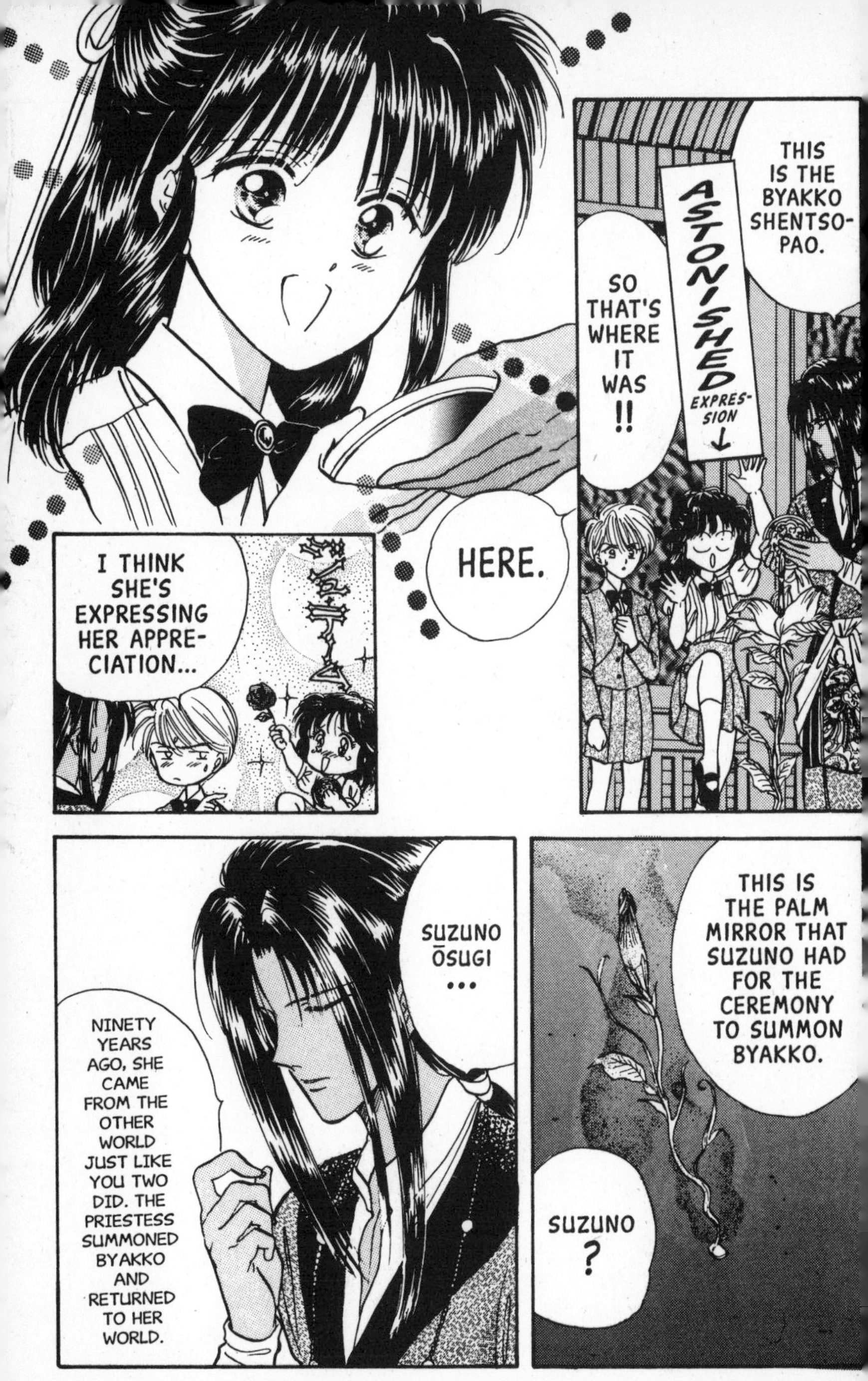
THIS IS THE BYAKKO SHENTSO-PAO.
SO THAT'S WHERE IT WAS!!
ASTONISHED EXPRESSION ↓
HERE.
I THINK SHE'S EXPRESSING HER APPRECIATION...
THIS IS THE PALM MIRROR THAT SUZUNO HAD FOR THE CEREMONY TO SUMMON BYAKKO.
SUZUNO?
SUZUNO ŌSUGI...
NINETY YEARS AGO, SHE CAME FROM THE OTHER WORLD JUST LIKE YOU TWO DID. THE PRIESTESS SUMMONED BYAKKO AND RETURNED TO HER WORLD.

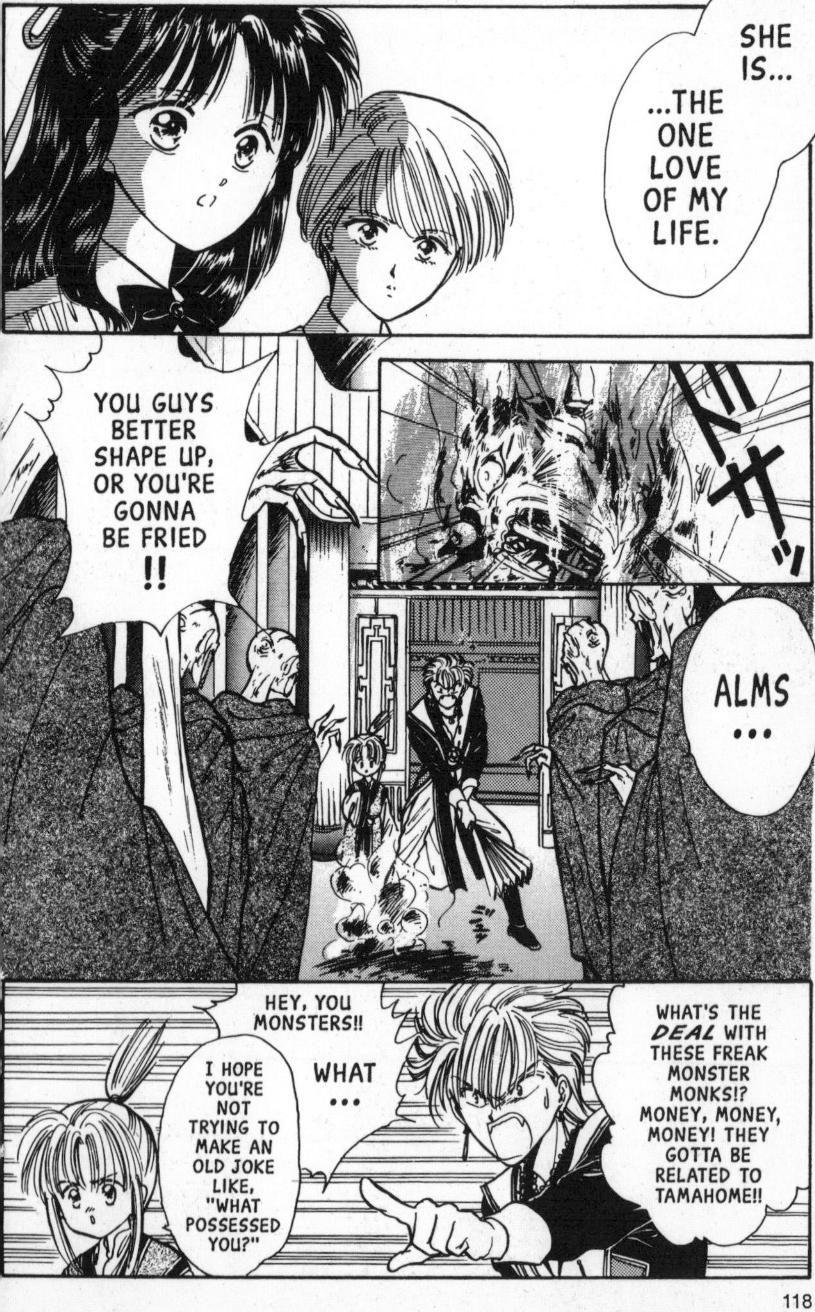
SHE IS... ...THE ONE LOVE OF MY LIFE.
ALMS...
YOU GUYS BETTER SHAPE UP, OR YOU'RE GONNA BE FRIED!!
WHAT'S THE *DEAL* WITH THESE FREAK MONSTER MONKS!? MONEY, MONEY, MONEY! THEY GOTTA BE RELATED TO TAMAHOME!!
HEY, YOU MONSTERS!!
WHAT...
I HOPE YOU'RE NOT TRYING TO MAKE AN OLD JOKE LIKE, "WHAT POSSESSED YOU?"

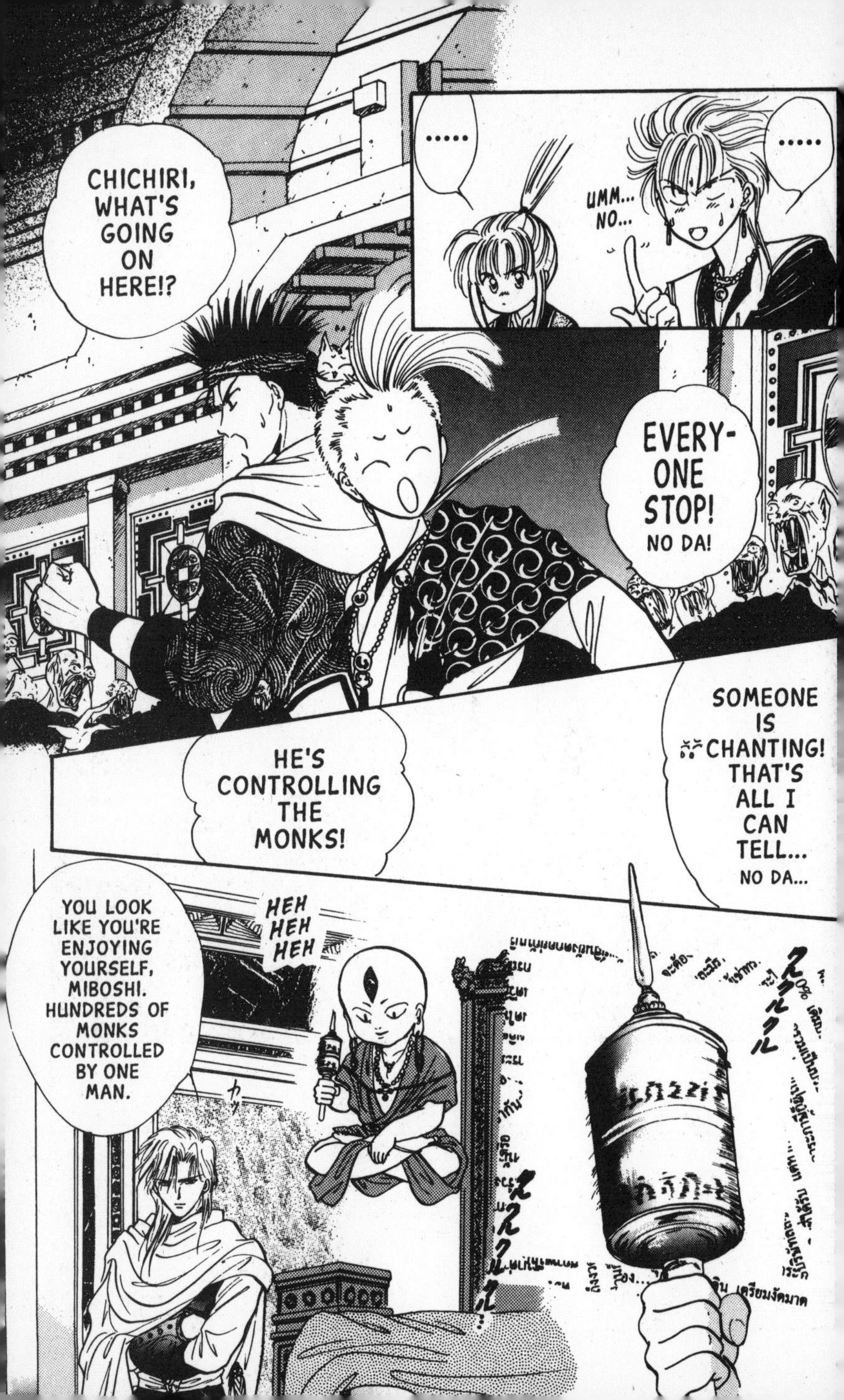
.....
UMM... NO...
.....
CHICHIRI, WHAT'S GOING ON HERE!?
EVERY-ONE STOP! NO DA!
SOMEONE IS CHANTING! THAT'S ALL I CAN TELL... NO DA...
HE'S CONTROLLING THE MONKS!
HEH HEH HEH
YOU LOOK LIKE YOU'RE ENJOYING YOURSELF, MIBOSHI. HUNDREDS OF MONKS CONTROLLED BY ONE MAN.

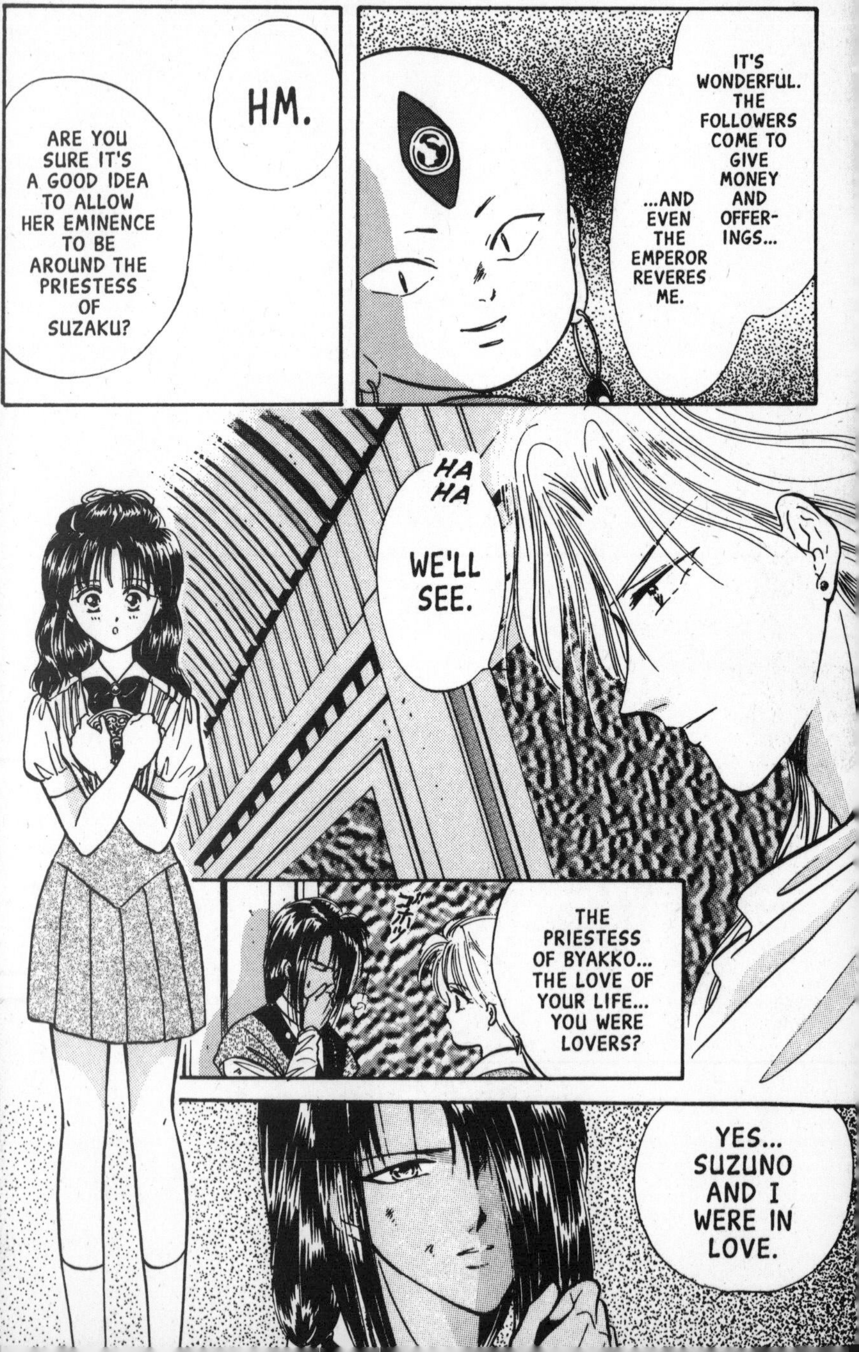

IT'S WONDERFUL. THE FOLLOWERS COME TO GIVE MONEY AND OFFER-INGS...
...AND EVEN THE EMPEROR REVERES ME.
HM.
ARE YOU SURE IT'S A GOOD IDEA TO ALLOW HER EMINENCE TO BE AROUND THE PRIESTESS OF SUZAKU?
HA HA
WE'LL SEE.
THE PRIESTESS OF BYAKKO... THE LOVE OF YOUR LIFE... YOU WERE LOVERS?
ゴホッ
YES... SUZUNO AND I WERE IN LOVE.

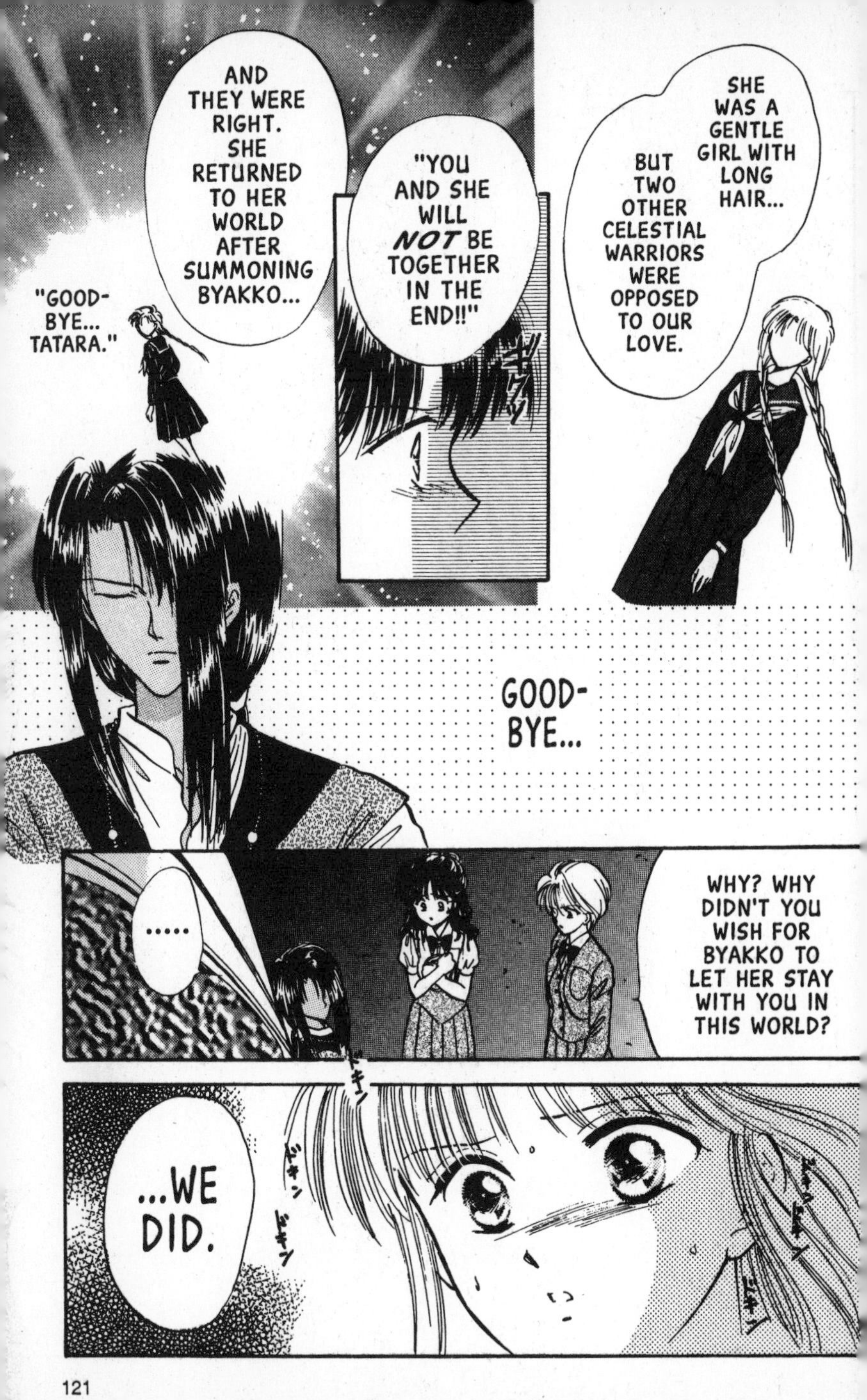

SHE WAS A GENTLE GIRL WITH LONG HAIR...
BUT TWO OTHER CELESTIAL WARRIORS WERE OPPOSED TO OUR LOVE.
"YOU AND SHE WILL *NOT* BE TOGETHER IN THE END!!"
AND THEY WERE RIGHT. SHE RETURNED TO HER WORLD AFTER SUMMONING BYAKKO...
"GOOD-BYE... TATARA."
GOOD-BYE...
WHY? WHY DIDN'T YOU WISH FOR BYAKKO TO LET HER STAY WITH YOU IN THIS WORLD?
.....
...WE DID.

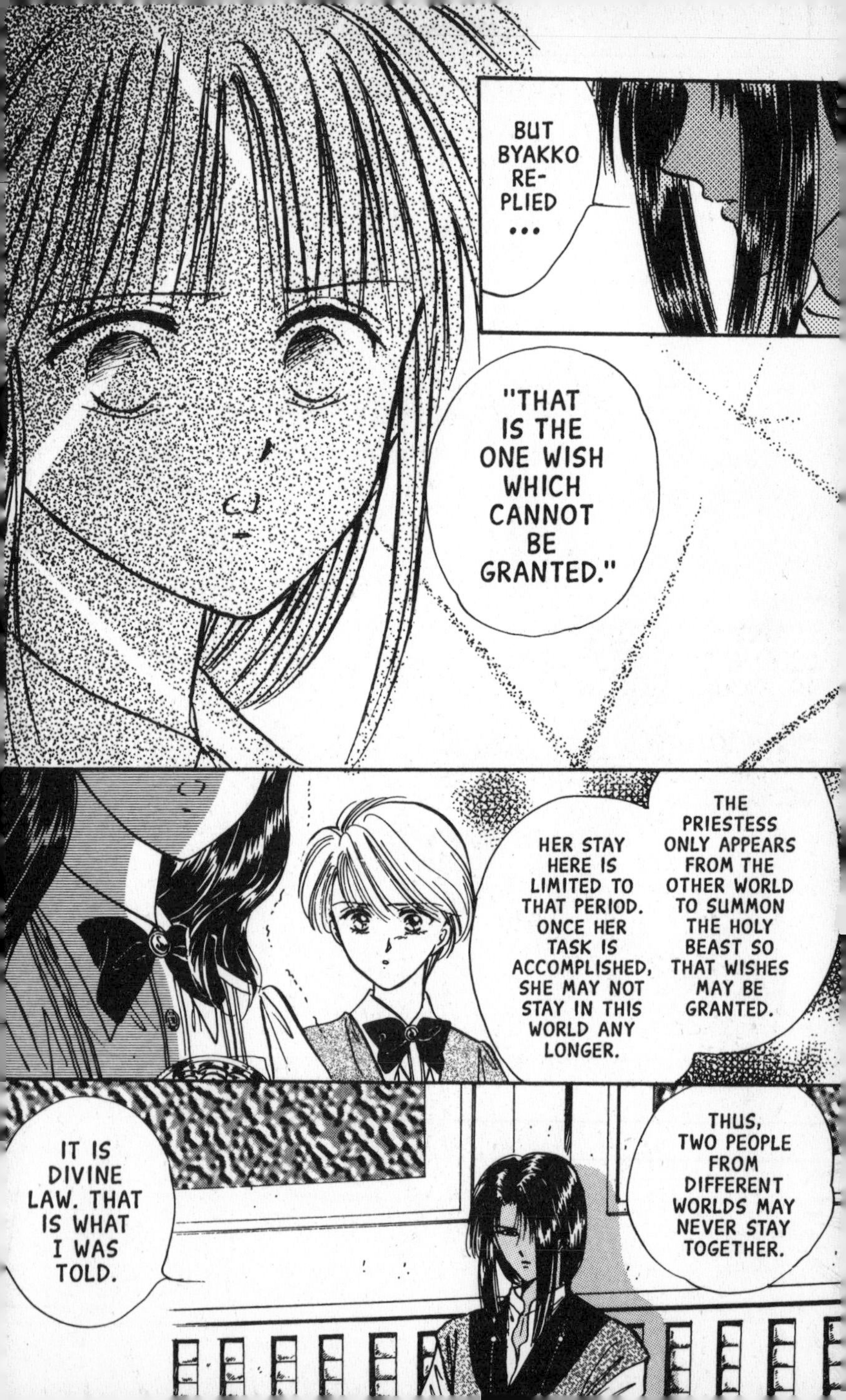
BUT BYAKKO RE-PLIED...
"THAT IS THE ONE WISH WHICH CANNOT BE GRANTED."
THE PRIESTESS ONLY APPEARS FROM THE OTHER WORLD TO SUMMON THE HOLY BEAST SO THAT WISHES MAY BE GRANTED.
HER STAY HERE IS LIMITED TO THAT PERIOD. ONCE HER TASK IS ACCOMPLISHED, SHE MAY NOT STAY IN THIS WORLD ANY LONGER.
THUS, TWO PEOPLE FROM DIFFERENT WORLDS MAY NEVER STAY TOGETHER.
IT IS DIVINE LAW. THAT IS WHAT I WAS TOLD.

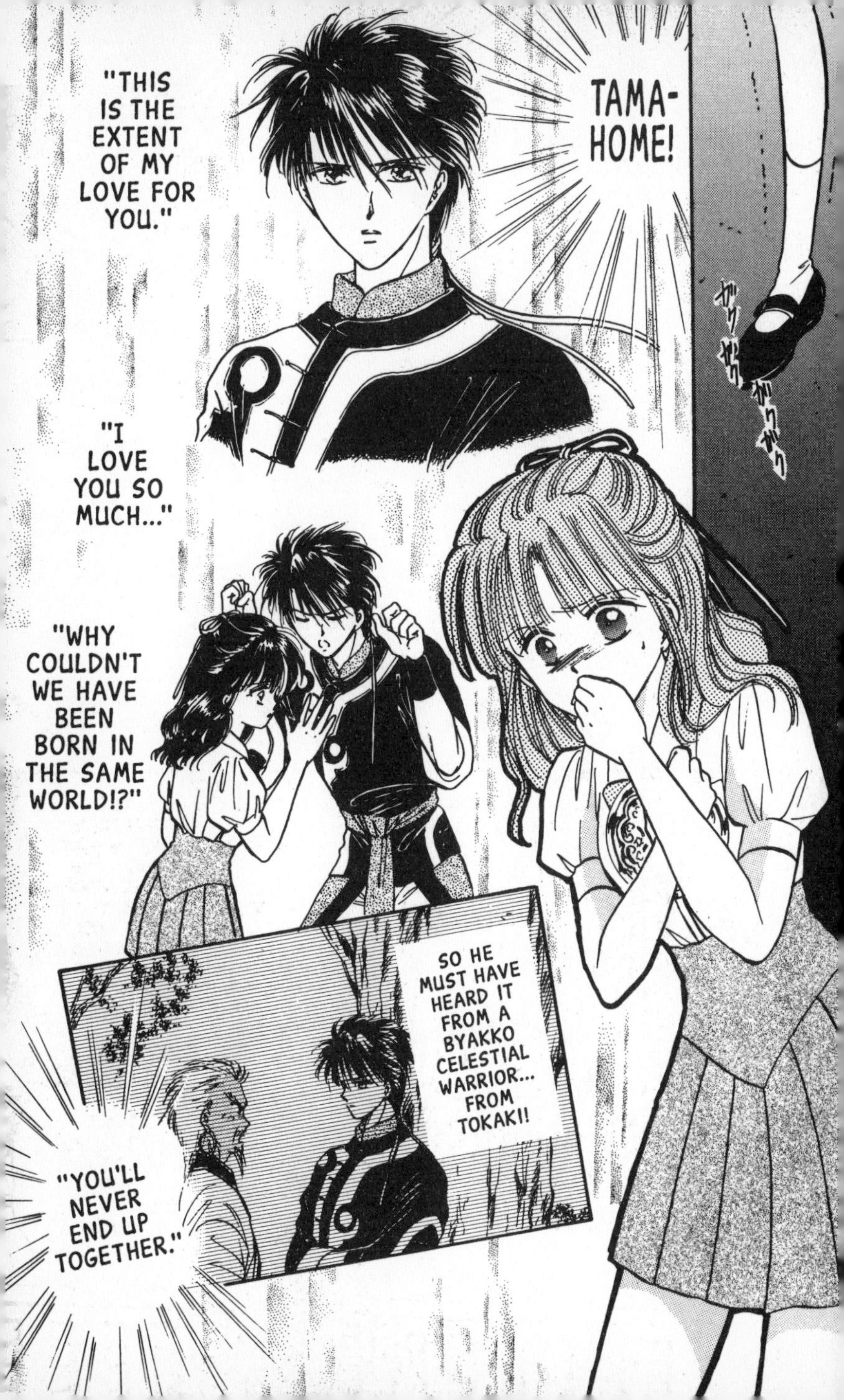
TAMA-HOME!
"THIS IS THE EXTENT OF MY LOVE FOR YOU."
"I LOVE YOU SO MUCH..."
"WHY COULDN'T WE HAVE BEEN BORN IN THE SAME WORLD!?"
SO HE MUST HAVE HEARD IT FROM A BYAKKO CELESTIAL WARRIOR... FROM TOKAKI!
"YOU'LL NEVER END UP TOGETHER."

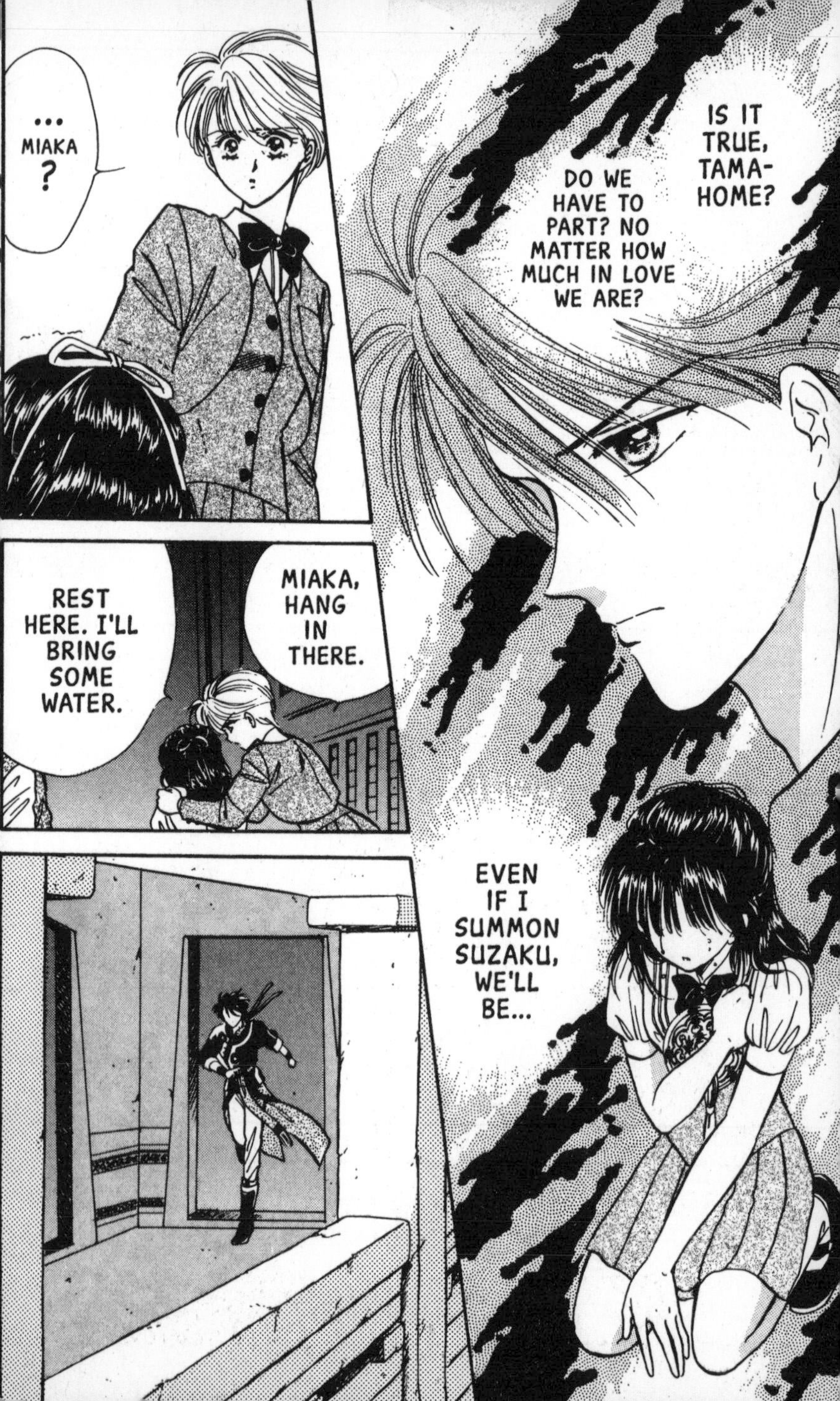

IS IT TRUE, TAMAHOME?
DO WE HAVE TO PART? NO MATTER HOW MUCH IN LOVE WE ARE?
EVEN IF I SUMMON SUZAKU, WE'LL BE...
... MIAKA ?
MIAKA, HANG IN THERE.
REST HERE. I'LL BRING SOME WATER.

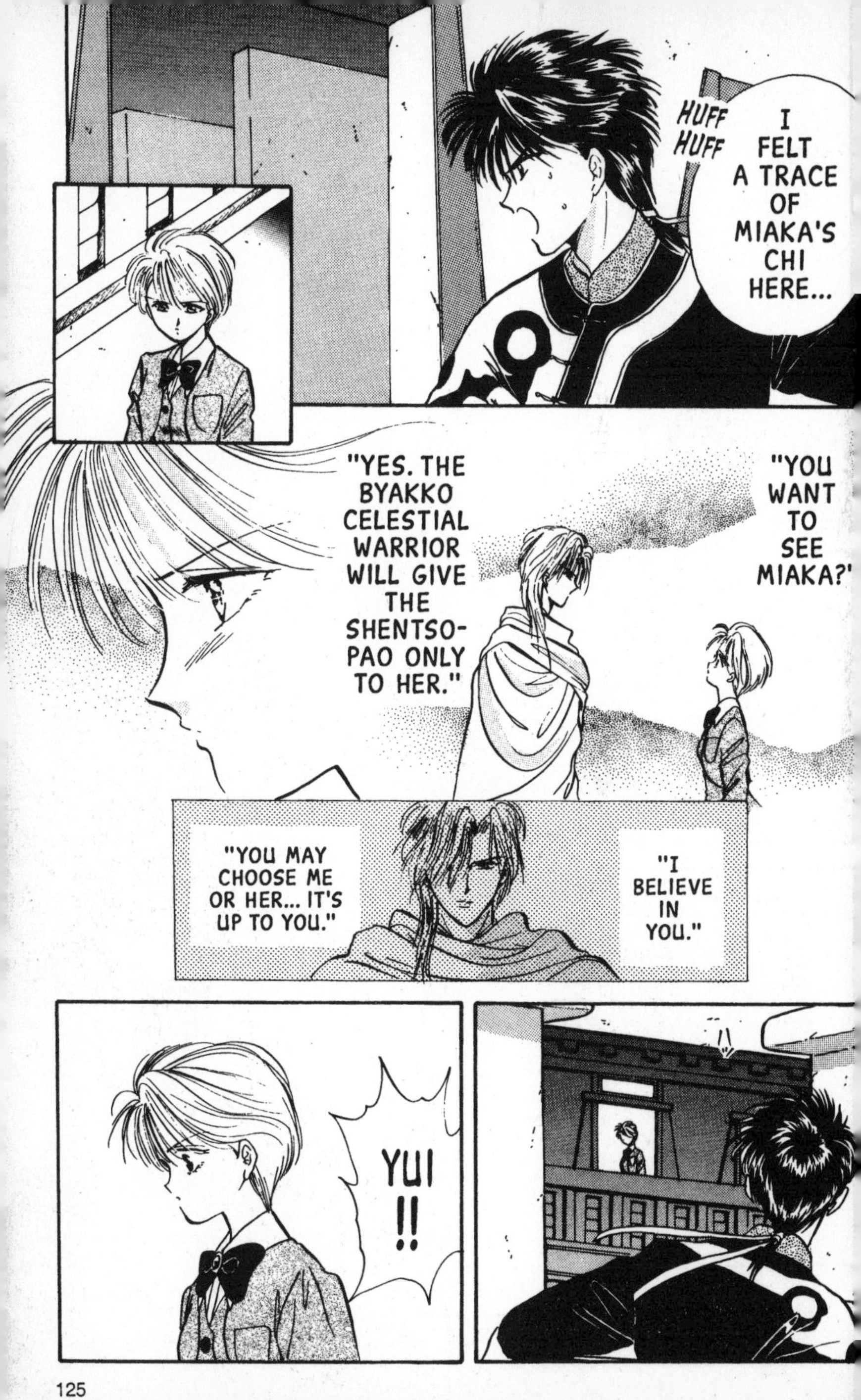
HUFF HUFF
I FELT A TRACE OF MIAKA'S CHI HERE...
"YOU WANT TO SEE MIAKA?'
"YES. THE BYAKKO CELESTIAL WARRIOR WILL GIVE THE SHENTSO-PAO ONLY TO HER."
"I BELIEVE IN YOU."
"YOU MAY CHOOSE ME OR HER... IT'S UP TO YOU."
YUI !!

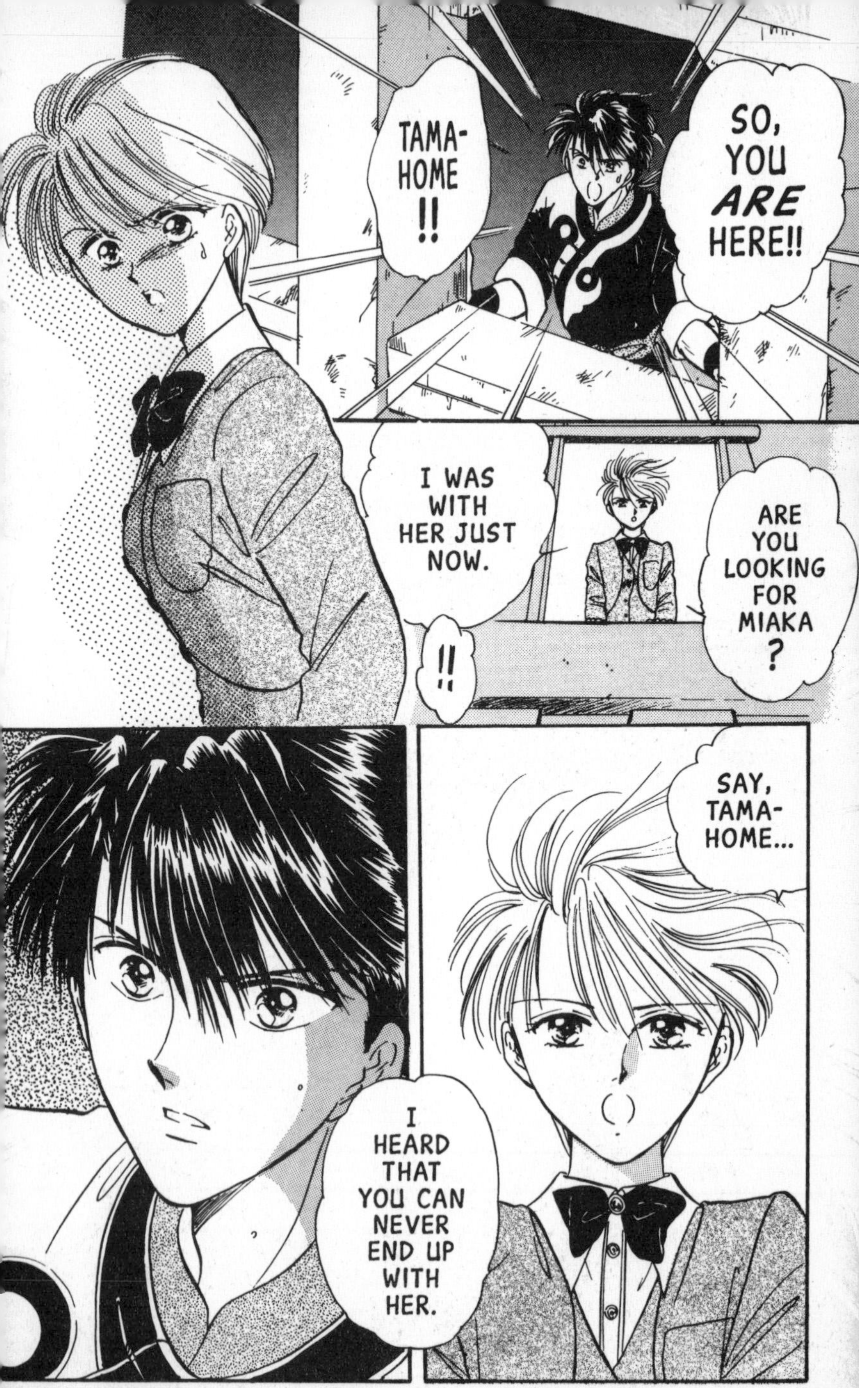
SO, YOU *ARE* HERE!!
TAMA-HOME!!
ARE YOU LOOKING FOR MIAKA?
I WAS WITH HER JUST NOW.
!!
SAY, TAMA-HOME...
I HEARD THAT YOU CAN NEVER END UP WITH HER.

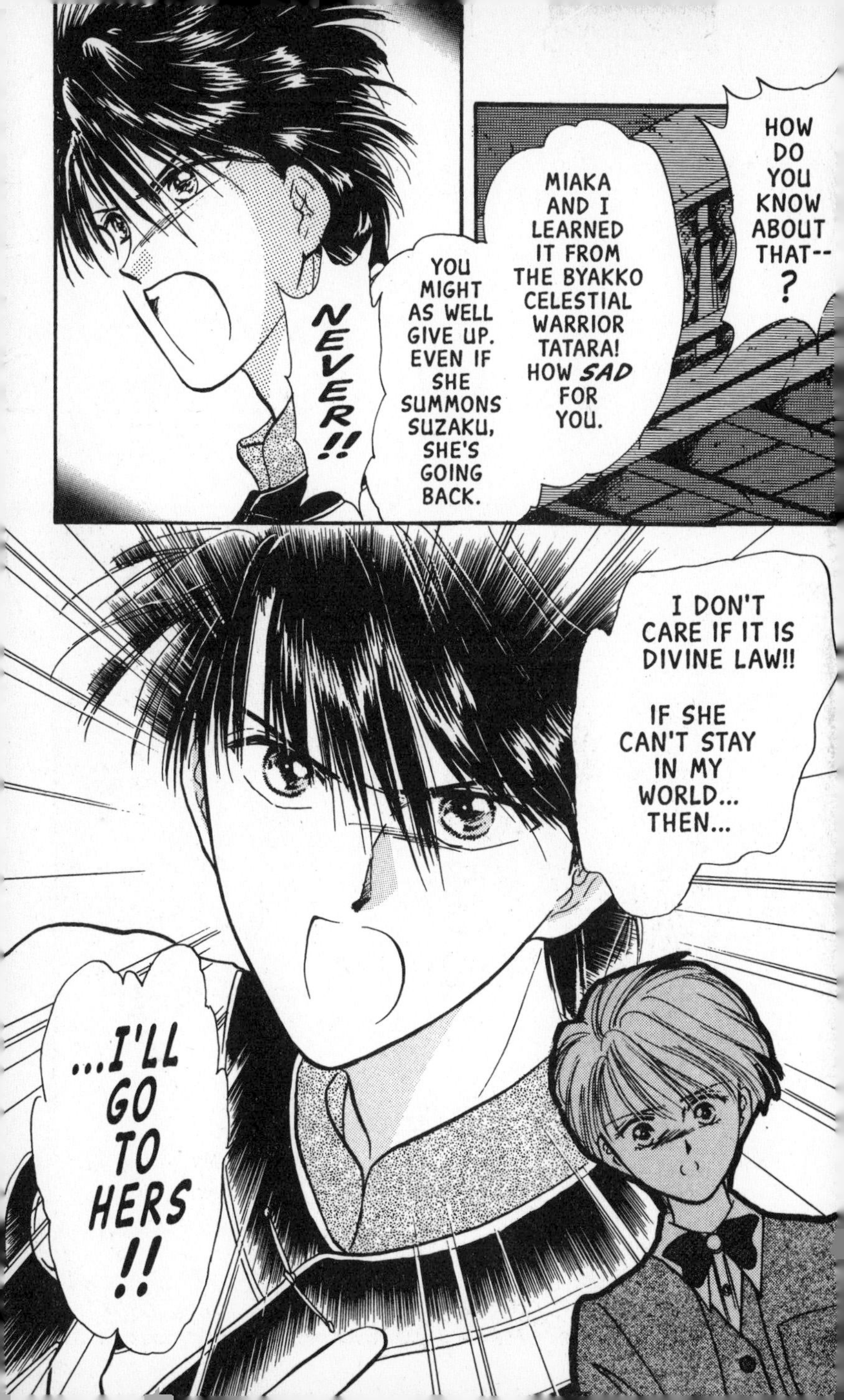
HOW DO YOU KNOW ABOUT THAT--?
MIAKA AND I LEARNED IT FROM THE BYAKKO CELESTIAL WARRIOR TATARA! HOW *SAD* FOR YOU.
YOU MIGHT AS WELL GIVE UP. EVEN IF SHE SUMMONS SUZAKU, SHE'S GOING BACK.
NEVER!!
I DON'T CARE IF IT IS DIVINE LAW!!
IF SHE CAN'T STAY IN MY WORLD... THEN...
...I'LL GO TO HERS!!

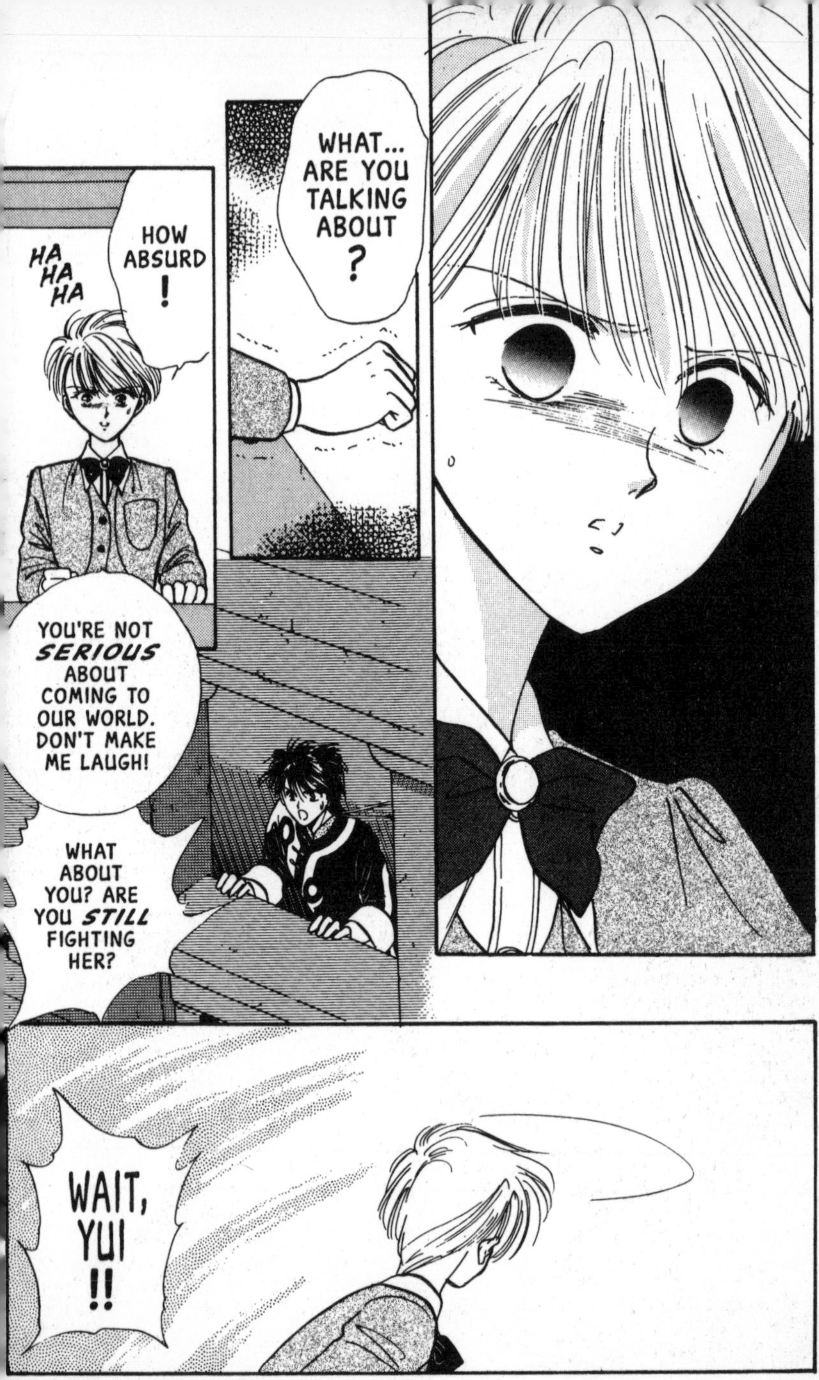
WHAT... ARE YOU TALKING ABOUT ?
HOW ABSURD !
HA HA HA
YOU'RE NOT *SERIOUS* ABOUT COMING TO OUR WORLD. DON'T MAKE ME LAUGH!
WHAT ABOUT YOU? ARE YOU *STILL* FIGHTING HER?
WAIT, YUI !!

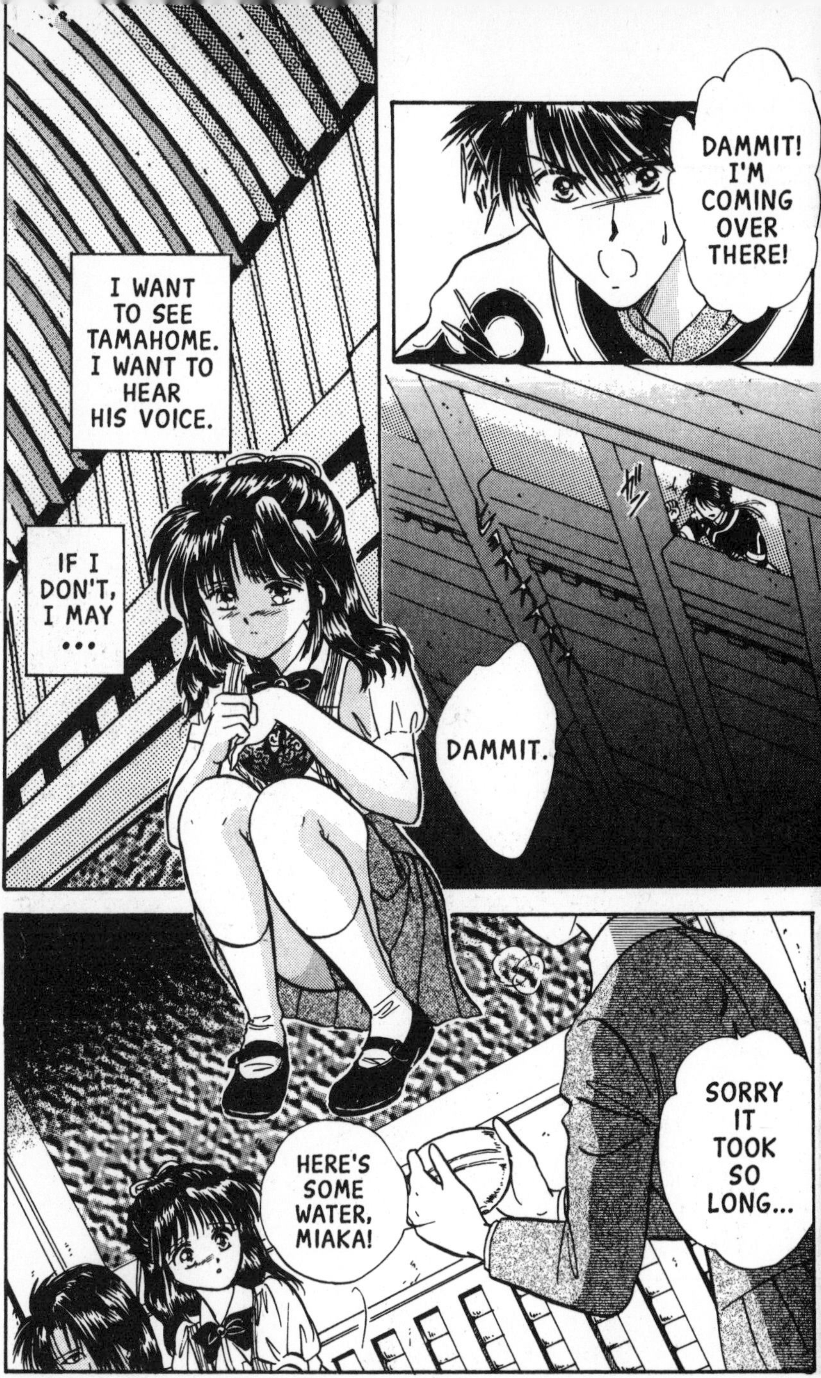
DAMMIT! I'M COMING OVER THERE!
DAMMIT.
I WANT TO SEE TAMAHOME. I WANT TO HEAR HIS VOICE.
IF I DON'T, I MAY ...
SORRY IT TOOK SO LONG...
HERE'S SOME WATER, MIAKA!

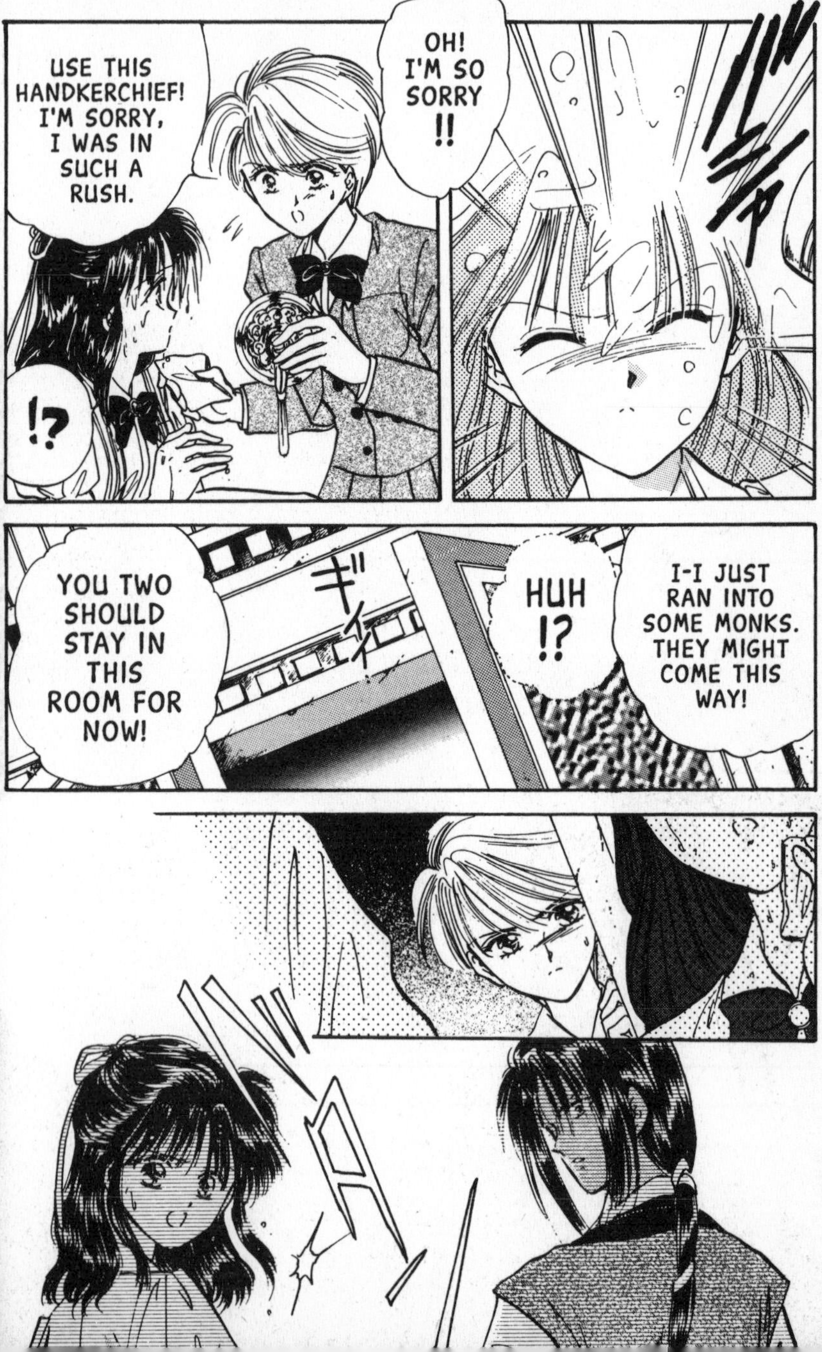
バシャ
OH! I'M SO SORRY !!
USE THIS HANDKERCHIEF! I'M SORRY, I WAS IN SUCH A RUSH.
!?
I-I JUST RAN INTO SOME MONKS. THEY MIGHT COME THIS WAY!
HUH !?
ギイィ
YOU TWO SHOULD STAY IN THIS ROOM FOR NOW!

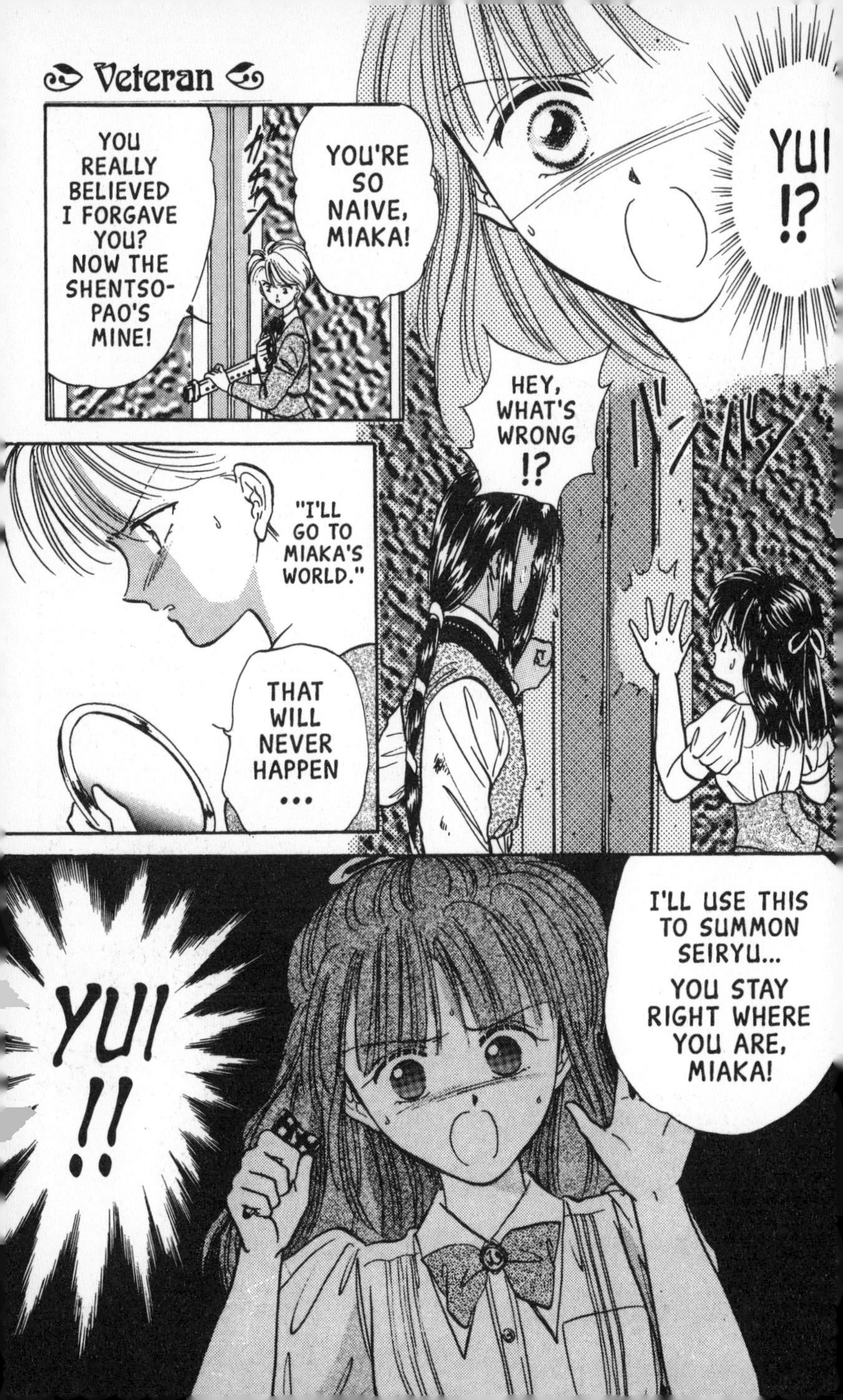
YUI !?
HEY, WHAT'S WRONG !?
YOU'RE SO NAIVE, MIAKA!
YOU REALLY BELIEVED I FORGAVE YOU? NOW THE SHENTSO-PAO'S MINE!
"I'LL GO TO MIAKA'S WORLD."
THAT WILL NEVER HAPPEN...
I'LL USE THIS TO SUMMON SEIRYU...
YOU STAY RIGHT WHERE YOU ARE, MIAKA!
YUI !!

THE SUDDEN--

ART CORNER!!

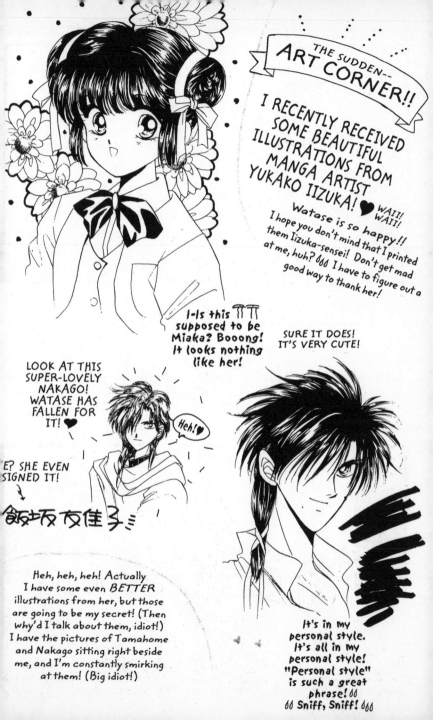

I RECENTLY RECEIVED SOME BEAUTIFUL ILLUSTRATIONS FROM MANGA ARTIST YUKAKO IIZUKA! ♥ WAI!! WAI!!

Watase is so happy!! I hope you don't mind that I printed them Iizuka-sensei! Don't get mad at me, huh? I have to figure out a good way to thank her!

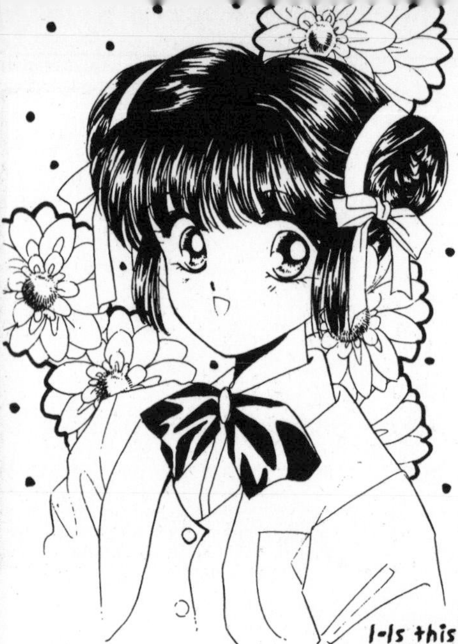

I-Is this supposed to be Miaka? Booong! It looks nothing like her!

SURE IT DOES! IT'S VERY CUTE!

LOOK AT THIS SUPER-LOVELY NAKAGO! WATASE HAS FALLEN FOR IT! ♥

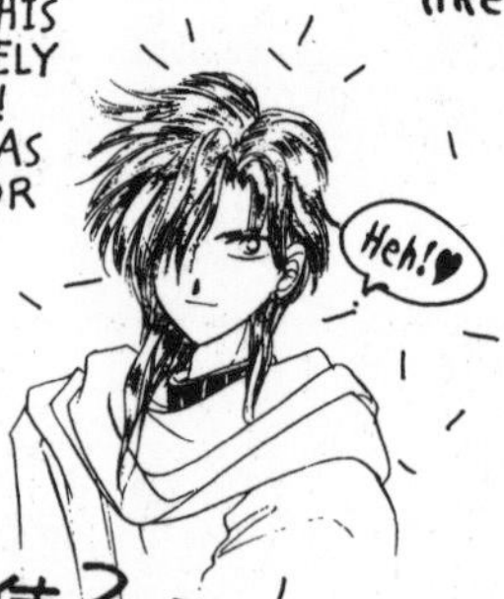
Heh! ♥

E? SHE EVEN SIGNED IT!

飯坂友佳子

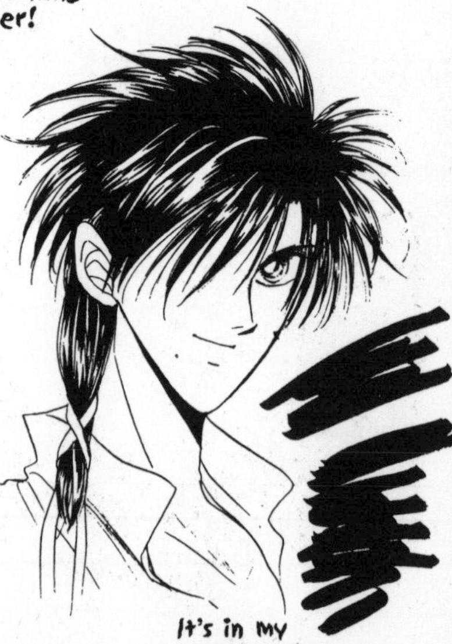

Heh, heh, heh! Actually I have some even *BETTER* illustrations from her, but those are going to be my secret! (Then why'd I talk about them, idiot!) I have the pictures of Tamahome and Nakago sitting right beside me, and I'm constantly smirking at them! (Big idiot!)

It's in my personal style. It's all in my personal style! "Personal style" is such a great phrase! Sniff, Sniff!

QUIZ!!

The bottom scene occurs one second after the top scene. How many items have changed?

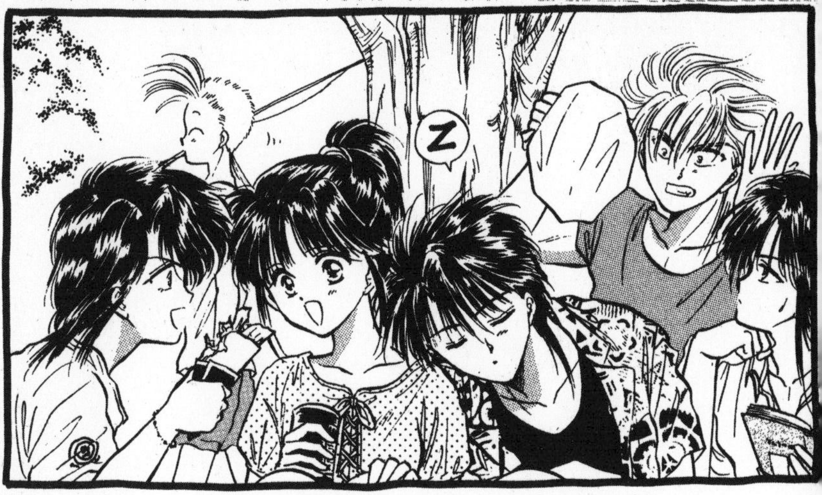
Z

CHAPTER SIXTY-FOUR
IMMINENT PARTING

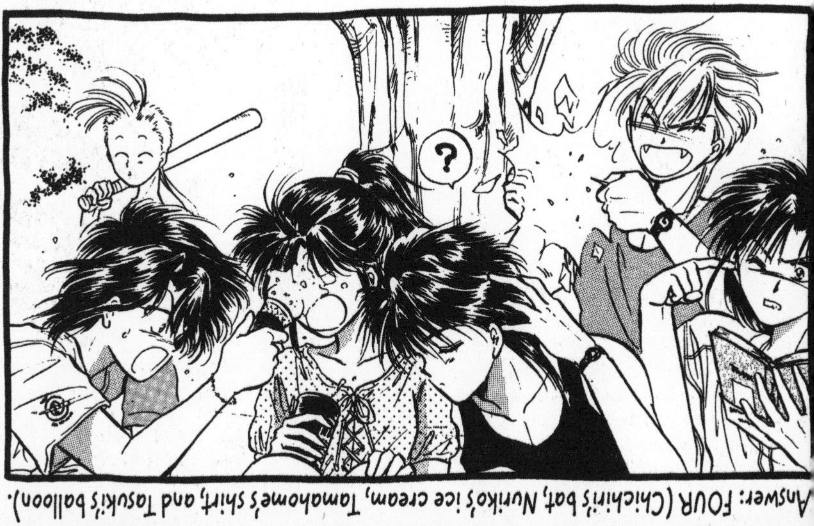
?

Answer: FOUR (Chichiri's bat, Nuriko's ice cream, Tamahome's shirt, and Tasuki's balloon).

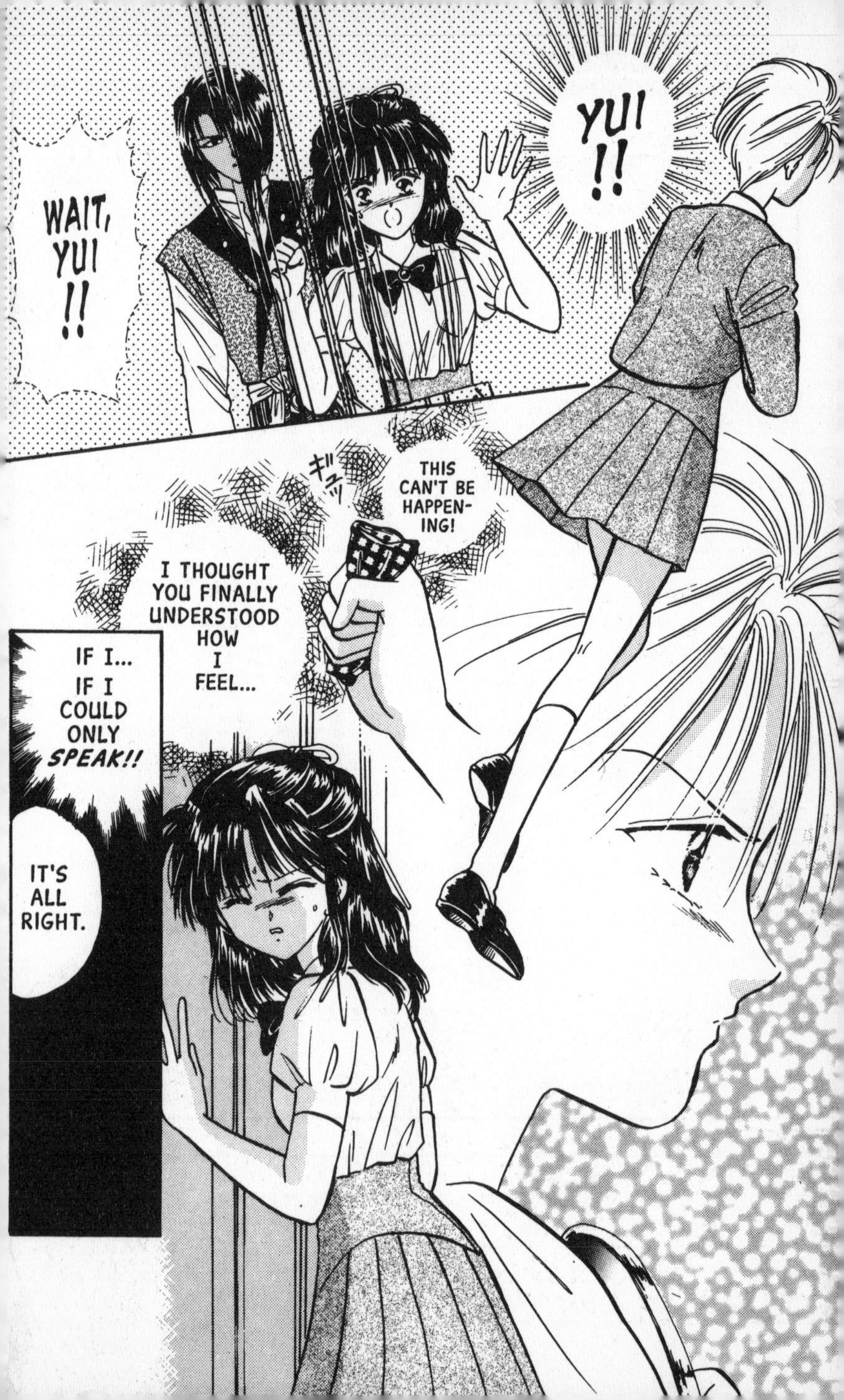
YUI !!
WAIT, YUI !!
ギュッ
THIS CAN'T BE HAPPEN- ING!
I THOUGHT YOU FINALLY UNDERSTOOD HOW I FEEL...
IF I... IF I COULD ONLY *SPEAK!!*
IT'S ALL RIGHT.

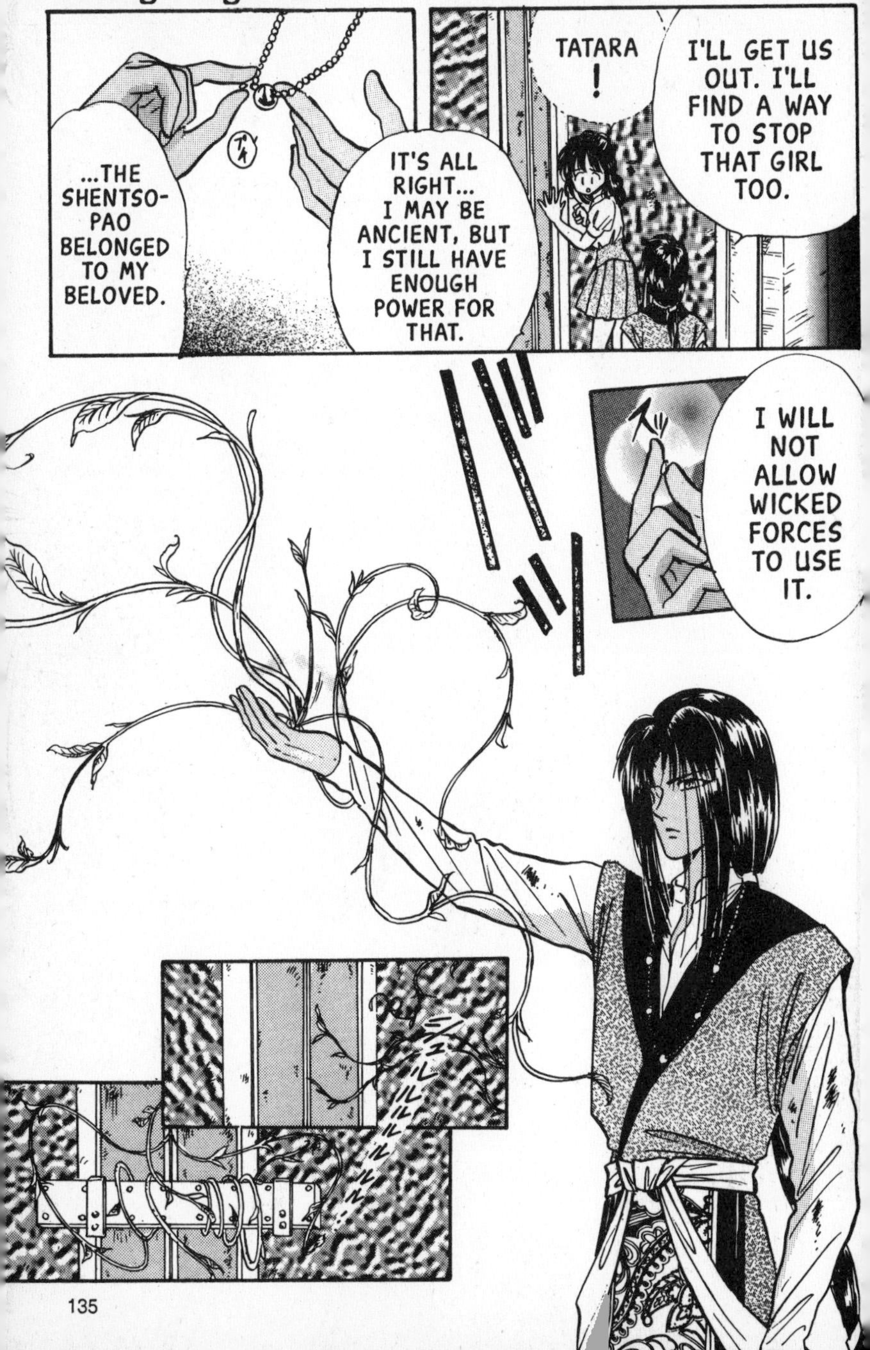
I'LL GET US OUT. I'LL FIND A WAY TO STOP THAT GIRL TOO.
TATARA!
IT'S ALL RIGHT... I MAY BE ANCIENT, BUT I STILL HAVE ENOUGH POWER FOR THAT.
...THE SHENTSO-PAO BELONGED TO MY BELOVED.
I WILL NOT ALLOW WICKED FORCES TO USE IT.

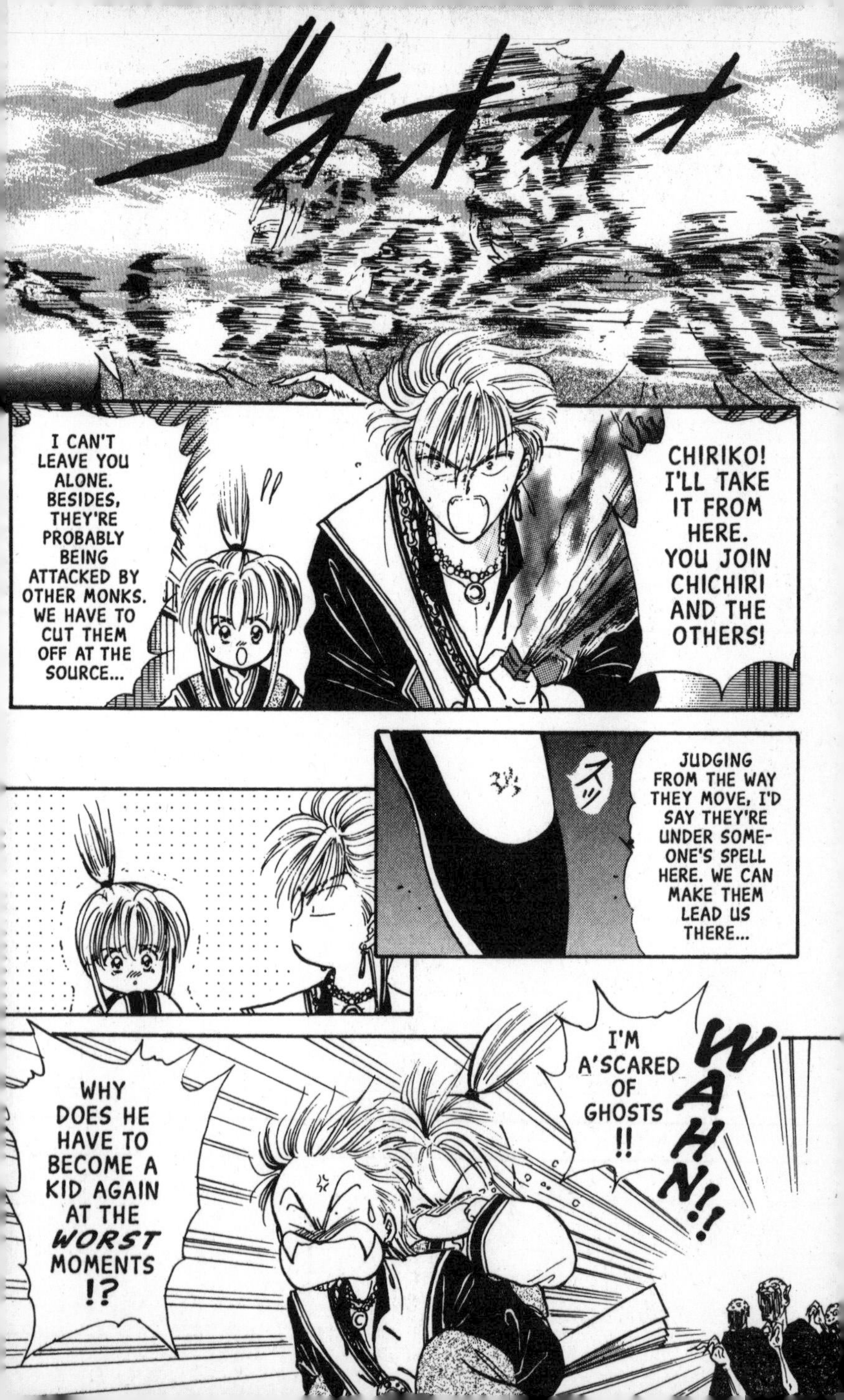
ゴオオオオ
CHIRIKO! I'LL TAKE IT FROM HERE. YOU JOIN CHICHIRI AND THE OTHERS!
I CAN'T LEAVE YOU ALONE. BESIDES, THEY'RE PROBABLY BEING ATTACKED BY OTHER MONKS. WE HAVE TO CUT THEM OFF AT THE SOURCE...
スッ
JUDGING FROM THE WAY THEY MOVE, I'D SAY THEY'RE UNDER SOME-ONE'S SPELL HERE. WE CAN MAKE THEM LEAD US THERE...
WAHN!!
I'M A'SCARED OF GHOSTS !!
WHY DOES HE HAVE TO BECOME A KID AGAIN AT THE *WORST* MOMENTS !?

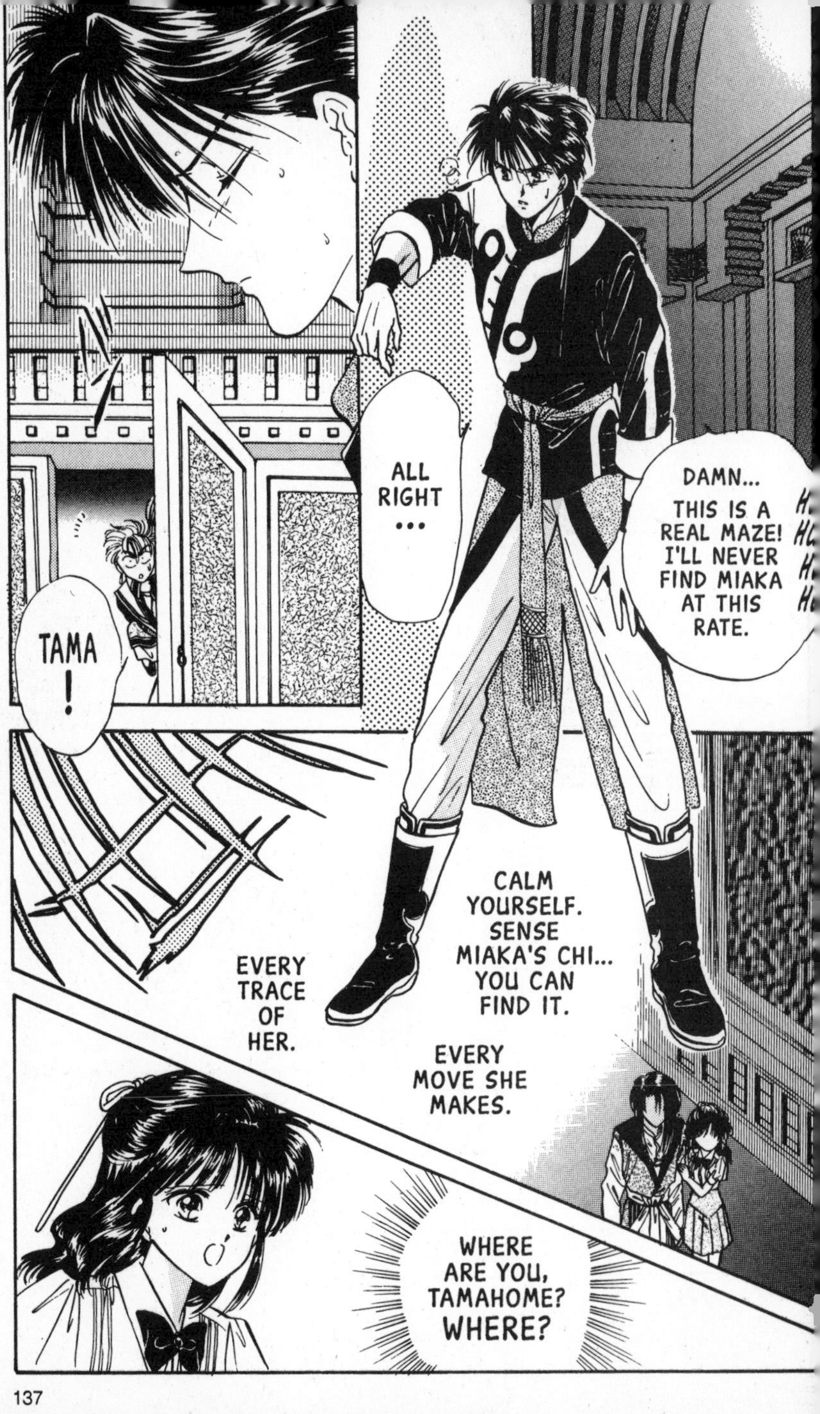
DAMN... THIS IS A REAL MAZE! I'LL NEVER FIND MIAKA AT THIS RATE.
ALL RIGHT ...
TAMA !
CALM YOURSELF. SENSE MIAKA'S CHI... YOU CAN FIND IT.
EVERY MOVE SHE MAKES.
EVERY TRACE OF HER.
WHERE ARE YOU, TAMAHOME? WHERE?

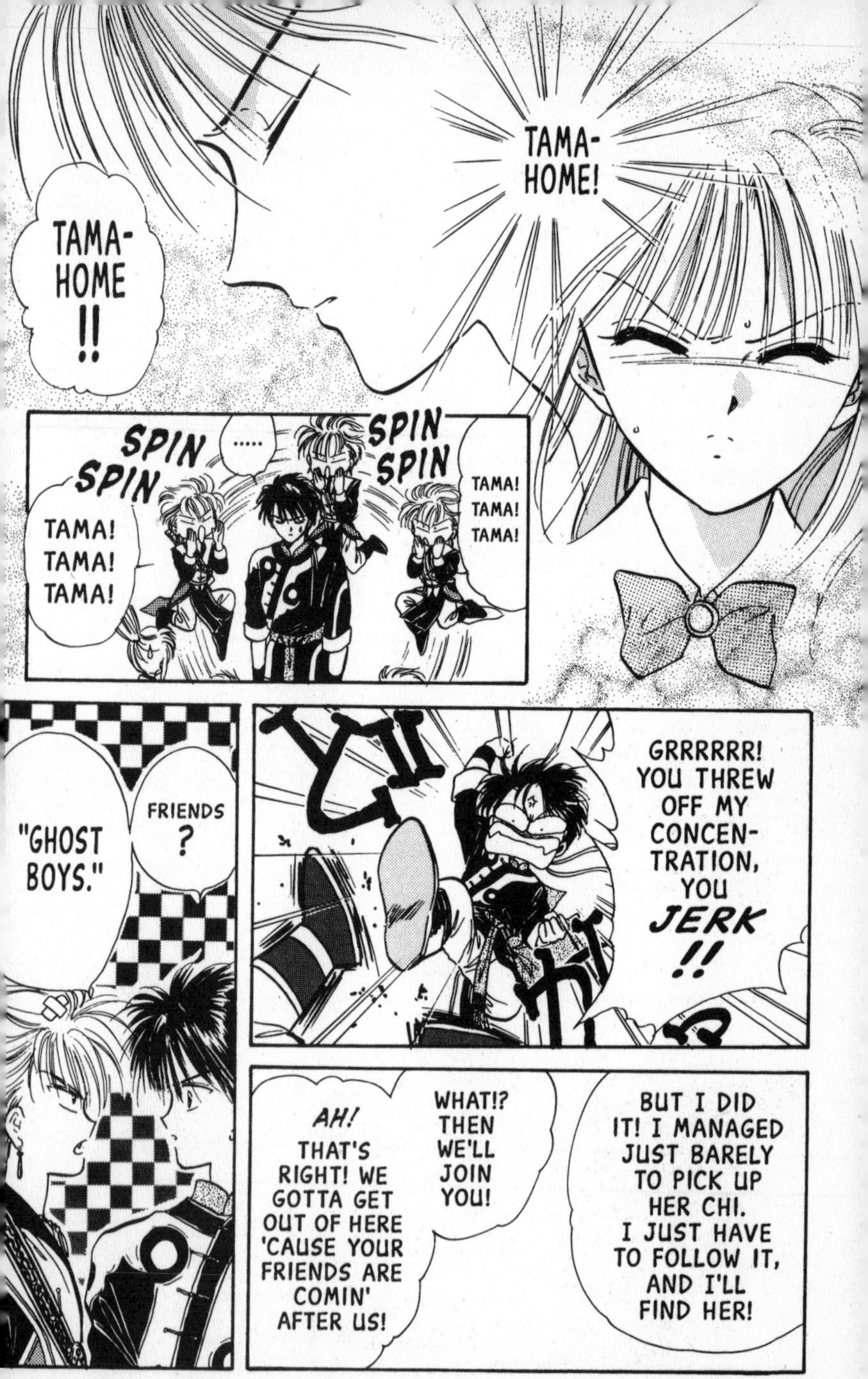
TAMA-HOME!
TAMA-HOME !!
SPIN SPIN
TAMA! TAMA! TAMA!
.....
SPIN SPIN
TAMA! TAMA! TAMA!
GRRRRRR! YOU THREW OFF MY CONCEN-TRATION, YOU JERK !!
BUT I DID IT! I MANAGED JUST BARELY TO PICK UP HER CHI. I JUST HAVE TO FOLLOW IT, AND I'LL FIND HER!
WHAT!? THEN WE'LL JOIN YOU!
AH! THAT'S RIGHT! WE GOTTA GET OUT OF HERE 'CAUSE YOUR FRIENDS ARE COMIN' AFTER US!
FRIENDS ?
"GHOST BOYS."

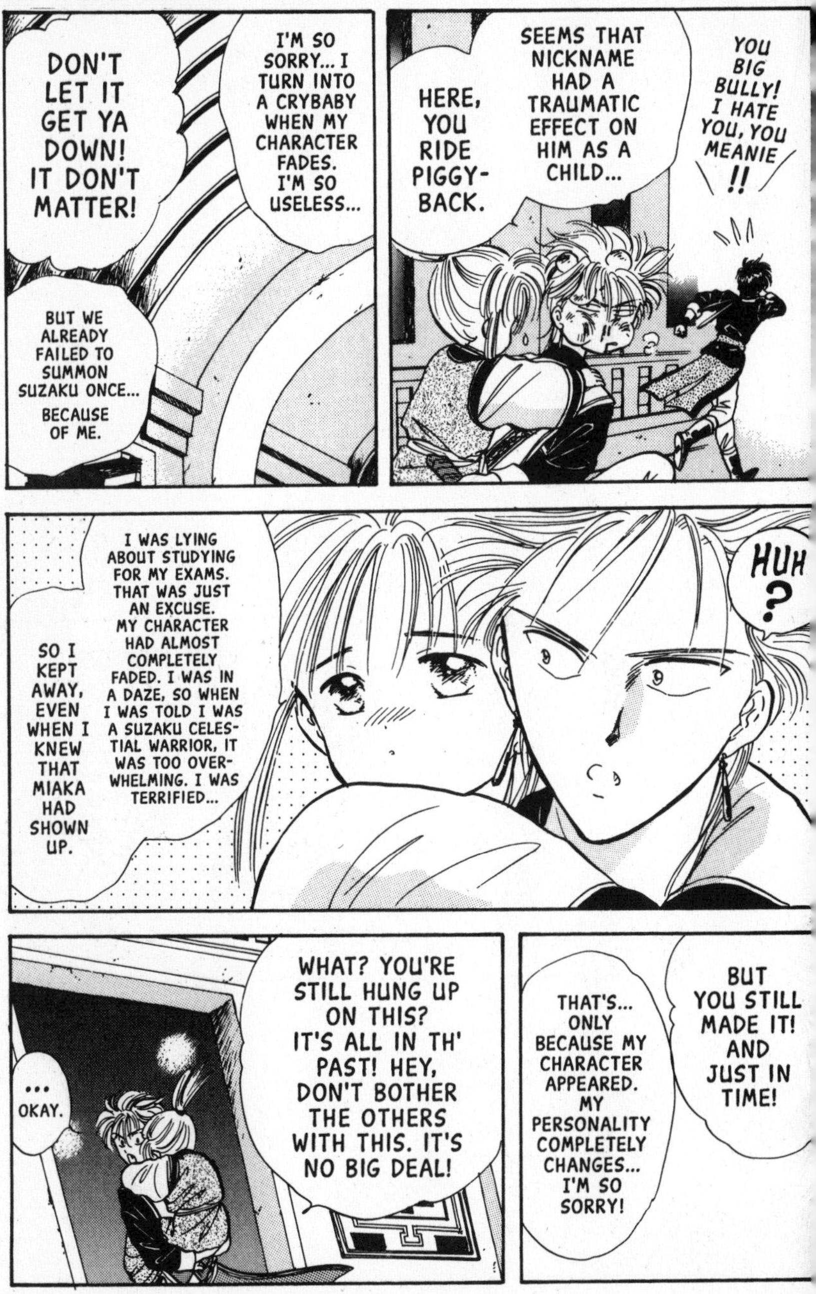
YOU BIG BULLY! I HATE YOU, YOU MEANIE!!
SEEMS THAT NICKNAME HAD A TRAUMATIC EFFECT ON HIM AS A CHILD...
HERE, YOU RIDE PIGGY-BACK.
I'M SO SORRY... I TURN INTO A CRYBABY WHEN MY CHARACTER FADES. I'M SO USELESS...
DON'T LET IT GET YA DOWN! IT DON'T MATTER!
BUT WE ALREADY FAILED TO SUMMON SUZAKU ONCE... BECAUSE OF ME.
HUH?
I WAS LYING ABOUT STUDYING FOR MY EXAMS. THAT WAS JUST AN EXCUSE. MY CHARACTER HAD ALMOST COMPLETELY FADED. I WAS IN A DAZE, SO WHEN I WAS TOLD I WAS A SUZAKU CELESTIAL WARRIOR, IT WAS TOO OVERWHELMING. I WAS TERRIFIED...
SO I KEPT AWAY, EVEN WHEN I KNEW THAT MIAKA HAD SHOWN UP.
BUT YOU STILL MADE IT! AND JUST IN TIME!
THAT'S... ONLY BECAUSE MY CHARACTER APPEARED. MY PERSONALITY COMPLETELY CHANGES... I'M SO SORRY!
WHAT? YOU'RE STILL HUNG UP ON THIS? IT'S ALL IN TH' PAST! HEY, DON'T BOTHER THE OTHERS WITH THIS. IT'S NO BIG DEAL!
... OKAY.

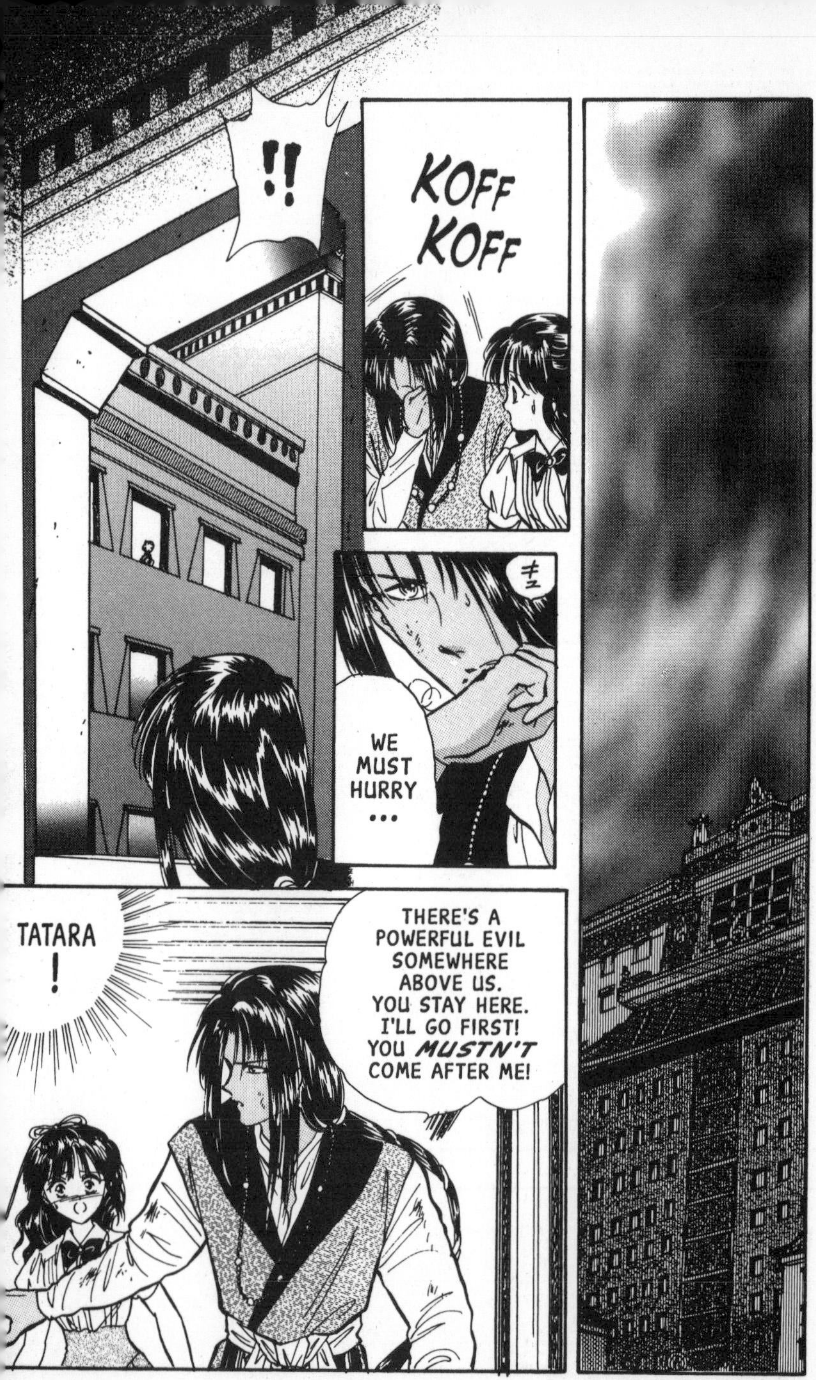
KOFF KOFF
キュ
WE MUST HURRY...
!!
TATARA!
THERE'S A POWERFUL EVIL SOMEWHERE ABOVE US. YOU STAY HERE. I'LL GO FIRST! YOU *MUSTN'T* COME AFTER ME!

Next is the No. 2 character in the CD survey, Tasuki. His Kansai dialect is a humorous touch. I wanted him to be different from the others. I had a wolf boy in mind, so his hair style and fangs were all part of that. It wouldn't have been interesting if he was just another handsome guy, a variation on "Tama" and "Hori." Still, my concept design for him changed several times. His personality was totally different in the first version, and the idea was that he was supposed to be a childhood friend of Tamahome's. The mountain bandit idea came to me because I wanted him to stand out from the usual cast of characters like farmer (peasant), emperor, monk, or doctor. There's one in Suikoden. And his harisen (fan) was another touch. I wanted something like the Basho harisen in Saiyuki, and then I was like, "speaking of Osaka," I came up with the idea of his accent. By the way, although you don't see it very often, Tasuki's a very fast runner. *Really!* You know how he just swept Miaka away when he first appeared. He's a strong fighter. He's not limited to just one strength like the other celestial warriors, he's incredibly strong in all regards.

I really wanted Chichiri to be very unique. He's based on the draft I did when I first came up with the story. I wanted someone light-hearted. Because he's a priest, he should be bald, but I ended up giving him an odd hairstyle. I claimed he had a Mohawk in volume 4, but it isn't really. It's just that he has very long bangs.

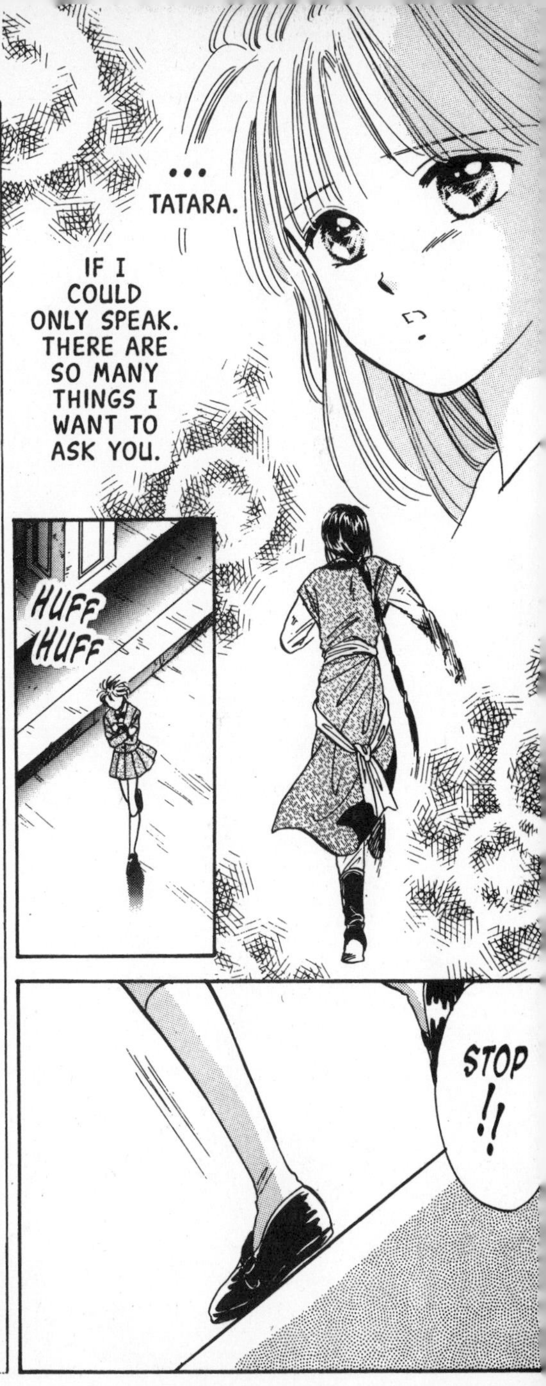
... TATARA.
IF I COULD ONLY SPEAK. THERE ARE SO MANY THINGS I WANT TO ASK YOU.
HUFF HUFF
STOP!!

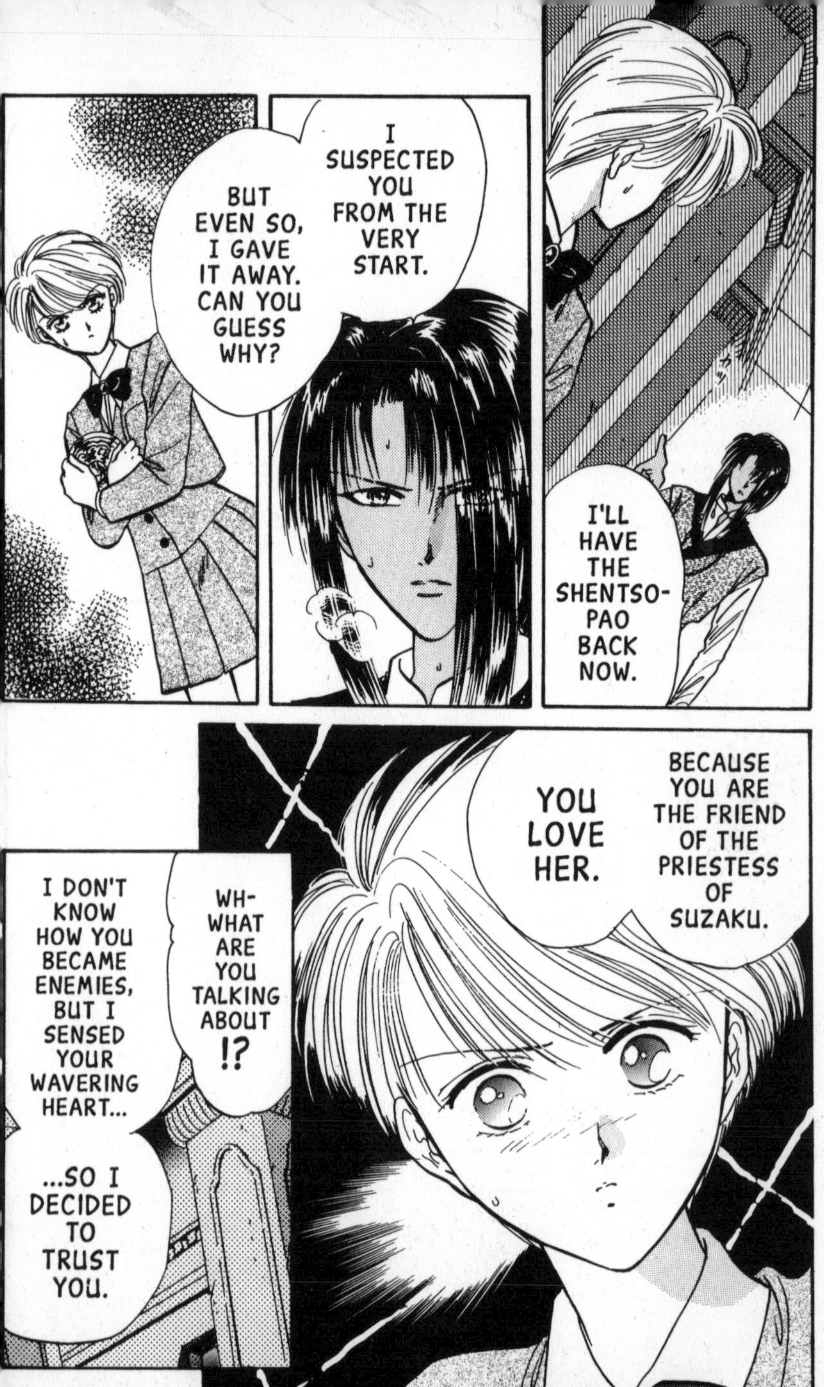
I'LL HAVE THE SHENTSO-PAO BACK NOW.
I SUSPECTED YOU FROM THE VERY START.
BUT EVEN SO, I GAVE IT AWAY. CAN YOU GUESS WHY?
BECAUSE YOU ARE THE FRIEND OF THE PRIESTESS OF SUZAKU.
YOU LOVE HER.
WH-WHAT ARE YOU TALKING ABOUT!?
I DON'T KNOW HOW YOU BECAME ENEMIES, BUT I SENSED YOUR WAVERING HEART...
...SO I DECIDED TO TRUST YOU.

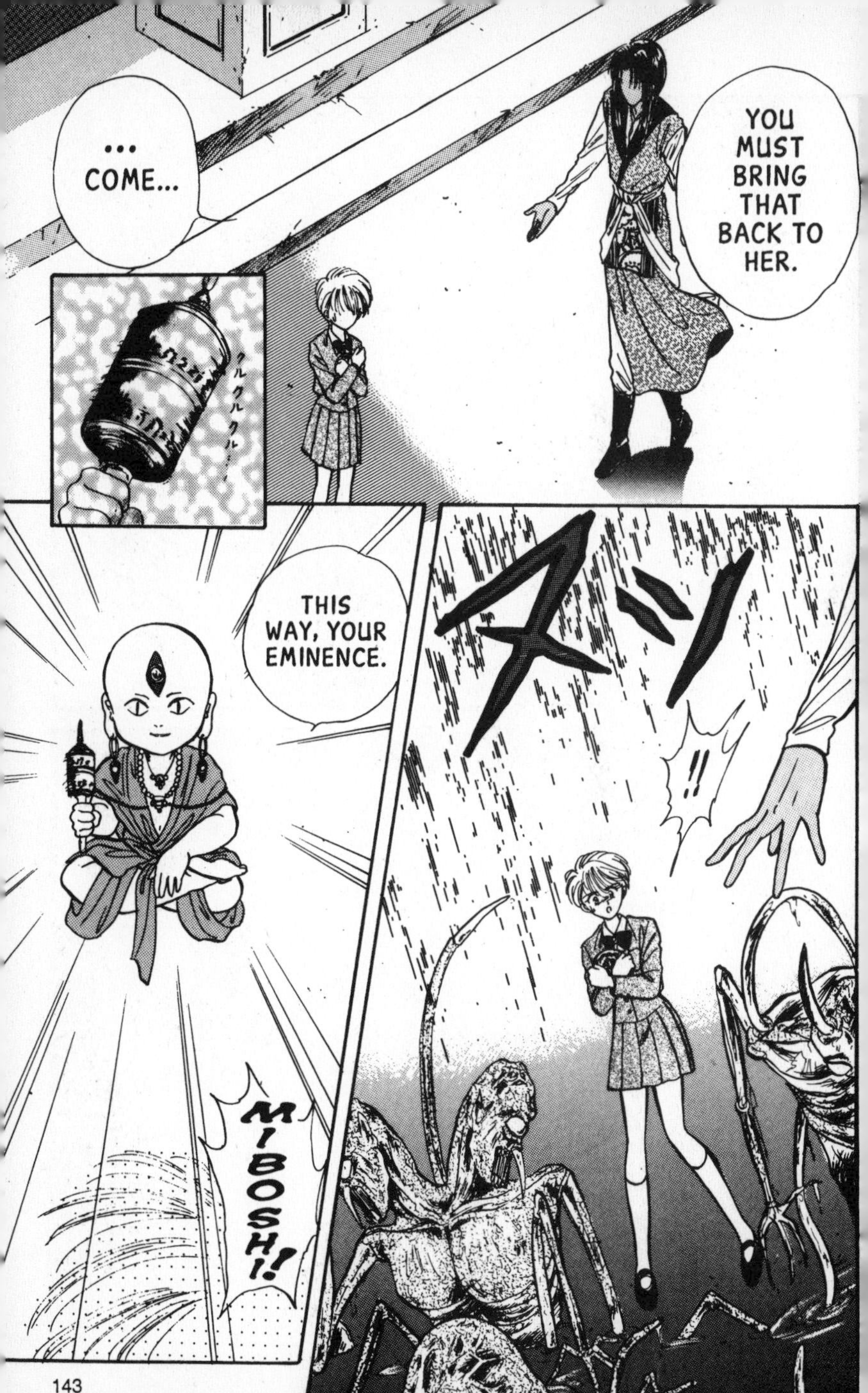
YOU MUST BRING THAT BACK TO HER.
... COME...
クルクルクル
スッ
!!
THIS WAY, YOUR EMINENCE.
MIBOSHI!!

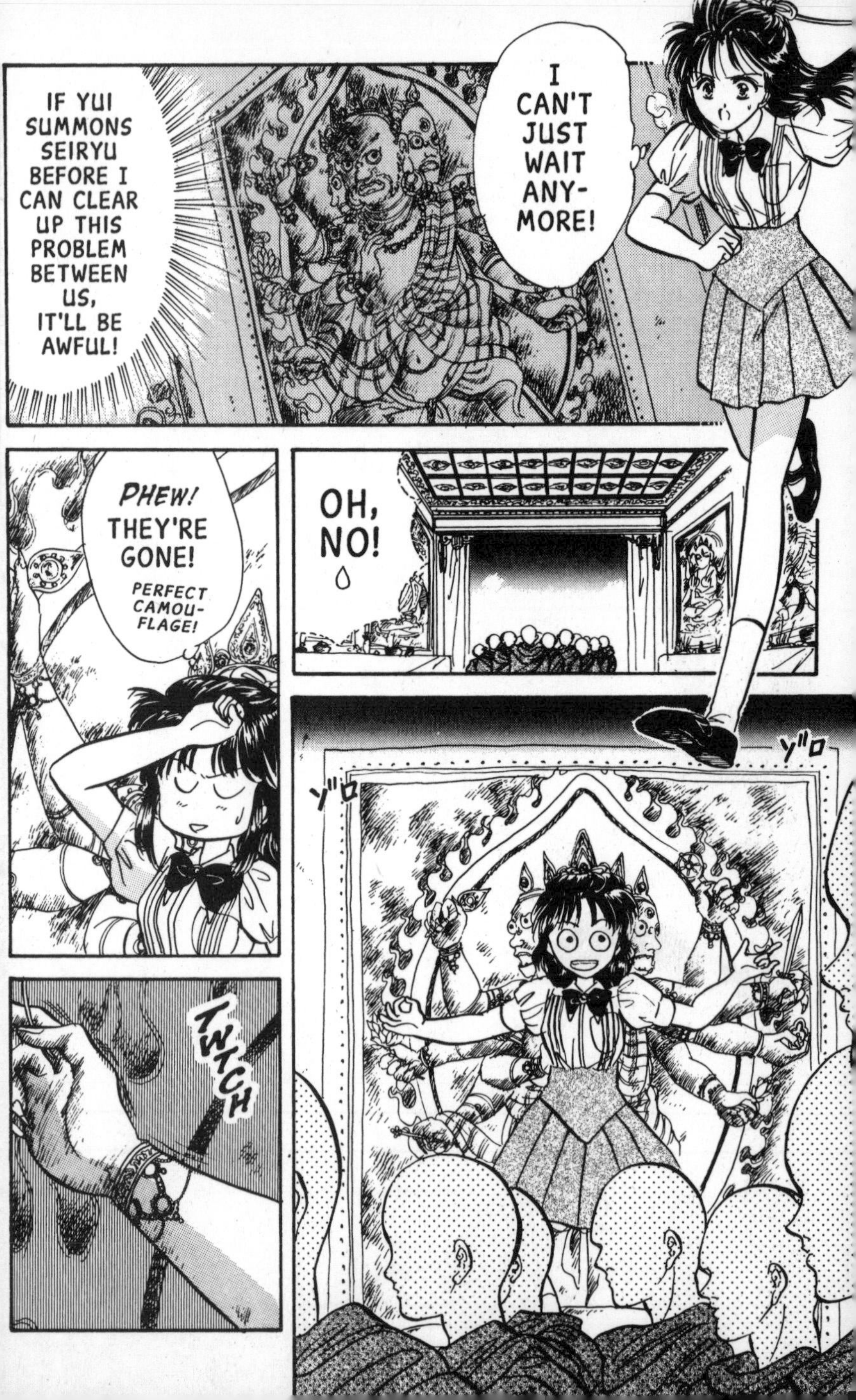
I CAN'T JUST WAIT ANY-MORE!
IF YUI SUMMONS SEIRYU BEFORE I CAN CLEAR UP THIS PROBLEM BETWEEN US, IT'LL BE AWFUL!
OH, NO!
PHEW! THEY'RE GONE!
PERFECT CAMOU-FLAGE!
ゾロ
ゾロ
TWITCH

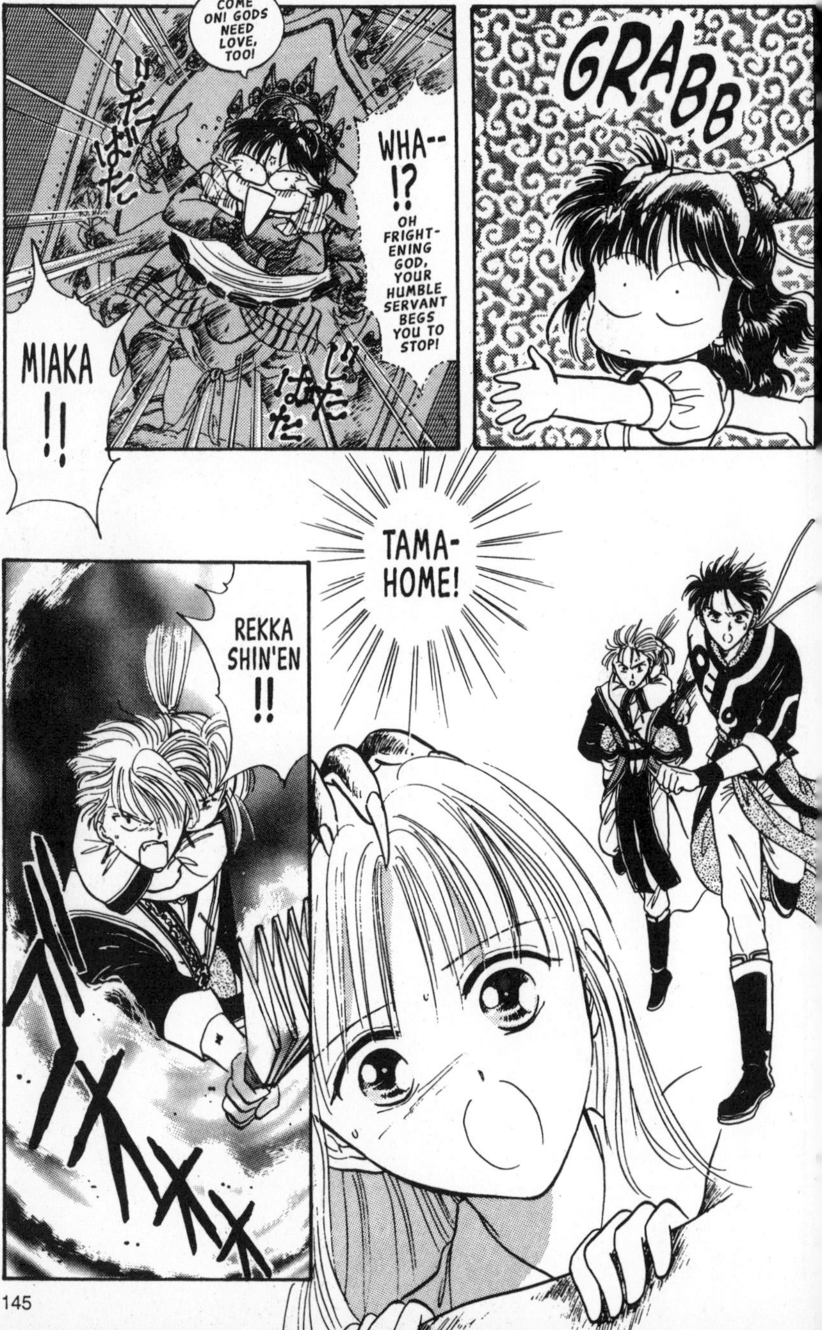
GRABB
COME ON! GODS NEED LOVE, TOO!
WHA--!?!! OH FRIGHTENING GOD, YOUR HUMBLE SERVANT BEGS YOU TO STOP!
MIAKA!!
TAMA-HOME!
REKKA SHIN'EN!!

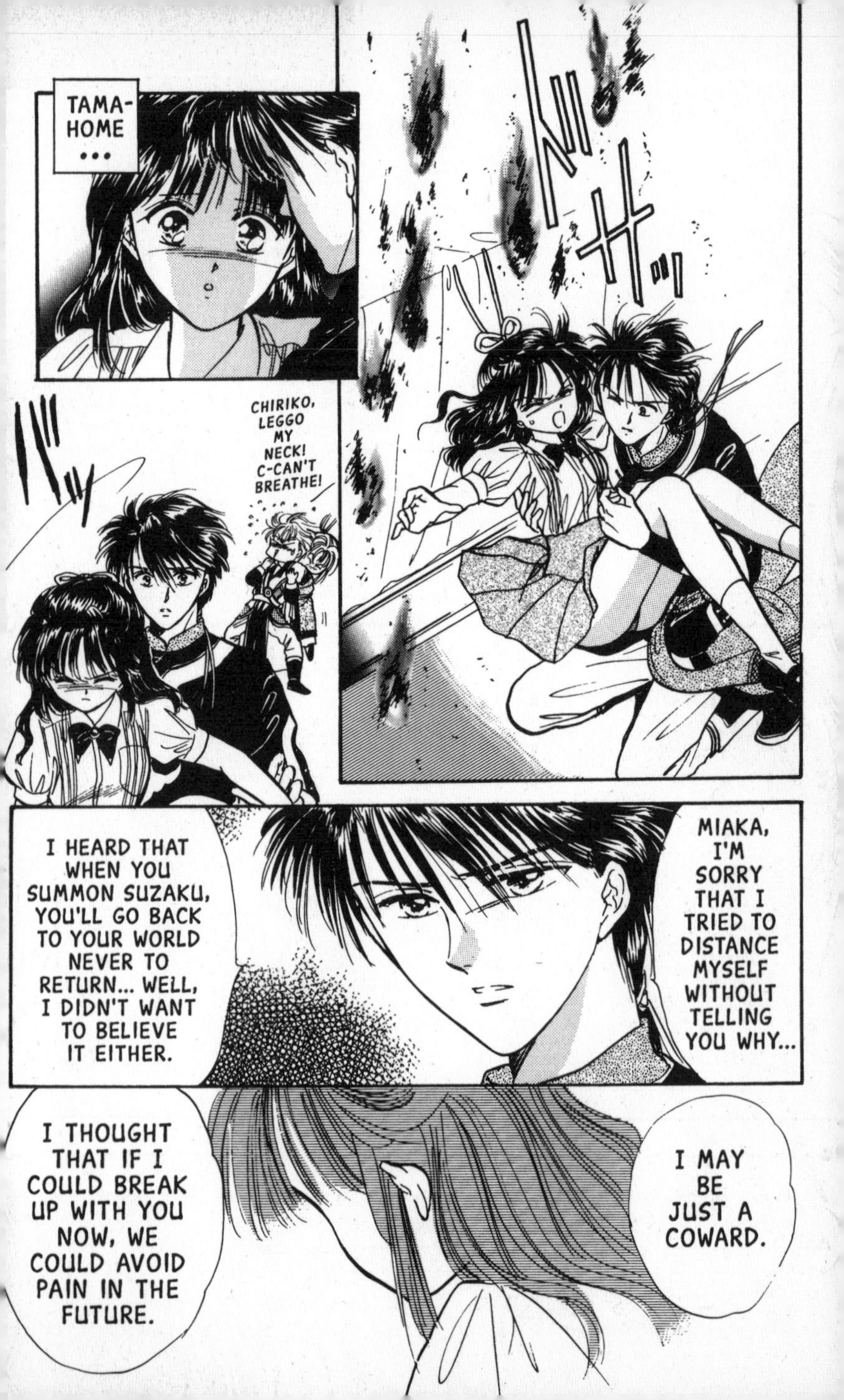
TAMA-HOME...
CHIRIKO, LEGGO MY NECK! C-CAN'T BREATHE!
MIAKA, I'M SORRY THAT I TRIED TO DISTANCE MYSELF WITHOUT TELLING YOU WHY...
I HEARD THAT WHEN YOU SUMMON SUZAKU, YOU'LL GO BACK TO YOUR WORLD NEVER TO RETURN... WELL, I DIDN'T WANT TO BELIEVE IT EITHER.
I MAY BE JUST A COWARD.
I THOUGHT THAT IF I COULD BREAK UP WITH YOU NOW, WE COULD AVOID PAIN IN THE FUTURE.

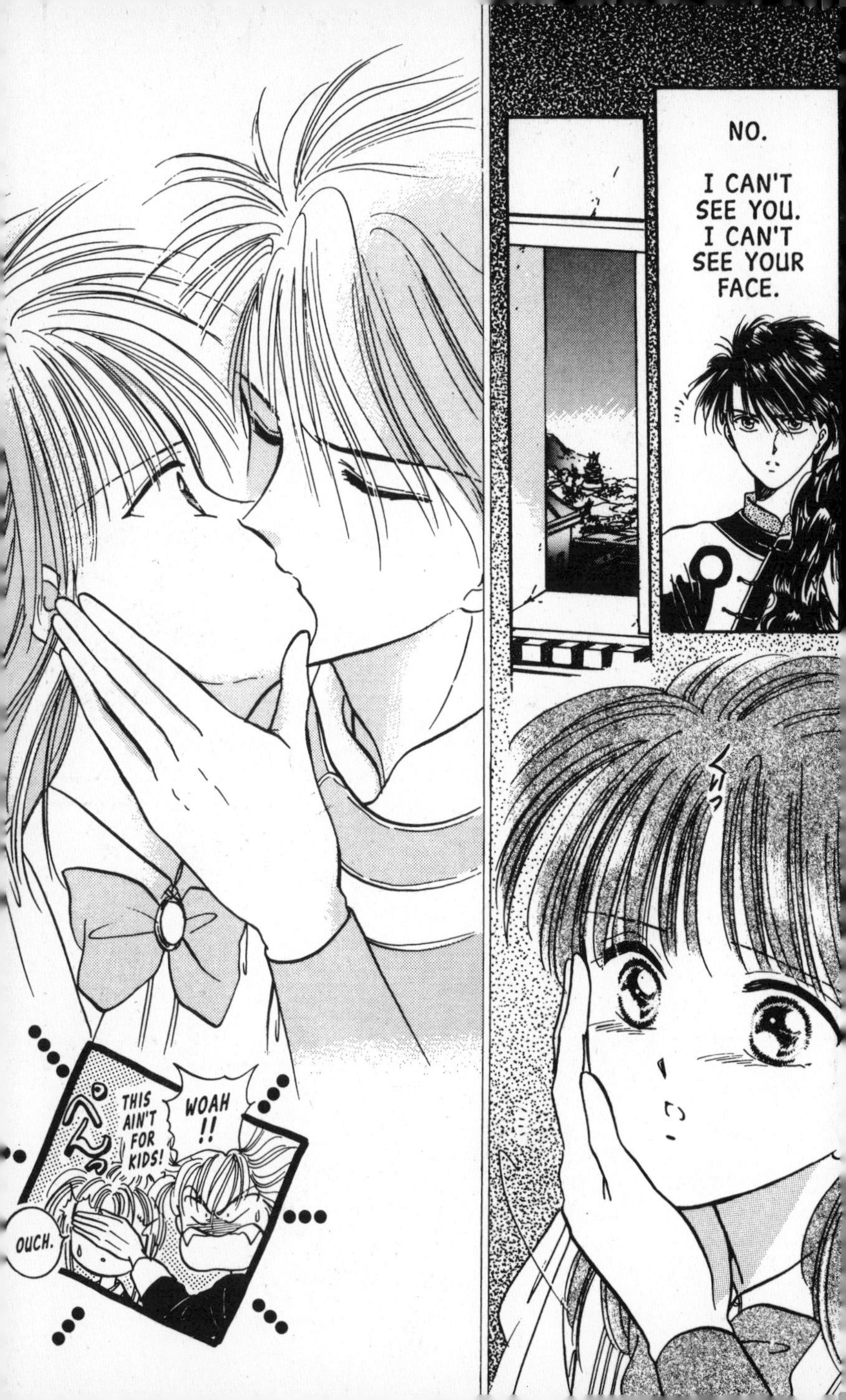
NO.
I CAN'T SEE YOU. I CAN'T SEE YOUR FACE.
WOAH !!
THIS AIN'T FOR KIDS!
OUCH.

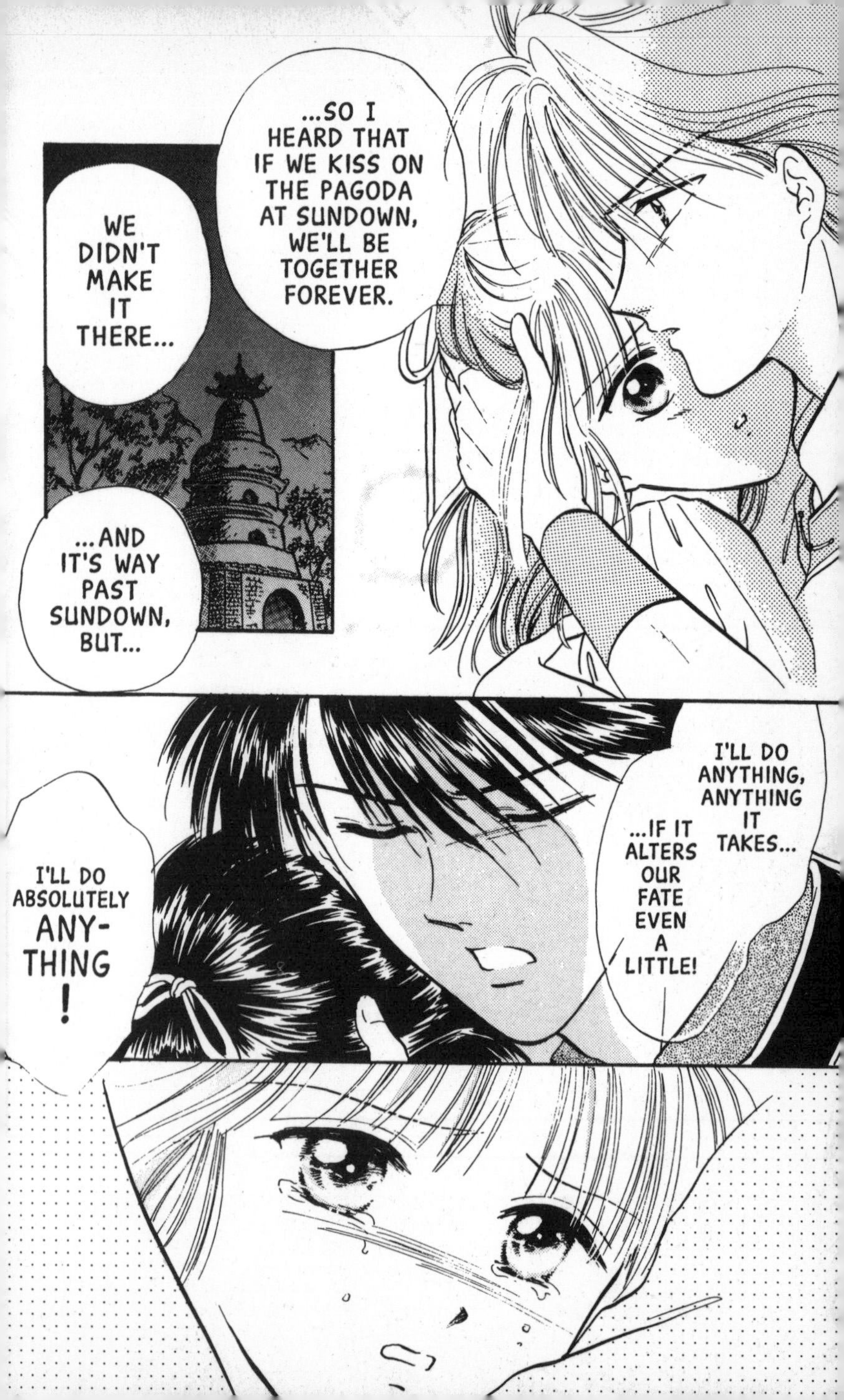
...SO I HEARD THAT IF WE KISS ON THE PAGODA AT SUNDOWN, WE'LL BE TOGETHER FOREVER.
WE DIDN'T MAKE IT THERE...
...AND IT'S WAY PAST SUNDOWN, BUT...
I'LL DO ANYTHING, ANYTHING IT TAKES...
...IF IT ALTERS OUR FATE EVEN A LITTLE!
I'LL DO ABSOLUTELY ANY-THING!

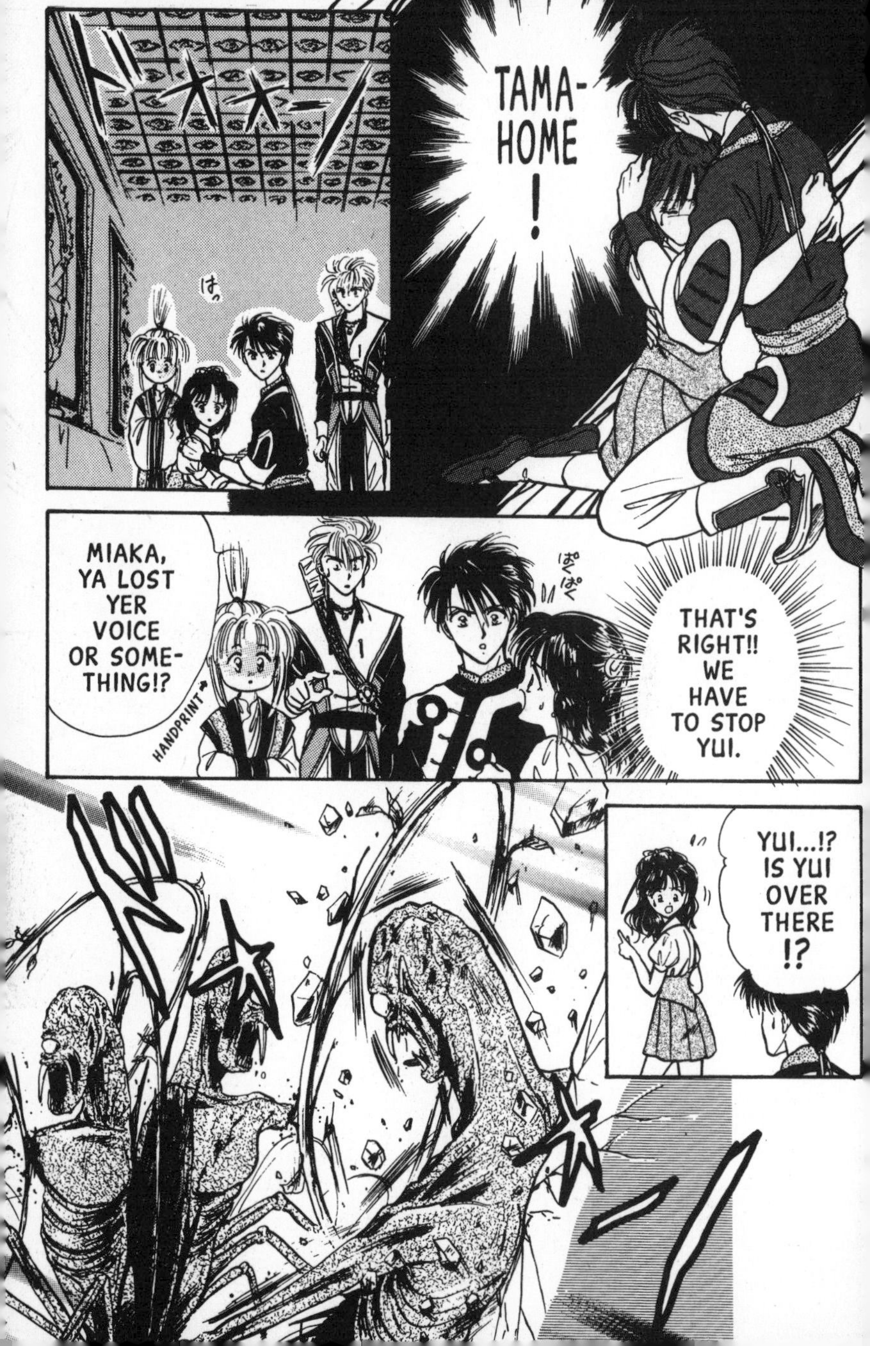
TAMA-HOME !
はっ
THAT'S RIGHT!! WE HAVE TO STOP YUI.
ぱくぱく
MIAKA, YA LOST YER VOICE OR SOME-THING!?
HANDPRINT
YUI...!? IS YUI OVER THERE !?

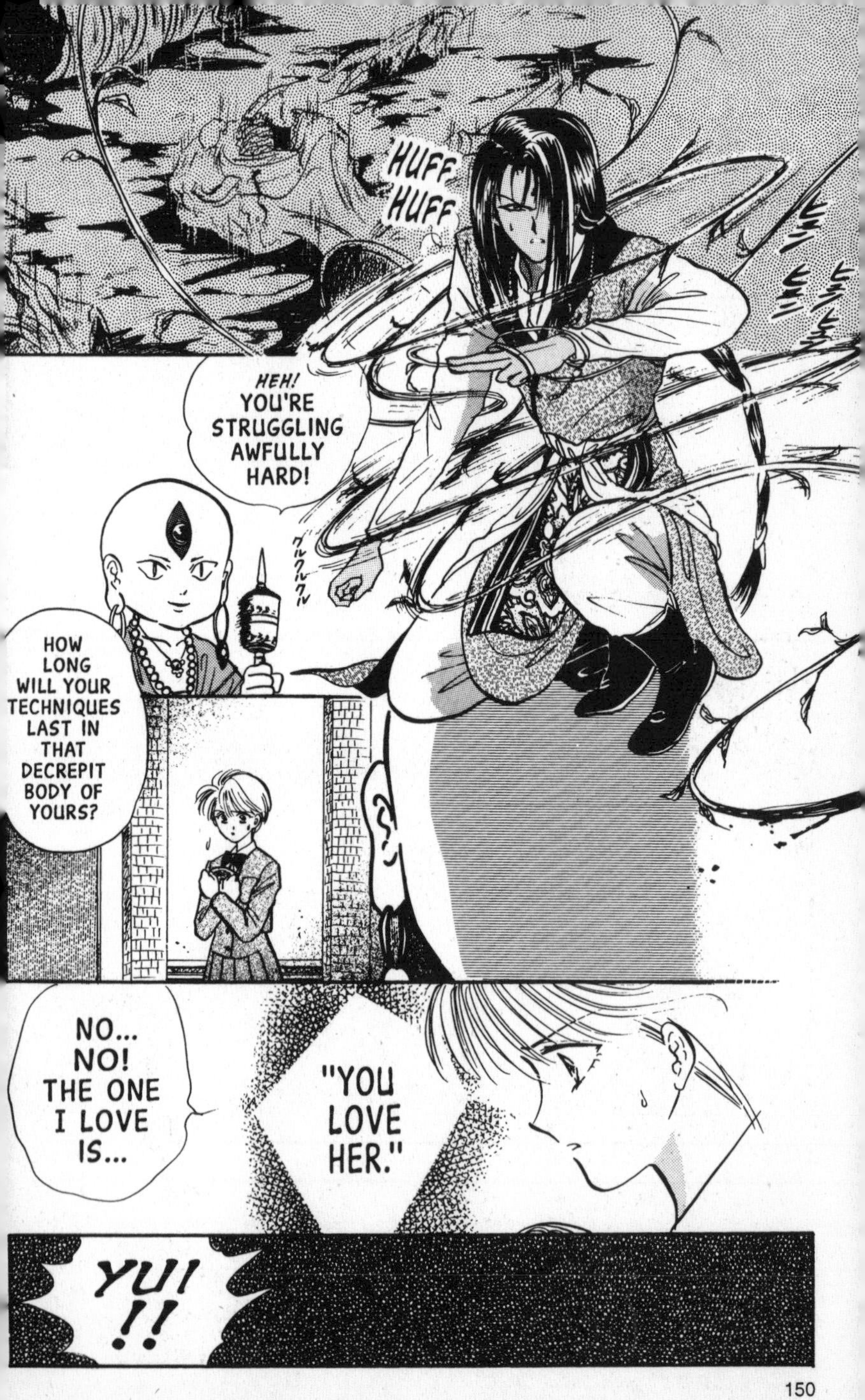
HUFF HUFF
HEH! YOU'RE STRUGGLING AWFULLY HARD!
HOW LONG WILL YOUR TECHNIQUES LAST IN THAT DECREPIT BODY OF YOURS?
"YOU LOVE HER."
NO... NO! THE ONE I LOVE IS...
YUI!!

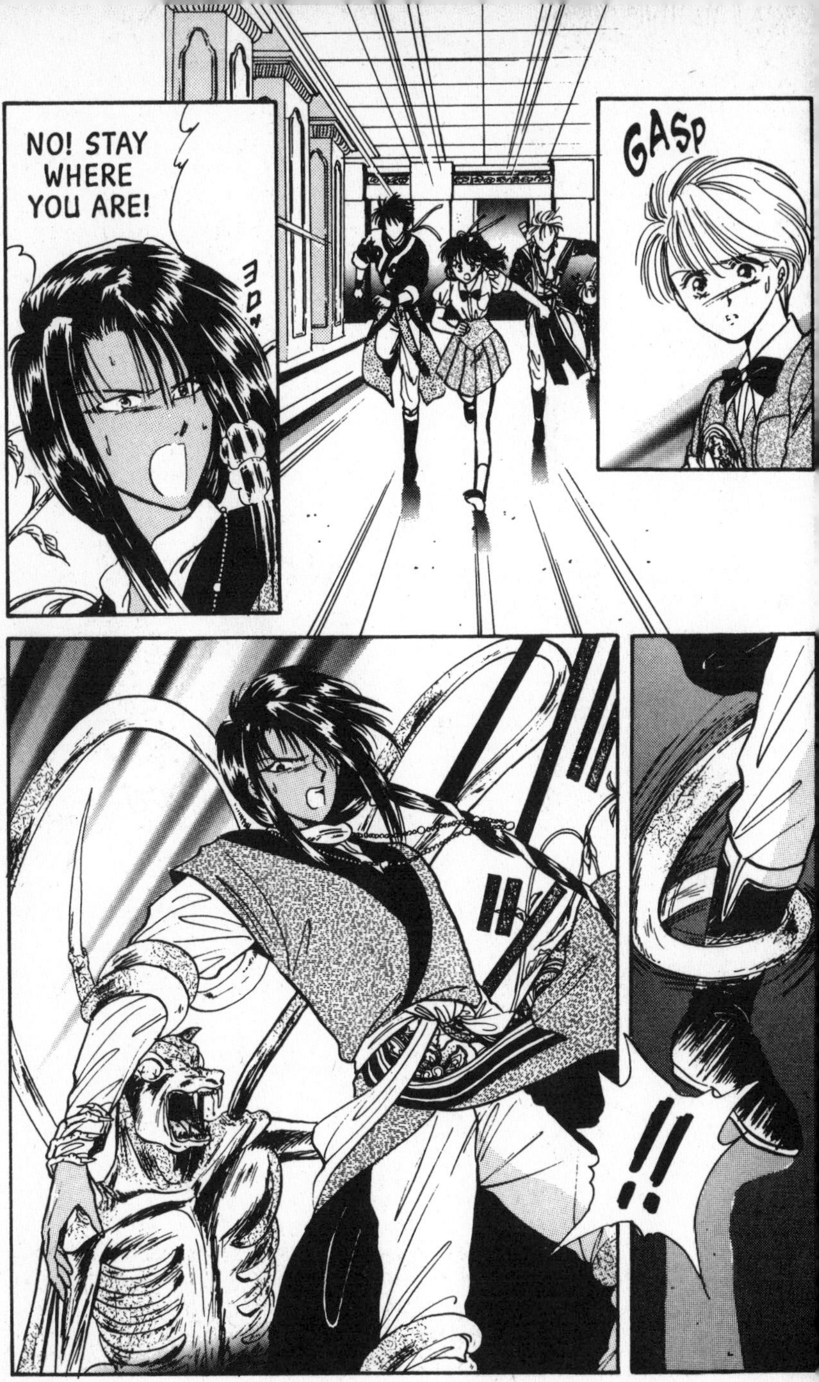
GASP
NO! STAY WHERE YOU ARE!
ヨロッ
!!

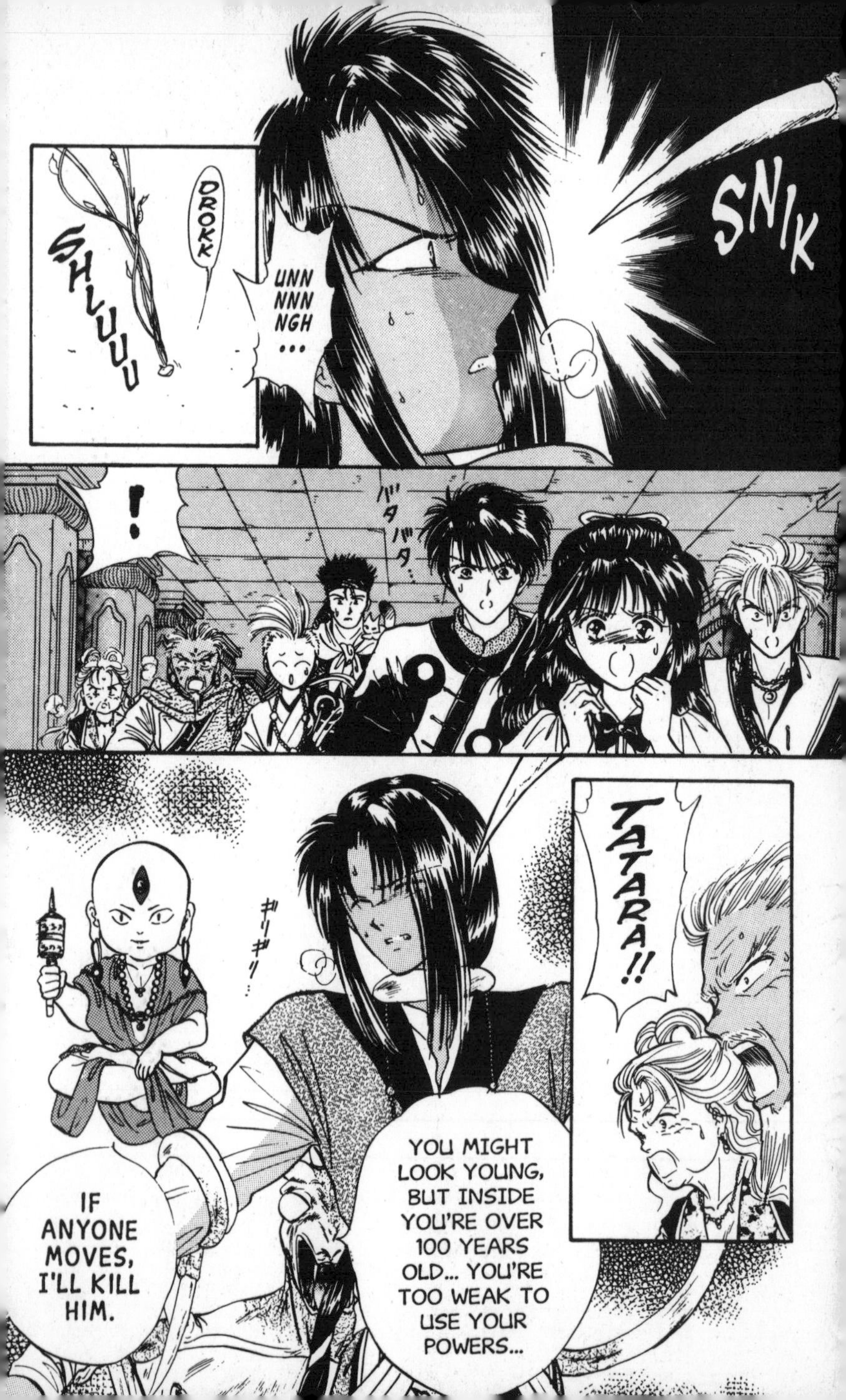
SNIK
UNN NNN NGH...
OROKK
SHLUUU...
!
バタバタ...
TATARA!!
YOU MIGHT LOOK YOUNG, BUT INSIDE YOU'RE OVER 100 YEARS OLD... YOU'RE TOO WEAK TO USE YOUR POWERS...
ギリギリ...
IF ANYONE MOVES, I'LL KILL HIM.

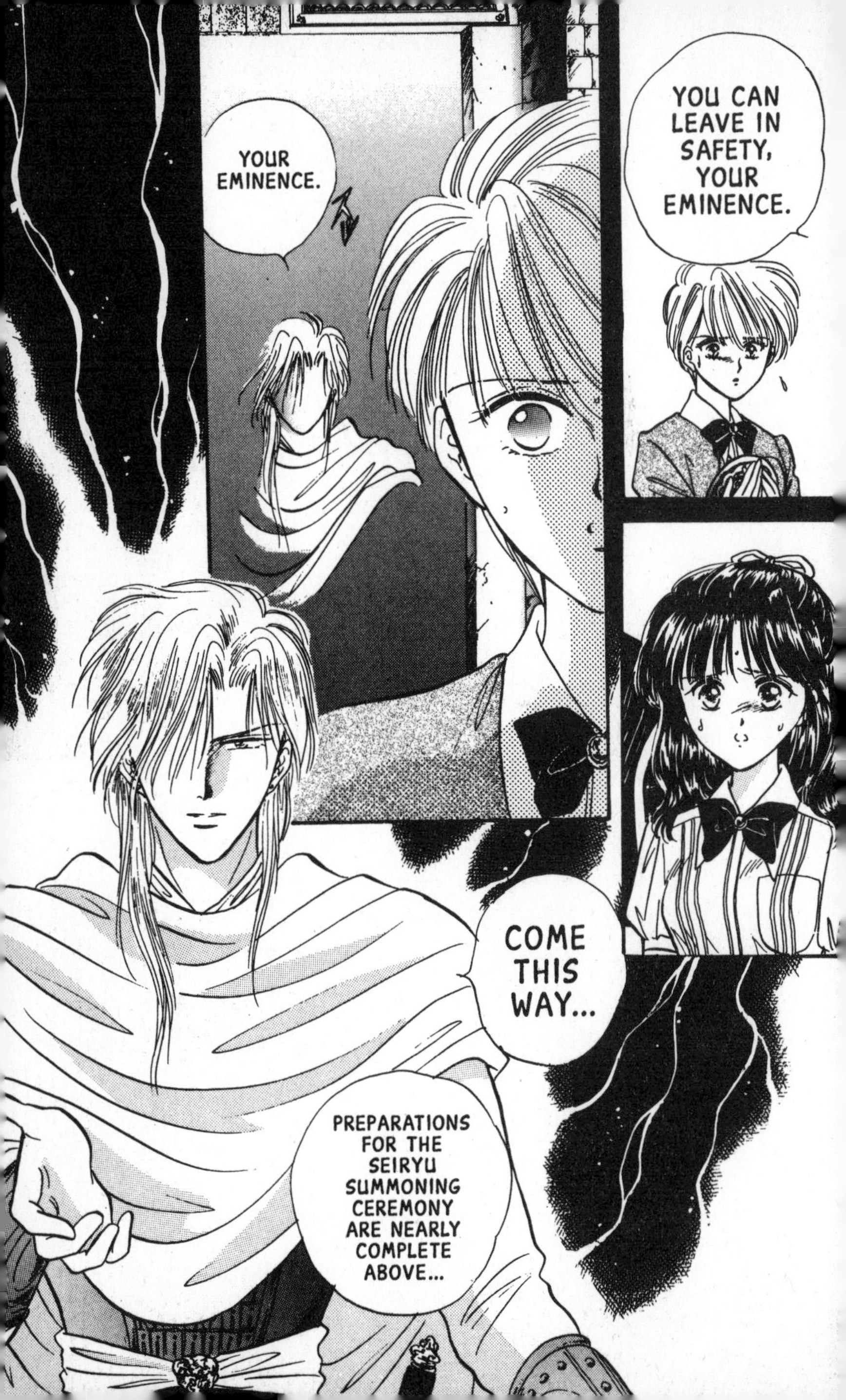
YOU CAN LEAVE IN SAFETY, YOUR EMINENCE.
YOUR EMINENCE.
COME THIS WAY...
PREPARATIONS FOR THE SEIRYU SUMMONING CEREMONY ARE NEARLY COMPLETE ABOVE...

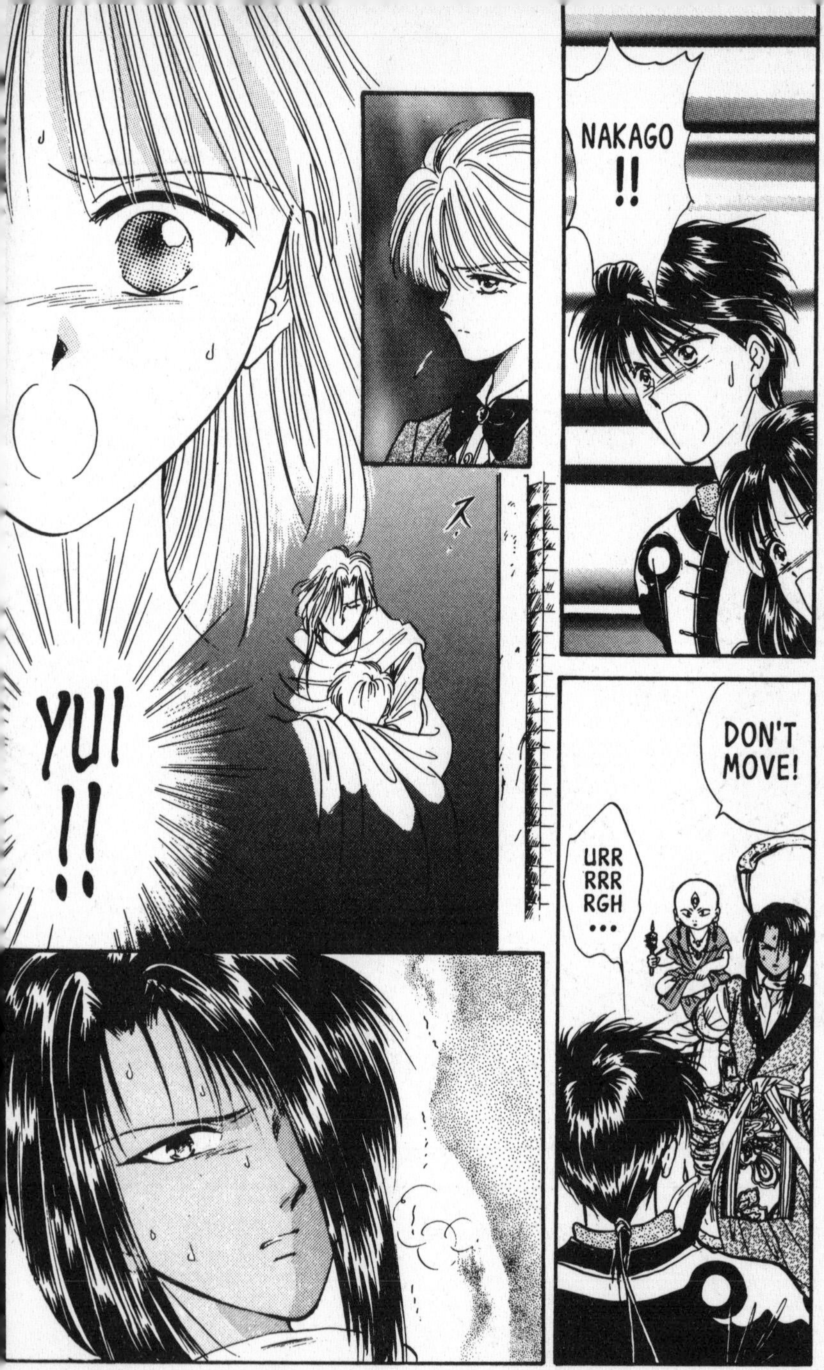
NAKAGO !!
ス
YUI !!
DON'T MOVE!
URR RRR RGH ...

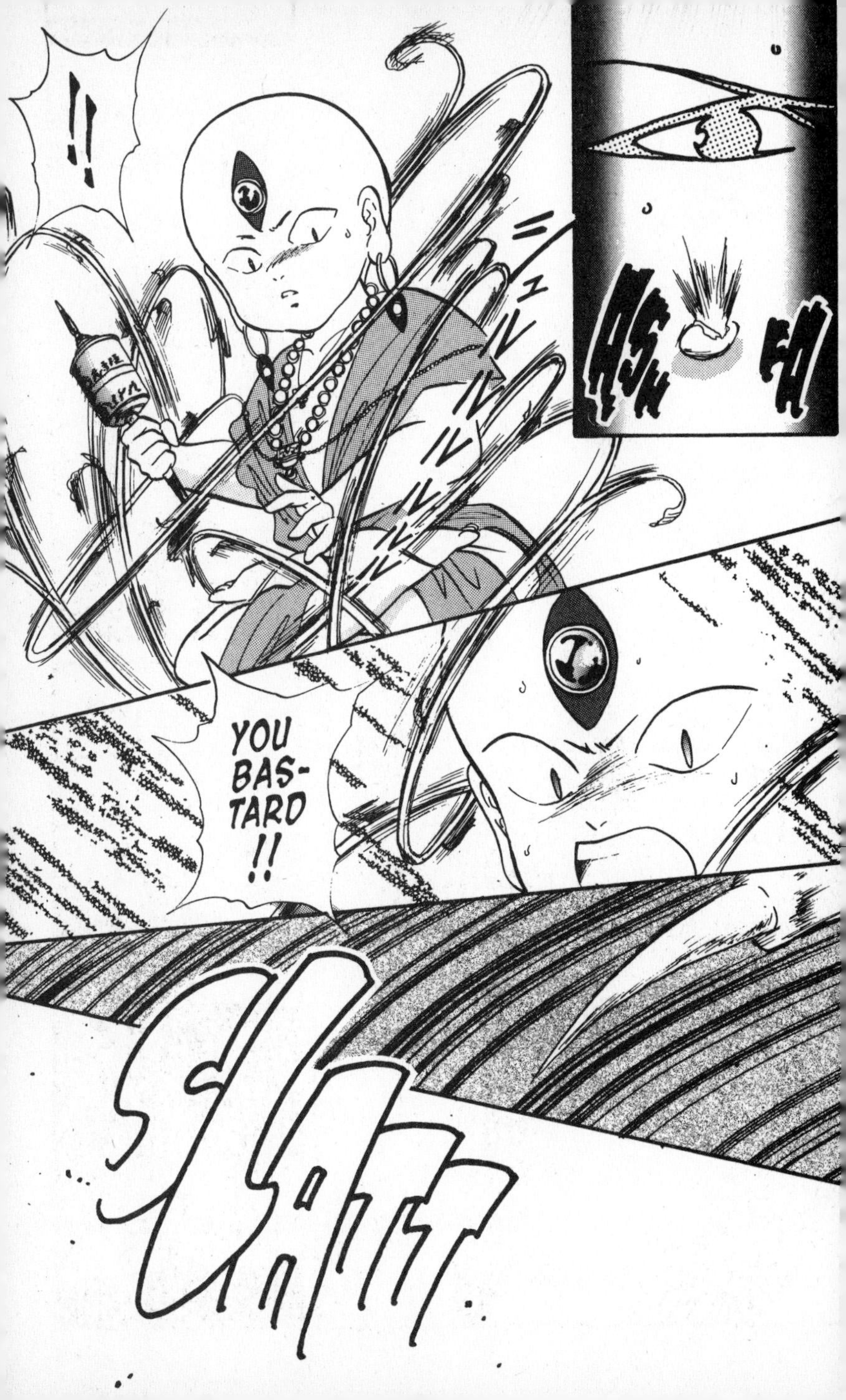
!!
YOU BAS-TARD !!

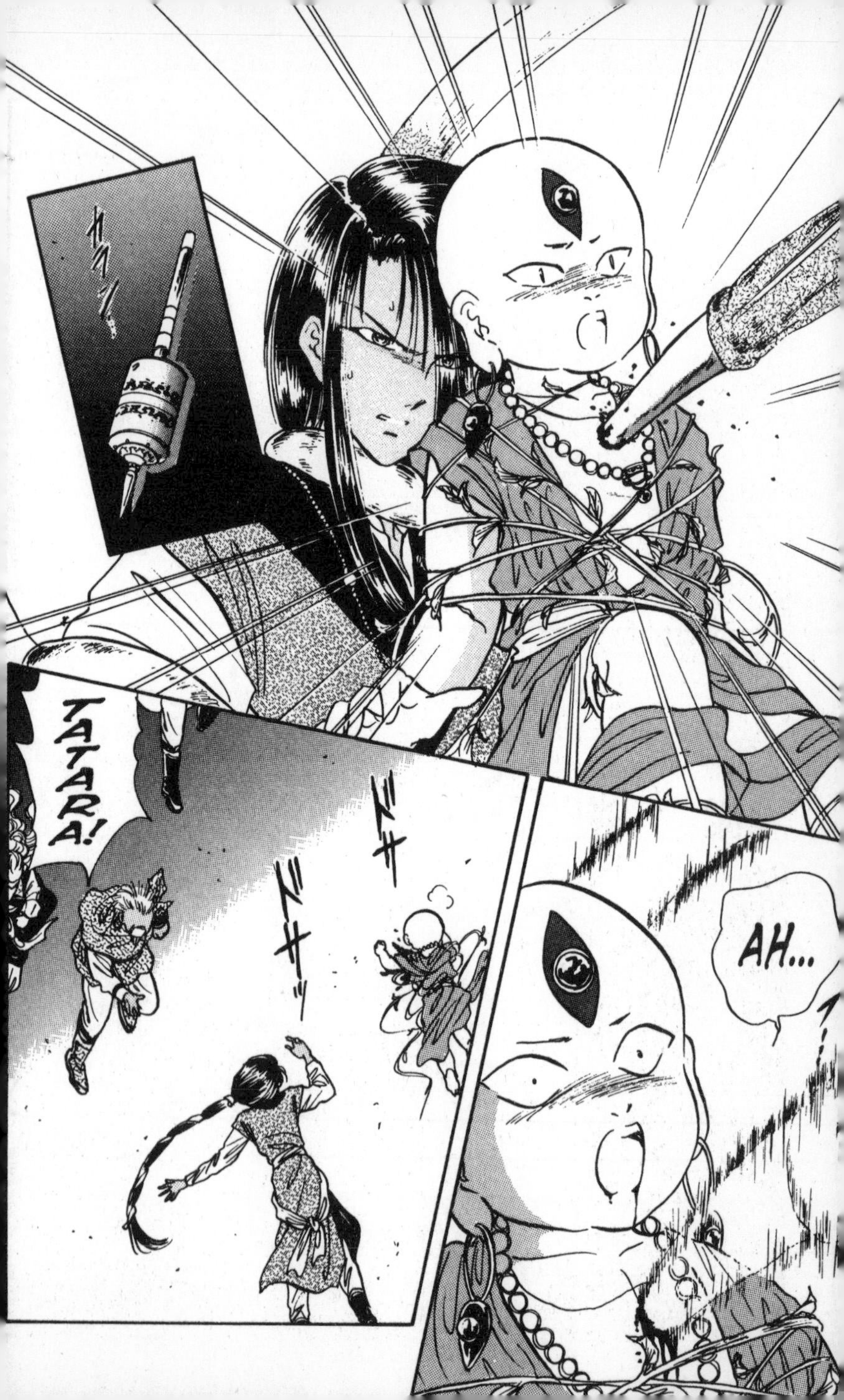
AH...
TATARA!

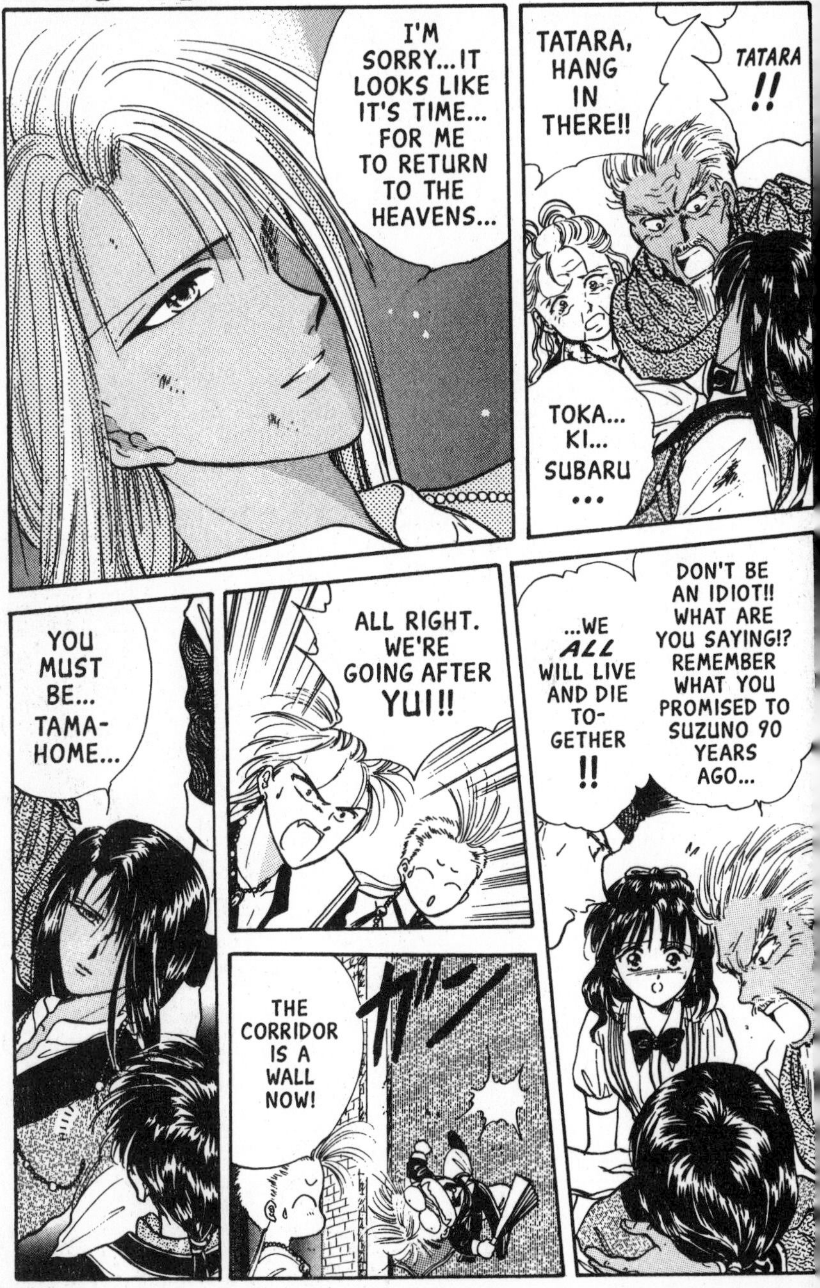
TATARA!!
TATARA, HANG IN THERE!!
TOKA... KI... SUBARU ...
I'M SORRY...IT LOOKS LIKE IT'S TIME... FOR ME TO RETURN TO THE HEAVENS...
DON'T BE AN IDIOT!! WHAT ARE YOU SAYING!? REMEMBER WHAT YOU PROMISED TO SUZUNO 90 YEARS AGO...
...WE ALL WILL LIVE AND DIE TO-GETHER!!
ALL RIGHT. WE'RE GOING AFTER YUI!!
THE CORRIDOR IS A WALL NOW!
YOU MUST BE... TAMA-HOME...

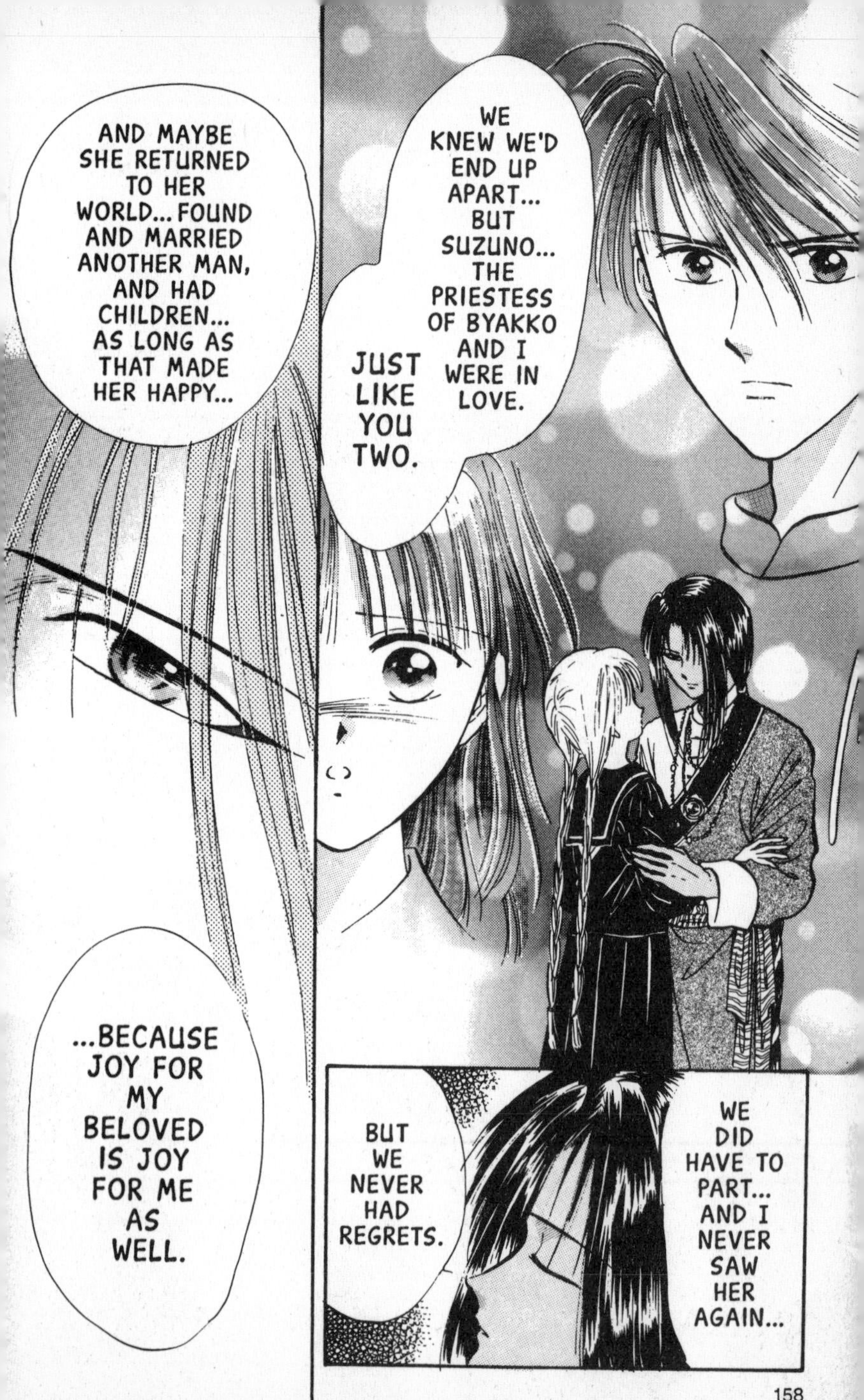
WE KNEW WE'D END UP APART... BUT SUZUNO... THE PRIESTESS OF BYAKKO AND I WERE IN LOVE.
JUST LIKE YOU TWO.
WE DID HAVE TO PART... AND I NEVER SAW HER AGAIN...
BUT WE NEVER HAD REGRETS.
AND MAYBE SHE RETURNED TO HER WORLD... FOUND AND MARRIED ANOTHER MAN, AND HAD CHILDREN... AS LONG AS THAT MADE HER HAPPY...
...BECAUSE JOY FOR MY BELOVED IS JOY FOR ME AS WELL.

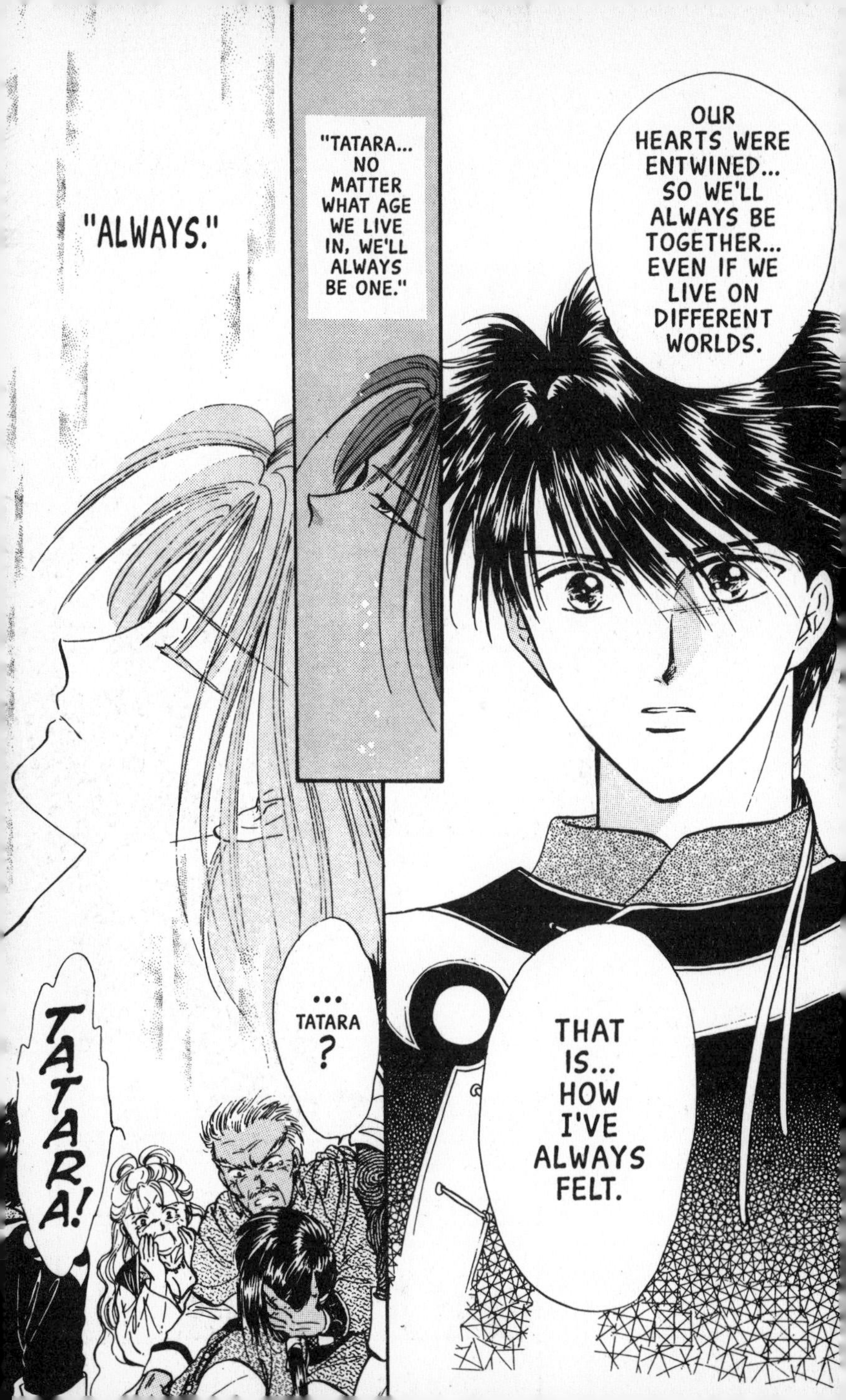
OUR HEARTS WERE ENTWINED... SO WE'LL ALWAYS BE TOGETHER... EVEN IF WE LIVE ON DIFFERENT WORLDS.
THAT IS... HOW I'VE ALWAYS FELT.
"TATARA... NO MATTER WHAT AGE WE LIVE IN, WE'LL ALWAYS BE ONE."
"ALWAYS."
...TATARA?
TATARA!

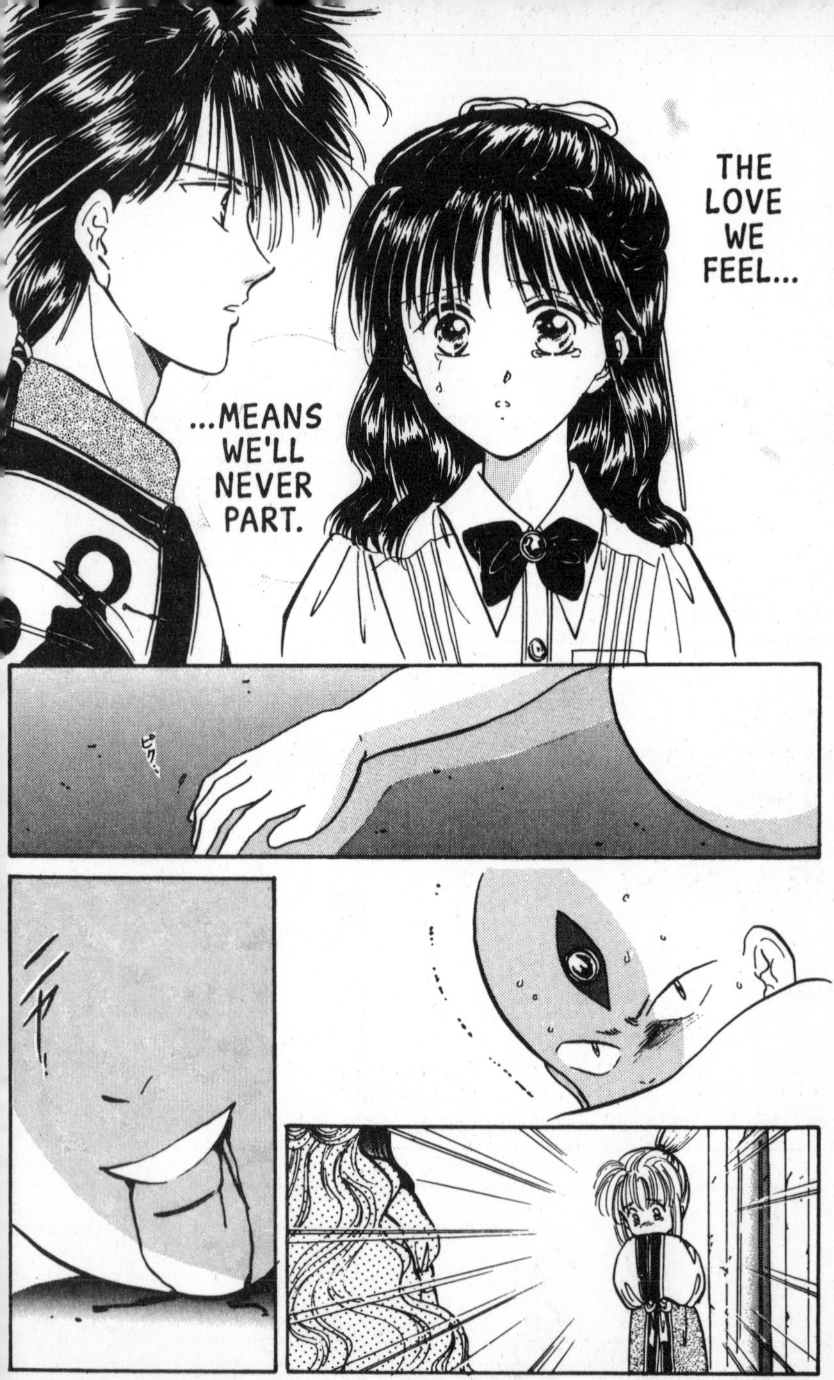
THE LOVE WE FEEL...
...MEANS WE'LL NEVER PART.
ピク…
ニヤ

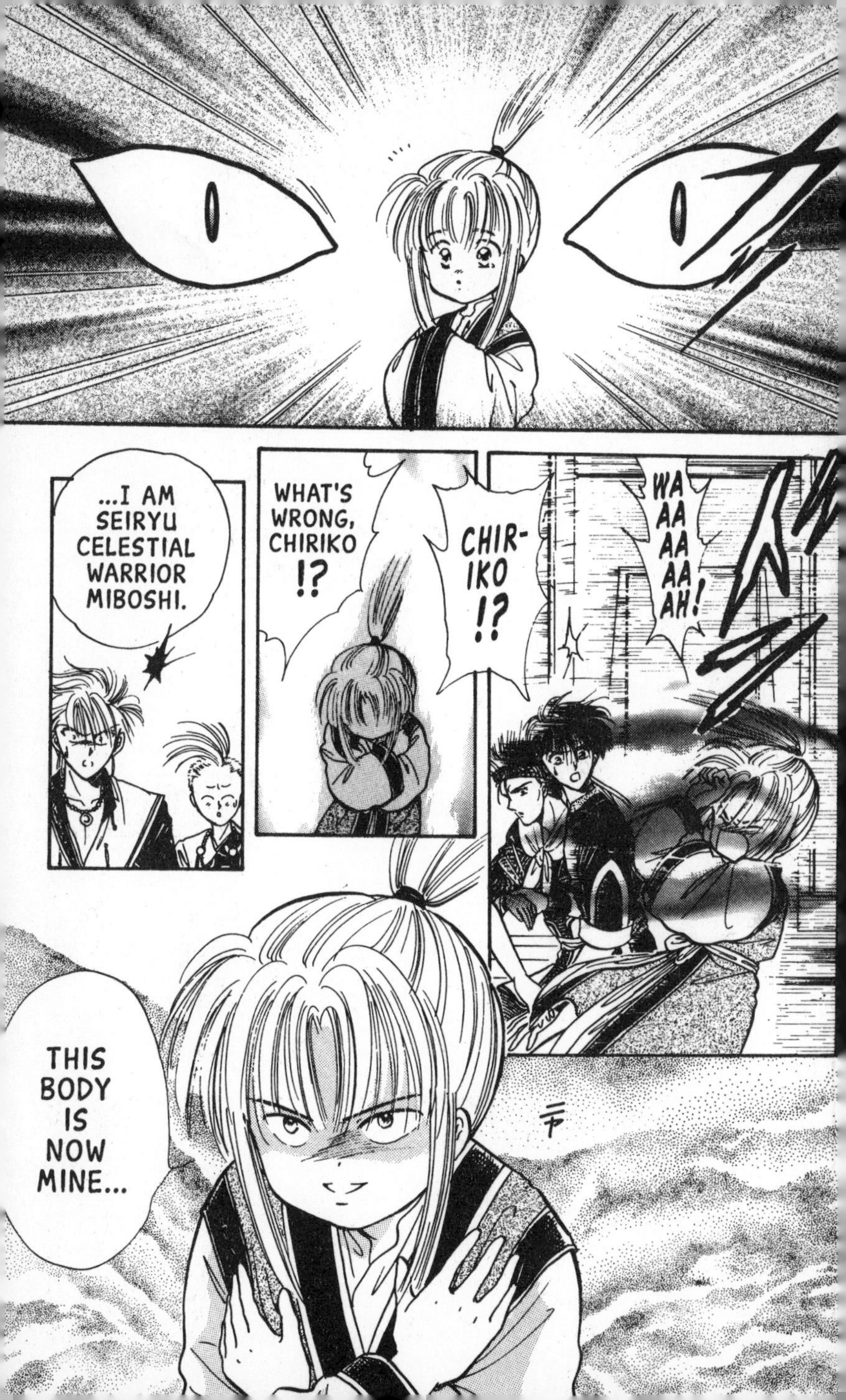
WAAAAAAAAH!
CHIRIKO!?
WHAT'S WRONG, CHIRIKO!?
...I AM SEIRYU CELESTIAL WARRIOR MIBOSHI.
THIS BODY IS NOW MINE...

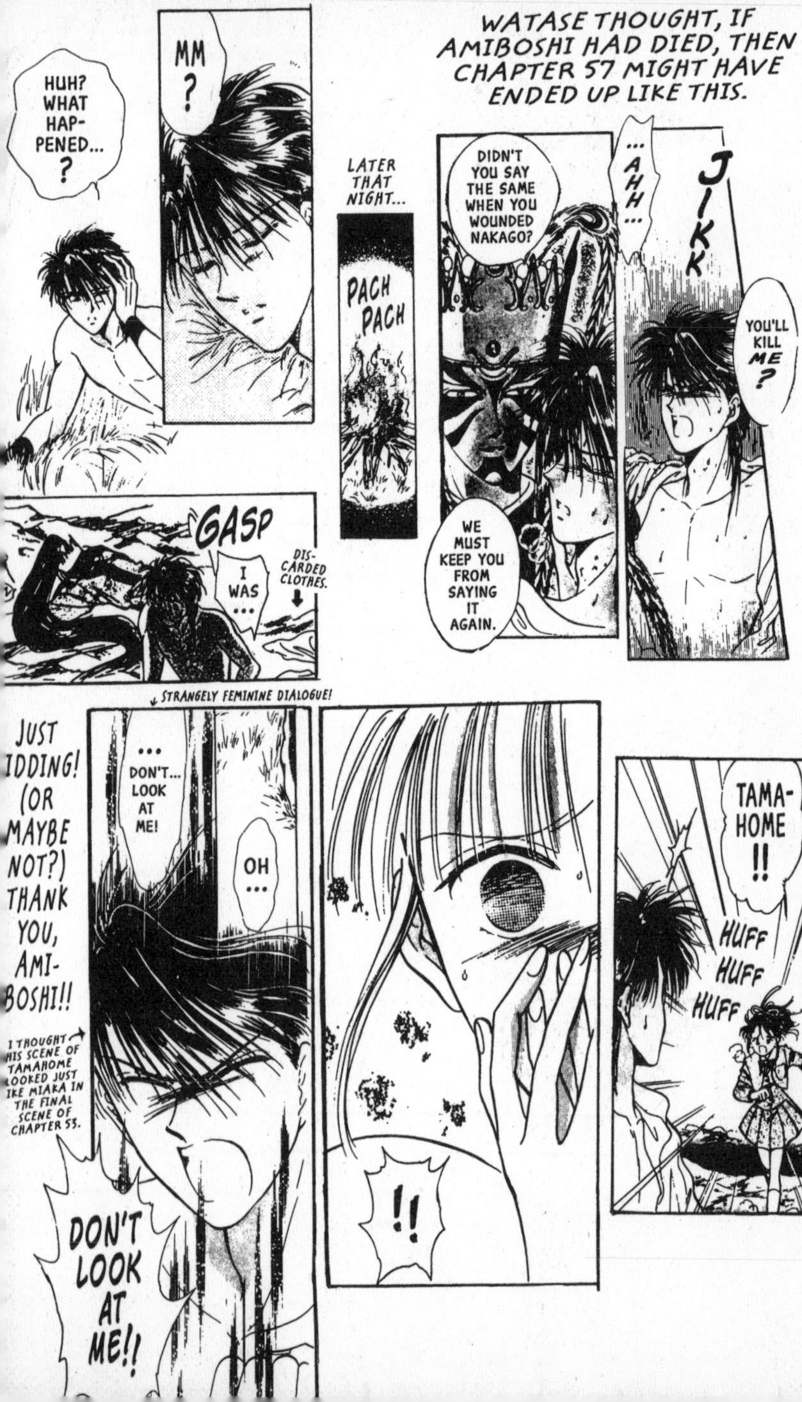
WATASE THOUGHT, IF AMIBOSHI HAD DIED, THEN CHAPTER 57 MIGHT HAVE ENDED UP LIKE THIS.
JIKK
...AHH...
YOU'LL KILL ME?
DIDN'T YOU SAY THE SAME WHEN YOU WOUNDED NAKAGO?
WE MUST KEEP YOU FROM SAYING IT AGAIN.
LATER THAT NIGHT...
PACH PACH
MM ?
HUH? WHAT HAP-PENED... ?
GASP
I WAS ...
DIS-CARDED CLOTHES.
TAMA-HOME !!
HUFF HUFF HUFF
!!
STRANGELY FEMININE DIALOGUE!
... DON'T... LOOK AT ME!
OH ...
DON'T LOOK AT ME!!
JUST IDDING! (OR MAYBE NOT?) THANK YOU, AMI-BOSHI!!
I THOUGHT HIS SCENE OF TAMAHOME LOOKED JUST IKE MIAKA IN THE FINAL SCENE OF CHAPTER 53.

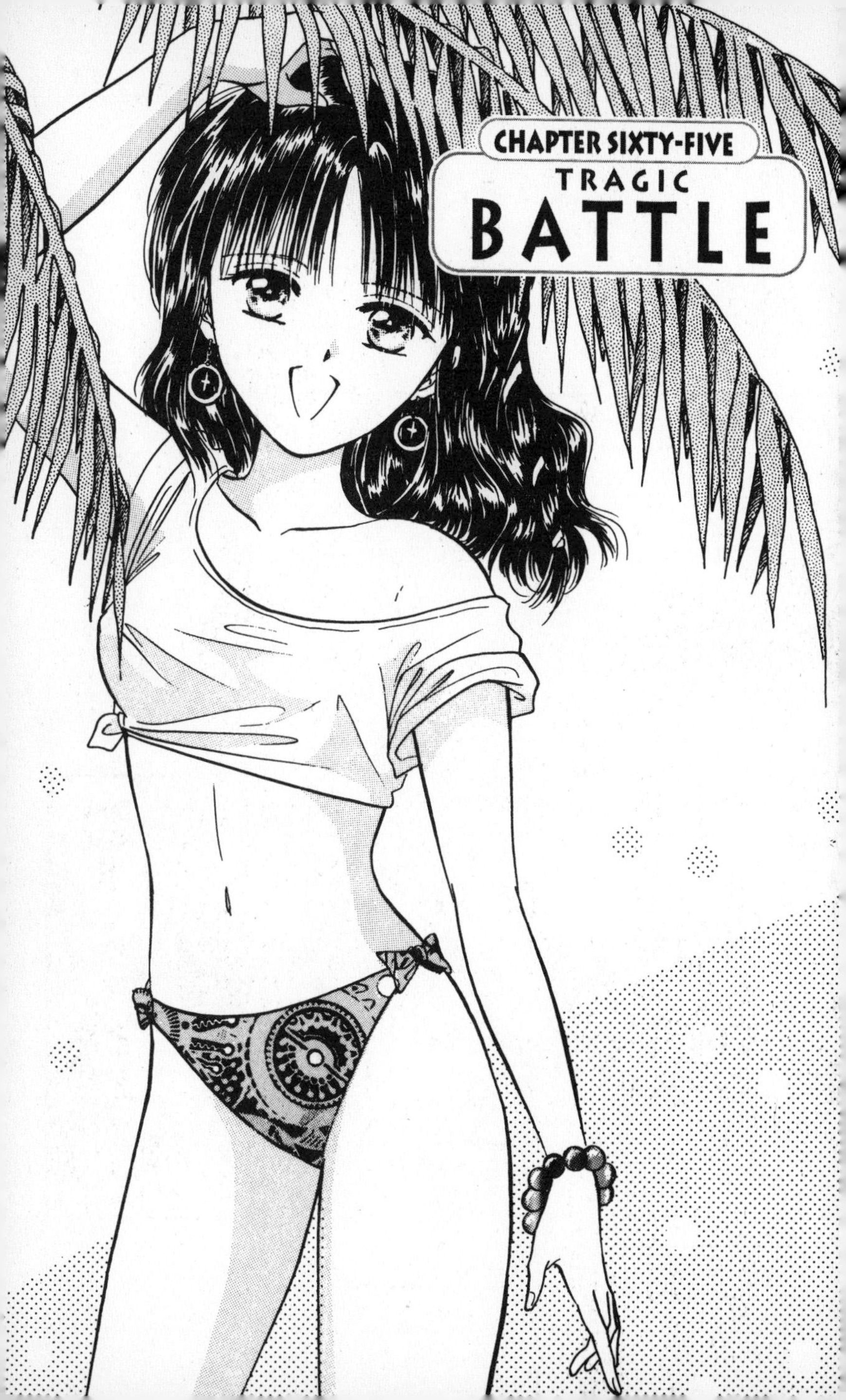
CHAPTER SIXTY-FIVE
TRAGIC
BATTLE

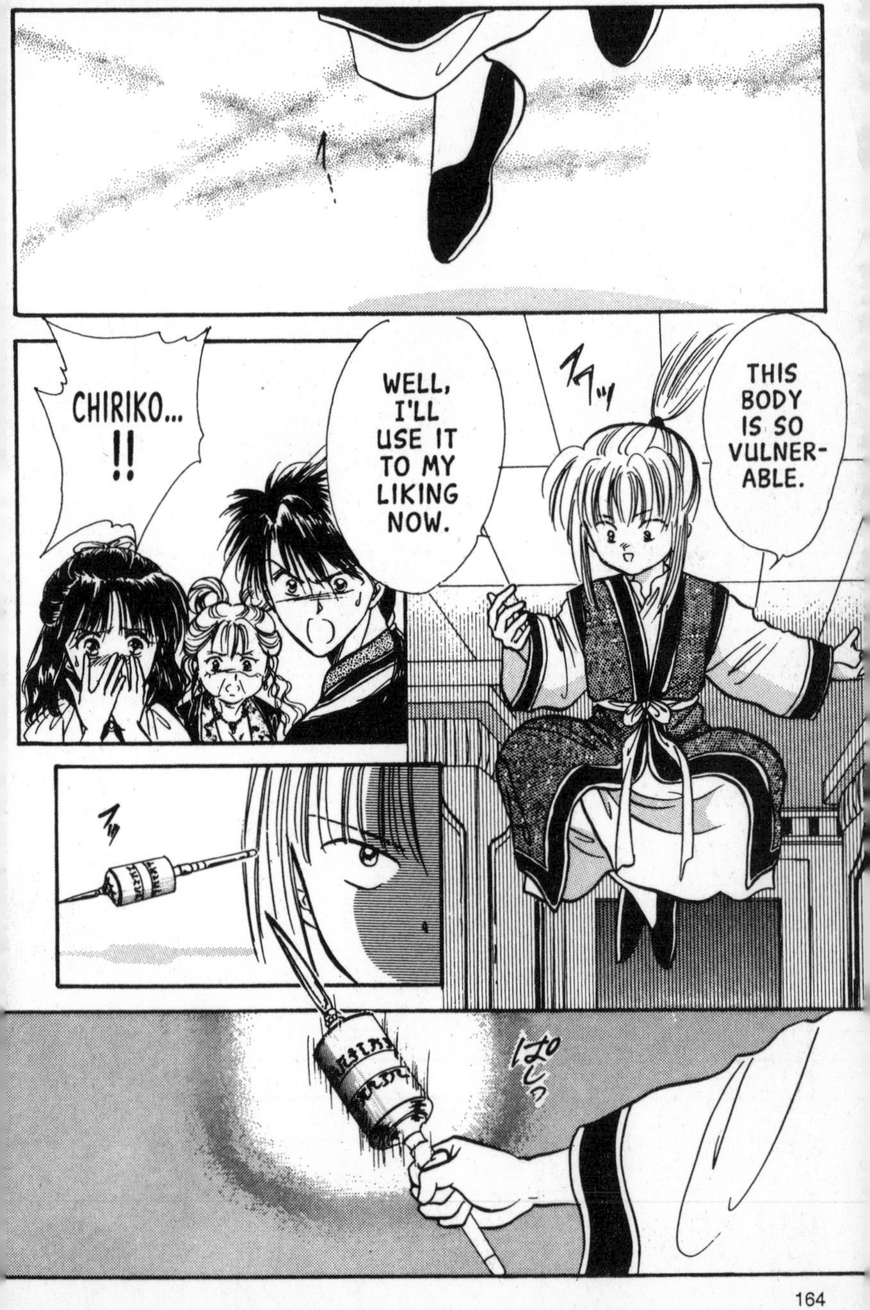

スッ
THIS BODY IS SO VULNERABLE.
WELL, I'LL USE IT TO MY LIKING NOW.
CHIRIKO... !!
フッ
ぱしっ

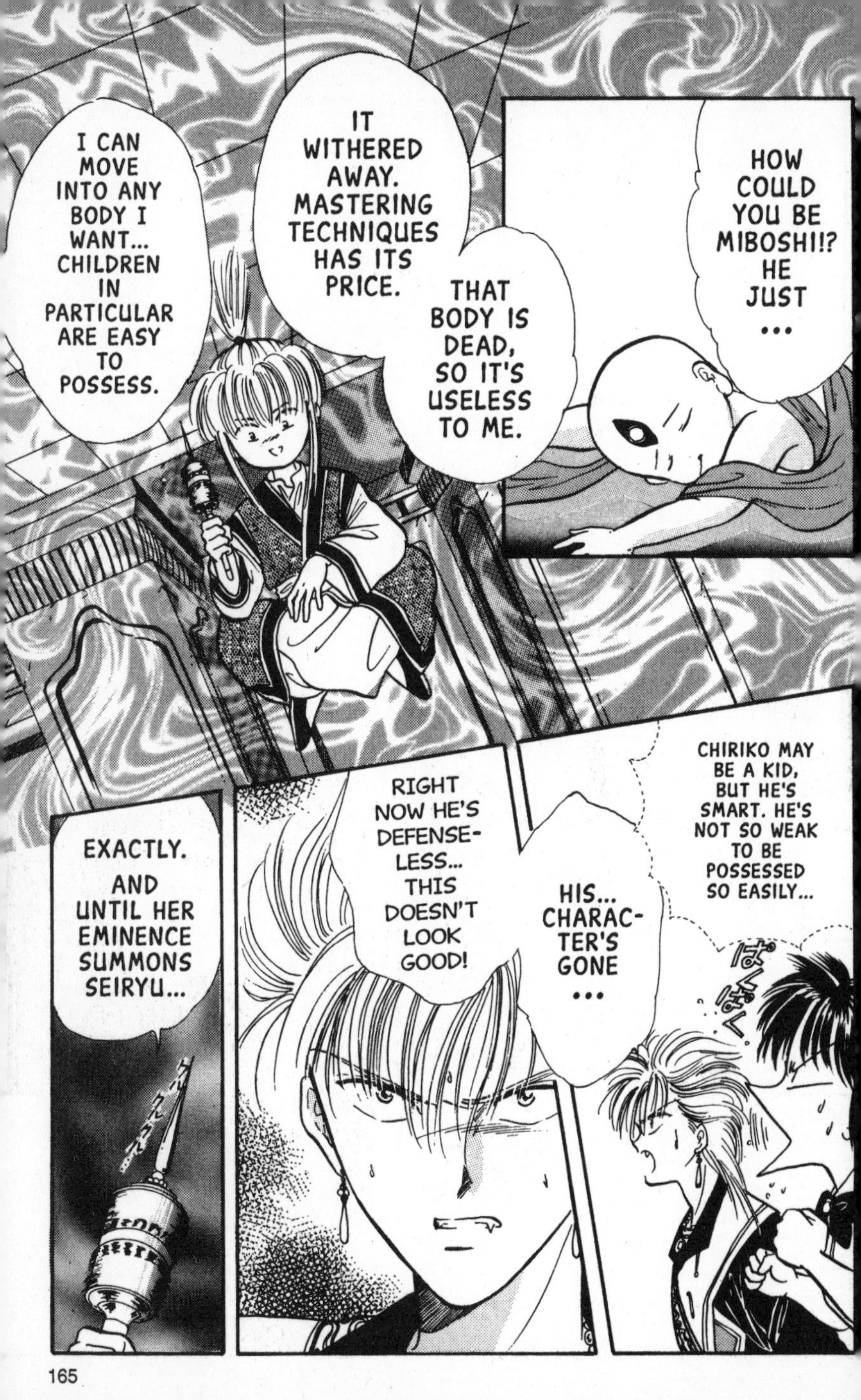
HOW COULD YOU BE MIBOSHI!? HE JUST ...
THAT BODY IS DEAD, SO IT'S USELESS TO ME.
IT WITHERED AWAY. MASTERING TECHNIQUES HAS ITS PRICE.
I CAN MOVE INTO ANY BODY I WANT... CHILDREN IN PARTICULAR ARE EASY TO POSSESS.
CHIRIKO MAY BE A KID, BUT HE'S SMART. HE'S NOT SO WEAK TO BE POSSESSED SO EASILY...
HIS... CHARACTER'S GONE ...
RIGHT NOW HE'S DEFENSE-LESS... THIS DOESN'T LOOK GOOD!
EXACTLY. AND UNTIL HER EMINENCE SUMMONS SEIRYU...

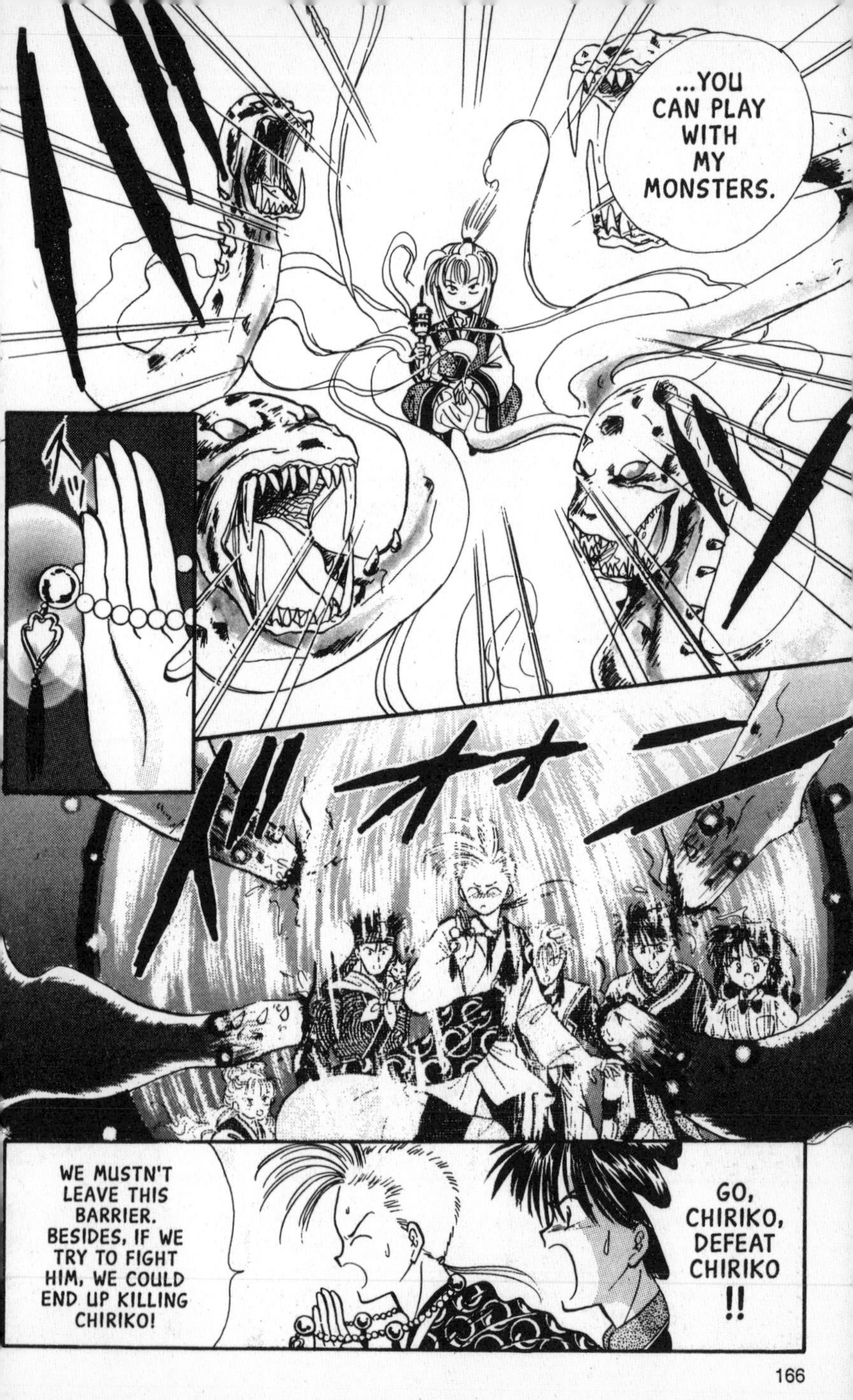
...YOU CAN PLAY WITH MY MONSTERS.
GO, CHIRIKO, DEFEAT CHIRIKO !!
WE MUSTN'T LEAVE THIS BARRIER. BESIDES, IF WE TRY TO FIGHT HIM, WE COULD END UP KILLING CHIRIKO!

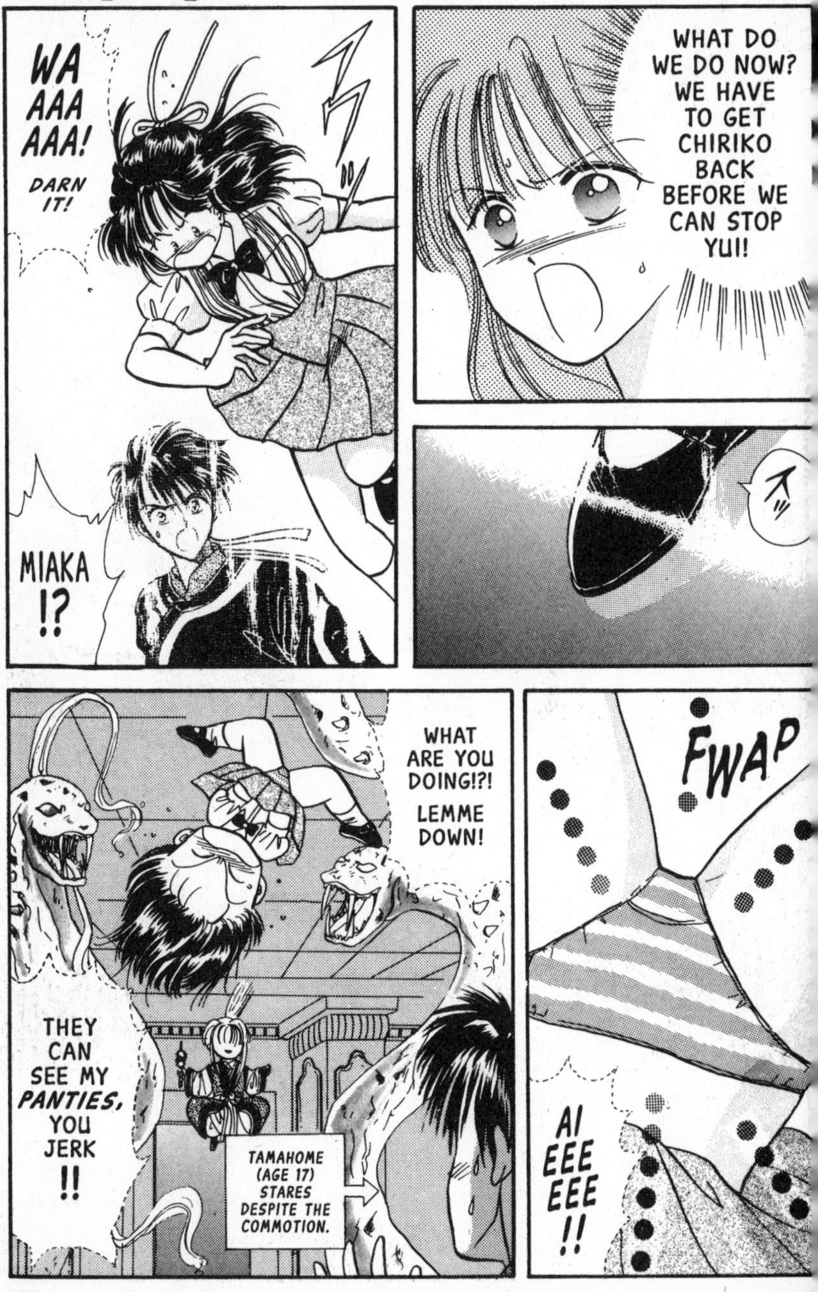
WHAT DO WE DO NOW? WE HAVE TO GET CHIRIKO BACK BEFORE WE CAN STOP YUI!
WA AAA AAA!
DARN IT!
MIAKA !?
FWAP
AI EEE EEE !!
WHAT ARE YOU DOING!?!
LEMME DOWN!
THEY CAN SEE MY *PANTIES*, YOU JERK !!
TAMAHOME (AGE 17) STARES DESPITE THE COMMOTION.

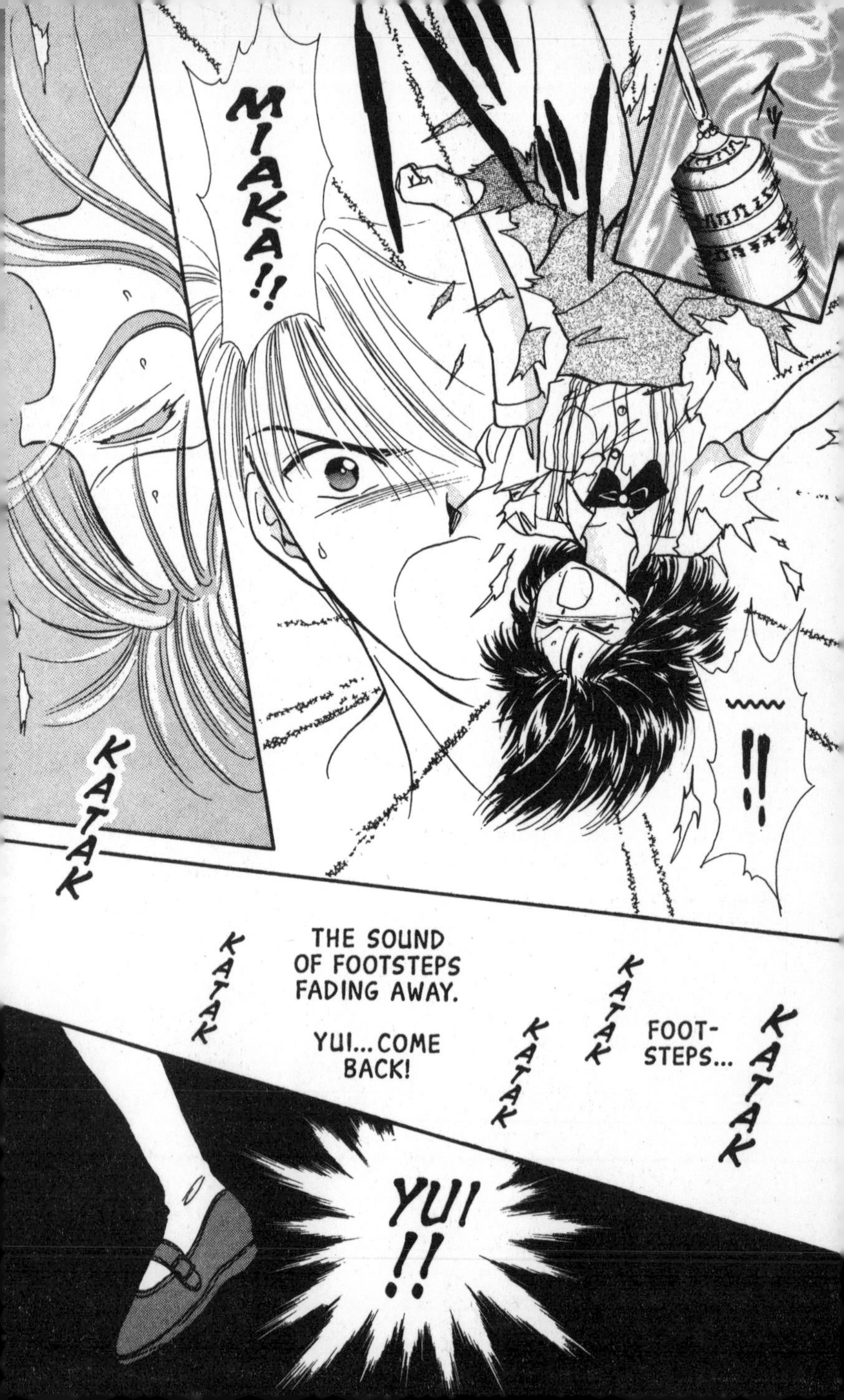
MIAKA!!
!!
KATAK
KATAK
FOOT-
STEPS...
KATAK
KATAK
THE SOUND
OF FOOTSTEPS
FADING AWAY.
YUI...COME
BACK!
KATAK
YUI
!!

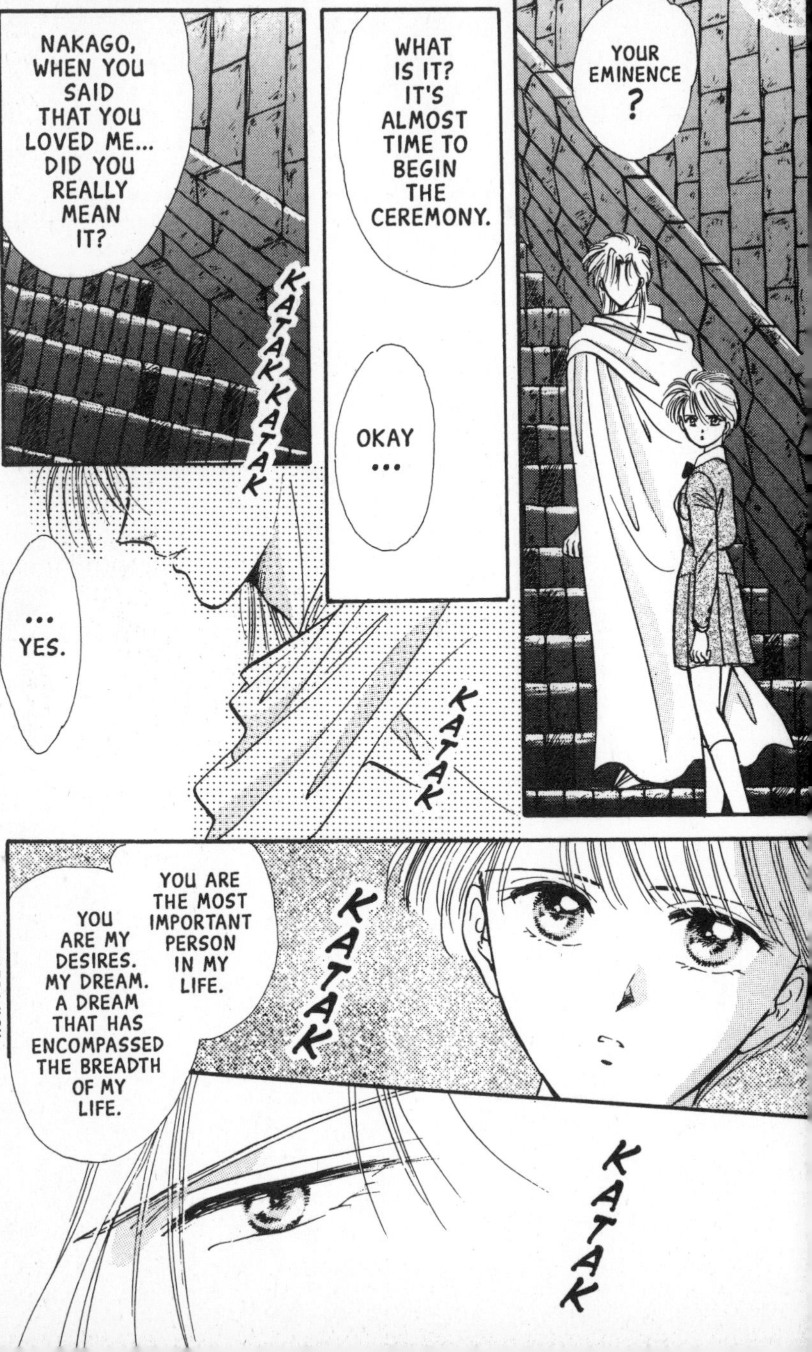
YOUR EMINENCE ?
WHAT IS IT? IT'S ALMOST TIME TO BEGIN THE CEREMONY.
OKAY ...
NAKAGO, WHEN YOU SAID THAT YOU LOVED ME... DID YOU REALLY MEAN IT?
KATAK KATAK
... YES.
KATAK
YOU ARE THE MOST IMPORTANT PERSON IN MY LIFE.
YOU ARE MY DESIRES. MY DREAM. A DREAM THAT HAS ENCOMPASSED THE BREADTH OF MY LIFE.
KATAK
KATAK

HOW POETIC...

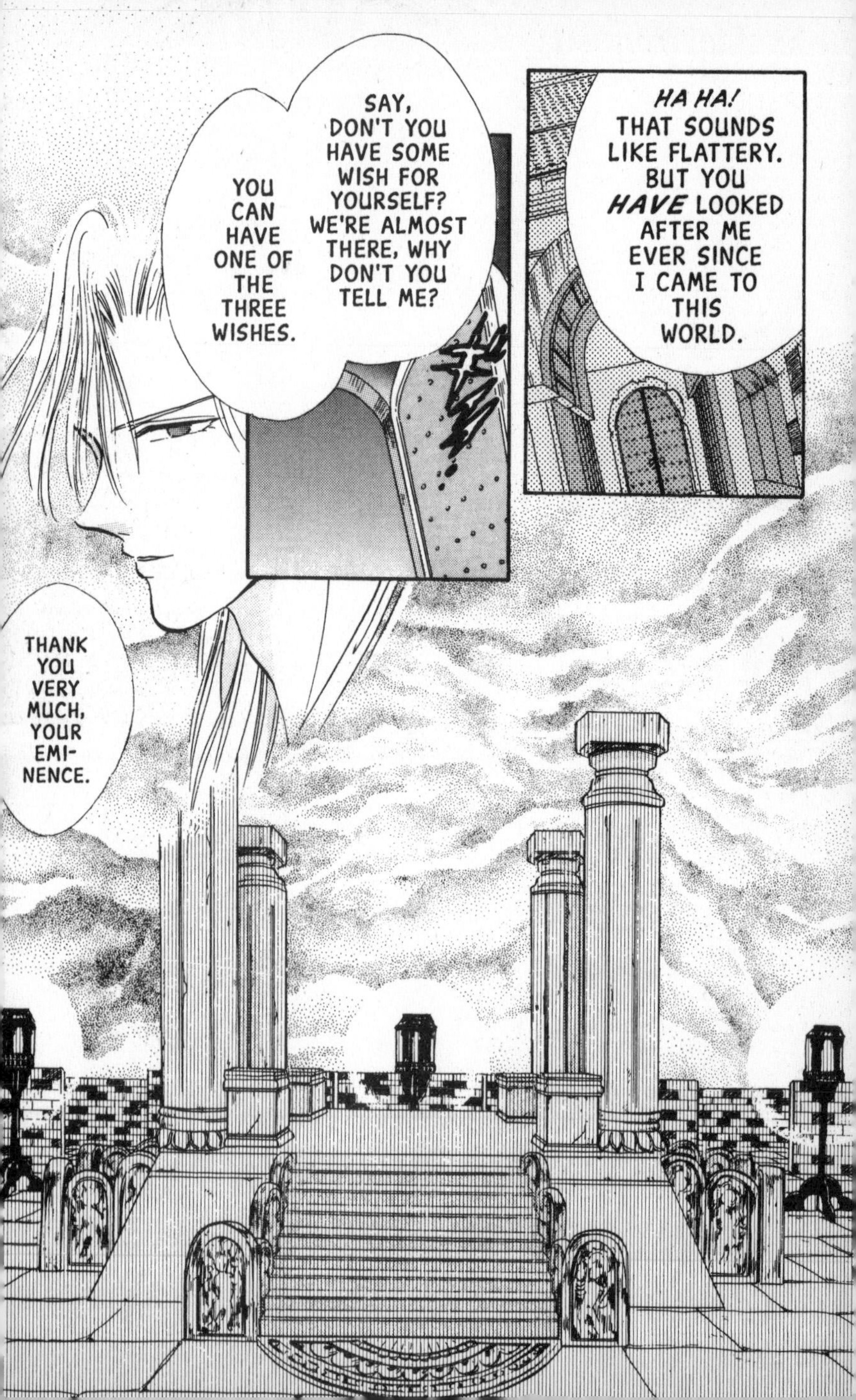
HA HA! THAT SOUNDS LIKE FLATTERY. BUT YOU HAVE LOOKED AFTER ME EVER SINCE I CAME TO THIS WORLD.
SAY, DON'T YOU HAVE SOME WISH FOR YOURSELF? WE'RE ALMOST THERE, WHY DON'T YOU TELL ME?
YOU CAN HAVE ONE OF THE THREE WISHES.
THANK YOU VERY MUCH, YOUR EMI-NENCE.

I knew that Chichiri's face would be a mask from the very start. I wanted him to be totally serious when the situation called for it, but at the same time be relaxed and not too concerned with the world. I bet the tone of his voice changes accordingly. I have to say, the times when he suddenly gets small are really popular.

Hey, I only managed to cover six of the warriors!! Well, that's about it for this volume. I'll continue this with volume 12. I'll cover the Seiryu celestial warriors too! Don't you want me to? Weeell, I will! I get the occasional fan mail where someone asks me why I have to pick on Miaka so much. I'm not so interested in picking on her as I am in showing her rise above her challenges. I guess it's all right for some people to have a protagonist who doesn't have to suffer...someone who's always nurtured...where everything works out fine. But I wanted Miaka to be challenged.
I mean, reality is hard! So I'm hoping my readers will be encouraged to do their best once they see her trying hard too. My readers are always supporting me, but I'm also trying to encourage my readers as well.
...since I can't respond to your letters.

Now, the 1995 calendar will be out in November. This time, there'll be five new drawings. That's one less than last time, but in exchange, I plan to draw a whole lot of new pictures for a book of illustrations! Also, the second novelization of Prepubescence will be out in November. Like the previous one, all the illustrations will be new. I hope you get a chance to pick one up.
See you.

'94 9/5

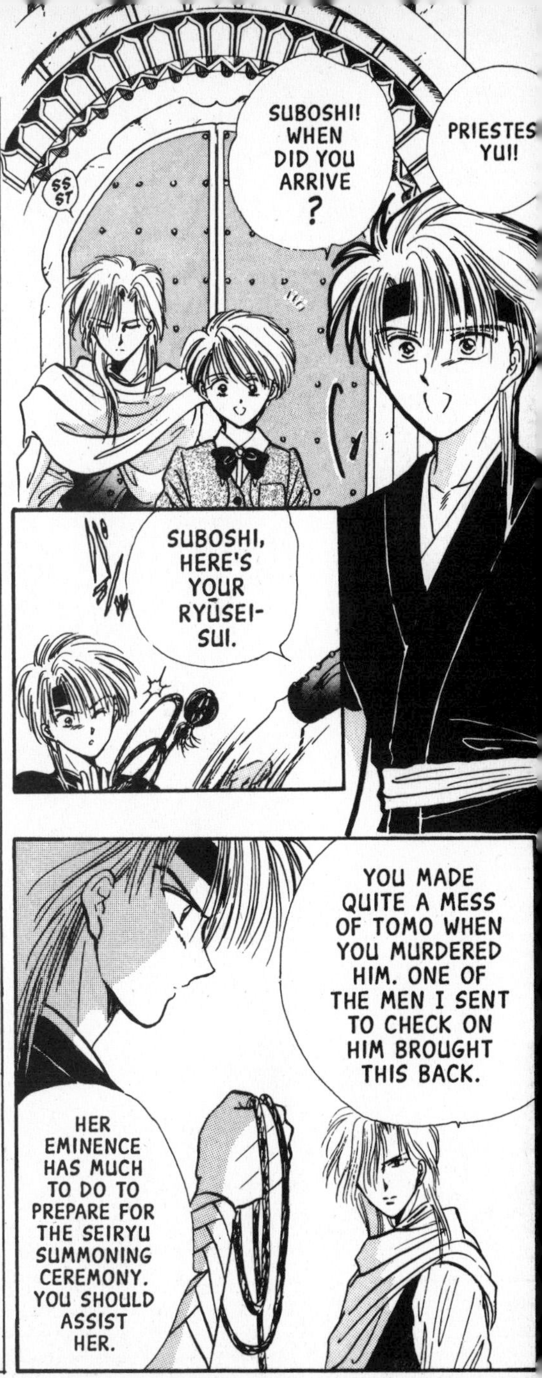
PRIESTES YUI!
SUBOSHI! WHEN DID YOU ARRIVE ?
SS ST
SUBOSHI, HERE'S YOUR RYŪSEI-SUI.
YOU MADE QUITE A MESS OF TOMO WHEN YOU MURDERED HIM. ONE OF THE MEN I SENT TO CHECK ON HIM BROUGHT THIS BACK.
HER EMINENCE HAS MUCH TO DO TO PREPARE FOR THE SEIRYU SUMMONING CEREMONY. YOU SHOULD ASSIST HER.

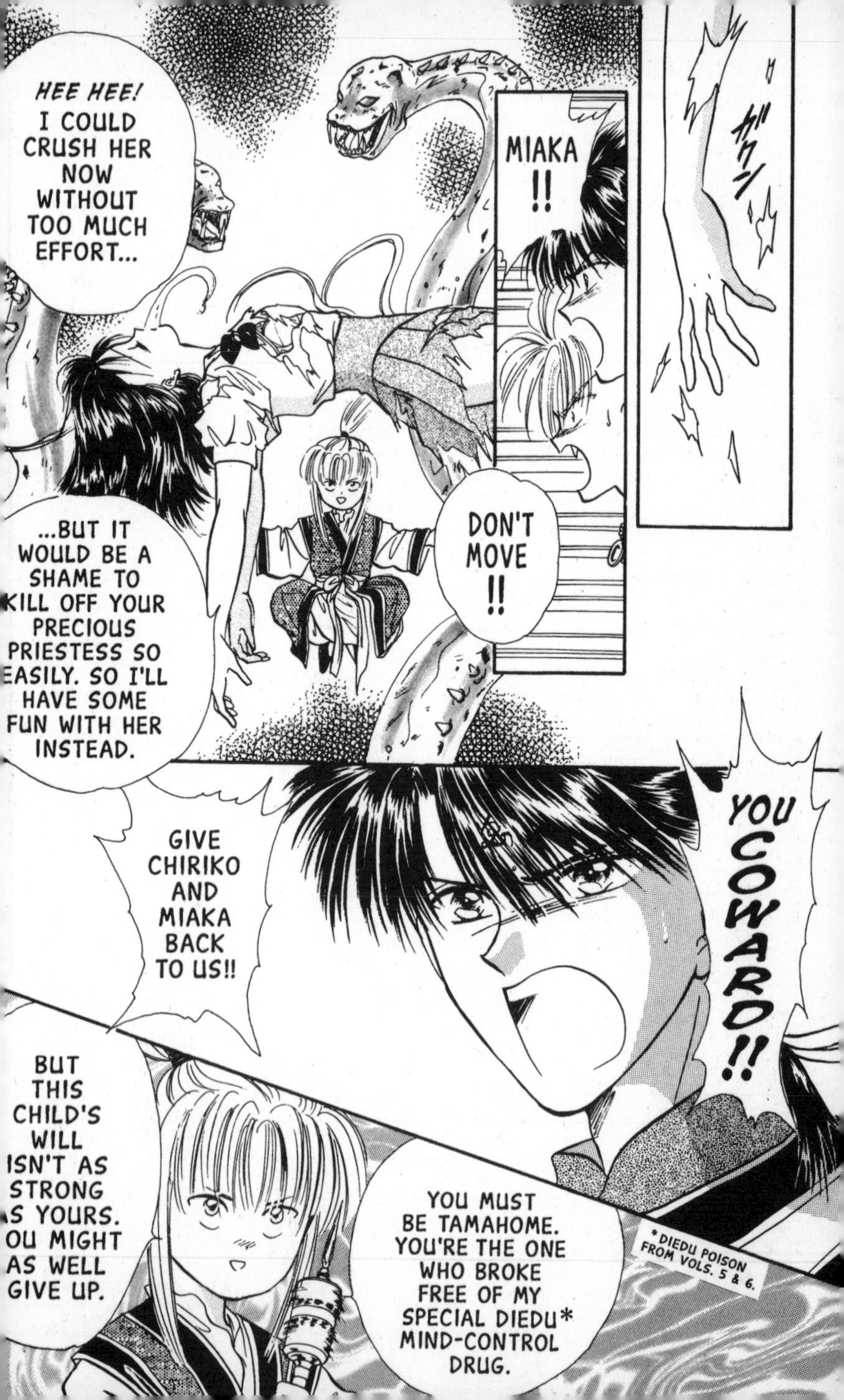
ガクン
MIAKA!!
DON'T MOVE!!
HEE HEE! I COULD CRUSH HER NOW WITHOUT TOO MUCH EFFORT...
...BUT IT WOULD BE A SHAME TO KILL OFF YOUR PRECIOUS PRIESTESS SO EASILY. SO I'LL HAVE SOME FUN WITH HER INSTEAD.
YOU COWARD!!
GIVE CHIRIKO AND MIAKA BACK TO US!!
YOU MUST BE TAMAHOME. YOU'RE THE ONE WHO BROKE FREE OF MY SPECIAL DIEDU* MIND-CONTROL DRUG.
*DIEDU POISON FROM VOLS. 5 & 6.
BUT THIS CHILD'S WILL ISN'T AS STRONG AS YOURS. OU MIGHT AS WELL GIVE UP.

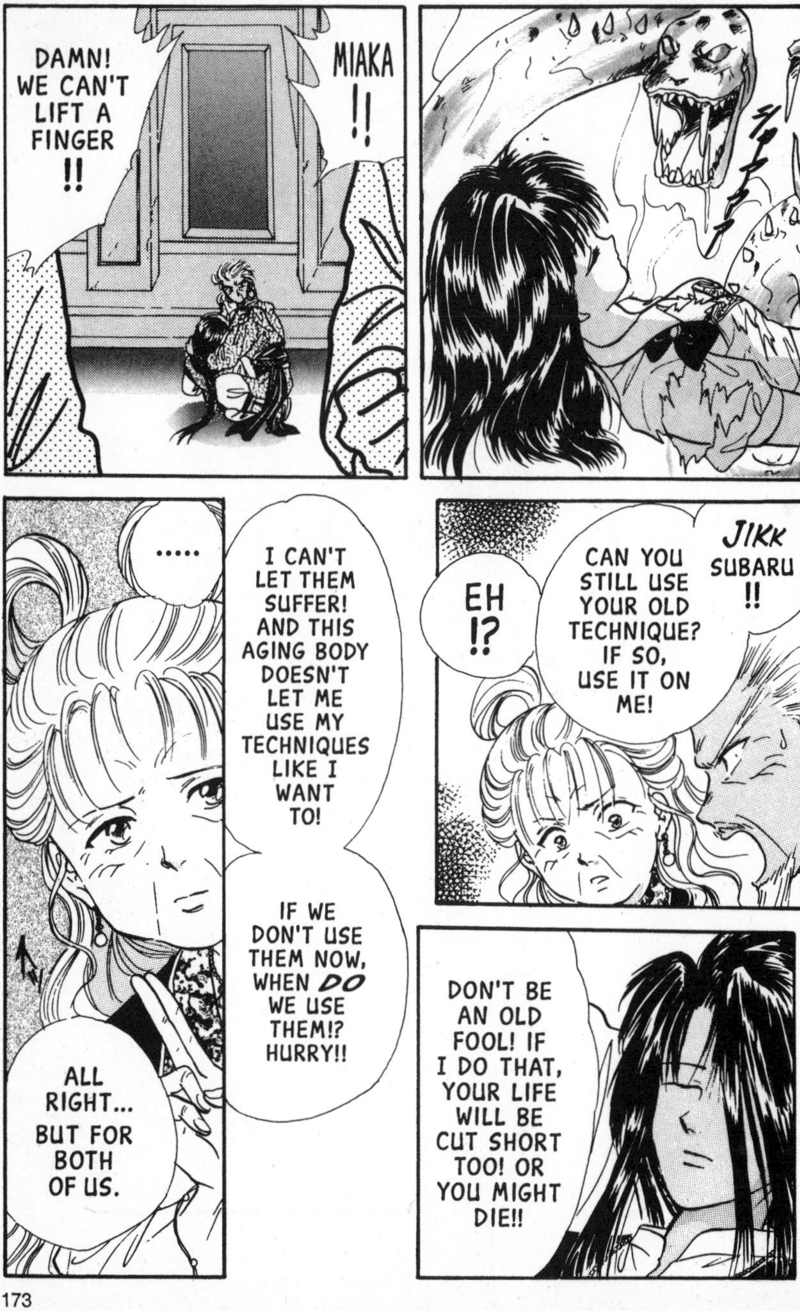
MIAKA!!
DAMN! WE CAN'T LIFT A FINGER!!
JIKK SUBARU!!
CAN YOU STILL USE YOUR OLD TECHNIQUE? IF SO, USE IT ON ME!
EH!?
DON'T BE AN OLD FOOL! IF I DO THAT, YOUR LIFE WILL BE CUT SHORT TOO! OR YOU MIGHT DIE!!
.....
I CAN'T LET THEM SUFFER! AND THIS AGING BODY DOESN'T LET ME USE MY TECHNIQUES LIKE I WANT TO!
IF WE DON'T USE THEM NOW, WHEN *DO* WE USE THEM!? HURRY!!
ALL RIGHT... BUT FOR BOTH OF US.

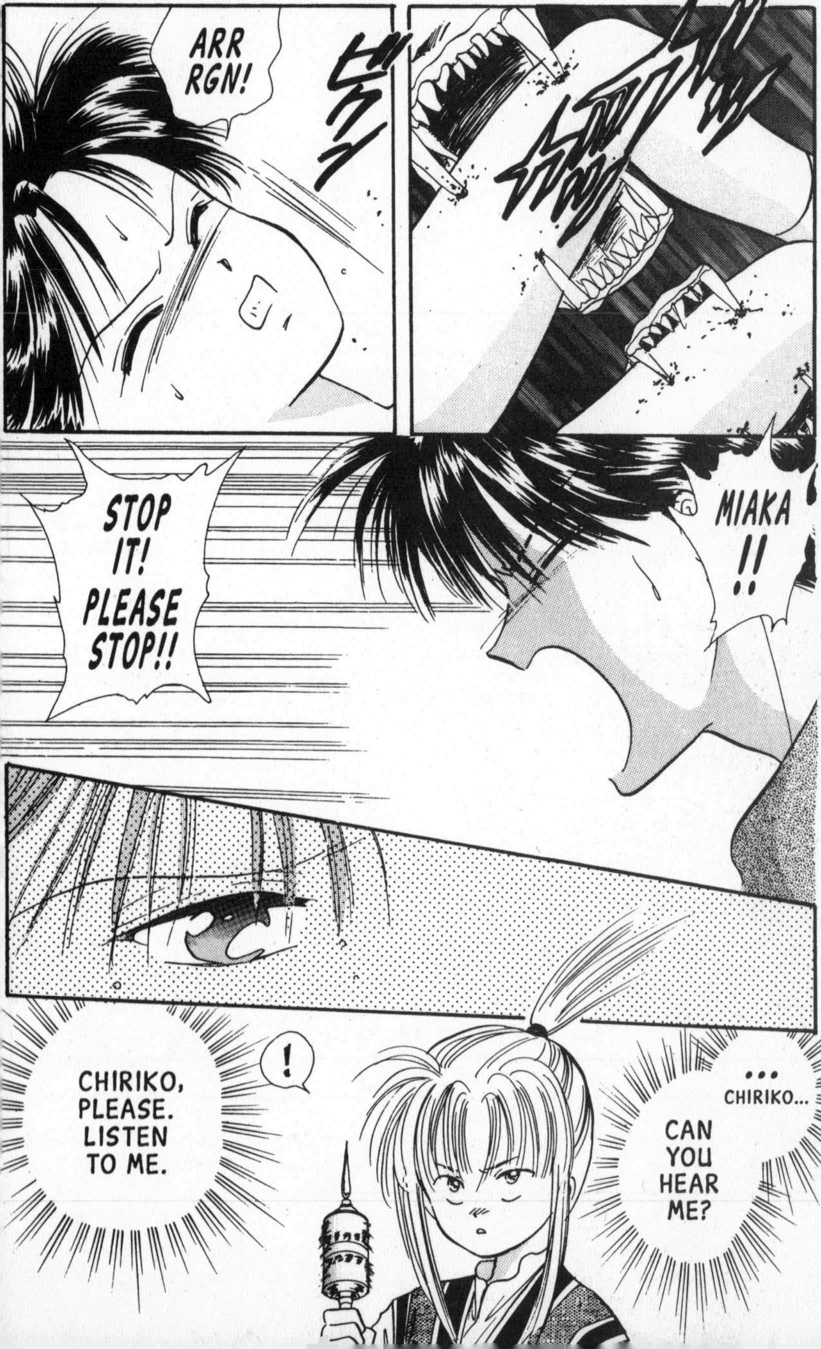
ARR RGN!
MIAKA !!
STOP IT! PLEASE STOP!!
... CHIRIKO...
CAN YOU HEAR ME?
!
CHIRIKO, PLEASE. LISTEN TO ME.

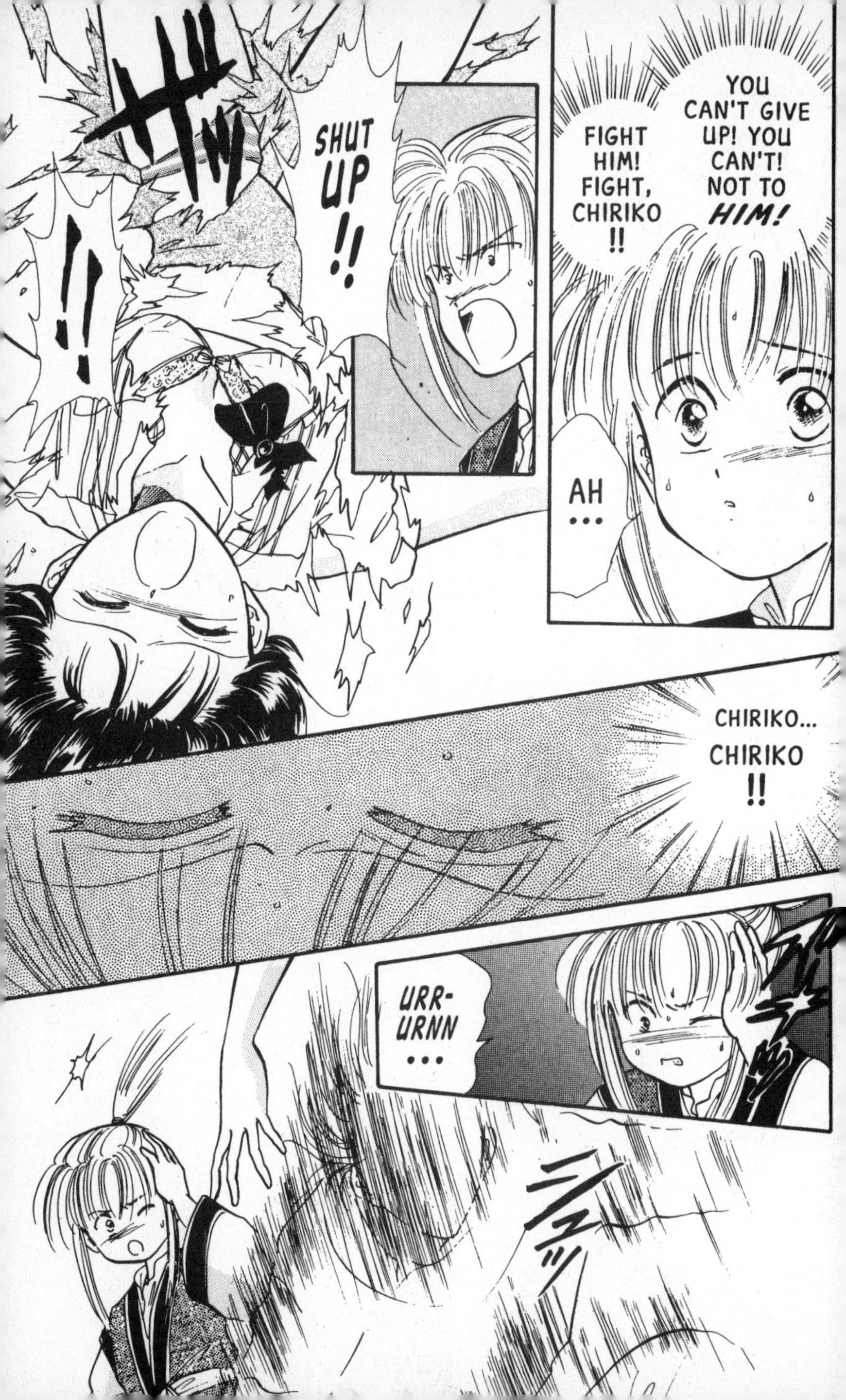
YOU CAN'T GIVE UP! YOU CAN'T! NOT TO *HIM!*
FIGHT HIM! FIGHT, CHIRIKO !!
AH ...
SHUT UP !!
!!
CHIRIKO... CHIRIKO !!
URR-URNN ...

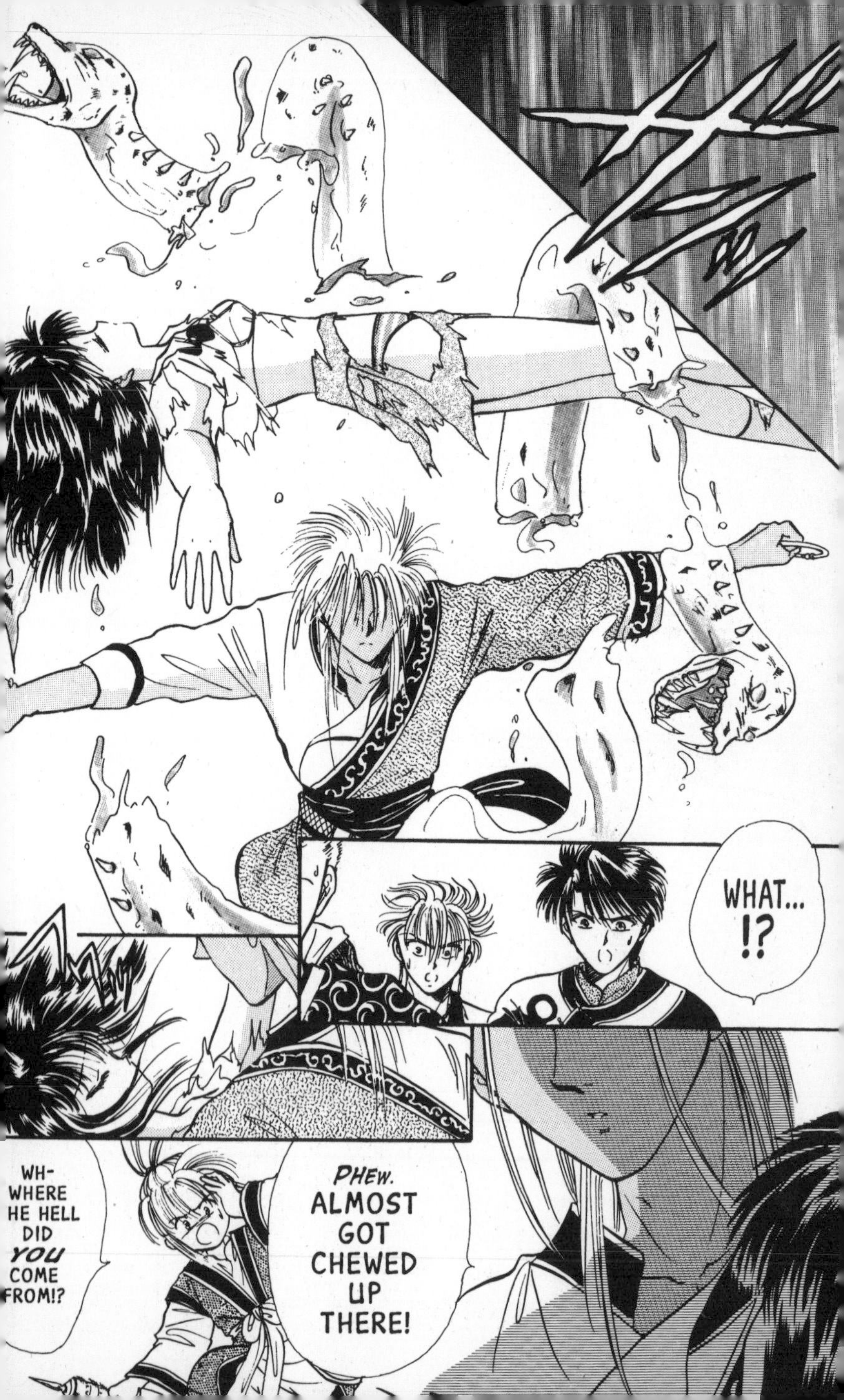
WHAT... !?
PHEW. ALMOST GOT CHEWED UP THERE!
WH- WHERE HE HELL DID YOU COME FROM!?

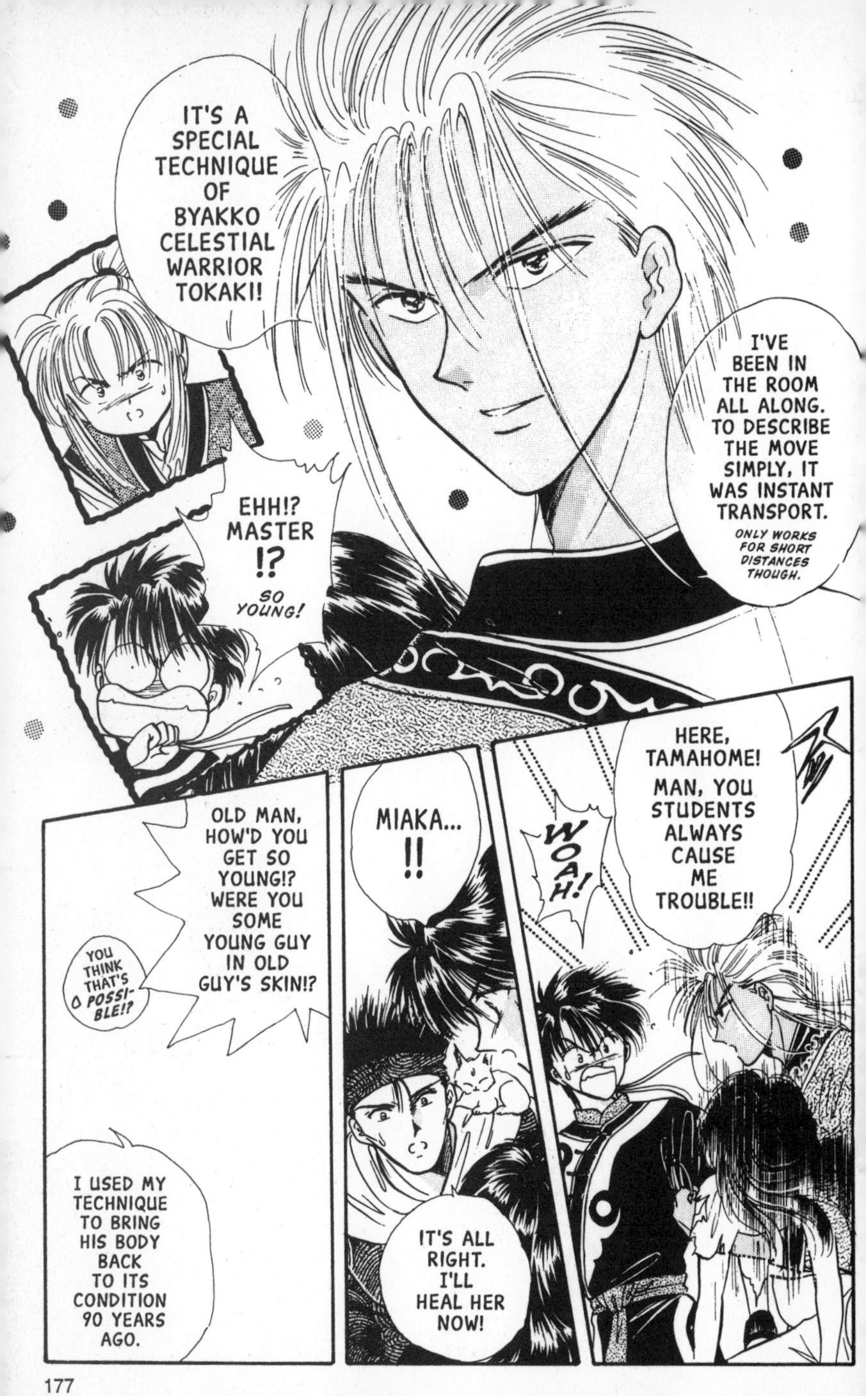
IT'S A SPECIAL TECHNIQUE OF BYAKKO CELESTIAL WARRIOR TOKAKI!
I'VE BEEN IN THE ROOM ALL ALONG. TO DESCRIBE THE MOVE SIMPLY, IT WAS INSTANT TRANSPORT.
ONLY WORKS FOR SHORT DISTANCES THOUGH.
EHH!? MASTER !?
SO YOUNG!
HERE, TAMAHOME! MAN, YOU STUDENTS ALWAYS CAUSE ME TROUBLE!!
WOAH!
MIAKA... !!
IT'S ALL RIGHT. I'LL HEAL HER NOW!
OLD MAN, HOW'D YOU GET SO YOUNG!? WERE YOU SOME YOUNG GUY IN OLD GUY'S SKIN!?
YOU THINK THAT'S POSSIBLE!?
I USED MY TECHNIQUE TO BRING HIS BODY BACK TO ITS CONDITION 90 YEARS AGO.

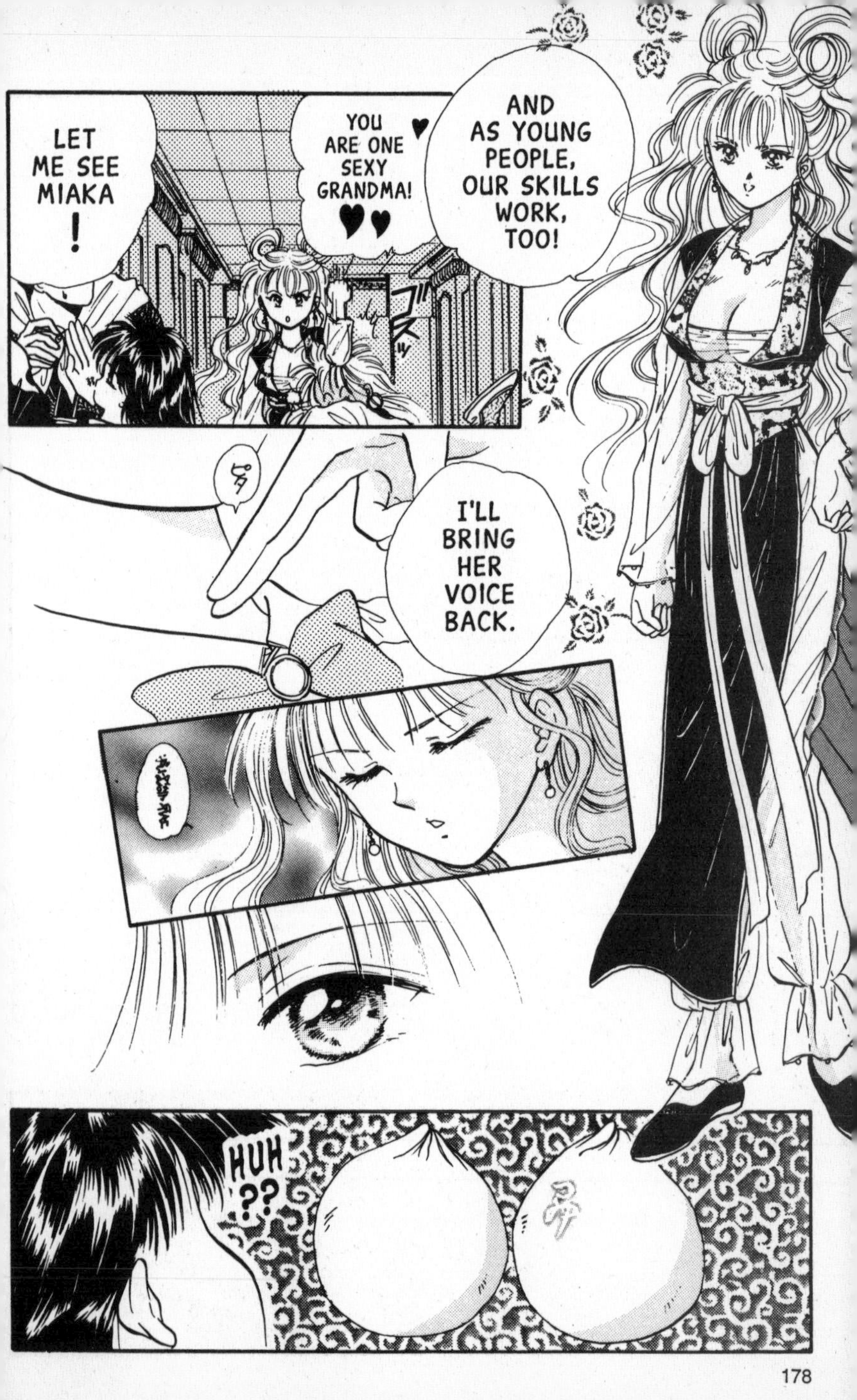
AND AS YOUNG PEOPLE, OUR SKILLS WORK, TOO!
YOU ARE ONE SEXY GRANDMA!
LET ME SEE MIAKA!
I'LL BRING HER VOICE BACK.
HUH ??

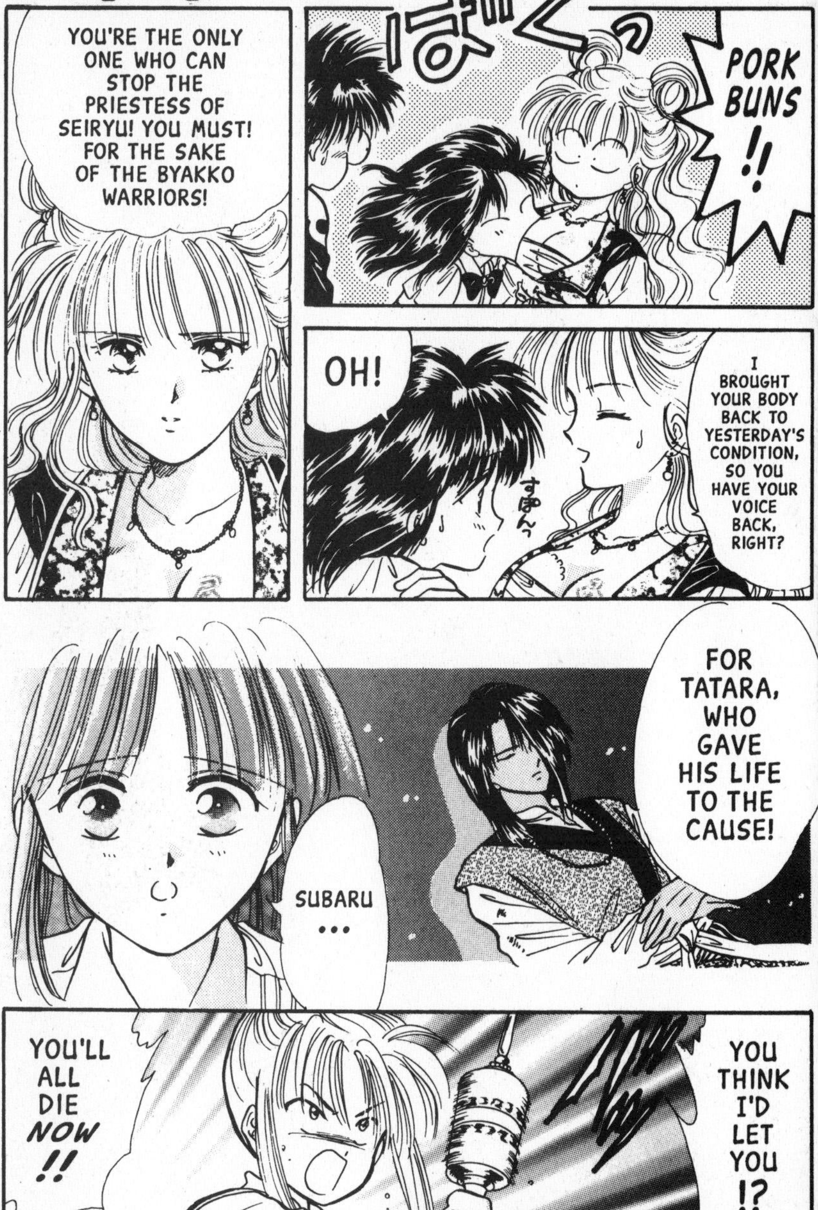
ぱくっ
PORK BUNS !!
I BROUGHT YOUR BODY BACK TO YESTERDAY'S CONDITION, SO YOU HAVE YOUR VOICE BACK, RIGHT?
OH!
すぽんっ
YOU'RE THE ONLY ONE WHO CAN STOP THE PRIESTESS OF SEIRYU! YOU MUST! FOR THE SAKE OF THE BYAKKO WARRIORS!
FOR TATARA, WHO GAVE HIS LIFE TO THE CAUSE!
SUBARU …
YOU THINK I'D LET YOU !?
YOU'LL ALL DIE NOW !!

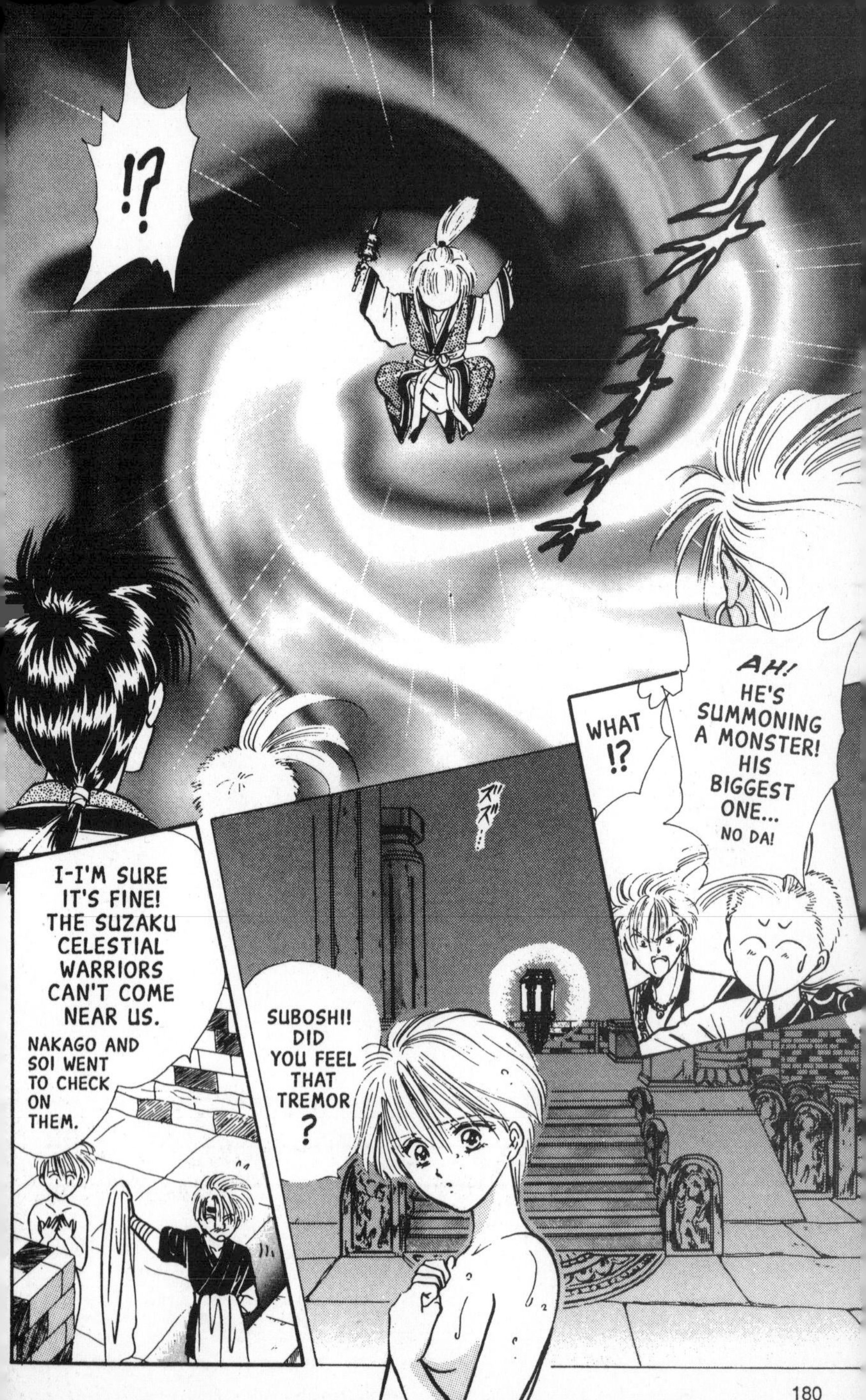
!?
AH! HE'S SUMMONING A MONSTER! HIS BIGGEST ONE... NO DA!
WHAT !?
SUBOSHI! DID YOU FEEL THAT TREMOR ?
I-I'M SURE IT'S FINE! THE SUZAKU CELESTIAL WARRIORS CAN'T COME NEAR US.
NAKAGO AND SOI WENT TO CHECK ON THEM.

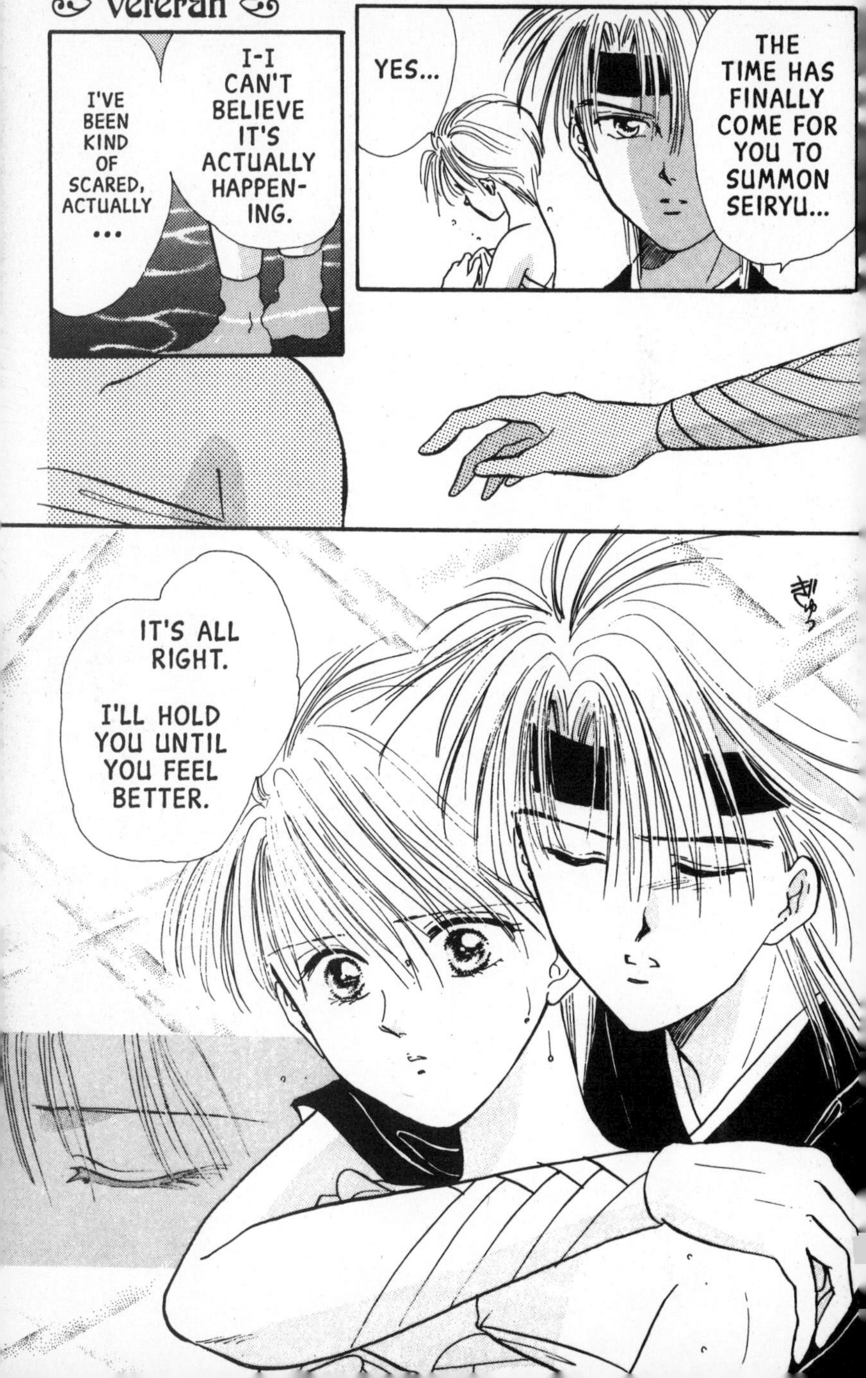
THE TIME HAS FINALLY COME FOR YOU TO SUMMON SEIRYU...
YES...
I-I CAN'T BELIEVE IT'S ACTUALLY HAPPEN-ING.
I'VE BEEN KIND OF SCARED, ACTUALLY ...
ぎゅっ
IT'S ALL RIGHT.
I'LL HOLD YOU UNTIL YOU FEEL BETTER.

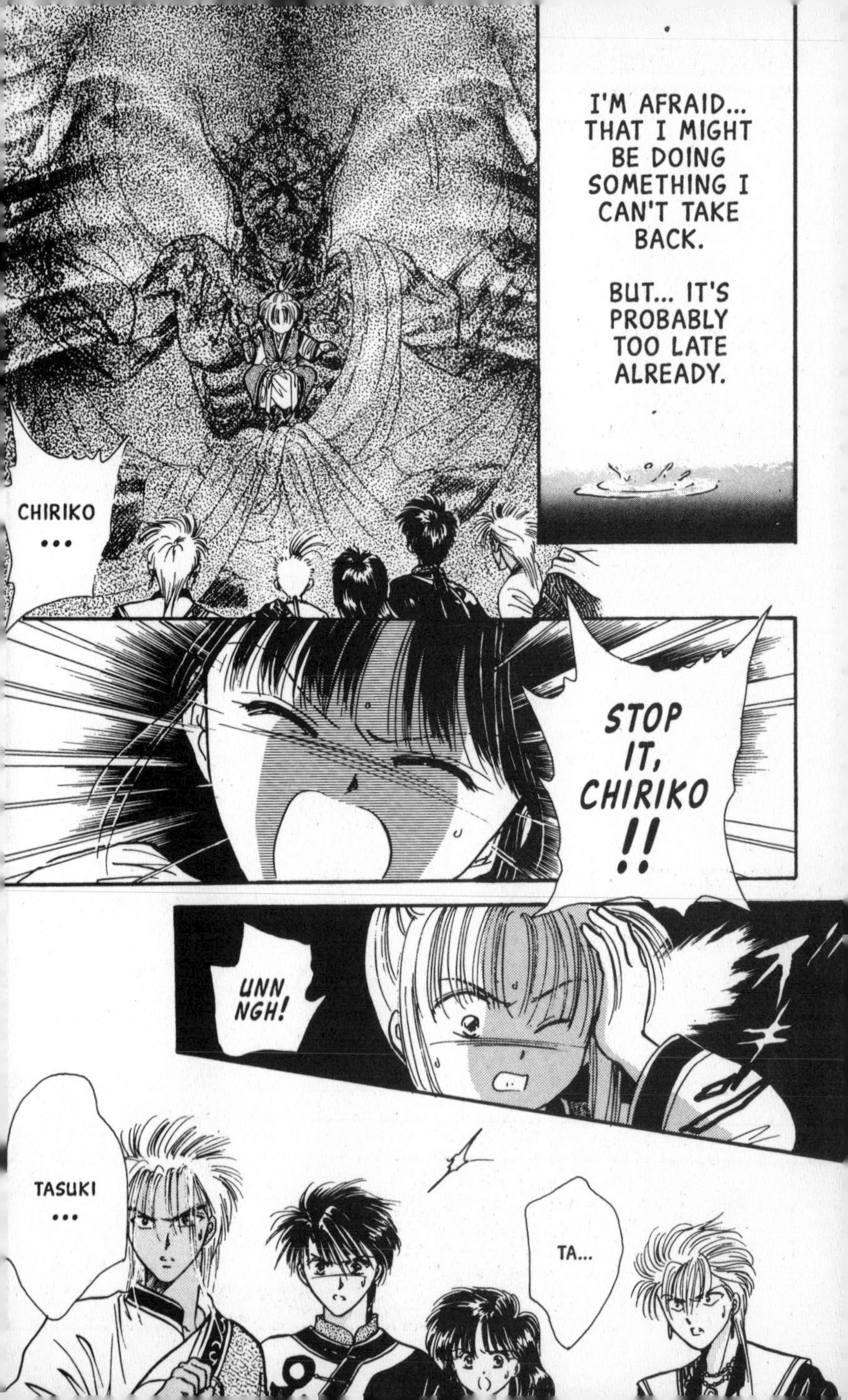
I'M AFRAID... THAT I MIGHT BE DOING SOMETHING I CAN'T TAKE BACK.
BUT... IT'S PROBABLY TOO LATE ALREADY.
CHIRIKO ...
STOP IT, CHIRIKO !!
UNN NGH!
TA...
TASUKI ...

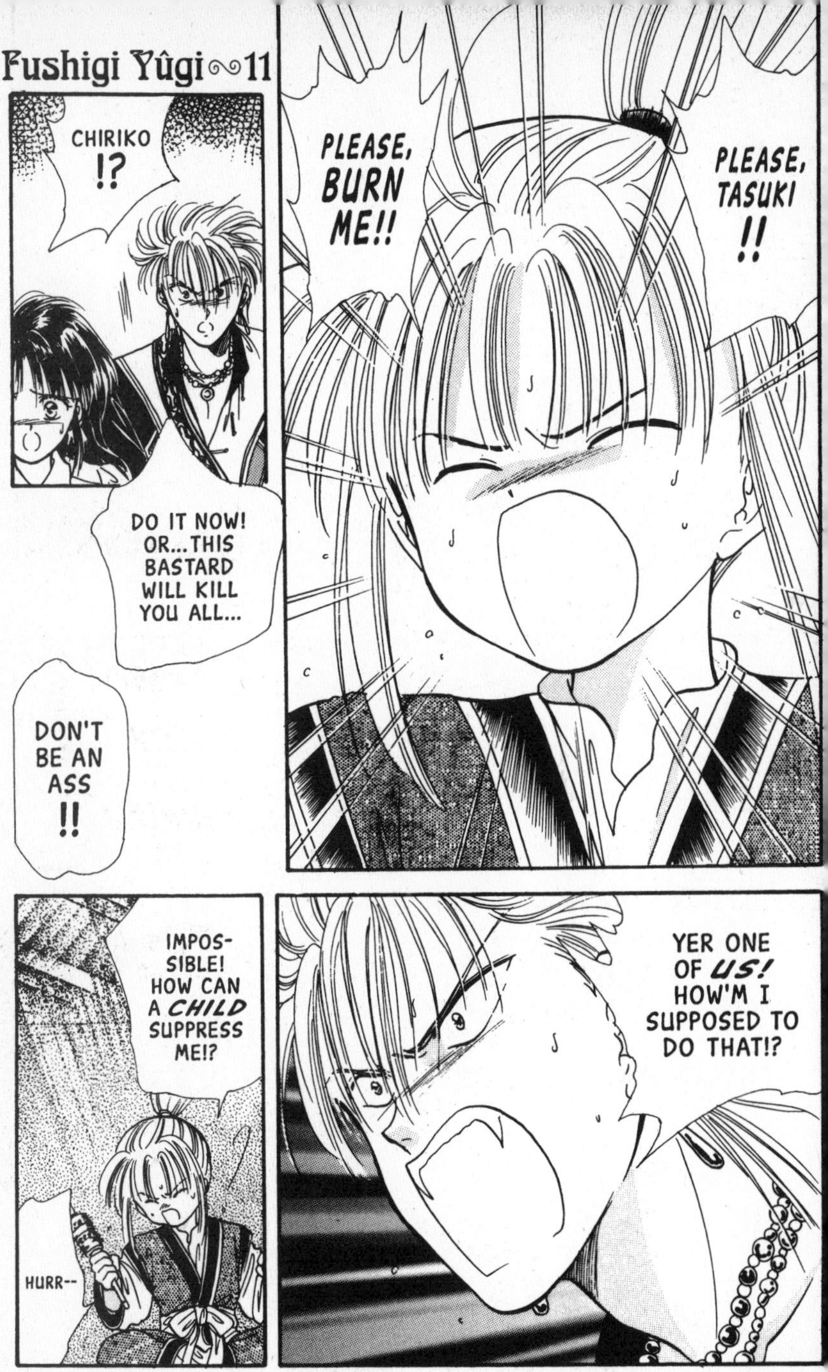
PLEASE, TASUKI !!
PLEASE, BURN ME!!
CHIRIKO !?
DO IT NOW! OR...THIS BASTARD WILL KILL YOU ALL...
DON'T BE AN ASS !!
YER ONE OF US! HOW'M I SUPPOSED TO DO THAT!?
IMPOSSIBLE! HOW CAN A CHILD SUPPRESS ME!?
HURR--

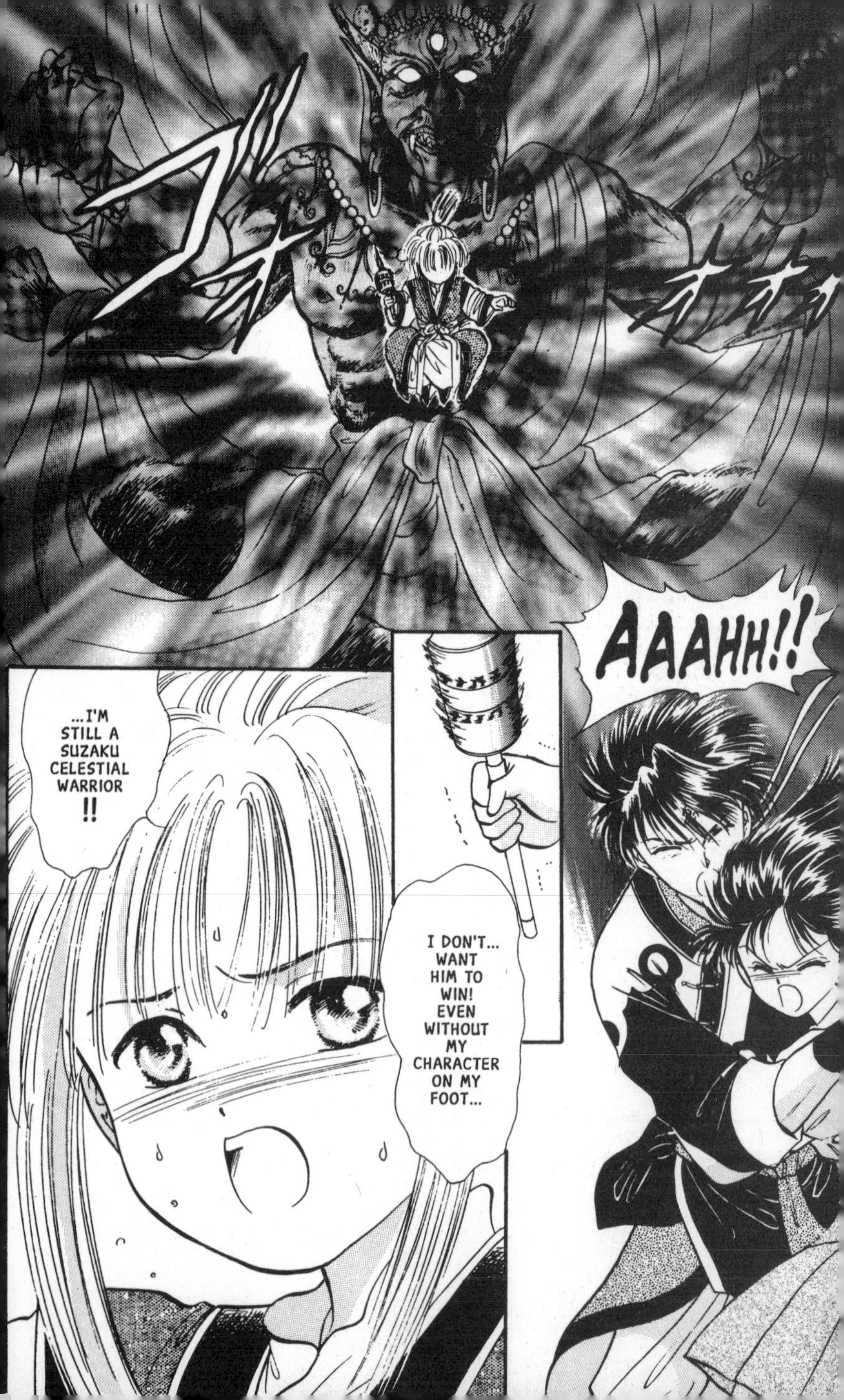
AAAHH!!
I DON'T... WANT HIM TO WIN! EVEN WITHOUT MY CHARACTER ON MY FOOT...
...I'M STILL A SUZAKU CELESTIAL WARRIOR !!

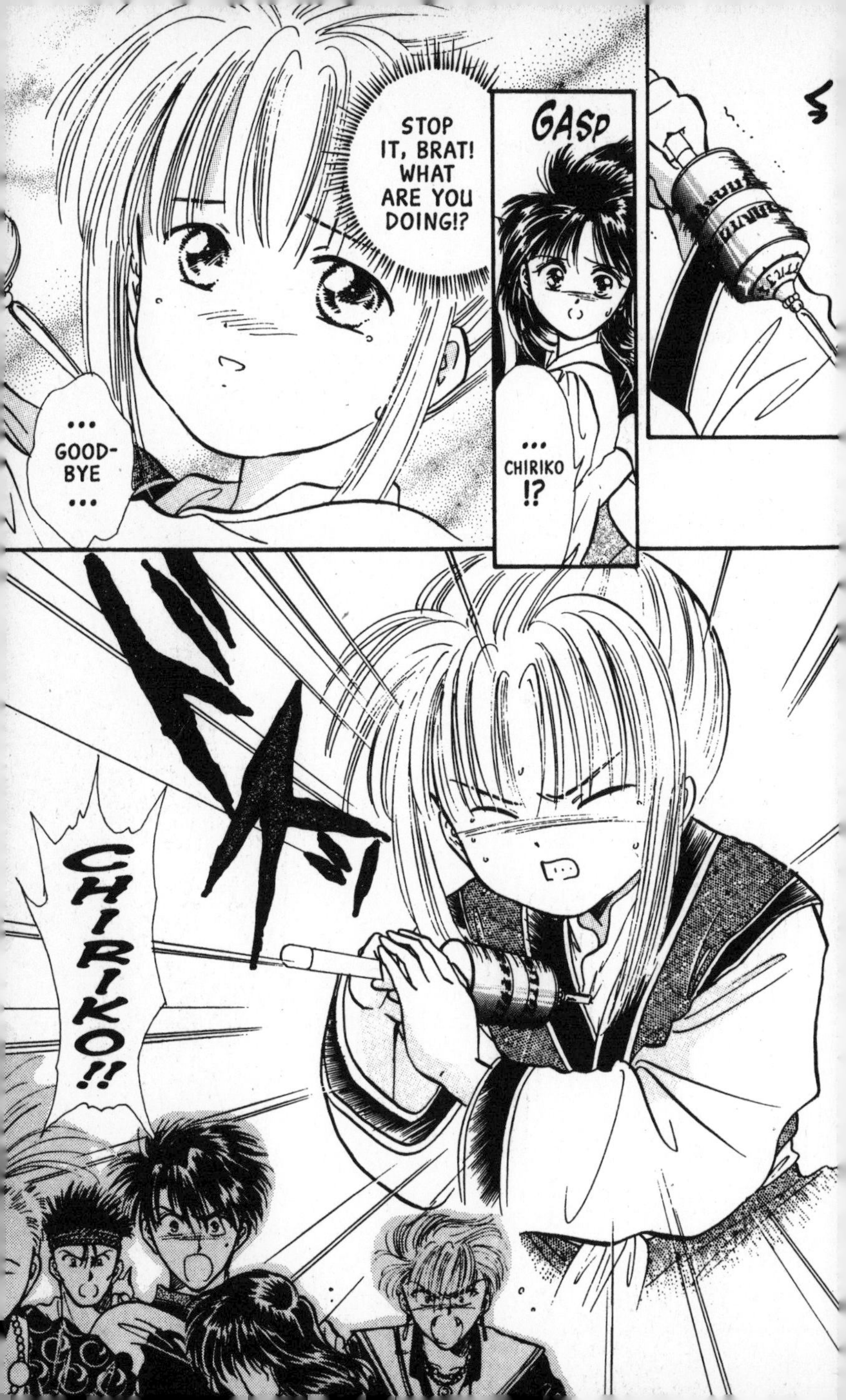
GASP
... CHIRIKO !?
STOP IT, BRAT! WHAT ARE YOU DOING!?
... GOOD-BYE ...
CHIRIKO!!

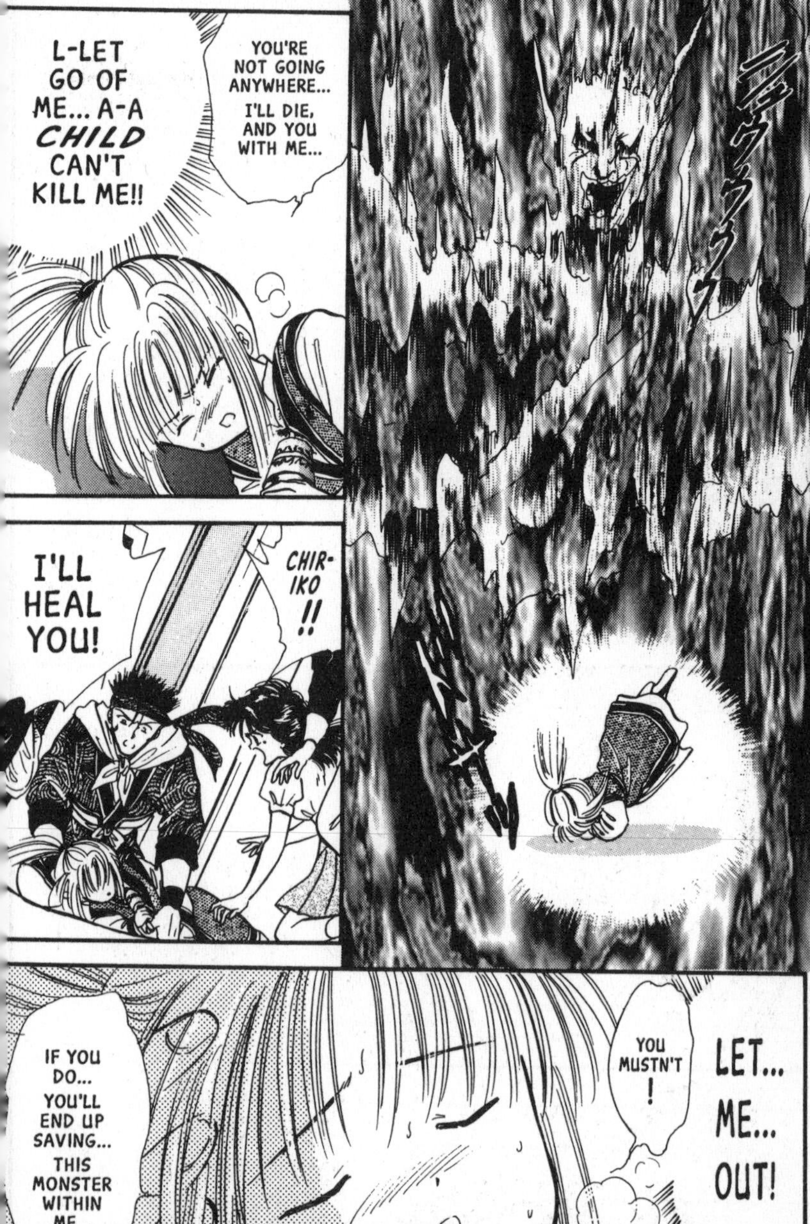
YOU'RE NOT GOING ANYWHERE... I'LL DIE, AND YOU WITH ME...
L-LET GO OF ME... A-A *CHILD* CAN'T KILL ME!!
CHIRIKO!!
I'LL HEAL YOU!
LET... ME... OUT!
YOU MUSTN'T!
IF YOU DO... YOU'LL END UP SAVING... THIS MONSTER WITHIN ME...

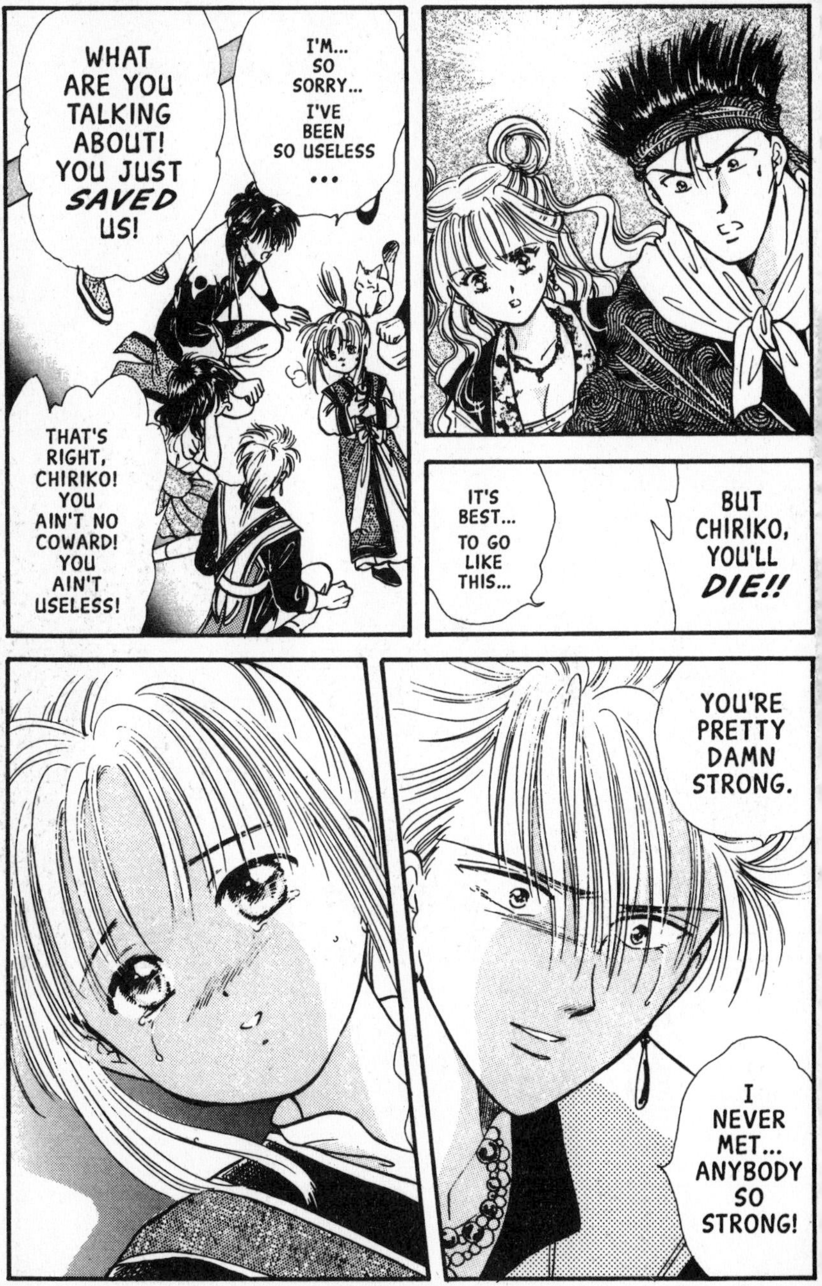
BUT CHIRIKO, YOU'LL *DIE!!*
IT'S BEST... TO GO LIKE THIS...
I'M... SO SORRY... I'VE BEEN SO USELESS ...
WHAT ARE YOU TALKING ABOUT! YOU JUST *SAVED* US!
THAT'S RIGHT, CHIRIKO! YOU AIN'T NO COWARD! YOU AIN'T USELESS!
YOU'RE PRETTY DAMN STRONG.
I NEVER MET... ANYBODY SO STRONG!

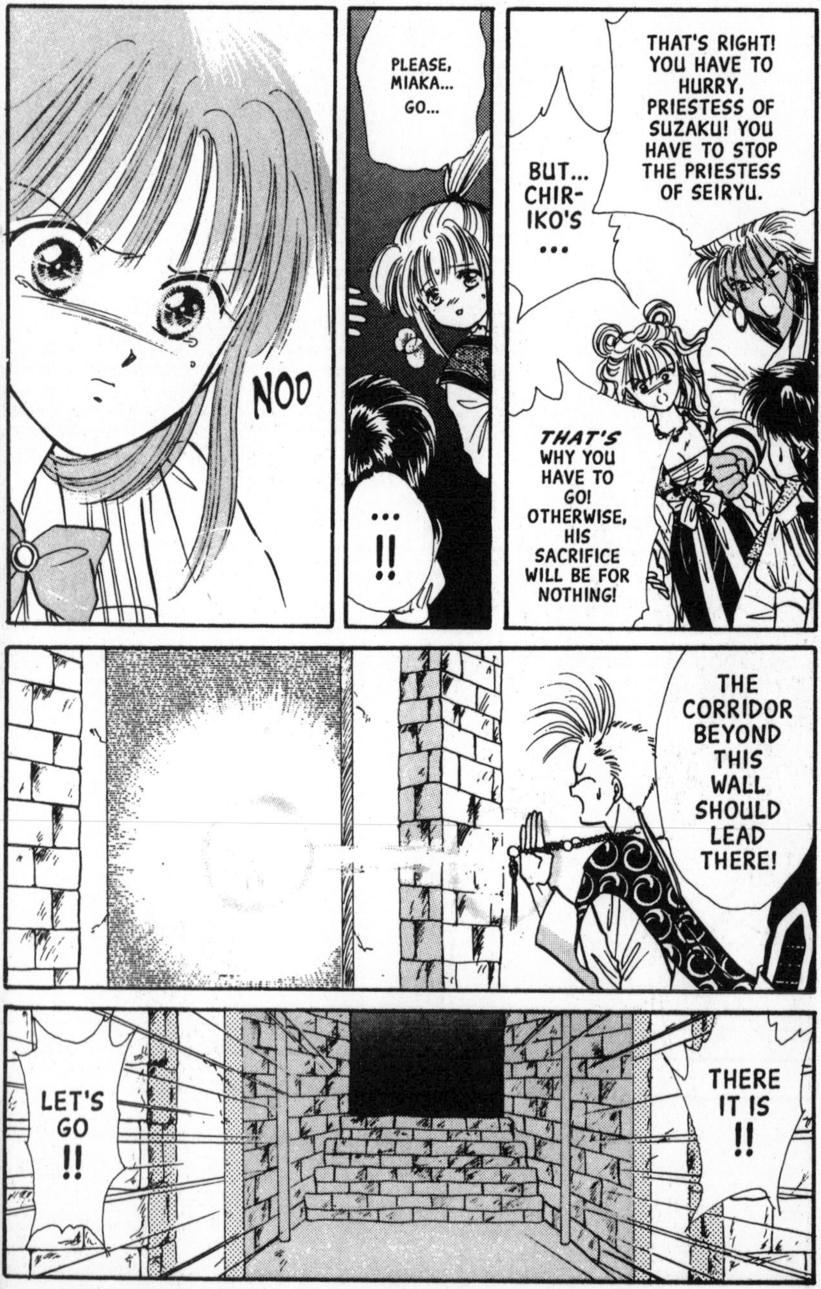
THAT'S RIGHT! YOU HAVE TO HURRY, PRIESTESS OF SUZAKU! YOU HAVE TO STOP THE PRIESTESS OF SEIRYU.
BUT... CHIRI-KO'S...
THAT'S WHY YOU HAVE TO GO! OTHERWISE, HIS SACRIFICE WILL BE FOR NOTHING!
PLEASE, MIAKA... GO...
...!!
NOD
THE CORRIDOR BEYOND THIS WALL SHOULD LEAD THERE!
THERE IT IS !!
LET'S GO !!

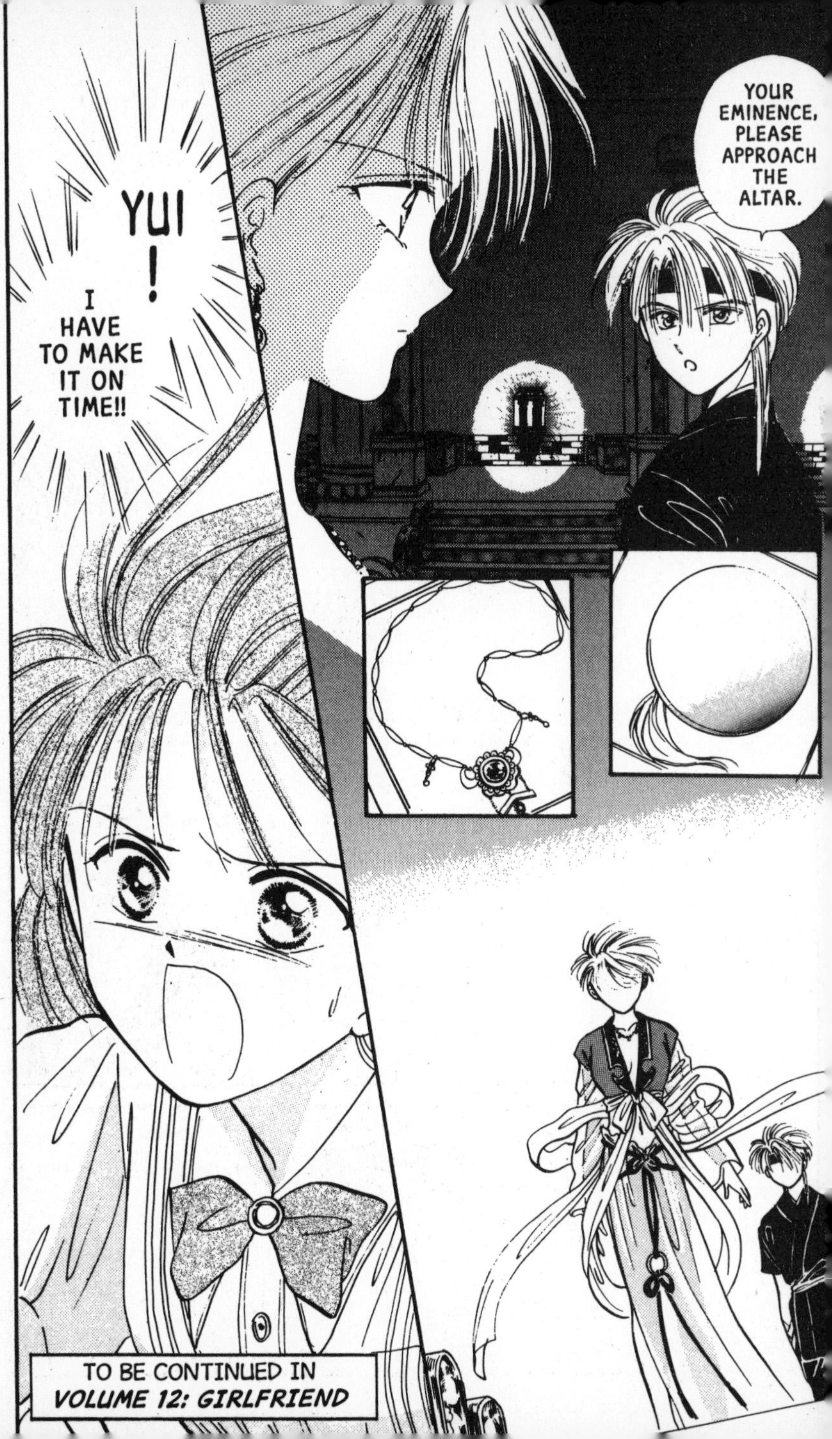
YOUR EMINENCE, PLEASE APPROACH THE ALTAR.
YUI!
I HAVE TO MAKE IT ON TIME!!
TO BE CONTINUED IN *VOLUME 12: GIRLFRIEND*

ABOUT THE AUTHOR

Yû Watase was born on March 5 in a town near Osaka, Japan, and she was raised there before moving to Tokyo to follow her dream of creating manga. In the decade since her debut short story, *PAJAMA DE OJAMA* ("An Intrusion in Pajamas"), she has produced more than 50 compiled volumes of short stories and continuing series. Her latest series, *ZETTAI KARESHI* ("He'll Be My Boyfriend"), is currently running in the anthology magazine *SHÔJO COMIC*. Watase's long-running horror/romance story *CERES: CELESTIAL LEGEND* and her most recent completed series, *ALICE 19TH*, are now available in North America published by VIZ. She loves science fiction, fantasy and comedy.

The Fushigi Yûgi Guide to Sound Effects

Most of the sound effects in FUSHIGI YÛGI are the way Yû Watase created them, in their original Japanese.

We created this glossary for a page-by-page, panel-by-panel explanation of the action and background noises. By using this guide, you may even learn some Japanese.

The glossary lists page and panel number. For example, page 1, panel 3, would be listed as 1.3.

22.4	FX: Zururu (sliding)
22.4	FX: Booo (listlessness)
23.3	FX: Sa (picking up)
24.3	FX: Poro poro (sob sob)
26.3	FX: Doka (kick)
26.4	FX: Dokoo (kick)
27.1	FX: Suu (quiet snoring)
27.1	FX: Gaa (loud snoring)
27.1	FX: Pee (cute snoring)
27.2	FX: Patan (door shutting)
29.2	FX: Zuda (falling)
29.5	FX: Fuwa (looming over)
30.1	FX: Zawa (leaves stirring)
31.1	FX: Dokun dokun (ba-dump)
31.1	FX: Dokun dokun (ba-dump)
31.2	FX: Dokun dokun (ba-dump)
31.3	FX: Zuru (sliding)
32.3	FX: Zaaa (swaying branches)

CHAPTER SIXTY-ONE:
A SAD FATE

37.2	FX: Shun (sulking)
38.5	FX: Sawa sawa (leaves stirring)
39.2	FX: Zukin (pang)
39.3	FX: Fu (blowing out)
40.1	FX: Fu (appearance)
42.1	FX: Batan (door opening)
44.2	FX: Ka (kneeling down)

CHAPTER SIXTY:
RAY OF RESURRECTION

6.2	FX: Dooo (explosion)
7.5	FX: Byu (burst)
7.6	FX: Ba (flute sound)
8.1	FX: Gua (burst)
8.2	FX: Kururu (spinning)
8.4	FX: Byu byu byu (shooting)
9.1	FX: Gusa (stab)
9.3	FX: Suu (appearing)
9.3	FX: Dosa (falling)
10.1	FX: Dosu (stab)
10.2	FX: Gobo (cough)
12.1	FX: Do (slashing)
12.1	FX: Dosu (stabbing)
12.1	FX: Dogo (blow)
12.3	FX: Dosa (falling)
14.6	FX: Koron (tipping over)
15.4	FX: Fu (fainting)
15.5	FX: Gaba (getting up)
16.2	FX: Ba (covering up)
17.1	FX: Gui (tug)
17.3	FX: Gohh (burst)
17.4	FX: Do (explosion)
19.3	FX: Gui (tugging)
21.1	FX: Gohh (roar)
21.2	FX: Ta (skip)
22.3	FX: Shan (clanking)

78.1 FX: Heta (exhaustion)

79.4 FX: Su (slight movement)

80.2 FX: Piku (detecting)

81.1 FX: Fu (smile)
81.5 FX: Jara (jangle)

83.4 FX: Gan (thump)
83.4 FX: Gon (thump)
83.4 FX: Dota (fall)
83.5 FX: Batan (shut)

84.1 FX: Ha (noticing)
84.3 FX: Kotsu kotsu (footsteps)
84.4 FX: Gui (tug)

85.2 FX: Pan (slap)

87.2 FX: Dosu (punch)

88.2 FX: Zuru (slip)

89.1 FX: Waku waku (excited)
89.3 FX: Giku (alarm)

90.1 FX: Pan (slap)
90.5 FX: Da (dashing out)

91.3 FX: Pichon (drip)
91.4 FX: Buru (shiver)
91.5 FX: Ha (waking)

92.2 FX: Gashaan (rattle)
92.3 FX: Ha (detecting)

93.1 FX: Dokidoki (excited)
93.5 FX: Geho (cough)

95.5 FX: Ban ban (slam slam)

97.3 FX: Ga (knock)
97.5 FX: Shiin (silence)

98.3 FX: Gu (clench)

100.4 FX: Shiin (silence)

101.3 FX: Hah (turning around)

45.2 FX: Dokun (ba-dump)

46.2 FX: Niya (smile)

47.5 FX: Fui (turning around)

48.4 FX: Kii (door opening)

52.2 FX: Deroron (ominous appearance)
52.4 FX: Doya doya (chatting)

53.3 FX: Tsun (turning away)
53.4 FX: Gata gata (furniture moving)

54.1 FX: Zazaaa (leaves blowing)
54.6 FX: Ha (oops)

55.3 FX: Gatan (rising)
55.5 FX: Bishi (pointing)

56.4 FX: Gatsu gatsu (eating)
56.5 FX: Sawa sawa (chatting at a distance)

68.1 FX: Zaza (bird fluttering)
68.2 FX: Doki doki doki (ba-dump ba-dump ba-dump)

69.2 FX: Biku (alarm)
69.3 FX: Dokun dokun dokun (ba-dump ba-dump ba-dump)
69.4 FX: Ba (hiding)
69.4 FX: Dokun dokun dokun (ba-dump ba-dump ba-dump)
69.4 FX: Dokun dokun (ba-dump ba-dump)
69.6 FX: Ka ka (galloping)

CHAPTER SIXTY-TWO: THE UNBREAKABLE WALL

74.3 FX: Gyu (tug)
74.4 FX: Zu (moving out)
74.5 FX: Zuru (slip)

75.2 FX: Shaa (pant)

76.1 FX: Ha (realization)
76.2 FX: Gooooh (flame)
76.3 FX: Booooh (sizzle)

77.2 FX: Chiiin (doooong)
77.3 FX: Chiiin (doooong)
77.3 FX: Dotatata (running over)

129.2 FX: Gan (knock)
129.2 FX: Hyohhh (whistling wind)

130.1 FX: Basha (splash)
130.5 FX: Batan (shut)

131.1 FX: Ban ban (thump thump)
131.2 FX: Gachan (door locking)

CHAPTER SIXTY-FOUR: IMMINENT PARTING

134.2 FX: Gyu (squeeze)

135.2 FX: Puchi (tear)
135.4 FX: Su (hold)
135.5 FX: Ba (popping out)
135.6 FX: Shururururu (swirl)

136.1 FX: Gooh (burn)
136.3 FX: Su (fade)

137.3 FX: Ban (door opening)

138.3 FX: Dokaa (kick)

140.3 FX: Kyu (wipe)

142.1 FX: Ka (footstep)

143.2 FX: Kuru kuru kuru (twirl twirl twirl)
143.3 FX: Nu (sudden appearance)

144.3 FX: Zoro zoro (mass movement)

145.2 FX: Jitabata jitabata (panic)
145.4 FX: Gooooh (flames)

146.1 FX: Dosa (landing)
146.3 FX: Ba (dramatic turn)

147.3 FX: Kui (gentle tug)
147.5 FX: Pen (slap)

149.1 FX: Doohn (burst)
149.1 FX: Ha (realization)
149.3 FX: Paku paku (mouth movement)
149.6 FX: Doohn (burst)

150.1 FX: Hyun hyun hyun hyun (wrapping around)
150.2 FX: Kuru kuru kuru (spin spin spin)

CHAPTER SIXTY-THREE: THE TRUTH REVEALED

106.1 FX: Gyuuu (choke)
106.2 FX: Geho geho (cough)
106.3 FX: Ku (snicker)

107.1 FX: Boro boro (sob sob)
107.3 FX: Gachan (click)

108.1 FX: Koku koku (nod nod)

109.1 FX: Ba (grab)
109.3 FX: Gakun (bow)
109.4 FX: Gaba (jerking up)

110.2 FX: Ba (toss)
110.5 FX: Seh seh (working hard)

111.4 FX: Geho geho (cough cough)
111.5 FX: Hah hah (huff huff)

113.2 FX: Ha (realizing)

114.4 FX: Su (extracting)

116.2 FX: Pah (opening up)
116.3 FX: Su (appearing)

118.2 FX: Dosa (falling)
118.3 FX: Ju (sizzle)

119.4 FX: Kuru kuru kuru (spin spin spin)
119.4 FX: Kuru kuru kuru kuru (spin spin spin spin)

120.3 FX: Fufu (snicker)
120.4 FX: Goho (cough)

121.2 FX: Giku (alarm)
121.6 FX: Dokin dokin dokin (ba-dump ba-dump ba-dump)
121.6 FX: Dokin dokin dokin (ba-dump ba-dump ba-dump)

123.1 FX: Gaku gaku gaku gaku (shake shake shake shake)

125.1 FX: Hah hah (huff huff)
125.4 FX: Ha (alarm)

128.3 FX: Ha ha (laughing)

174.1 FX: Ga ga (stab stab)
174.2 FX: Bikun (pain)
175.5 FX: Zuki (pain)
175.6 FX: Shu (flash)

176.1 FX: Zan (slice)
176.4 FX: Fuwa (float)

177.4 FX: Su (flash)

178.2 FX: Gosu (elbow)
178.3 FX: Pita (touch)

179.1 FX: Baku (biting)
179.2 FX: Supon (bounce back)
179.5 FX: Ba (fling)

180.1 FX: Gooohhh (whirlwind)
180.3 FX: Zu zu (rumble rumble)

181.4 FX: Gyu (hug)

182.4 FX: Zukin (pain)

184.1 FX: Gooohhh (roar)

185.1 FX: Ku (grab)
185.4 FX: Dosu (stab)

186.1 FX: Shuuu (fizzing out)
186.1 FX: Dosa (landing)

151.3 FX: Yoro (stagger)
151.5 FX: Ba (grab)

152.4 FX: Bata bata (stomp stomp)
152.6 FX: Giri giri (squeeze squeeze)

153.3 FX: Su (emerge)

154.4 FX: Su (fade)

155.2 FX: Shururururururu (whizzing around)

156.2 FX: Karan (thump)
156.3 FX: Fu (fading)
156.4 FX: Dosa dosa (falls)

157.5 FX: Gan (bump)

160.2 FX: Piku (twitch)
160.5 FX: Niya (smile)

161.1 FX: Kah (flash)
161.2 FX: Don (bump)
161.5 FX: Niya (smile)

164.1 FX: Fu (rising)
164.2 FX: Fuwa (float)
164.4 FX: Fu (appearing)
164.5 FX: Pashi (grasp)

165.3 FX: Paku paku (mouth movement)
165.5 FX: Kuru kuru kuru (spin spin spin)

166.1 FX: Ban (burst)
166.2 FX: Su (wave)
166.3 FX: Doohn (burst)

167.2 FX: Su (snag)
167.3 FX: Fuwa (floating)

168.1 FX: Su (twirl)
168.2 FX: Ba (tearing apart)

170.2 FX: Giii (creak)

171.3 FX: Pashi (hit)

172.1 FX: Gakun (arm falling)

173.1 FX: Shaaa (hissing)
173.6 FX: Su (finger motion)

EDITOR'S RECOMMENDATIONS

Did you like *FUSHIGI YÛGI*? Here's what VIZ recommends you try next:

ALICE 19TH is Yû Watase's recent series about a seemingly normal teenage girl. One day, Alice hears strange voices telling her to save a rabbit. She almost loses her life rescuing the bunny, and soon finds out it's a magical entity with great powers that has a special message for Alice.

SAIKANO is a compelling love story. A few days after they start dating, Shuji discovers his girlfriend Chise has a secret—she's been secretly engineered by the military to transform into a powerful weapon. Chise is becoming increasingly powerful as the Ultimate Weapon, and is torn between her life as a fighting machine and living as an ordinary teenager.

REVOLUTIONARY GIRL UTENA draws the reader into the world of a princess who wants to become a prince, just like the man who saved her as a little girl. Seven years later, while trying to find the prince who rescued her, Utena finds out things are not as they appear and is forced to fight duels for the power to revolutionize the world.

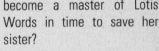

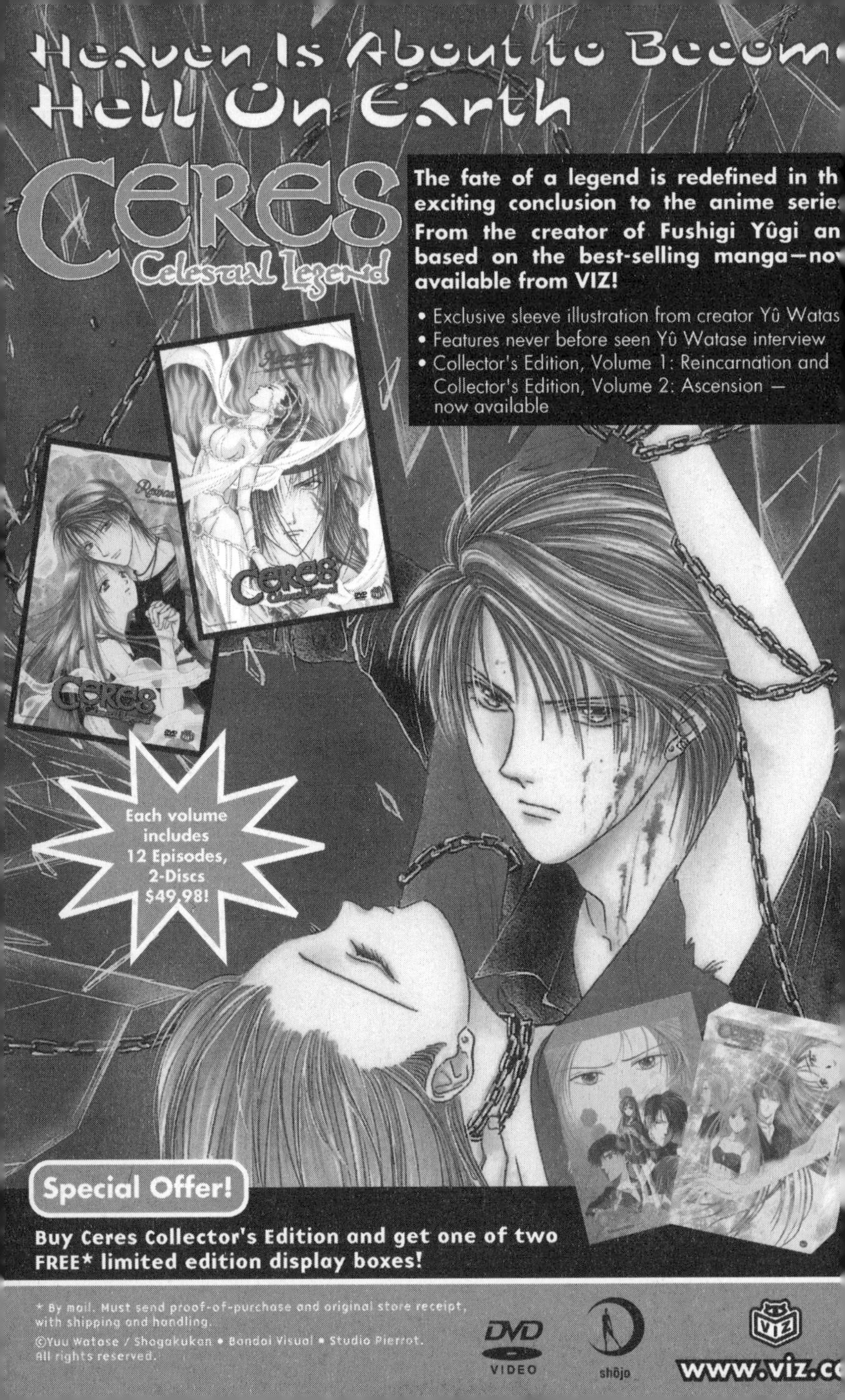
Heaven Is About to Becom
Hell On Earth
Ceres
Celestial Legend
The fate of a legend is redefined in th
exciting conclusion to the anime serie
From the creator of Fushigi Yûgi an
based on the best-selling manga—no
available from VIZ!
• Exclusive sleeve illustration from creator Yû Watas
• Features never before seen Yû Watase interview
• Collector's Edition, Volume 1: Reincarnation and Collector's Edition, Volume 2: Ascension — now available
Each volume includes 12 Episodes, 2-Discs $49.98!
Special Offer!
Buy Ceres Collector's Edition and get one of two FREE* limited edition display boxes!
* By mail. Must send proof-of-purchase and original store receipt, with shipping and handling.
©Yuu Watase / Shogakukan • Bandai Visual • Studio Pierrot. All rights reserved.
DVD VIDEO
shōjo
VIZ
www.viz.c

COMPLETE OUR SURVEY AND LET
US KNOW WHAT YOU THINK!

☐ Please do NOT send me information about VIZ products, news and events, special offers, or other information.

☐ Please do NOT send me information from VIZ's trusted business partners.

Name: _____

Address: _____

City: _____ **State:** _____ **Zip:** _____

E-mail: _____

☐ Male ☐ Female **Date of Birth** (mm/dd/yyyy): ___ / ___ / _____ (Under 13? Parental consent required)

What race/ethnicity do you consider yourself? (please check one)

☐ Asian/Pacific Islander ☐ Black/African American ☐ Hispanic/Latino

☐ Native American/Alaskan Native ☐ White/Caucasian ☐ Other: _____

What VIZ product did you purchase? (check all that apply and indicate title purchased)

☐ DVD/VHS _____

☐ Graphic Novel _____

☐ Magazines _____

☐ Merchandise _____

Reason for purchase: (check all that apply)

☐ Special offer ☐ Favorite title ☐ Gift

☐ Recommendation ☐ Other _____

Where did you make your purchase? (please check one)

☐ Comic store ☐ Bookstore ☐ Mass/Grocery Store

☐ Newsstand ☐ Video/Video Game Store ☐ Other: _____

☐ Online (site: _____)

What other VIZ properties have you purchased/own? _____
_____

How many anime and/or manga titles have you purchased in the last year? How many were VIZ titles? **(please check one from each column)**

ANIME	MANGA	VIZ
☐ None	☐ None	☐ None
☐ 1-4	☐ 1-4	☐ 1-4
☐ 5-10	☐ 5-10	☐ 5-10
☐ 11+	☐ 11+	☐ 11+

I find the pricing of VIZ products to be: **(please check one)**

☐ Cheap ☐ Reasonable ☐ Expensive

What genre of manga and anime would you like to see from VIZ? **(please check two)**

☐ Adventure ☐ Comic Strip ☐ Science Fiction ☐ Fighting

☐ Horror ☐ Romance ☐ Fantasy ☐ Sports

What do you think of VIZ's new look?

☐ Love It ☐ It's OK ☐ Hate It ☐ Didn't Notice ☐ No Opinion

Which do you prefer? **(please check one)**

☐ Reading right-to-left

☐ Reading left-to-right

Which do you prefer? **(please check one)**

☐ Sound effects in English

☐ Sound effects in Japanese with English captions

☐ Sound effects in Japanese only with a glossary at the back

THANK YOU! Please send the completed form to:

NJW Research
42 Catharine St.
Poughkeepsie, NY 12601

All information provided will be used for internal purposes only. We promise not to sell or otherwise divulge your information.

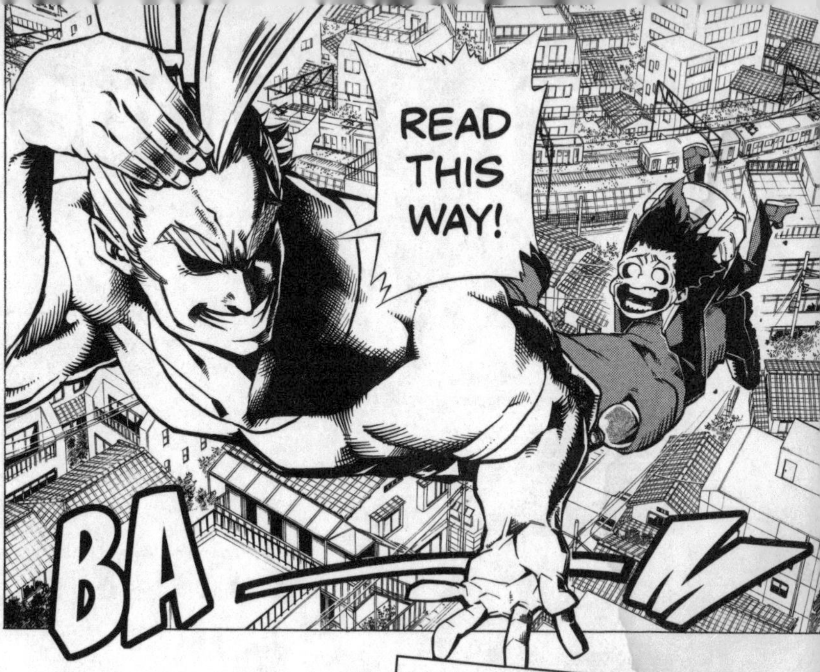
READ THIS WAY!
BA—M

MY HERO ACADEMIA

reads from right to left, starting in the upper-right corner. Japanese is read from right to left, meaning that action, sound effects and word-balloon order are completely reversed from English order.

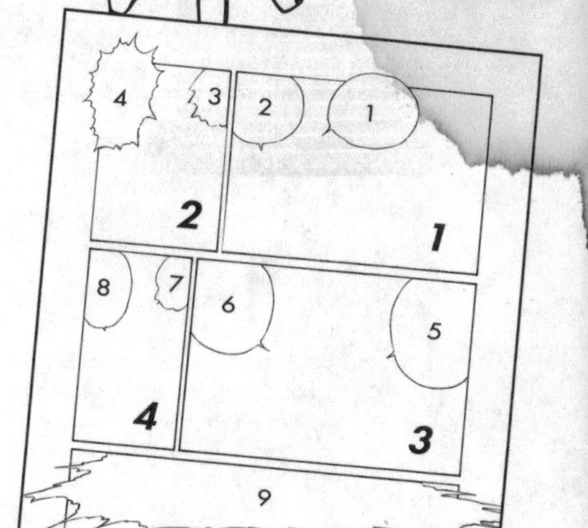
1
2
1
3
4
2
5
6
3
7
8
4
9
5
142

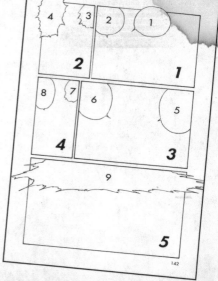

Black Clover

STORY & ART BY YŪKI TABATA

Asta is a young boy who dreams of becoming the greatest mage in the kingdom. Only one problem—he can't use any magic! Luckily for Asta, he receives the incredibly rare five-leaf clover grimoire that gives him the power of anti-magic. Can someone who can't use magic really become the Wizard King? One thing's for sure—Asta will never give up!

SHONEN JUMP   VIZ media
www.viz.com